MNI SOTA MAKOCE

Minnesota Historical
Society Press

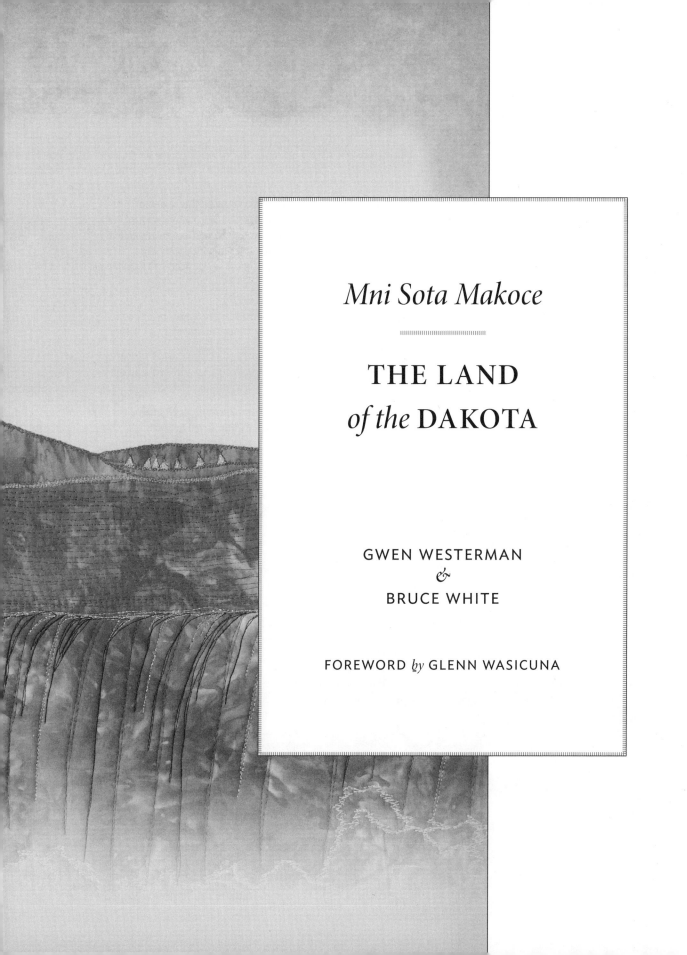

Mni Sota Makoce

THE LAND *of the* DAKOTA

GWEN WESTERMAN
&
BRUCE WHITE

FOREWORD *by* GLENN WASICUNA

CLEAN
WATER
LAND &
LEGACY
AMENDMENT

www.mhspress.org
The Minnesota Historical Society Press is a member
of the Association of American University Presses.
Manufactured in the United States of America

10 9 8 7 6 5 4 3 2 1

♾ The paper used in this publication meets the minimum requirements
of the American National Standard for Information Sciences—
Permanence for Printed Library Materials, ANSI Z39.48-1984.

International Standard Book Number
ISBN: 978-0-87351-869-7 (paper)
ISBN: 978-0-87351-883-3 (e-book)

Library of Congress Cataloging-in-Publication Data

Westerman, Gwen.
Mni sota makoce : the land of the Dakota / Gwen Westerman and Bruce White ;
foreword by Glenn Wasicuna.
p. cm.
Includes bibliographical references and index.
ISBN 978-0-87351-869-7 (pbk. : alk. paper) — ISBN 978-0-87351-883-3 (e-book)
1. Dakota Indians—Minnesota—History. 2. Dakota Indians—Minnesota—
Social life and customs. 3. Minnesota—History. 4. Minnesota—
Social life and customs. I. White, Bruce M., 1951– II. Title.
E99.D1W63 2012
977.6—dc23
2012022469

Contents

Ina, ohiŋni uŋnikiksuyapi.

Foreword

My father, Heḣaka Cuwi Maza, said, "It's hard to be an Indian."

At the time, I agreed with him but I didn't really know why. Now, decades later, working with researchers, writers, and interviewees and looking into myself for *Mni Sota Makoce: The Land of the Dakota,* I can see the meaning come into focus. While working on this project, we were asked by people of all ages the one question that has become so familiar to us: "Why didn't the schools teach us about Dakota people?"

The response to this question could not be a simplistic one. The answers are many and varied. But the most important and certainly the best answer we have as Dakota people is "Thank you." Thank you for asking that one question that will open up decades, generations of stories, information, answers, and ideas that we have to share with the world.

Some know the brutal history of the Dakota people. Some know dates, places, and events. Others delight in dazzling us with misspelled, misinterpreted Dakota words and names: Shakopee. Owatonna. Chaska. Winona. Although we can appreciate what has been written about us, it does not go far enough. It does not capture Dakota thought or feeling. As Dakota people we are honorable. We listen. We were told not to be who we are and we listened. We settled in every city, town, village, and hamlet imaginable. We are accountants, doctors, athletes, teachers, lawyers, professors, and journalists. In Mni Sota Makoce, know that the next time you land at Minneapolis–St. Paul International Airport, your plane could be guided in by a world-renowned championship powwow dancer in the fancy dance category. We are everywhere.

We were told not to speak our language and we listened. Now, in 2012, we are told that our language is on the verge of extinction. Somebody else told us we were "Sioux," and we said, "Yes, sir, we are Sioux." Somebody else came along and said, "No, you are Dakota," and we said, "We are Dakota." Others along the way said we are Aboriginal, Natives, Indians, Native Americans, Native Canadians. We listened politely to these things, knowing that we are ikce wicaṡta, meaning "common man."

Are we the only nation in this world that allows our language to be misspelled, misinterpreted, and mispronounced? What would the good folks of, say, Bloomington do if such mistakes were applied to their language?

As Dakota people, we were exiled, banished forever from Mni Sota Makoce. It is like being put on "pause." While the rest of the world goes on, we are on pause. Now it is 2012, time to celebrate 150 years of—being put on pause? The anniversary date for the Dakota–U.S. War is looming, and suddenly we are on "play." We look at each other and think all different kinds of thoughts. It reminds me of a time years ago when I accompanied a group of high school students to a museum. They saw the usual "Indian" artifacts on display. At the end of the tour I asked them, what can we put in here today to tell people who we are? We all looked at each other. We did not know what to say.

We as Dakota people believe in the power of prayer. We believe in the Creator. Everything we do on a daily basis is guided by prayer. The project that developed into *Mni Sota Makoce: The Land of the Dakota* began and was sustained with prayer because that is the Dakota way. The people involved were guided sometimes unknowingly by the Creator. It has been an eye-opening, thought-provoking, and illuminating experience for all of us.

Thank you for picking up this book. Look at us. We have been here all this time. Talk to us. We have something to tell you. We are ikce wicaṡta—common man. We hurt. We cry. We laugh. We are people.

Heḣaka Cuwi Maza, it is hard to be an Indian because you told me also that being Dakota means every step you take is a prayer.

Wambdi Wapaha Glenn Wasicuna
GOOD THUNDER, MINNESOTA

MNI SOTA MAKOCE

Introduction

Minnesota is a Dakota place. The Dakota people named it and left their marks in the landscape and in its history. Yet the relationship of the Dakota people to their traditional lands in Minnesota is little understood by Minnesotans today. Many history books describe the Dakota as a fierce, warlike people who lived in Minnesota prior to the arrival of whites, then disappeared. Others tell the story of the 1862 Dakota–U.S. War as though those events were the only ones of significance in Dakota history.

Among the Dakota people, the importance of this place to their history and identity is well known. It is part of the oral tradition and knowledge of the people. In the written record of European encounters with Dakota people that go back three hundred years, explorers and missionaries described the Dakota, this region, and places in it, though perhaps sometimes in incomplete and garbled form. Even from these sources, the enduring eloquence of Dakota people about their connection to the land can be heard.

In an account from around 1720, an unknown Frenchman recorded the Dakota belief that the first of their people came from the ground on the prairie between the mouth of the Minnesota River and the Falls of St. Anthony. In April 1754 Dakota chiefs gathered with a French diplomat, Joseph Marin, at a fort along the Mississippi River to complain about incursions by Ojibwe into their territory. One of the chiefs laid before Marin a map of the region and said,

> No one could be unaware that from the mouth of the Wisconsin to Leech Lake, these territories belong to us. On all the points and in the little rivers we have had villages. One can still see the marks of our bones which are still there, which are the remains from the Cristinaux [Cree] and the Sauteux [Ojibwe] having killed us. But they never can drive us away. These are territories that we hold from no one except the Master of Life who gave them to us. And although we have been at war against all the nations, we never abandoned them.[1]

Such statements about the Dakota's connection to this region continued, reported by many writers, whether French, British, or American. William

H. Keating, a geologist who came to the Minnesota area on an exploratory expedition in 1823, observed, "The Dacotas have no tradition of having ever emigrated, from any other place, to the spot upon which they now reside; they believe that they were created by the Supreme Being on the lands which they at present occupy." A writer in the early 1850s, probably one of the white missionaries among the Dakota, reported that "One great natural fact which perhaps ought to be recognized and recorded at the start, is this, viz: That the mouth of the Minnesota river (Watpa Minisota [Mni Sota Wakpa]) lies immediately over the center of the earth and under the centre of the heavens." The writer of that statement may have been the missionary Stephen R. Riggs, who later stated, "The Mdewakantonwan think that the mouth of the Minnesota River is precisely over the center of the earth and that they occupy the gate that opens into the western world."[2]

The Dakota connection was not only to the entire region of Minnesota but also to specific places, rivers, lakes, rocks, landforms, and village sites, all imbued with meaning by generations of experience and knowledge. At treaty negotiations at Prairie du Chien in 1825, Dakota leaders were asked to describe their territory so that federal officials could differentiate the lands of various nations. Dakota chiefs gave eloquent accounts of where they lived and where they belonged. A Waḣpetuŋwaŋ leader known as "the Little" stated, "I am of the prairie. I claim the land up the River Corbeau [Crow River] to its source & from there to Otter Tail Lake. I can yet show the marks of my lodges there and they will remain as long as the world lasts." Tataŋka Nażiŋ, Standing Buffalo, a Sisituŋwaŋ leader from Lake Traverse and Lac qui Parle, stated that his lands commenced at Ottertail Lake and ran north to Pine Lake and the Pine River, which emptied into the Red River.[3]

Wanataŋ, the Ihaŋktuŋwaŋ leader from Lake Traverse, said, "I am from the plains and it is of that part of our Country of which I speak. My line commences where Thick Wood River empties into Red River thence down Red River to Turtle River—up Turtle River to its source, thence south of the Devils Lake to the Missouri at the Gros Ventre Village." Çaŋ Sagye, a Waḣpekute leader whose territory lay in present-day south-central Minnesota and northern Iowa, stated, "I will now point out the boundary of the land where I was born. It commences at the raccoon fork of the Des Moines River at the mouth of the Raccoon River, thence up to a small lake, the source of Bear River & thence following Bear River to its entrance into the Missouri a little below Council Bluffs (supposed to be Bowyer's [Boyer] river)."[4]

Even in the nineteenth century, as forces they could not control took their lands from them, Dakota people did not fail to speak of the importance of their homelands. At the Traverse des Sioux treaty negotiations in 1851, government officials put great pressure on Dakota leaders to be quick about signing a treaty in which they would give up all their lands west of the Mississippi River in return for a reservation much smaller than where most of the Dakota had ever lived. Government commissioners believed the question was "a simple one": whether the Dakota would sell all their lands and get in return what would "make them comfortable for many years" or whether they would starve in the midst of a wide country "destitute almost of game." Ištaȟba, Sleepy Eye, the elder statesman in the region of Traverse des Sioux, rose to make a few observations: "Your coming and asking me for my country makes me sad; and your saying I am not able to do any thing with my country makes me still more sad."[5]

A few weeks later at the 1851 Mendota treaty negotiation, Wakute spoke of his fears about the treaty and whether, however good the treaty might be, it would be changed after it was signed, just as other treaties had been changed. After signing a treaty in 1837, he said, Dakota leaders found the provisions were "very different from what they had been told and all were shamed." He then said of the reservation that had been picked for them by government officials, "I was not brought up in a prairie country but among woods and I would like to go to a tract of land called Pine Island which is a good place for Indians. I want you to write this in the treaty." Pine Island, located on the Zumbro River, had been a wintering place for Dakota from Wakute's band for generations. Perhaps at this moment of decision he felt a lingering hope that he could return to that place where he might be left alone by the forces of white colonization and settlement.[6]

Even after they were exiled in 1863, following the Dakota–U.S. War, the Dakota continued to speak about their homelands, in stories told by exiles and by the Dakota who returned to those places they had been forced to leave. Explaining, in 1864, the contributing causes of the events of 1862, Tataŋka Nażiŋ, Standing Buffalo, namesake of the earlier Sisituŋwaŋ leader from Lake Traverse, stated, "I loved my lands, it was on them that I had been raised and fed, it was the land of my fathers." In the years following, Dakota people went back to places they valued, among them the places where their ancestors had been buried for generations. Anthropologist Ella Deloria wrote about her conversations with Minnesota Dakota in the 1930s: "Dakota felt pulled to the region where their dead were put to rest. A survivor of the 1862 Minnesota Uprising reported in her interview the following: 'We were driven out of Minnesota wholesale, though the majority of our people were innocent. But we could not stay away so we managed to find our way back, because our makapahas were here.' The term means earth-hills and is the Santee idiom for graves."[7]

And today Dakota people continue to tell, in many ways and in many places, the stories of their enduring connection to their lands in Minnesota.

The relationship of a people to the lands where they live is crucial for understanding their history and culture. How people use and name the features in their landscapes—and the way this creates their common history—is a topic of great interest in the fields of history, anthropology, folklore, linguistics, and geography. The philosopher Edward S. Casey wrote that a people's sense of place and time is contained in places, the places they inhabit and use. He wrote that "space and time come together in place. Indeed they arise from the experience of the place itself." Folklorist Keith C. Ryden has noted that a place "is much more than a point in space . . . A sense of place results gradually and unconsciously from inhabiting a landscape over time, becoming familiar with its physical properties, accruing a history within its confines."[8]

History comes from stories, accounts, anecdotes, legends, traditions, and folktales. No matter who gives these accounts, or whether they are written or not, they come with the perspective of the teller and the teller's culture, position, and situation. Some are "master stories," stories that express the important values of a people. And some of those master stories are dominant ones, given priority because of the tellers' status. The Dakota connection to this region goes back beyond human memory and written history, but Europeans did not know of the Dakota people until the mid-1600s. Since then, French, British, and American observers have created a written history of the Dakota from a European and white perspective. They tell of the Dakota living in the present-day state of Minnesota and in areas of what is now Canada and in Wisconsin, Iowa, and the Dakotas, including the Mississippi and Minnesota river regions they would continue to inhabit in the nineteenth century.

Rare during the last three hundred years have been histories written to communicate the Dakota point of view about their homelands. Even rarer were histories that communicated the Dakota point of view about the white history of the Dakota people. The white versions of history demonstrate the specific personality of those who wrote and the sometimes haphazard nature of their relationships with the Dakota. While war between the Dakota and other peoples was often described in great detail, the names of Dakota groups, where they lived, and their culture were given random treatment. White visitors often came to Dakota country on brief visits, without seeing the Dakota use of the land from one season to the next and without understanding the rich seasonal patterns that nourished their lives. One account from a single season or year does not provide a full record of the patterns in Dakota use of the region and its resources. Similarly, European visitors had little knowledge of the cultural links between Dakota places or the layers of meaning of each Dakota place. Occasionally they learned of Dakota stories connected to places, but they had little inkling of what those stories actually meant. Missionaries gave small credence to Dakota beliefs, offering biased accounts of seasonal ceremonies. Together these histories—and their shortcomings—show the precarious nature of any solid conclusions one might draw from this information, especially without the traditional history and knowledge of the Dakota themselves.

In writing about Dakota people, non-Dakota historians have often looked for information about particular themes, such as when the Dakota people reached the locations where they lived in the nineteenth century and how they got there. This interest may derive in part from neighboring Ojibwe traditional accounts, such as those recorded in William Warren's *History of the Ojibway People,* which describe the Ojibwe claim that they forced the Dakota to the Mississippi Valley from the Mille Lacs area at some point in the eighteenth century—a claim about which there are differing Dakota points of view. Another topic of investigation has been the subsistence strategies of Dakota people in the past and whether they planted crops such as corn. Dakota oral tradition and the early written records about the Dakota can answer some of these questions. Contrary to historians' assertions, for example, Dakota traditions tell of growing corn at Mille Lacs and at Spirit Lake in what is now Iowa. But there are also questions that arise from the oral tradition itself and the themes that have been and are important to Dakota people in the past and today, such as the significance of traditional cultural places. It is important to guide research by the concerns and understandings of Dakota people themselves.

Europeans in the Minnesota region were not mere observers. They came as traders, government representatives, and missionaries, with goals of changing Dakota people's lives. The consequence was that by their interaction they affected the patterns of Dakota people in the use of the land. As shown in the accounts of Pierre Le Sueur, the French presence on the Mississippi and Minnesota rivers in the 1600s drew the attention of Dakota who lived farther north. Missionaries and government agents encouraged Dakota people to spend more time growing crops and less time hunting and gathering. It is often difficult from such early accounts to obtain a full and complete view of the patterns of Dakota land use.

The histories of the nineteenth-century treaties signed by Dakota leaders which set the stage for the forced removal of the Dakota in 1863 are yet another example of the pitfalls of a narrowly European perspective on Dakota history. These histories generally are told from the incomplete perspective of government negotiators. Yet the Dakota people and the government agents who negotiated and signed the treaties had radically different points of view about their meaning. Instead of being a straightforward account of two peoples coming together to negotiate, the narratives reflect a clash of points of view and of the stories that the different signers had about land and culture. For example, the land transferred in these treaties is usually referred to in legal terminology as *cessions*. However, this term privileges the non-indigenous side of the negotiating table. Instead, because of the way Dakota wishes were often ignored in such treaties, it might be more accurate to call them *seizures*. To make legal or political assertions about the meaning of such treaties today—without examining a fuller history of how these treaties came to be—is as precarious as the cultural conclusions many draw only from written historical accounts.

The dominance of a non-Dakota master story about the Dakota people continues to pose challenges today as Dakota people seek to reclaim the legacy of their history and their places. Many Dakota burial sites and sacred and cultural sites in Minnesota have been damaged, built upon, and impacted in assorted ways by farming, development, and suburbanization. Even in the case of public lands, Dakota assertions about the importance of such places to their history and culture are often treated with skepticism by public agencies given the duty to protect these sites. Widespread ignorance about the Dakota's role in Minnesota and the impact of their exile from Minnesota means that many public agencies and the wider public must be educated before such sites can be protected properly.

The answer to many of the problems presented by Dakota history as it has been written in the past is to try to achieve a more complete account, one that gives full appreciation to the Dakota oral tradition but also makes a concerted effort to read between the lines of written records to search for Dakota points of view and Dakota meanings. This effort also requires a close reading of place and landscape within Minnesota to understand the nature of this place as the Dakota homeland. This approach is especially necessary for nonverbal sources of information, such as archaeological sites, burial mounds, and petroglyphs. Dakota history is often encoded in such places, which bring alive the stories sometimes ignored by historians who call them legends and leave them out of written history.

Oral tradition, written sources, information coded in the landscape—all these pieces of information can be seen as complementary, creating a resonant history in which there are multiple voices, including the eloquent voices of Dakota people past and present. Surprising as it may seem, the written records of British, French, and American visitors to Dakota country contain within them clues to and pieces of a parallel but largely unwritten narrative, documenting the long cultural tradition of the Dakota in the region of Minnesota. In the place names detailed by early French explorers are the accounts of a people who knew these locations well. French records demonstrate that Mni Sota Makoce was a Dakota place when the French first arrived, and despite all that has happened in the last 150 years, it is still a Dakota place today.

DESCRIPTION OF THE PROJECT

To fully explore and renew the theme of the Dakota people and their relationship to their homelands in Minnesota requires much more than the efforts of one person, one perspective, or one project. Many voices are required. This book is the product of a four-year collaboration among people of many backgrounds to study the history and the land of the Dakota people in Minnesota. Each person, whether Dakota or of European ancestry, brought a different perspective to this work, but our goal was the same: to study the heritage of the Dakota people and to make all Minnesotans aware that Minnesota was and is the homeland of the Dakota.

In 2007 a group of Dakota people met to form the Two Rivers Community Development Corporation, a nonprofit entity with a mission to research alternative approaches for the recovery of historic Dakota lands and stories and to advocate for Dakota involvement in the development of places with Dakota connections, such as the Fort Snelling area. In the fall of 2007, Syd Beane and Sheldon Wolfchild, acting as representatives of Two Rivers CDC, met with the Indian Land Tenure Foundation (ILTF) to seek funding for research relating to the recovery of historic Dakota lands. ILTF representatives invited Two Rivers CDC representatives to submit a grant request for this purpose. With the help of Bruce White, Two Rivers wrote and submitted a proposal to ILTF in October 2007.

This proposal to research Dakota land history in Minnesota before 1862 was funded by ILTF starting in the spring of 2008, through Two Rivers' fiscal sponsor, the Native American Community Development Institute (NACDI), with Syd Beane acting as project director and Gwen Westerman and Bruce White as research co-chairs. Other research participants included Katherine Beane, Erin Griffin, Thomas Shaw, Howard Vogel, and Glenn Wasicuna. Over the next year and a half, work involving oral history interviews and archival research continued. Project participants met regularly in St. Paul, Mankato, and on the shores of Lake Pepin to discuss the work and its broader meanings.

As the grant came to a close in 2009, project participants submitted an application to the Minnesota Historical Society to complete the research and interviews and to produce a book manuscript with anticipated publication in

2012, the 150th anniversary of the events of 1862. A major goal of the proposal was to produce a book with a much richer perspective on Dakota history before 1862 than has previously existed. The Minnesota Historical Society made a generous award to the project through Minnesota's Arts and Cultural Heritage Fund in January 2010. With this grant, project participants renewed their research with fresh energy and by the end of June 2011 had completed a draft manuscript. This manuscript was further revised and submitted to the Minnesota Historical Society Press, which accepted it for publication. Over the following months, work continued to expand and hone the narrative.

Working carefully with fluent first-language Dakota speakers, we chose to use the contemporary Dakota orthography developed at the University of Minnesota in the 1990s under the guidance of Waȟpetonwiŋ, Carolynn Schommer. We have also updated, when possible, the spellings of Dakota names and words to correct the centuries of phonetic misspellings and presumptions about meanings propagated in other sources. Where multiple historic spellings occur and require clarification, we have provided explanations in the endnotes and hope they will generate more discussion. Our title, *Mni Sota Makoce,* uses the Dakota adjective *sota* with a regular "s," meaning "clear" or "sky-colored," so that it translates as "land where the waters are so clear they reflect the clouds." Just one of the forms of the name, it was also chosen so readers would be able to pronounce it correctly.

The present form of this book is the product of many people, not just the project participants. We are grateful to all those who contributed to and influenced this work over the last five years, especially the many Dakota people who generously shared their stories of the land and of our people. Glenn Wasicuna not only served as our cultural and language advisor but also helped us ground our efforts in a spiritual way that opened our eyes and our hearts. In particular we want to thank the funding agencies—the Indian Land Tenure Foundation, the Minnesota Arts and Cultural Heritage Fund, the Minnesota Historical Society, and the fiscal agent NACDI—for their generous support of this work. We are also grateful to the Minnesota Historical Society Press and its warm, helpful, and highly competent and patient editor Shannon Pennefeather for seeing the merit in what we wanted to do and helping to make it happen.

PRONUNCIATION GUIDE

||||||||||||||||||||||||||||||||||

This Dakota orthography, or way of representing the language's sounds in written symbols, was created at the University of Minnesota. This orthography is one of many used by Nakota, Lakota, and Dakota speakers. All written forms of Dakota are good for learning the language.

Absent from the Dakota language are these English consonants: f, j, l, q, r, v, and x.

	PRONOUNCED	SOUND
a	a	as in *father*
aŋ	aŋ	as in *honk*
b	ba	as in *boy*
c	ca	*ch* sound, but soft (unaspirated), almost like a *j*
ç	ça	*ch* sound, but hard (aspirated), as in *chalk* and *chop*
c'	c'a	*ch* sound with a pause (glottal stop) before a vowel (a, aŋ, e, i, iŋ, o, u, uŋ)
d	da	as in *dog*
e	e	as *a* in *stay*
ġ	ġa	guttural *g* sound
g	ga	only used when *k* is contracted, ex., waŋyaka to wayag
h	ha	as in *help*
ħ	ħa	guttural *h* like *ch* in German (*machen*)
i	i	as in *see*
iŋ	iŋ	as in *pink*
k	ka	soft (unaspirated) *k*, almost like a *g*
ķ	ķa	hard (aspirated) *k* as in *kite*
k'	k'a	*k* with a pause (glottal stop) before a vowel
m	ma	as in *mom*
n	na	as in *noon*
o	o	as in *open*
p	pa	soft (unaspirated) *p*, almost like a *b*
p̣	p̣a	hard (aspirated) *p* as in *pop*
p'	p'o	*p* with a pause (glottal stop) before a vowel
s	sa	as in *simple*
s'	s'a	*s* with a pause (glottal stop) before a vowel
ṡ	ṡa	*sh* sound as in *shop*
ṡ'	ṡ'a	*sh* sound with a pause (glottal stop) before a vowel
t	ta	soft (unaspirated) *t* as in *storm*, almost like a *d*
ṭ	ṭa	hard (aspirated) *t* as in *top*
t'	t'a	*t* with a pause (glottal stop) before a vowel
u	u	as the *oo* sound in *loop*
uŋ	uŋ	as in *tune*
w	wa	as in *water*
y	ya	as in *yellow*
z	za	as in *zap*
ż	ża	as the *s* sound in *pleasure*

CHAPTER ONE

Homelands

"The power of the Dakotas had always dwelt in the land,
from the great forest to the open prairies. Long before the white man
ever dreamed of our existence, the Dakota roamed this land."

Waŋbdi Wakiya

Mni Sota Makoce. The land where the waters are so clear they reflect the clouds. This land is where our grandmothers' grandmothers' grandmothers played as children. Carried in our collective memories are stories of this place that reach beyond recorded history. Sixteen different verbs in the Dakota language describe returning home, coming home, or bringing something home. That is how important our homeland is in Dakota regardless of where our history has taken us. No matter how far we go, we journey back home through language and songs and in stories our grandparents told us to share with our children.

"Back home" implies a return, a cycle of returning, as if it is expected, natural, a fact of life. Families gather around kitchen tables and remember the generations before us or journeys we make to or away from home. It is there, back home, where we are trying to return, where we belong, where the landscape is as familiar as our childhood beds and our mothers' hands, where our roots are the deepest. It is there, back home, where we hear the repeated stories that make us who we are. So deep is that connection to the land that the word for *mother* and for the earth are the same in the Dakota language: Ina.

Indeed, the stories—oral histories and oral traditions—are reflected in the place names of this region where Dakota people have lived for millennia and where they still maintain powerful connections to the land. Place names around us—Maŋkato, Owotaŋna, Winuna, Shakpe, Mni Sota—repeat these stories. Existing in different versions, carried forward by multiple storytellers, the message is the same: Mni Sota is a Dakota place.

For Dakota people, stories are often tied to places in the landscape and the skies rather than to groups of people or specific bands, which were fluid and mobile. While common misconceptions perpetuated in European and later American historical accounts portray the Dakota as nomadic people, we were in fact purposeful in our seasonal migrations, following ancient and rhythmic cycles. That rhythm included not only when to harvest wild and cultivated foods and the best time to hunt and trap so the meat was good but also when to tell stories. Ceremonies were conducted and stories told based upon generations of observing the constellations.

No clear boundaries seem to exist between many of these stories and which group they "belong" to unless they are associated with a specific place, person, or historical event. There are many stories, many perspectives, and many generations of oral tradition to be told and re-told. In "Grandmother to Granddaughter: Generations of Oral History in a Dakota Family," Waziyatawiŋ stresses that "these are not merely interesting stories or even the simple dissemination of historical fact. They are, more importantly, transmissions of culture upon which our survival as a people depends. When our stories die, so will we."[1]

The stories gathered here represent a broad base of knowledge of Dakota people from every band—Bdewakaŋtuŋwaŋ, Waȟpekute, Waȟpetuŋwaŋ, Sisituŋwaŋ, and Ihaŋktuŋwaŋ—that span Minnesota, Nebraska, South Dakota, North Dakota, Saskatchewan, Alberta, and Manitoba. To add to the body of knowledge represented by more widely known storytellers and tribal historians, we sought out elderly fluent speakers and traditional people who were willing to share what they knew about the land. Over a period of three years, we conducted interviews with many Dakota people who were eager to share the stories they knew because they had not been asked to tell them before. Our collaborators ranged in age from thirty to one hundred years old. With other accounts taken from nineteenth- and twentieth-century oral history collections, we have brought together numerous stories and multiple viewpoints of this place and our people into a continuous narrative. At once singular and collective, they create an account of Dakota history from "beyond remembering" to today. They endure as Dakota stories and histories of how we came to be in this land, Mni Sota Makoce, how we are a part of this land, and what our responsibilities are to each other and to our Ina. Through these stories we are taught how to live, and through these stories we will continue to live.[2]

Otókahe / The Beginning

[ERIN GRIFFIN] **Stories and theories** written by explorers, missionaries, historians, and anthropologists locate Dakota origins in numerous places. One version is that Dakota people came from the North. Some Dakota accounts gathered from missionaries suggest that Bde Wakaŋ (Spirit Lake, or what is known today as Mille Lacs) is the origin place and the center of the earth. Reports from early French explorers give details about Dakota people and their activities around this region. Other accounts place Dakota people even farther north than Bde Wakaŋ. Nineteenth-century missionary Stephen R. Riggs suggested that Dakota people lived as far north as Hudson Bay and the Arctic Ocean. Similarly, missionary Samuel W. Pond proposed that Dakota people once lived so far north that they knew of "the habits of the Esquimaux, for whom they had a name, calling them 'Eaters of raw food.'"[i]

While there is no question that the Dakota nation traveled and spread out over great distances, claims of Dakota origins in places other than Mni Sota Makoce conflict with Dakota oral narratives and ultimately undermine Dakota connections to the land. Mni Sota is the original homeland of the Dakota, and our own oral history of the events of our creation remains the most important to us. This region was the home of Dakota people generations before us, and for generations after us it will remain our homeland. We are told that we were brought here to this land from the stars to the place where the Minnesota and Mississippi rivers meet. This place known as Bdote is our place of genesis. We have recognized Bdote as the center of the earth and of all things, and historical accounts tell of it as a meeting place where massive gatherings of lodges took place annually. From here, our Oyate expanded into the four bands of Mdewakaŋtuŋwaŋ, Waĥpekute, Waĥpetuŋwaŋ, and Sisituŋwaŋ and over time spread out across much of what is today Minnesota, North and South Dakota, Nebraska, into Iowa and Wisconsin, and the provinces of Manitoba, Saskatchewan, and Alberta in Canada.[ii]

Though the bands were spread out, Dakota life was dictated by kinship, which is the essence of Dakota culture. According to Dakota anthropologist Ella Deloria,

> The ultimate aim of Dakota life, stripped of accessories, was quite simple: One must obey kinship rules; one must be a good relative. No Dakota who has participated in that life will dispute that . . . Without that aim and the constant struggle to attain it, the people would no longer be Dakotas in truth. They would no longer even be human. To be a good Dakota, then, was to be humanized, civilized. And to be civilized was to keep the rules imposed by kinship for achieving civility, good manners, and a sense of responsibility toward every individual dealt with.

A person's relatives were not limited to the nuclear family; instead, Dakota kinship allowed for something much larger. A father's brothers were counted as one's fathers; a father's sisters were aunts. A mother's sisters were counted as one's mothers and her brothers would be uncles. Correspondingly, their children would be considered one's brothers and sisters. According to this practice, no matter how distant, a relative would be claimed. This inclusiveness was tioṡpaye, the extended family. Following kinship rules was a way of life, far more complex than just knowing one's relations. In this way, a Dakota person could undoubtedly find a relative almost anywhere when traveling within the Dakota nation. Kinship rules also provided a sense of security and an acknowledgment of the laws by which the people were governed.[iii] ∎

It is through our stories that we all understand where we come from, regardless of heritage or background or religion. "Mythology, next to language," said missionary Stephen R. Riggs, "affords the most reliable evidence as to the origin or relationship of a people; for peoples have been slow to change their gods." While *mythology* may have negative connotations in today's society, it is through myths that we try to explain the unexplainable or to understand a time before we were in existence. The similarities in those stories, according to early-twentieth-century Dakota oral historians, indicate that "the Dakota and the white man must be closely related, since they tell nearly the same story about creation." Throughout human culture, creation stories provide an explanation of how the world began.[3]

THE CREATION OF OUR SOLAR SYSTEM

Hekta ehaŋna, long ago, our people were camped together. The chief wanted to know if there was an end to this land and called his council. They chose four young men—tall, strong, fast, not yet with women—gave them extra moccasins, and sent them toward the direction of the setting sun to find the answer. The young men traveled for a few days and then slept on the side of a hill. Not on the top, not on the bottom, but the middle. If they came straight down, it might appear to someone watching from across the way that they were hostile. So they descended back and forth across the hill to seem friendly.

Early in the morning, one young man awoke to a noise. "Wake up," he said, "I thought I heard something." They looked down the hill. A strange man, strange because he was not Dakota, was sitting there facing the other way, toward where the sun sets. He wore a white blanket and had hair on his face. One of them said, "Let's go see this mysterious man. There's a reason we came across him." As they were trying to decide what to do, the man said, "Hiyu po! Taku ociciyakapi kte bduhe do. Come on down here. I have something to tell you."[4]

To hear this stranger speak their language was unexpected, and the young

---

Not One Creation Story, but Many

[WAKIŊYAŊ ZI SAPA, CURTIS CAMPBELL] **"So depending on** where you live at or how you've grown up, each place had their creation story. There were different types of values that came out of these different histories of the creation stories. I don't hold any one of them above the others; they're all equally important. And there's no right or wrong among any of them. But that's the way it is, you know. You go further down south, down river and go further north, either way, we're all the same people. We're all Dakota people, you know."[iv] ∎

men were uncertain about what to do next. One wanted to continue on their original journey and reminded the others they still had a long way to go. Another thought it was a trick to lure them into a trap and that it couldn't be good. While they were talking, the stranger again said, "You four up there, come down here. I have something to tell you." They suddenly realized the stranger knew their language and, despite facing away from them, knew there were four in their party. Then one young man whispered, "This is unexplainable. He must be a sacred being." They agreed to go and talk with him.

The man had a small fire going and said, "You sit here on the south side. I have something to tell you." Then he spent all day teaching them about the world where they lived. He spoke of how the suns—there were many suns, not just one—the stars, the moons, and the planets were put together and how they were to work together. The stranger explained how all of these things came to pass. And the young men said he told them, after he had talked all day, to remember his words:

> These things I am telling you, always remember these as long as you can in the future, tell each other every year, every generation, and your grandchildren and your great-grandchildren, continue telling each other . . . Those who walk with commitment, they will walk in that path of what they remember.

THE CREATION OF THE EARTH

When the world was created, Kuŋśi Maka, Grandmother Earth, was just a rock, and she was chosen to hold life. The moons, the planets, the stars, and the sun agreed to help her with the task she had been given. Before the earth was made there was water everywhere; no land was to be seen. The Creator then made the animals that have fur and those that swim in the water. This was the beginning of everything.

While the world was still covered in water, the Uŋkteȟi, a powerful water spirit, sent some of the animals down into the water one by one to reach the bottom to find some clay. Many animals tried but were unsuccessful and died in the effort. The muskrat took his turn, dove into the water, and after a long time surfaced with a paw full of clay. From this small amount, land was made and placed on the turtle's back.[5]

Dakota oral traditions also describe how uŋkteȟi battled with the wakiŋyaŋ, or thunder beings, who caused storm winds and lightning. Uŋkteȟi would churn up the surfaces of rivers and lakes, creating whitecaps and rolling waves, until the Sun brought peace to the world again, holding a rainbow, like a flag of many colors, in his hand. The uŋkteȟi could travel along underground waterways from Lake Traverse and Big Stone Lake along the Minnesota and Mississippi rivers to Ṭaku Wakaŋ Tipi. Dakota people were familiar with the routes and may have also used them for safety and escape when required.[6]

Dakota men seated in the "profound deliberation" of a council were the subject of a painting by George Catlin, who visited southern Minnesota in 1835 and 1836. The exact location is not recorded, but the scene resembles some of the islands of wood in the region's prairies.

WE ARE A PART OF THIS LAND

The search for the origin of humans in this world is a shared quest in almost every culture. Many of the stories that explain where we came from involve not only the creation of a body from the dust or mud of the earth itself but also the element of a spirit or breath from the Creator.

THE SPIRIT ROAD

Dakota people are called Wicaŋhpi Oyate, Star People. Our spirits come from the Creator down the Caŋku Wanaǧi, the "spirit road," more commonly known as the Milky Way. At death, we return where we came from along that same road. In the PBS series *The Elegant Universe*, physicist Michio Kaku discussed the theory of the moment of creation when a star explodes and becomes bits of matter that float into space and are drawn to another star to form planets and ultimately life. He explained that life comes from light and energy and therefore we are made of stardust. But as Dakota people, we knew that. Our creation stories tell us that long ago we came to this earth along the Milky Way.[7]

BDOTE

The place of first creation is at the confluence of the Minnesota and Mississippi rivers, where the Dakota people came from the stars to be on the earth. Two bluffs were formed from the earth, one called Caśke Taŋka and the other Caśke Cistiŋna. The Earth opened herself in that way, and from the mud the Creator made the first Dakota man and woman. Because Dakota were made from the Earth, she is called Ina, mother. In 1720 a French account recorded that the Dakota "say that the first Sciou and the first woman of their tribe came out of the earth, which brought them forth on the prairie below St. Anthony Falls." This statement is perhaps the first written record of the importance to the Dakota of the area around Bdote. More than one hundred years later, missionary Stephen R. Riggs wrote, "The Mdewakanton think that the mouth of the Minnesota River is precisely over the center of the earth, and that they occupy the gate that opens into the western world."[8]

The importance of water is significant. In the beginning, the water—Mni— was pure, part of the land, and therefore part of the people. It was the first medicine given to our people because water keeps everything alive. Water that comes from within the earth is pure and as such is considered wakaŋ or sacred. This region where the rivers come together plays a significant role in the history of the Dakota people in Mni Sota Makoce, as it contains Ṭaku Wakaŋ Tipi, Mni Sni or Coldwater Spring, and Oheyawahi or Pilot Knob.

In this place, the Dakota people flourished. We respected our homeland and our Creator. Our numbers increased. Our winter camps became villages, and we became the people of the Oçeti Śakowiŋ, the Seven Council Fires.[9]

ḢE MNI ÇAŊ

As the people spread out from Bdote, a cultural hub was established at Ḣe Mni Çaŋ (Barn Bluff, near present-day Red Wing) on the Mississippi River. Fog often rises up from the rivers in this area, and it was known as I saŋ ti, "where they live under the fog." Each group of people possessed a great spiritual strength and had their responsibilities to the larger community. The Bdewakaŋtuŋwaŋ were the spiritual people who lived by the water, as did the Sisituŋwaŋ, the medicine people. The Waḣpekute were warriors who protected the medicine people. Waḣpetuŋwaŋ people were dwellers in the forest, and the Iḣaŋktuŋwaŋ lived at the edge of the great forest. Iḣaŋktuŋwaŋ were scattered at the edge of the forest. It was to this hub that people from the east and north came. Some decided to stay and lived among the Dakota. Others visited for a while, then left and went west and south. Dakota people also left with them.[10]

Many people lived in that area, working together, gathering medicines, and hunting, year in and year out. The land belonged to everyone, and everyone used it in harmony. Then there were disagreements about who should pick

Bdote Mni Sota / Mouth of the Minnesota River

The area of Bdote (or Mdote) Mni Sota is located at the mouth of the Minnesota River where it flows into the Mississippi midway between the downtowns of Minneapolis and St. Paul. It is, according to Dakota oral traditions, a place of creation. The mouth of the Minnesota's broad valley is located in a break in the high banks of the Mississippi corridor, a gorge deeply carved by the Falls of St. Anthony in its million-year journey up the river. This place was Bdote Mni Sota: bdote meaning "mouth"; mni sota referring to the clarity of the water and its reflection of the sky. The exact boundaries of Bdote Mni Sota are hard to determine. Sites generally considered to be within this sacred district include Mni Sni (Coldwater Spring) and Oheyawahi (Pilot Knob). Some Dakota include Ṭaku Wakaŋ Tipi (Carver's Cave) and Mounds Park within this region as well.[v]

In 1689 a French document claiming possession of the region mentions a Mantanton Dakota presence at the mouth of the Minnesota River and also suggests the possibility of a village site there. The later village known as Black Dog may have been located near the mouth of the Minnesota River before Fort Snelling was built. Trader James H. Lockwood, who arrived in the Upper Mississippi region in 1816, wrote, "There was another small band who had their village at Mendota, which signifies the meeting of the waters, whose chief was called Black Dog." After the construction of Fort Snelling, Indian Agent Lawrence Taliaferro resisted attempts by various Dakota to locate a village there, perhaps thinking he would be forced to show favoritism toward those villagers.[vi]

A 1960s construction project led to a new river channel connecting the Minnesota to the Missis-

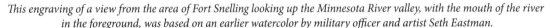

This engraving of a view from the area of Fort Snelling looking up the Minnesota River valley, with the mouth of the river in the foreground, was based on an earlier watercolor by military officer and artist Seth Eastman.

sippi River adjacent to Pike Island. This adjustment changed the mouth of the Minnesota, creating a back channel where the old river mouth had been. What used to be the east bank of the river and the location of the first U.S. military camp in 1819 is now known as Picnic Island and is accessible by road within Fort Snelling State Park.[vii] ■

The mouth of the Minnesota River, at left, underneath the Mendota Bridge, viewed from an airplane in 1935, shows the river as it was before a channel was cut through the bend at the river's mouth, to the right, in the 1970s. The land cut off by this channel is now Picnic Island in Fort Snelling State Park.

medicine in the area. Some of the Dakota claimed that area, and other people said it had always been theirs. The argument escalated until they were ready to fight one another. The two groups faced each other to do battle over the contested ground.

The ground started to shake. A mist rose up out of the area, and the people fell unconscious to the ground. After a while, as the mist started to lift, they came back to their senses and remembered they were ready to do battle. But as they looked at their opponents, they saw that they were separated by a valley with water running through there. The Creator had shown them this land was given for everyone to use and not to fight over it. From that moment on they called those Dakota groups, all the different villages regardless of which side of the river they were on, Kiyuksa. And so they lived that way, going back and forth across the river since both groups had relatives on both sides. And they realized their argument over the land was foolishness and nothing can be settled through fighting.

And so the people continued to live up and down the river until they fell away from the Creator and no longer knew how to behave. The uŋktehi were called upon to flood the land and cleanse it of the people's disrespectful actions. Flood stories, numerous across the world and among the many indigenous groups of North America, usually result from a violation of cultural or religious mores. As explained by Dakota oral traditions, the people were restored to land in different places, and the blood of those who perished became the sacred red stone from which our ceremonial pipes are made to this day.

Ŝuŋǧi, Reverend Gary Cavender relates that "In our Creation myth we the Dakota, the Seven Fires of the Dakota, came from the belt of Orion—the seven planets of the belt of Orion, the seven stars—and arrived at the convolution of the Minnesota and Mississippi Rivers, and so in some respects it is our Eden, and the land around there is sacred as well."[viii]

Dakota people belonged to one of the seven fires, or bands, that made up the Oyate, or Nation. Each band was designated by where they lived or what their responsibilities were. ■

In a Dakota creation story, the Seven Fires of the Dakota or Oçeti Ŝaḳowiŋ came from the constellation of Orion, which includes seven major stars.

Bdewakaŋtuŋwaŋ	Mdewakanton	The spiritual people who live by the water
Sisituŋwaŋ	Sisseton	The medicine people who live by the water
Waħpekuṭe	Wahpekute	The warriors who protected the medicine people and could shoot from among the leaves
Waħpeṭuŋwaŋ	Wahpeton	The people who live in the forest
Ihaŋktuŋwaŋ	Yankton	The people who live at the edge of the great forest
Ihaŋktuŋwaŋna	Yanktonai	Those scattered at the edge of the forest
Tituŋwaŋ	Teton	Dwellers of the plains

Dakota tradition maintains that when the Creator sent the Uŋkteȟi to flood the earth, the people who perished had forgotten how to behave as human beings. Their blood became the sacred red stone which is still used today for our ceremonial pipes used for prayer. Archeological evidence indicates that indigenous peoples have been excavating the stone for three thousand years. By the 1700s, the Dakota controlled the quarry, located in Pipestone County in southwestern Minnesota. Joseph Nicollet stated that the Dakota name for "this very sacred quarry" was "iyanska K'api; that is to say, the place where one digs the red rock," or "Chanduhuppa Shak'api—there where one digs the red pipes." An early written reference to the pipestone quarry and its importance to the Dakota occurred in Pierre Le Sueur's notes from around 1700, where he recorded that the "Hinhanctons" (Ihaŋktuŋwaŋ or Yanktons) were known as the village "of the stone (because of a red stone quarry that is found near them in the middle of a prairie)."[ix]

In his journal of a visit to the Minnesota River region in 1766–67, Jonathan Carver wrote that on the plains between the Minnesota and Missouri rivers was "a large mountain of red marble where all the neighbouring nations resort for stone to make pipes of. Even those who hold perpetual wars in all other parts meet here in peace." His later published narrative reported that in addition to using the stone to make the bowls of their pipes Indian people mixed "the red stone powdered" with the blue clay which Le Sueur had sought on the Blue Earth River, "to paint themselves different colors" for use when involved in "their sports and pastimes." Among the first non-Indians to write an account of visiting the quarry was the artist George Catlin, who in 1836 recorded the area and the process of quarrying in a series of paintings, at the same time managing to obtain false credit for "discovering" the quarry, which

led geologists to name pipestone *catlinite*. In 1838 Joseph Nicollet recorded the Dakota names for the quarry, noting that the Dakota told him the quarry "was opened by the great spirit of thunder, and one cannot visit it without his rumblings, and the lightings and storms that accompany them." Nicollet and his party, which included the explorer John Charles Fremont and the Odawa French trader Joseph Laframboise, spent several days in the area of the quarry, leaving their names carved on a rock. In 1849 the Minnesota territorial legislature sent a slab of pipestone to be used in the construction of the Washington Monument, accompanied by a letter from Representative Henry H. Sibley objecting to Catlin's claim to have been the first white man to visit the quarry and to the use of the term *catlinite* to refer to the rock. He ɱadȩ the point that a Dakota term for the rock was inyan ṡa or red stone.[x]

The Yankton treaty, signed in Washington, DC, in April 1858 and ceding Yankton lands in present-day South Dakota, contained in Article 8 the provision that the Yanktons "shall be secured in the free and unrestricted use of the red pipe-stone quarry, or so much thereof as they have been accustomed to frequent and use for the purpose of procuring stone for pipes; and the United States hereby stipulate and agree to cause to be surveyed and marked so much thereof as shall be necessary and proper for that purpose, and retain the same and keep it open and free to the Indians to visit and procure stone for pipes so long as they shall desire." A federal Indian school established at Pipestone in 1893 led to litigation involving the Yanktons, who objected to its creation without their permission, for which they ultimately received damages. In 1937 the Pipestone National Monument was established to preserve the quarry and surrounding area. Federal regulations limit quarrying to members of federally recognized tribes.[xi]

Mille Lacs is called Bde Wakaŋ by the Dakota, which is sometimes translated as "Spirit Lake." The name indicates that the lake was a particularly important sacred space, one associated with a portion of the Bdewakaŋtuŋwaŋ people, whose name may have come to refer to a larger group than in its original designation for Mille Lacs. Missionary Stephen R. Riggs wrote of the Dakota belief that there was a fearful Ṭaku Wakaŋ (that is, Uŋkteȟi) in the lake that appeared at planting time. The Bdewakaŋtuŋwaŋ "dreamed of it and no more feared it." A similar explanation appears in the Lakota accounts collected by James R. Walker.[xii]

The full relationship of the Dakota to Mille Lacs is difficult to document completely. Knife Lake is located near the southeast shore of Mille Lacs, at the headwaters of the nearby Snake River, in present-day Kanabec County near its border with Mille Lacs County. This lake is said to have been known to the Dakota as Isaŋti mde, referring to a place where stone was found to make the knife blades the Dakota used before they acquired metal goods. This name may be the origin of the term *Santee*, which was applied to all the eastern Dakota, particularly by western peoples. Father Louis Hennepin, in his account of a visit to the region in 1685, called the people he visited the Issatis. Jean-Baptiste Louis Franquelin's 1697 map of the Minnesota region and Pierre-Charles Le Sueur's records show multiple Dakota villages on Mille Lacs and in the surrounding region. They were accessible through a variety of rivers and portages connecting the lake to the Mississippi, St. Croix, St. Louis, and other rivers.[xiii]

The Mille Lacs area was rich in resources. Some ethnohistorians have suggested that large rice harvests are enough to explain its importance as a population center, but the maple groves along the south shore, the plentiful fish in the lake, the fur-bearing animals in the swamplands, and many other resources contributed as well. Archaeologist Mary K. Whelan, in an analysis of the animal and plant remains at Mille Lacs, found Late Woodland– and

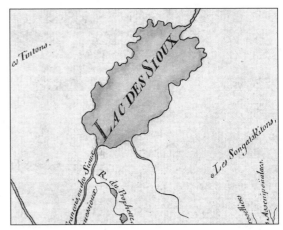

Two maps by Jean-Baptiste Louis Franquelin, from 1685 and 1688, provide the earliest French records of the Dakota presence at Bde Wakaŋ or Mille Lacs Lake, identifying the lake first as the "Lac des Sioux" or Lake of the Sioux and later as "Lac de Buade," from the family name of Louis de Buade, Comte de Frontenac, the Governor General of New France during this period. The second map also names the lake "Issatis," an early version of the name Santee, applied to eastern Dakota communities.

early historic–period sites suggesting the people living there could reside in the area year round. In contrast, Dakota sites on the Minnesota and Mississippi rivers were more likely summer villages. In the winter, the Dakota of these villages moved into the woods to live in small family groups.[xiv]

Archaeologist Jacob Brower, who traveled around Mille Lacs in 1900, mapped the locations of a number of mound groups as well as what he described as ancient village sites. At the end of his journey, he noted in his diary, "it is now my deliberate opinion that the nation of mound-builders who constructed the earthworks at Mille Lacs were the ancient Sioux villagers who for unknown ages occupied the shores of that lake." At Garrison in May 1900, Brower surveyed an "ancient earthwork" consisting of embankments hundreds of feet long that formed a kind of enclosure. Such an earthwork surrounding a village site may explain Franquelin's term for the Quiocpeton, or a nation refermé, suggesting an enclosed village.[xv]

Few of the mounds and earthworks Brower identified at Mille Lacs were excavated, and many have been destroyed. In any case, correlating these locations with Dakota groups in the seventeenth century is problematic. The most thorough excavations have occurred in the area of the three lakes below the outlet of Mille Lacs. Douglas Birk and Elden Johnson support the idea that the Dakota people at Mille Lacs resided in a series of small permanent villages throughout the area. Large gatherings might have occurred at particular times of the year, but contrary to Father Hennepin's suggestion, there was probably no single "great village" on the lake's shore. Perhaps he referred to those several villages, taking them to be united as one.[xvi] ∎

MILLE LACS

After the flood, some of the people lived under the water at Bde Taŋka or Bde Wakaŋ. One day, a young boy and his sister were walking together. The boy looked up and saw mniyomni to, a blue whirlpool, above them and reached up for it. The whirlpool pulled him up to the surface and threw him out onto the shore, a beautiful place of trees and hills. His sister followed the bubbles of the mniyomni, reached up, and was also thrown ashore. She followed her brother's footprints, eating roots and berries along the way, and picked up a small stone to suck in order to quench her thirst. Amazed at the beauty of the place, she was distracted and swallowed the stone. It traveled through her body and was born a child called Iŋyaŋ Hokśida, Stone Boy. This is how the people walked out of the lake and became people who walk on the land again.

BIG STONE LAKE

When the uŋkteȟi were called on to flood the land, the eagle picked up a young woman who was clinging to a tree and took her to where a large rock stood out from the water. He placed her on Iŋyaŋ Taŋka, the big rock, and showed her that the water from there—the center of the earth—flowed in all directions,

The Dakota called this place Owamniyomni or "whirlpool." Father Louis Hennepin is given credit for naming the Falls of St. Anthony. In an account of his trip in 1680–81, Hennepin provides the first written record of the Dakota view of the falls. He noted that one of the Dakota in his party climbed an oak tree and made an offering of a beaver robe decorated with porcupine quills, saying, "You, who are a spirit, grant that our tribe pass by here tranquilly without mishap. Grant that we may kill many buffaloes, destroy our enemies, and bring here captives, some of whom we will sacrifice to you."[xvii]

More than a hundred years later, Jonathan Carver reported that a Winnebago, that is, Ho-Chunk "prince" who had come to the region to visit the Dakota accompanied him to the falls and made an offering of his pipe and the ornaments he was wearing, throwing them into the water while asking for the Great Spirit's protection during their travels.[xviii]

Though incomplete, these descriptions indicate the veneration in which the falls were held and the sense that they housed a powerful being or beings. Gideon Pond wrote that a sudden flood of water over the falls in the 1820s following the breakup of ice was attributed to Uŋkteħi, and that a soldier who was carried away from the cabin below Fort Snelling had served to feed this being.[xix]

The falls were used in the late nineteenth century for water power for flour milling and other purposes, hastening the destruction of the falls, which were destined, in any case, to disappear for geological reasons. The falls today bear little resemblance to those of 150 years ago. ■

Owamniyomni or the Falls of St. Anthony was a site for ceremonies by Dakota people long before Father Louis Hennepin named it in 1681. Jonathan Carver recorded this view of the falls in 1778, prior to the extensive engineering that destroyed its earlier form.

The Bdewakaŋtuŋwaŋ Dakota village found lowest on the Mississippi River was that of the Kiyuksa band, at Wabasha's village or Wapasha's Prairie, shown here in a Seth Eastman watercolor from the 1840s, now the location of the city of Winona.

to the north and east and to the south and west. From there the people again multiplied and flourished.

OWAMNIYOMNI AND SPIRIT LAKE

Some of the Dakota people went to Owamniyomni, called St. Anthony Falls, for ceremonies because of the power associated with the falls along Ḣaḣa Wakpa. From there was a road to Spirit Lake in what is now known as Iowa. The people would walk or ride horses, and soon the different groups of Dakota spread out to the south and west of Bdote and lived all through the prairies, where they hunted buffalo and elk. Many villages were established around Spirit Lake. The Wapiya Wicaṡṭa, the medicine people, talked for quite a while about the times when the people would be short of food because so many of them lived in that area.

They remembered that long ago they had been told that at the bottom of the lake was a person who could help the people survive. So they asked the families there to send one of their daughters to volunteer to go into the lake. Some of the people did not believe in the old story and did not want to sacrifice their young girls for such a futile task. However, there were people who did believe what the Wapiya Wicaṡṭa were saying. One family stepped forward with their daughter.

They told the young girl to swim to the bottom, where she would meet someone who would help her. A lot of people thought she would drown because it was an impossible task. But she and her family believed, and she went with the Wapiya Wicaṡṭa in a small boat to the middle of the lake. They told her what to do and said they would be waiting there for her to return. So she went into the water and swam toward the bottom. There she saw a woman dressed in white buckskin who held a bowl in each hand. The woman said, "These will help your people. When you plant them, they will grow and then you can eat them." The young girl took the gifts from the woman and swam up, up, up to where the Wapiya Wicaṡṭa were waiting for her. They took her out of the water, and she placed the bowls in their hands and explained what the woman had told her.

The gift was seeds of corn: four male seeds in one bowl and four female seeds in the other. The young girl instructed them to plant the seeds one row male, one row female, one row male, one row female. And they would grow and the people would not run out of food again. There was a big crowd along the shore, with her family and those others who were sure she was going to drown. The medicine people explained to everyone how to plant the corn. From those first rows they planted, they harvested some and they saved some of the seeds to plant the following year.

The Dakota people from that time forward would have plenty of corn. Because the holy being, the sacred woman, lived there under the water and gave them the gift of corn, they called it Spirit Lake. They gave thanks to the creator and held the first green corn dance. The road between Spirit Lake and St. Anthony Falls was well traveled by Dakota people from that time forward.

Dakota women made use of birch-bark canoes to harvest wild rice throughout the Minnesota region, as archaeology, tradition, and written sources tell us. This view—which would likely have been accurate for the Dakota and neighboring Ojibwe, who both used such canoes for this purpose—was drawn by artist and scientist Robert O. Sweeny in the 1850s.

The Dakota spread across the land from Ḣe Mni Çaŋ throughout the northern Great Plains. Evidence of their pottery can be found in what is now western Wisconsin, Minnesota, western Ontario, and eastern Manitoba dating from 1150 CE. By the early eighteenth century, the Dakota controlled the areas around Lake of the Woods and Rainy Lake, hunting and traveling as far east as Kaministikwia, near Thunder Bay, Ontario, and as far northwest as the head of the Churchill River in Saskatchewan. According to Cree history, the Dakota came north along the Ballantyne River, known by the Cree as Puatsipi or Dakota River, on raids against the Cree and Assiniboine long before 1774, when the Hudson's Bay Company established its first inland post.[11]

One of the earliest written accounts of the migration of Dakota people away from the Mille Lacs area was recorded in Dakota language by Wambdi Oḳiya in 1837. Writing to the missionary Thomas Williamson, Wambdi Oḳiya said,

> From the beginning when the Dakotas grew, the present Chippewa country belonged to the Dakotas, they say . . . My fathers told it thus. What is called Knife Lake was the Mdewakantons planting ground, they say; and Wazina Ha Wakpa [Pine Bark River] used to be the land of the Wahpetons, they say. They planted there, they say . . . but for some unknown reason, they came here and remained, because there was much buffalo on the open prairie, and the Chippewas came and took up their home there, it is said. Because all the wise men are now dead, nobody mentions these things, and so it is.[12]

Moving to where the game was more plentiful, and isolated in the deep woods of the Upper Mississippi, the Dakota knew about the French from their interactions with the Ojibwe and Odawa long before they actually met them for the first time. By the early 1800s, trade goods began to filter in through the Ojibwe and Odawa, including iron pots, knives, blankets, and guns, so that by the time French voyageurs entered the Upper Mississippi Valley, "the Dakotas had no reason to be either shocked or frightened. They had no illusions that these were superior beings sent by the Great Spirit, though they were deeply impressed by their wondrous technology." It is no surprise, then, that they were called Waṡicuŋ, or people who had done well for themselves. And events were set into motion that would change the face of Mni Sota Makoce forever.[13]

CHAPTER TWO

Reading Between *the* Lines *of the* Historical Record

Minnesota is rich with Dakota places. Dakota history is encoded in the land and landscape of the state and the surrounding region. The challenge is to find that history wherever and however it is recorded—and to understand it. Historians usually begin their account of the Dakota in Minnesota in the seventeenth century, with the arrival of the French, basing the narrative on written records. Yet the Dakota people say they have always been in this region, a belief recorded both in their oral tradition and in the land itself.

DAKOTA INSCRIPTIONS ON THE LAND

Throughout Minnesota, the many mounds along the banks of rivers and lakes give tangible evidence of the history of the Dakota people. The mounds were a mystery to nineteenth-century whites, who could not believe that Indian people of that time built them or were related to those who did. Major Stephen Long traveled up the Mississippi and Minnesota rivers in June 1823. His account makes frequent mention of the mounds along the riverbanks and bluffs. "Near our encampment of last evening," he wrote, "there were several antique mounds of artificial structure arranged in nearly a right line along the margin of the river. The[y] are of inconsiderable height but cover a large surface." Beyond the mouth of the Whitewater River, Long noted, "In this beautiful spot are located numerous indian mounds of high antiquity." At the mouth of the Zumbro he observed "a numerous and crowded assemblage of antient tumuli." At the Cannon River, Long "crossed several small plains on which are seen antient tumuli more numerous than I ever before witnessed." In the 1840s German artist Henry Lewis described the view at the present site of Wabasha: "The countless mounds, enthroned on the hilltops like monuments of a long-gone race, form an immeasurable cordon along the blue horizon." Many experts speculated that the mounds had been built by a vanished race, a belief that persisted into the twentieth century. But James E. Colhoun, who accompanied Long in 1823, had already reached the conclusion, now commonly accepted, that the mounds were not the product of a vanished people but rather had been built by the "immediate ancestors of the Indians or by a similar race of men."[1]

In the 1850s missionary Stephen R. Riggs wrote about the mounds of the Minnesota Valley, pointing out their connection to the Dakota. He wrote that the Dakota preferred to bury people on a "*paha,* or conspicuous point" near villages, first erecting a scaffold where the body would lie before burial. Graves were shallow and the earth was mounded up over them, resulting, Riggs theorized, in the creation of mounds. He believed that existing mounds continued to be used for burial by the Dakota and were found near all Dakota villages.[2]

Later archaeologists, however, in the absence of written documentation, created their own names to describe the people who built the mounds, the patterns in their construction, and the archaeological evidence found during mound and site excavations, such as the Laurel, St. Croix, and Onamia ceramic patterns. As anthropologist Guy Gibbon pointed out, "archaeologists have not found a reliable way to distinguish social identities in the archaeological record." More recently, archaeologists have explored the mounds' connection to the Dakota people. Elden Johnson argued for an association between the seventeenth-century Dakota living at Mille Lacs and what was called the Psinomani archaeological complex, a name derived from the Dakota phrase for gatherers of wild rice, an important resource for people living there. Such associations have yet to be explored fully.[3]

In 1984 archaeologist Scott Anfinson, echoing Riggs over a century earlier, noted that the location of burial mounds along the Minnesota and Mississippi rivers corresponds very well to the locations of Dakota villages. He wrote, "Perhaps the strongest cultural correlation with mound distribution in Minnesota is with the early historic distribution of the Dakota," with the greatest concentration of mounds adjacent to major Dakota village sites. In any case, whether or not the Dakota built all of the mounds, they held the mounds to be sacred and buried their own dead within them.[4]

Anfinson pointed out that if the Dakota were "the most prolific mound builders of Minnesota," then much of the state's early ethnographic and archaeological record must be reexamined. According to Anfinson, it was a "popular misconception" that the Dakota "were *all* woodland dwellers at the time of white contact and that soon after contact they were forced out of their central Minnesota homes by the better-armed Ojibwa." He and other scholars contended that "the western Dakota or Santee were at least seasonally on the prairies of Minnesota" and that only the Bdewakaŋtuŋwaŋ and some of the Sisituŋwaŋ, Waḣpetuŋwaŋwan, and Waḣpekute "were truly forced out of their homes by the Ojibwa, although other Dakota groups may have had their seasonal movements into the woodlands restricted by the Ojibwa intrusion."

Anfinson was one of a handful of archaeologists to make connections between the written and three-dimensional records in looking at Dakota history. More precise correlations may be possible based on the location of burial mounds. Some village and mound sites in areas around Mille Lacs have been investigated, but many possible village sites have yet to be explored. And little attempt has been made to correlate the archaeological record with documentary information, whether written or oral. Archaeologists and historians, for different reasons, have resisted such efforts. Archaeologist David Mather wrote in 2004 about Dakota cultural connections to the Fingerson burial mound near Glenwood, overlooking the shore of Lake Minnewaska in Pope County. The mound, sixty feet in diameter and over seven and a half feet tall, was excavated in the 1940s and appeared to have some connection with Dakota ceremonies. Mather concluded that "ancient earthworks are not just piles of dirt any more than a cathedral is just a building. The mounds were constructed in a deliberate and symbolic way, as resting places for deceased loved ones, and also much more."[5]

Historical accounts of mound locations in the nineteenth century often noted their presence on bluffs above Dakota village sites, which suggests, conversely, that burial mounds not associated with known villages may be evidence of unidentified village locations. Numerous mounds along the wild-rice-filled Rice Creek corridor in Anoka and Ramsey counties, for example, which includes present-day Mounds View and Arden Hills, support the possibility that this area was a major village site for the Dakota in the seventeenth century and earlier, a presence suggested also in Dakota oral tradition (see page 58). The location on the St. Croix River known as Catfish Bar, which featured an adjacent effigy mound, establishes another connection between oral traditions, historical accounts, and archaeological sites (see page 73). These and other sites show the potential for a much wider collaborative archaeological, cultural, and historical study of the Dakota presence throughout Minnesota over many centuries.[6]

Written records about the Dakota begin with French explorers' accounts. The French first learned of the Dakota people through the ancestors of the present-day Ojibwe, known as the Saulteur, Sauteux, or Sauteur because of their residence around Sault Ste. Marie. The Ojibwe called the Dakota the Nadouesioux, a name spelled in multiple ways and later shortened to *Sioux*. In the 1830s explorer and mapmaker Joseph Nicollet wrote that the term referred to rattlesnakes and was intended to suggest the furor "with which an animal or men fight each other." Historian William Warren, who was of Ojibwe ancestry, said that based on nineteenth-century Ojibwe oral tradition, the name implies "our enemies."[7]

Early French accounts about the Dakota were not very detailed, but as time went on they provided more information, some of it contradicting previous reports. Some interpreters have concluded that these differences are evidence of cultural and geographic change among the people described. But, while it is true that all peoples undergo such changes, the fragmented and shifting record may simply represent evolving understanding as the French gained more extensive contact with the Dakota. Similarly, though the French viewed the shape of Lake Superior in multiple ways before mapping it accurately, one would not conclude that their records indicate a change in the lake's actual shape.[8]

Information on the range of the Dakota homelands at the time of the French arrival in the seventeenth century is difficult to extract from existing documents. The French recorded information in a haphazard manner, based on the interest of the particular observer. Documents are often a hodgepodge of information about locations, technology, social structure, marriage customs, and healing practices. Much of what was written about the Dakota, especially by French government officials, was shaped by their preoccupation with the wars among American Indian groups. Some writers were interested only in certain customs of the Dakota, others in their manner of living, but few recorded in detail the territory they occupied.

1642–43
French Jesuits at Sault Ste. Marie, on the eastern end of Lake Superior, learn of a group they called the "Nadouessis" who lived, they said, eighteen days' journey to the west.

THE JESUITS AND THE FIRST TRADERS

Some of the earliest accounts of the Dakota come from *Jesuit Relations*, a compilation of reports sent home to France by Jesuit missionaries working in the Great Lakes area. The 1642–43 account reports that Fathers Charles Raymbaut and Isaac Joques arrived at Sault Ste. Marie to make one of the first French visits to the homeland of the ancestors of the present-day Ojibwe. While there the priests learned of a group they called the Nadouessis, who lived, they said, eighteen days' journey to the west. "These Peoples till the soil in the manner of our Hurons, and harvest Indian corn and Tobacco. Their Villages are larger,

Roy de La grande Nation *p.8*

des Nadouessiouek, Il est armé f. 12. de sa Masue de guerre quön nomme pakamagan, Il Regne dans un grand Païs au delà de la mer de mail

A pictorial record from around 1720 called the Codex Canadiensis, *by Father Louis Nicolas, recorded "King of the Great Nation of Nadouessiouek" holding a pipe and a war club, exemplifying the stereotypical French view of the Dakota as a warlike people who used the pipe in their ceremonies.*

and in a better state of defense, owing to their continual wars with the Kiristinons [Cree], the Irinions [Illinois], and other great Nations who inhabit the same Country." The reference to Dakota people growing corn contradicts some later accounts, though it does suggest that some Dakota groups were growing corn at this date.[9]

According to Dakota tradition, the Dakota and Lakota people first grew corn either at Mille Lacs in Minnesota or at Spirit Lake in present-day Iowa. The acidic soils of the Mille Lacs region are not conducive to preserving plant remains, but archaeological evidence of corn (maize) has been found in residues on ceramic pots there dating to more than fifteen hundred years ago as well as in other more recent remains. Some archaeologists have suggested this evidence was the result of trade rather than cultivation, but it was certainly possible to grow varieties of corn at Mille Lacs, as the Ojibwe did in the nineteenth century. There is also evidence for the cultivation at Mille Lacs of squash, tobacco, chenopodium (also known as goosefoot, lamb's-quarters, or pigweed), and amaranth (also sometimes known as pigweed), still-common weeds that supplied an edible green and a grain used by native peoples for thousands of years. Although Dakota bands may not have grown these plants consistently, anthropologists have noted that while agriculture and horticulture were an important shift in the culture of many groups, there are few in which the shift to growing crops was sudden and permanent. Many groups made growing crops part of a mixed hunting and gathering way of life, as did early white settlers in Minnesota more than two hundred years later.[10]

French trader and government diplomat Nicolas Perrot gave an account in his memoirs of his experiences among the Dakota starting in the 1660s and of those who preceded him in the region in the late 1650s. As a government official, Perrot was concerned with the multiple relationships among American Indian groups and their effect on the fur trade and on France's own relationship with England. Thus, much of Perrot's narrative was about war, with incidental cultural descriptions.[11]

Perrot reported that after attacks by the Iroquois broke up Huron villages on Georgian Bay starting in 1649, some Huron and Odawa people sought refuge in the Mississippi River region, first among the Iowa, along the present-day Iowa River, then farther north along the Mississippi among the Dakota. Some of the refugees were captured by the Dakota and taken back to their villages. The Huron had brought with them iron tools and guns, something it was said the Dakota had not yet seen. According to Perrot, the Dakota perceived iron to be "a divinity." Similarly, the Dakota thought the people who carried these goods might have some supernatural power. They greeted those who brought them—first the Huron and Odawa, then the French—as wašíçuŋ, a term often translated as "spirits," though it referred to these people's prosperity and the goods they brought rather than to a belief in their innate superiority.[12]

According to Perrot, the Huron and Odawa settled on an island in the Mississippi River said to have been bare of trees, which some have suggested was Prairie Island. They lived there for several years, but relations between them and the Dakota broke down when a Huron hunting party killed some Dakota. Believing the Dakota were an easy target and desiring more territory, the Huron and Odawa went to war against them. Even without iron or guns, the Dakota fought back and forced the intruders up the Black River to its source and beyond, to Chequamegon on Lake Superior.[13]

1649
Breakup of Huron villages on Georgian Bay by the Iroquois causes some Huron and Odawa to take refuge in the years following on the Mississippi River, in Dakota country.

In the following years, the Dakota sent war parties toward Lake Superior. In response, the Huron and Odawa came to attack the Dakota in their villages. The account of the resulting battles provides a sense of where the Dakota were located in the mid-seventeenth century. Perrot wrote that "the country where they roam" consisted of "nothing but lakes and marshes, full of wild rice; these are separated from one another by narrow tongues of land, which extend from one lake to another; thirty or forty paces, and sometimes no more than five or six."[14]

Perrot noted that the Dakota lived in small villages scattered through the lakes and marshes, making use of the rice for survival and trapping the animals that inhabited the region. The area comprised more than "fifty leagues square" (100 to 150 square miles) through which the Mississippi took its course and into which the lakes and marshes flowed. Other parts of the region drained east into the nearby St. Croix River or south into the Minnesota River. The reference to the marshy region along the Minnesota shows that the Dakota were already making use of the area to the south and west of Mille Lacs in the seventeenth century while continuing to inhabit the Mille Lacs region. Thus much, if not all, of present-day Minnesota—not just the north-central part—was Dakota country prior to French arrival.[15]

1650s
Dakota are making use of the areas south and west of Mille Lacs as well as along the Minnesota River.

Perrot described how the Dakota made use of the land in fighting the Huron and Odawa, hiding in the midst of the wild rice marshes when necessary and luring the Huron into surprise attacks. He also noted that the Dakota were less cruel than their opponents, until they learned how brutally those opponents treated Dakota captives. In passing, Perrot commented that the wild rice eaten by the Dakota "was better tasting than rice."[16]

French trader and explorer Pierre Radisson and his brother-in-law Médard Chouart des Groseilliers spent the winter of 1659–60 in the region south of Lake Superior, in present-day northwestern Wisconsin. Radisson later wrote an account of these and other experiences, though it is believed a certain amount of his writing was embellished to impress his patrons in England (where Radisson was later instrumental in forming the British Hudson's Bay Company). Radisson wrote extensive descriptions of ceremonies shared by Ojibwe and Dakota over the course of the winter. He referred to the Dakota as Nadoneseronons, or "the nation of the beefe," in reference to their practice of buffalo hunting. Radisson described the Dakota's great interest in establishing trade with the French to obtain iron and other European merchandise. A delegation of Dakota visited Radisson's post bringing wild rice and Indian corn, further evidence of early corn cultivation by the Dakota.[17]

1659–60
Pierre Radisson and his brother-in-law, Médard Chouart des Groseilliers, spend the winter in the region south of Lake Superior, in present-day north-western Wisconsin.

Radisson's account provides evidence of an ongoing alliance between the Dakota and Ojibwe who were moving into the region. During the winter Dakota visitors took part in a Feast of the Dead with the Ojibwe, cementing a relationship of peace that may have begun even earlier. Historian Michael Witgen pointed out that Radisson appears to suggest this event was the beginning of the Dakota-Ojibwe relationship, based on the Dakota desire to obtain French merchandise through the Ojibwe. But it is not certain when the Dakota alliance with the Ojibwe began. William Warren, in his *History of the Ojibway People*, later cited Ojibwe tradition, saying that prior to 1700 the Dakota and Ojibwe coexisted peacefully and intermarried, particularly in the region around the St. Croix River, an area marked by many mound groups. Warren mentions a Dakota village site on Lake St. Croix, a portion of the river between its mouth and present-day Stillwater. The Maingan or Wolf clan of the Ojibwe, which still exists today, includes descendants of Dakota men who married Ojibwe women.[18]

Radisson's account also told of going to an unknown location, possibly a fortified village, containing seven thousand men, living in "cabbans most covered [with] skins and other close matts," seven days' journey from where he had wintered. He described it as a place where no trees grew, requiring the inhabitants to burn moss for fires, and where "they sowe corne, but their harvest is small." Radisson stated that the inhabitants hunted buffalo in the valleys in this region but traveled north to the woods in the winter where they hunted beavers. While some of the description might fit the region southwest of Mille Lacs, Radisson's account is suspect for a number of reasons. He wrote in a perfunctory way of the region's geography, and he also claimed to have traveled extensively to the north of Lake Superior in the same year, something that appears to be impossible given the amount of time he was known to have been in the region. Radisson's account was not published until the nineteenth century, and so it is unknown how widely this information circulated after his visit.[19]

Further testimony about the developing trade relationship between French, Dakota, and Ojibwe is found in a book written by historian Claude-Charles Le Roy, Bacqueville de La Potherie, in 1702, which was published in 1722. He described among other things the exploits of Nicolas Perrot, who in 1665 made his first appearance as a trader in the region of Green Bay and the Upper Mississippi River. La Potherie's account, like Perrot's own memoirs, is shaped by a preoccupation with the details of wars between American Indian groups. The period appears to have been one of great flux in the western Great Lakes. The French attempted to establish trade with all tribes separately, sometimes at the expense of former middlemen, which may have led to wars between various groups. La Potherie's account suggests that some of the French were trading directly with the Dakota along the Mississippi River but provides little detailed information about the Dakota there. No direct trade appears to have been taking place to the north at Mille Lacs.

La Potherie stated, accurately, that the Dakota had a village near 46 degrees

1665

Nicolas Perrot makes his first appearance as a trader in the region of Green Bay and trades directly with the Dakota along the Upper Mississippi River.

north latitude and noted that they "share their land and hunt with the Sauteurs." He wrote that the abundance of beaver and other animals made the Ojibwe forget their homeland. They wintered in the woods to hunt, then in the spring frequented Lake Superior, "where they sow Indian corn & squash." During this period and for decades later the Dakota continued to be allied with the Ojibwe who had migrated west from the area of Sault Ste. Marie to Chequamegon. La Potherie also stated the alliance was based on the fact that the Ojibwe brought French merchandise to the Dakota. He wrote, "They have made peace by which they are obliged to share daughters in marriage, one with the other. This is a great link to preserve perfect accord." However, as noted, Radisson's account suggests this was not a new relationship.[20]

The Jesuits meanwhile maintained a mission with the Ojibwe at Lake Superior, where they also sought to reach out to the Dakota. The *Jesuit Relations* of 1666–68 gave an account of a mission to the Nadouesiouek, reporting that they lived near "the great river Messippi" in a country "full of prairies, rich in all kinds of game." The Jesuits stated that these Dakota cultivated fields but did not grow corn, only tobacco. Instead of corn they obtained "a kind of marsh rye," or wild rice, which "grew in certain small Lakes that are covered with it." The priests seemed surprisingly unfamiliar with wild rice, given that it grew and was harvested by other tribes to the east. However, they reported tasting it when they encountered some Dakota at the head of Lake Superior. The Jesuits recorded a sampling of cultural information about the Dakota: they did not have guns; they used bows and arrows; they lived in cabins covered by deerskin, not bark; and they were "above all the rest, savage and wild," an enduring opinion reported by many later European sources.[21]

The 1669–70 *Jesuit Relations* was equally random, reporting on the Dakota's ceremonial use of the pipe commonly described as the calumet and noting their politeness to visitors, who were "fed with a wooden fork, as one would a child." Furthermore, "they have wild oats [rice], use little canoes, and keep their word inviolate." The 1670–71 report characterized the Dakota in terms similar to those used earlier by Perrot, stating that they were akin to the Iroquois of the country beyond Lake Superior but less "perfidious," not attacking until they had been attacked. The report repeated the information that the Dakota preferred wild rice to any cultivated plants but did not mention tobacco, as earlier missives had. It stated that the Dakota occupied "no fewer than fifteen Villages" near the Mississippi but provided no precise information.[22]

FRENCH "POSSESSION" OF THE GREAT LAKES

In June 1671 the Jesuits, along with Perrot and others, brought together representatives of various native groups in the western Great Lakes for a ceremony in which the French took possession of the region in the name of the king. The

1666–68
Jesuit priests make contact with the Dakota of the Minnesota region. Dakota and Ojibwe share peaceful relations in the region, including intermarriage.

June 1671
French at Sault Ste. Marie take ceremonial possession of the western Great Lakes region in a ceremony in which Dakota people are not present.

event was planned for the French government by Simon Francois Dumont, Sieur de St. Lusson, who had been instructed to proceed to the region of Lake Superior to search for copper and to plant a cross in the first village he found. St. Lusson erected his cross at the village at Sault Ste. Marie and took possession of Lakes Huron and Superior, their tributaries, and the lands adjacent discovered and undiscovered, stating that the region was henceforth dependent on the king of France and subject to his laws and customs.[23]

As historian Patricia Seed noted, European powers all used various techniques to lay claim to sections of the New World, each emphasizing a slightly different approach. The French preferred theatrical rituals, with ceremonies incorporating both European and native symbols. Seed wrote that these events were "carefully choreographed—from the order and hierarchy of marchers to objects carried by its participants." Planting a cross, giving a formulaic speech, shouting "Vive le roy! (Long live the king!)," and shooting off muskets were all necessary contributions to the event. Seed noted that for the French, ceremony was not an empty ritual but rather doing something "according to the rules." And according to those rules, a key part of the ceremony was the supposed consent of native participants, which was in many cases manufactured or obtained through subterfuge.[24]

The French used legal formulas to produce a written record of these theatrical events. The result was a prise de possession, or "taking possession," in the form of a procès-verbal, a formulaic written document representing the European legal fiction called the Doctrine of Discovery. The procès-verbal presented the facts of the event, including details about the region in question and the peoples who inhabited it and their supposed consent. These documents were cited decades later to demonstrate conquest and authorize the transfer of hegemony from one European power to another. When the French claimed the Lake Superior region in 1671, representatives of fourteen nations added pictographic signatures to the document, but it does not appear that any Nadouesioux or Dakota were there. How the Dakota and the other tribes perceived the event is unclear, but most likely they saw it merely as a means of improving trade with the French. Neither the Dakota nor the other native people who were actually present would have considered the possibility that they were giving up possession of their homelands.[25]

In the early 1670s, various Jesuits, including missionary Father Jacques Marquette, explored the Mississippi region, traveling to Green Bay, into the Fox-Wisconsin river network, to the Mississippi, and then south without visiting the Dakota. There is little record of contacts with the Dakota until 1678, when Daniel Greysolon, Sieur Dulhut, set out to "make the discovery of the Nadoueciou and Asinipoulaks, who were unknown to us, and to make peace with all the nations around Lake Superior who live under the domination of our Invincible monarch." In July 1679 he "planted the arms of his majesty" at the "great village of the Nadouesioux called Izatys," where he said no Frenchman had ever been. Dulhut may have intended by planting this coat of arms to claim the land for France, but he is not known to have prepared a document of possession, only a "memoire" of his discoveries and a letter addressed to French officials.[26]

The name Izatys—which was oddly misread by later historians as *Kathio*—appears to be a variation of the word Isaŋti, which would later come to be spelled *Santee*, referring to the eastern Dakota. Some sources suggest the name refers to Knife Lake, or Isaŋti Mde, on the southeast side of Mille Lacs, where the Dakota found stone to make knife blades.[27]

Dulhut also claimed to have been to another location never visited by the French, the village of the Songaskitons and Houtetbatons, located 120 leagues (a league was the equivalent of two to three miles) from Izatys, where he also planted the king's arms. In later sources the Songaskitons or Songasquitons were described as "the village of the fort," from a Dakota word meaning "a fence," because they were said to have lived in a fortified village north of Mille Lacs, a possibility recorded in later French sources and in the archaeological record. The Houtetbatons may be from the Wakpa, for river, indicating the "River Sioux," who later lived along the St. Croix. Neither location is the equivalent of two to three hundred miles from Mille Lacs, however, unless this distance takes into account an extensive and circuitous journey. (It is also possible Dulhut's knowledge was inaccurate or his use of the measure inconsistent.) Also, no other source implies these two groups shared a common village, though both appear to have been living between Mille Lacs and Lake Superior. The suggestion that no Frenchman had been to these villages shows that even if Pierre Radisson had been in the area, the record of his visit almost twenty years earlier had not survived.[28]

Dulhut called a meeting with the Assiniboine and other nations to the north for September 15, 1679, at the head of the lake, in the present-day Duluth-Superior area, to make peace with the Dakota, "their common enemy." He stated that all the nations came and that he urged them to cement their alliances with each other through intermarriage. The following winter he also encouraged mutual assembly for hunting and feasting, "by this means creating a closer friendship." In both cases the emphasis on the need for closer ties seems to have been on the relations between the Cree and the southern groups, not between the Dakota and the Saulteur, or Ojibwe of Lake Superior, who at this point were already allied.[29]

In June 1680 Dulhut set off in two canoes with a native interpreter and four other Frenchmen, traveling through a river, possibly the Brule, that flowed into Lake Superior around twenty-four miles from the head of the lake. They went up this river and portaged into another—probably the St. Croix—which

July 1679
Daniel Greysolon, Sieur Dulhut, goes to Mille Lacs and the "great village of the Nadouesioux called Izatys." The following spring on the Mississippi River he encounters Father Louis Hennepin, who arrived at Mille Lacs after Dulhut's departure and spent part of the winter and spring there.

discharged into the Mississippi. Near the river's mouth they encountered eight Dakota cabanes, or tepees, and received word of the presence of missionary Father Louis Hennepin, who had come west with the expedition of René-Robert Cavalier, Sieur de la Salle, in 1679. Hennepin was diverted to the north on the Mississippi by Dakota warriors on a war party against the Illinois.[30]

Hennepin would later report on his journey in an account published in France in 1683 and reprinted in other European languages in the years following. He claimed he was captured by the Dakota and forced to accompany them back to Mille Lacs, but his description suggests their interest had to do with European technology, as described in Perrot's earlier account of their first acquisition of French iron tools. Rather than treating him like an enemy, they attended to him with great honor in hopes that he could provide them with this new knowledge and equipment.[31]

At the time Dulhut encountered him, Hennepin claimed he had spent the winter and spring of 1679–80 at Mille Lacs, which he reached after an arduous journey from the Mississippi across frozen rivers. In his account, Hennepin called the people he visited the Issatis—similar to Dulhut's Izatys. Hennepin also mentioned but did not visit other groups said (probably erroneously, based on later evidence) to be located on rivers and lakes around Mille Lacs, including the Tinthonha, or men of the prairie, and the Chongaskethon, similar to Dulhut's Songaskitons, though Hennepin calls them the tribe of the dog or wolf—perhaps a reference to šuŋka, the Dakota word for "dog."[32]

Hennepin suggested that the Dakota he visited lived in a solitary "great village" on the south side of Mille Lacs. It was on an island, possibly in the course of the present-day Rum River through the three lakes which lie below the outlet of Mille Lacs—perhaps present-day Aquipaguetin Island, which was named much later after the chief who was Hennepin's host. Hennepin estimated that when he traveled south with the band to go buffalo hunting, the party comprised eighty cabanes or tepees of people, including one hundred thirty families with two hundred fifty warriors, suggesting a population for the village of over a thousand people. The band's chief was Ouasicoudé, or, rather, Wazikute, meaning, he said, "pierced pine," from wazi, "pine," and kute, "shoot," a name later listed for a Dakota chief in 1750 and for several Dakota bands.[33]

Hennepin's account is often sparse in detail, although it is certainly more specific than earlier French sources. Upon arrival at Mille Lacs, Hennepin was suffering from the exertions of the trip. A sweat lodge was constructed for him, and he and four Dakota entered. The leader, Aquipaguetin, "began to sing in a thundering voice and others joined him." After undergoing this sweat three times, Hennepin "felt as strong as formerly." Though this reference may be the first to the Dakota ini ceremony (sometimes called inipi, or "they sweat"), he described only the outward manifestations and its effect, not its spiritual significance.[34]

Hennepin spent time at Mille Lacs in late winter and early spring, followed by a brief return visit in August. He did not witness all of the group's subsistence activities, but he did list some of their food resources, noting, for example, being fed a bark platter of wild rice seasoned with dried blueberries and smoked fish eggs cooked in an earthen pot. Hennepin also mentioned that the people trapped beavers and in the spring and summer left Mille Lacs and went south and west to hunt buffalo along the Mississippi River, going as far as the Chippewa River, known to them as the Buffalo River because of the number of buffalo seen there. Hennepin accompanied them on one such journey. He described gathering various kinds of fruit, hunting deer, and catching turtles, catfish, and paddlefish or sturgeon for food along the way. Some of the seasonal subsistence practices of the Dakota at Mille Lacs shared features with those of the Ojibwe in the region more than a hundred years later. For example, in the nineteenth century the Dakota were described as using mainly dugout canoes, even though when living earlier at Mille Lacs, where birch trees were plentiful, they made canoes of birch. Hennepin stated that the Dakota at Mille Lacs grew no crops but that while he was there he planted tobacco and vegetables.[35]

Hennepin's accounts show that the Mille Lacs Dakota were familiar with the region to the south and west. He also noted that the "great chief of the Issati"

During summer or winter travel, Dakota people lived in tepees made of buffalo skins, which could be taken down and easily transported in canoes or on land. The image is an engraving based on a painting by Seth Eastman.

Spring 1680

A Dakota chief
shares his knowl-
edge by drawing a
map to guide
Hennepin to the
"French settle-
ments" as far as
Michilimackinac.

showed his knowledge by drawing a map to guide Hennepin to the "French settlements," at least as far as the French mission at Michilimackinac: "He marked with a pencil on a paper I gave him the route we should follow for 400 leagues of the way." Hennepin described the Dakota's veneration for the powerful spirit present in the Falls of St. Anthony, suggesting his familiarity with the site. He did not mention the Minnesota River by name, but his writings show the Dakota would have often passed through the area of Bdote, its mouth. In any case, whether Hennepin mentioned particular details of culture or geography is not a good indicator of their importance for the Dakota people. Given earlier and later accounts, it is quite likely that many other Dakota groups lived along the Minnesota and Mississippi rivers apart from Mille Lacs at this time.[36]

It was while Hennepin was with the Dakota hunting buffalo that he encountered Dulhut, who had descended the St. Croix River to the Mississippi. There at an encampment of eight tepees Dulhut first received word of Hennepin's presence in the area. From the Dakota encampment he set off eighty leagues (or several hundred miles, clearly an exaggeration) along the river to where he found Hennepin, along with what he estimated to be a thousand or eleven hundred Dakota. Together they all returned to Mille Lacs, where Dulhut said he scolded the Dakota for the maltreatment Hennepin told him he had received. He then refused the two pipes they presented to smoke with him, wishing to convey his disapproval of their actions. The Dakota danced in front of him by way of apology—something not mentioned by Hennepin in his narrative. Together Dulhut and Hennepin traveled east to the key French post at Michilimackinac, in the straits between Lakes Huron and Michigan, and later back to Quebec. Hennepin never returned to the Upper Mississippi. Dulhut received a commission to the region of the western Great Lakes, where he returned in 1685, but further record of where he may have gone in the Upper Mississippi region is sparse.[37]

After Dulhut and Hennepin, little information was recorded about the Dakota until the late 1680s. However, La Salle, on his journey down the Mississippi River in 1682, mentioned the Dakota, even without visiting them. Reaching the river's mouth in April, he laid claim to the entire river and its watershed for the king of France in a ceremony similar to that of 1671 at Sault Ste. Marie. Perhaps to add to the event's credibility, La Salle had brought with him notary Jacques de la Metairie, who prepared a procès-verbal.[38]

The document was a lengthy account of La Salle's expedition down the Mississippi River from Lake Michigan, naming the places he reached and the tribes he visited. Following that was the description of the ceremony and La Salle's speech, in which he announced, among other things, that he was taking possession of all the country of Louisiana, including all the branches of the Mississippi, from "its source beyond the country of the Sioux or the Nadouessioux, and this with their consent, and the consent" of other tribes in the region "with whom also we have made alliance either by ourselves or by others." No Dakota were present and La Salle of course had not met them, so perhaps the statement was meant to take into account the meetings between the Dakota and Hennepin and Dulhut. No record exists of the Dakota consenting to La Salle taking possession of the entire Mississippi River to its headwaters.[39]

A few years later, in 1685, French trader Nicolas Perrot returned to the Upper Mississippi River as commandant of Baie des Puants (Green Bay) and the neighboring regions. He was soon sent east again but returned in 1688 as commander of a post among the Dakota to establish peace and trade with various western nations. In the spring of 1689 he built a fort, later named Fort St. Antoine, on Lake Pepin. On May 8, 1689, he led a ceremony there to take possession, in the name of Louis XIV, of the entire Upper Mississippi region. The details of the claim include a kind of inventory of Dakota groups and suggestions about where they were located. Perrot stated that the French had visited and thereby claimed

> the country of the Nadouesioux on the banks of the River St. Croix, and the entry of the River St. Peter, on the bank of which were the Mantantaun and farther up in the lands to the northeast of the Mississippi as far Menchokatoux [or possibly Menehokatoux, possibly from Mni çoka tuŋwaŋ, meaning "village in the center of the water," probably Mille Lacs] where live the greatest part of the Songeskitons and other Nadouesioux who are to the north east of the Mississippi.

This inventory was preceded by the proviso that the claim included not only those places to which the French went but also those "where they will go." This statement makes any interpretation of the Dakota geography based on French visits problematic. However, the reference to the St. Peter or St. Pierre River confirms that the French had, in the years after Hennepin's and Dulhut's visits, become aware of the river's existence. Later evidence suggests the French had first entered the river in the mid-1680s.[40]

It is not clear how many Dakota were present at the ceremony or how they might have viewed the event. But the French clearly considered not only the region to the northeast of the Mississippi River, including Mille Lacs, but also the St. Croix and the Minnesota rivers to be part of Dakota country, although historians often suggest the Dakota did not travel there until later. The group called the Mantantaun, a version of the name of the Mantantons, would later be described as connected with the area around Mille Lacs, related to the larger Bdewakaŋtuŋwaŋ Dakota. This official French document places them already at Bdote, the mouth of the Minnesota River. In fact, the document lists no other groups or tribes associated with the Minnesota River, which makes clear that from the French point of view this region was part of the Dakota homelands.

1685

Nicolas Perrot returns to Dakota country, bringing with him Frenchmen, such as Pierre-Charles Le Sueur, who in following years enter the Minnesota River for the first time.

1689

Nicolas Perrot builds a fort, to be named Fort St. Antoine, on Lake Pepin. On May 8 he leads a ceremony to take possession, in the name of Louis XIV, of the entire Upper Mississippi region.

This sequence of maps shows the increasing knowledge of the western Great Lakes and the Dakota country in the Upper Mississippi Valley during the seventeenth century, culminating in maps drawn from the knowledge of Pierre Le Sueur.

Right: In 1650, when Nicolas Sanson drew this map of the western Great Lakes, the French had little knowledge of the extent of "Lac Superieur," Lake Superior, or "Lac des Puans," which later was understood to be Lake Michigan.

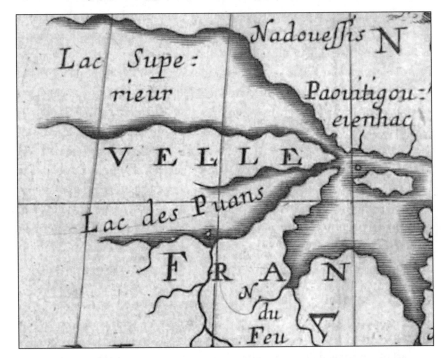

Below: Explorations by the Jesuits in the Mississippi Valley in the 1670s provided the French with a more accurate view of Lake Superior and a rudimentary knowledge of the Mississippi Valley, including the presence of buffalo, depicted as resembling French cattle, and the "Siou," who were placed next to a lake which may have represented Mille Lacs.

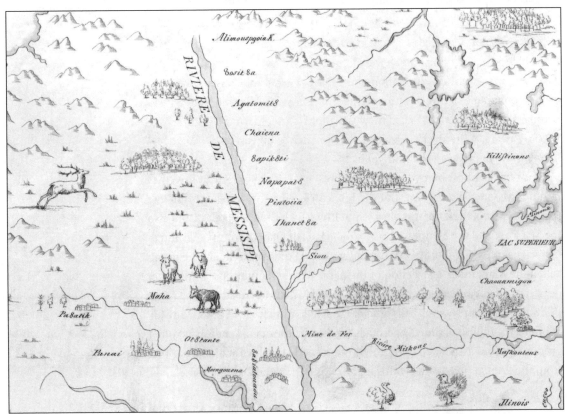

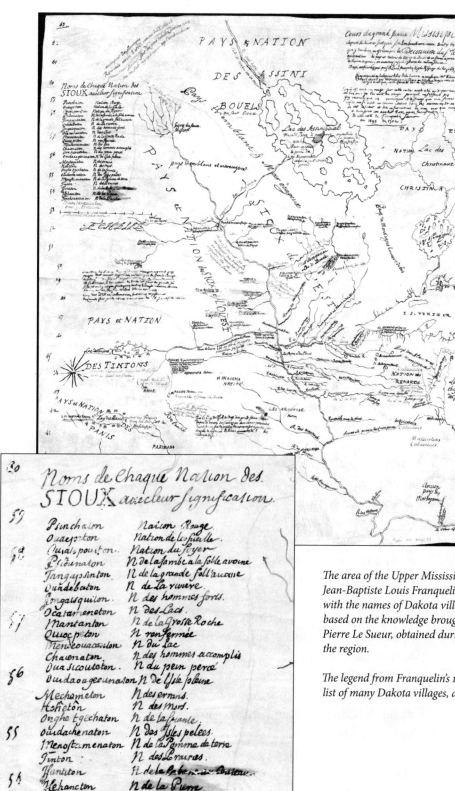

The area of the Upper Mississippi River recorded in Jean-Baptiste Louis Franquelin's 1697 map is filled with the names of Dakota villages and landmarks, based on the knowledge brought back to France by Pierre Le Sueur, obtained during his many years in the region.

The legend from Franquelin's 1697 map contains a list of many Dakota villages, described as "nations."

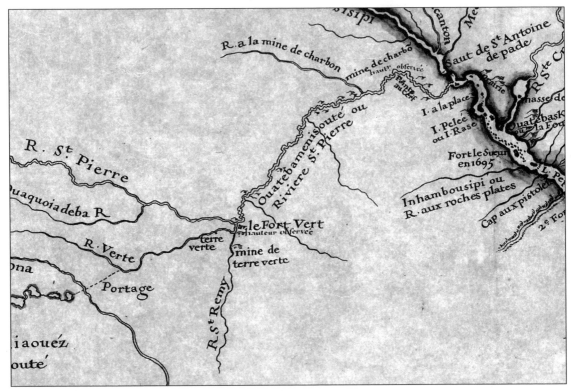

Guillaume Delisle's 1702 map of the Mississippi also records the valley of the Minnesota River, known to the Dakota as the "Outabemenisoute" or Mni Sota Wakpa and to the French as the Rivière St. Pierre or St. Peters River. Like Franquelin, Delisle based his map on Pierre Le Sueur's knowledge, though with more geographic accuracy. Delisle did not show the locations of Dakota villages, but he did record Le Sueur's Fort Vert, on the Blue Earth River, where he mined for what he thought was copper.

As in the 1671 event, the Dakota may have wanted to establish a relationship with the French for a variety of purposes, particularly for trade. But giving up claim to their territory was far from anything they would have thought was involved in such French ceremonies. Beyond that, the French taking possession was simply another example of the implementation of the Doctrine of Discovery (see page 136).

PIERRE LE SUEUR AND THE MINNESOTA RIVER REGION

Among those French Perrot brought to the Upper Mississippi may have been Pierre-Charles Le Sueur, who first came to the region in 1683, traveling through the Great Lakes, Green Bay, and the Wisconsin River to reach the Mississippi. Later evidence suggests Le Sueur was among the first Frenchmen to enter the Minnesota River. He was one of the signers of Perrot's possession document in 1689. Ten years later, Le Sueur claimed to have lived for seven years at various times in the Dakota country. In 1695 he was sent by Louis de Buade, Comte de Frontenac, the Governor General of Canada, to build a fort on an unnamed island above the mouth of the Cannon River—possibly Prairie Island—to help support continuing peace between the Dakota and Ojibwe. Le Sueur later reported that the Ojibwe were then living on a large lake one hundred leagues east of the Mississippi—apparently Lake Superior—

while the Dakota were living on the river's upper reaches. Later that year Le Sueur returned to Montreal with an Ojibwe chief from Chequamegon named Chingouabé, a Dakota chief named Tioścaté, and at least one Dakota woman, the wife of a chief who had been captured by another tribe and returned to her people by the French at Michilimackinac. They were said to be the first of the nation "who had ever been to settlements of the French." The visit appears to have been part of an initiative to establish trade via Lake Superior to avoid attempts by the Fox in the Wisconsin River area to cut off the Dakota, who were their enemies.[41]

The party arrived in Montreal in July 1695 and met with Frontenac. Tioścaté spread out a beaver robe, then another on top of that, and placed a tobacco pouch and otter skin over both, asking to be adopted so that Frontenac would take pity on him and give him iron goods. He then laid on the beaver robe twenty-two arrows, one for each village of his nation, asking that they all receive Frontenac's protection. He had learned from the Ojibwe that Frontenac was the "Master of Iron" and that he had a big heart to receive all nations. Such speeches were the standard of diplomacy through which nations like the Dakota sought to establish a relationship with the French that would lead to trade. Frontenac agreed to take the Dakota as his children as long as they obeyed him—which in this context appears to have meant keeping the peace with the nations with which the French were at peace and fighting against those, like the Iroquois, with whom the French were at war. Frontenac also promised to send Le Sueur back to them carrying "necessaries," since he alone was acquainted with their language.[42]

Unfortunately, Tioścaté died during the winter in Montreal and, despite his best efforts, Le Sueur was unable to return to Dakota country until four years later. In the meantime he went to France. There he encountered the mapmaker Jean-Baptiste Louis Franquelin, who in 1697 drew a map of the Upper Mississippi showing the locations of a number of Dakota bands and villages. Le Sueur also met the geographer Claude Delisle, who quizzed him about the geography of the Upper Mississippi River. When Le Sueur returned to France in 1702, Delisle was able to ask him further questions and to transcribe portions of his journal. That year Delisle's son Guillaume, a cartographer, drew a map of the Mississippi River based on Le Sueur's knowledge. Then or later the Delisles made a tracing of the earlier Franquelin map, supplementing it with their own documentation, providing the only surviving version of the 1697 map.[43]

Le Sueur had previously traveled to Dakota country through the Great Lakes, but in 1699 he sailed from France with the second expedition to Louisiana of Pierre Le Moyne d'Iberville—to whom Le Sueur was related through marriage—reaching the mouth of the Mississippi River in December. From there he traveled by boat and canoe upriver with a party of Canadian and

1695
Pierre Le Sueur builds a fort on an island above the mouth of the Cannon River and then returns to Montreal with an Ojibwe chief, a Dakota chief named Tioścaté, and at least one Dakota woman. They are said to be the first Dakota to go there.

1699
Ihaŋktuŋwaŋna winter count records "they lived with a white man on the Blue Earth River."

1700

Pierre Le Sueur returns to Dakota country. He descends the Mississippi the following year, never to return. He records Dakota place names in the region.

French workers, possibly hoping to reestablish trade with the Dakota. The French government had suspended trade in the region because of the glut of pelts, but Le Sueur claimed to have discovered copper ore in the "blue and green earth" found in what is now the Blue Earth River near present-day Mankato. The fact that Le Sueur knew of this site through his experiences with the Dakota suggests that at this time, if not much earlier, the Dakota were already living on the Upper Minnesota River. Le Sueur's narratives and French maps drawn with his help provide further evidence of the full extent of the Dakota homelands in Minnesota.[44]

Le Sueur encountered Dakota people as he traveled north along the Mississippi even before reaching the Minnesota region, although he said very little about them in his journal. Instead, he provided a general description of the Dakota based on his previous encounters with them. At this time, according to Le Sueur, the Dakota lived on either side of the Mississippi River above the Falls of St. Anthony. He appears to have been the first to divide them into two major groups, reflected in the 1697 Franquelin map based on his information. He reported the Dakota included the Sioux of the East, made up of three hundred cabanes, meaning bark summer houses or tepees, and the Sioux of the West, who numbered a thousand cabanes, although Le Sueur admitted he had only seen a part of the latter. The dividing line between these groups, according to the map, appears to have been the Mississippi River, though Le Sueur does not make clear whether this division had any cultural importance for the Dakota.[45]

Le Sueur described the buffalo-hide tepees used by the Dakota and noted that two or three men and their families lived in each tepee. He said the eastern group did not cultivate the soil but in September and October harvested a large amount of wild rice, which nourished them a good part of the year. The rice grew in the many small lakes near the Mississippi River, and the Dakota harvested it with light bark canoes that held only two or three people. The Sioux of the West, according to Le Sueur, did not use canoes and did not cultivate the soil or harvest wild rice. The lived along the upper reaches of the Mississippi and along the Missouri River, where they survived only by hunting. Le Sueur stated that the Sioux of the East were "the masters of all the other Sioux, as well as of the Aiaouez [Ioway] & the Octotaba [Oto] because they were the 1st with whom we had commerce and to whom we gave arms, hence they are well armed."[46]

Le Sueur's two groups of Dakota reflect later eighteenth-century French descriptions of the Sioux of the Lakes or Woods and the Sioux of the Prairies. However, these divisions do not necessarily match similar distinctions made by nineteenth-century observers. Le Sueur categorized some of the groups, such as those who appear to correspond to the present-day Waḣpekute and Waḣpetuŋwaŋ, as Sioux of the West, although later sources sometimes categorized them as part of the eastern Dakota, or Santee.

LE SUEUR AND PLACE NAMES

In addition to providing information on the various bands or villages that made up the Dakota people, Le Sueur's narrative provides a wealth of Dakota place names. Everywhere Le Sueur went, he recorded the knowledge of a people who had been in the region for a long time and who knew the details of its landscape. Sometimes Le Sueur recorded this information without really knowing what it meant. In early September 1700, for example, he passed the mouth of a river flowing into the Mississippi from the west below the present location of Wabasha. He had seen a quantity of grapes growing at the river's mouth on a previous visit and so called it Rivière aux Raisins, "river of grapes." In fact this was the Zumbro River, known later to the French as the Embarrass, a reference to downed trees and other obstacles. But elsewhere Le Sueur gave the correct Dakota name for it, "Outaba Ouasiaujou" or Wazi Ožu Wakpa, meaning "river where the pines grow," referring to an unusual grove of pine trees found in the upper reaches of the river at a place later known as Pine Island.[47]

On September 14, 1700, after passing through Lake Pepin, Le Sueur reached a place he called Hinhanbousnata, his version of Iŋyaŋ Bosdatu, the Dakota name for the Cannon River. The term refers to a prominent perpendicular rock—Castle Rock—located in the river's headwaters. It was just beyond there, probably around present-day Prairie Island, that Le Sueur had built his fort in 1695. He mentioned it on his return in 1700, although he did not say whether it was still standing at the time.[48]

Le Sueur then passed the mouth of the St. Croix River, named, he said, Otebakesou or Ohanonghetaouateba, the latter a version of Hoġaŋ Owaŋka Kiŋ, "where the fish lies," referring to a Dakota legend about a place on the lower river. Le Sueur also mentioned a mine containing pure copper, which the Dakota cut pieces of to make balls for their guns when they lacked lead.[49]

On September 19, Le Sueur and his party entered the St. Peters (St. Pierre) or Minnesota River, which he called the Outebaminisouté, for Mni Sota Wakpa. It is quite likely Le Sueur, in the 1680s, was among the first Frenchmen to enter this river, the existence of which Hennepin was apparently unaware. Le Sueur said the river was given its French name because "it was discovered some time ago on St. Peter's [St. Pierre] Day [June 29] and because of the five of us at the time, a Jes[uit] & 4 adventurers, there were 3 named Peter [Pierre]." Le Sueur gave no date for this event except to say that he first came to the Dakota country in 1683. When the French claimed the region in 1689, they made reference to the mouth of the river and the presence of the Mantantons there.[50]

Le Sueur and his men took ten days to ascend as far as the mouth of the present-day Blue Earth River. This whole area, according to Le Sueur, was within the territory of the Sioux of the West. He noted that soon after he

continued on page 54

Iŋyaŋ Bosdatu Wakpa / Cannon River and Wazi Ożu Wakpa / Zumbro River

These two rivers and their tributaries, stretching from west to east across present-day southeastern Minnesota, were major links in the Dakota transportation network. Each had important geographical landmarks on them. The Dakota names of both rivers were first recorded by French trader Pierre Le Sueur around 1700, although he did not explore them beyond their mouths.

Iŋyaŋ Bosdatu Wakpa (Cannon River) enters the Mississippi River west and upriver from Ḣe Mni Çaŋ (Barn Bluff) and the city of Red Wing. The river's name, meaning "standing rock," referred to Castle Rock, a prominent landmark near the river almost thirty miles above the mouth, a rocky column rising forty-four feet above the prairie in present-day Dakota County. The rock formation was said to resemble a castle. Although the base of the rock still stands, the upper column fell in the 1890s. The sources of the river are found far to the west in Le Sueur County, within twenty miles of the Minnesota River and even closer to various streams flowing into it, making the river a useful shortcut connecting the lower Minnesota and Mississippi rivers in southeastern Minnesota. The river valley was used by various Dakota bands, but its upper reaches and the region to the south were said to be Waḣpekute country.[i]

Wazi Ożu Wakpa (Zumbro River), meaning "river where the pines grow," has its mouth below Lake Pepin. The Dakota named it for the grove of pine trees found on the middle branch of the river, near the present-day site of Pine Island in Goodhue County. The modern name of the river came from the French Rivière aux Embarrass, meaning a river with obstructions. This site was a wintering place for Dakota of various bands. Wakute, the chief of Red Wing village, stated at the 1851 treaty negotiation that this was "a good place for Indians," preferred over the new Dakota reservations federal officials had proposed. Survey records for the township just east of Pine Island also note that an earlier farm there had been used by the people of Wabasha's village. With its various forks and branches, the Zumbro River was linked by portage to several other river systems in the region, including the Cannon and the Whitewater rivers and the Cedar, a source of the Des Moines.[ii] ■

Castle Rock or Iŋyaŋ Bosdatu, located along the course of the Cannon River near present-day Northfield, provided the Dakota name for the river, Iŋyaŋ Bosdatu Wakpa. This photo was taken in the 1860s, before the upper pillar of stone had been destroyed.

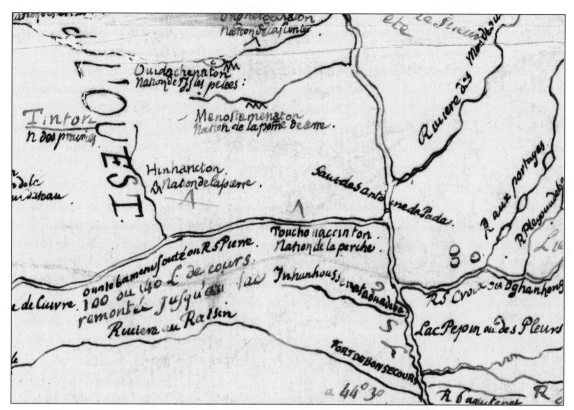

The Cannon and Zumbro rivers are shown in the center, below the Minnesota River, on Franquelin's 1697 map, based on information supplied by Pierre Le Sueur and other French travelers. Le Sueur correctly gave a version of the Dakota name for the Cannon River, Wakpa Iŋyaŋ Bosdatu, although he did not realize this river was much longer than the Zumbro, which he called the "River of the Grapes." Le Sueur's notes, however, recorded a version of the Dakota name Wazi Ożu Wakpa, which refers to the pine trees that grow along the river.

continued from page 51

entered the Minnesota and began to travel upriver, some of the Sioux of the East followed to try to persuade him to return to the Mississippi so they could trade with him as they had done in the past. They stated it was not their custom to hunt in that region without being invited by those to whom it belonged; if they had to come to trade with him at the Blue Earth River, they ran some risk. They preferred instead that he establish himself at the mouth of the Minnesota River—clearly a significant and strategic place for the various Dakota villages, a place where all the nations of the east and the west could come to meet. In response Le Sueur pointed out that he was not there to trade for beaver with them, but to mine, which was not the answer they sought. To mollify them he gave presents of tobacco, powder, and ammunition.[51]

Despite the discouragement, the eastern Dakota continued up the Minnesota River after him. He called the leader of the group Ouacan-tapai, from Wakaŋtoŋpi, which may mean "sacred birth" or "sacred born" according to several sources. Wakaŋtoŋpi appears to have been a Mantanton, an eastern group from the neighborhood of Mille Lacs whose name meant "village of a great lake which discharges into a little one"—apparently the same group mentioned in the 1689 possession document at the mouth of the Minnesota River. Also with Le Sueur were the Oouiatespouitons—a western group whose name is defined as "a village dispersed in many little bands." Both groups claimed relationship with Tioscaté, the eastern chief Le Sueur had taken with him to Montreal in 1695. During the winter Wakaŋtoŋpi and his band gave a feast in which he served buffalo and deer meat, along with wild rice and dried blueberries.[52]

Despite the sharp division Le Sueur makes between the eastern and western groups of Dakota, aspects of his narrative undermine that distinction. The simple fact that the Mantantons spent part of the winter near him on the Blue Earth River, despite their stated unwillingness to be there, suggests a certain mobility among the various Dakota groups and their willingness to share territory with each other. It also shows that the French presence may have been a powerful factor in drawing the Dakota south from Mille Lacs, but it provides no evidence to disprove the idea that many Dakota were spending much of the year in the region already.

Le Sueur also noted that warriors from both parties would unite sometimes to go to war against enemies to the west. According to a report he gave to Delisle in 1699, "the two nations of Sioux, that is of the East and the West, assembled one time & went on a ninteen-day's journey to the west to make war on nations who were their enemies, . . . [and] in this country there were forts along the sea" where the people dressed in long robes and made knives that were different from those of the French. For Le Sueur and Delisle, who like many of the French sought information about a passage to a western sea, this information was significant, and their version of the story overlooks a great deal of the cultural context. More recently the Dakota elder Ota Kute, Eli Taylor, gave a rich and much more detailed account about Dakota young men who left on a similar journey to the west. In Taylor's version the point of the story was not the place where the young men went but the spiritual knowledge they gained.[53]

Another eastern group Le Sueur called the Mendeouacantons, or "the village of the lake of the spirits," a version of the name Bdewakaŋtuŋwaŋ, also came to the fort during the course of the winter. According to one version, they were invited there by Wakaŋtoŋpi, part of his concerted effort to persuade Le Sueur to renew trade with the eastern groups. Heretofore they had stayed away because, frustrated by Le Sueur's journey up the Minnesota River, they had plundered the goods from one of his men. When they arrived at the fort, the Mendeouacantons brought gifts to make amends, including four hundred pounds of beaver skins. Further, "they promised that in the following summer, after they had made canoes and gathered in their harvest of wild rice, they would come to settle near the French."[54]

This substantial gift of beaver skins, which Le Sueur might have expected from his earlier encounters with the Dakota, indicates he was unlikely to travel in Dakota country without exchanging anything, whether it was furs, food, or merchandise. Le Sueur knew that simply coming into the Dakota country to mine would create opportunities for trade, if only as a diplomatic measure.

Le Sueur clearly defined the Hinhanctons, the Ihaŋktuŋwaŋ or Yanktons, as western Dakota. They were said to live in the area of a red stone quarry, a reference to the pipestone deposits to the southeast. They came to settle near the fort along with the Ouacpecoutetons, "a village of people who practice shooting at the leaves." These may be the Waȟpekute, and Le Sueur classified them, along with the Ouacpetons, or Waȟpetuŋwaŋ, "the village of the leaf," as Sioux of the West. It is interesting to note that an Ihaŋktuŋwaŋna winter count belonging to John K. Bear records one year, dated from internal evidence to around 1699, when "Makato wakpa ed wasicun kicitipi," or "They lived with a White man on the Blue Earth River."[55]

Le Sueur's accounts suggest these various groups of Dakota had been in the Minnesota River region for a long time. Le Sueur had come to the Blue Earth River because he believed the "blue and green earth" found there contained copper ore. His information came from the Dakota themselves, who used this earth as body paint. Le Sueur noted that the Dakota made no distinction between blue and green, using the same Dakota word to apply to both. In fact, Le Sueur called the Blue Earth River the Green River as he recounted the following story:

Around 2 leagues above the mouth of the Green River in the St. Peters River there is a steep rock where the Sioux often make sacrifices because their ancestors, according to their traditions, obtained the first green ochre [vert de montagne] that they had ever seen and so since that time they have always traded it with their neighbors and allies who like the Sioux paint their faces and all their bodies in assemblies of ceremonies. The other mines of the same material were not discovered until much later than this one, and it is only when a rock crumbled and they feared it would be crushed that they looked elsewhere for it.[56]

This account suggests the Dakota were not recent arrivals in the region. It further shows how Le Sueur's knowledge of the place was nourished by the Dakota's oral traditions. Over a century later, British geologist George William Featherstonhaugh, who traveled on the Minnesota River in 1835, mentioned encountering "an elderly chief" who told him there was "a place near the mouth of the Terre Bleu [Blue Earth] to which the Indians resorted to collect a green earth which they used to paint themselves, and that he had seen it himself in place." When Featherstonhaugh, traveling by canoe, reached the mouth of the Blue Earth River, he encountered a Sisituŋwaŋ family camping on a sandbar. They directed him to one such location on a fork of the river. He described the colored stone as a "silicate of iron of a blueish-green colour," which formed a seam dividing a layer of limestone from one of sandstone. Featherstonhaugh concluded that Le Sueur's claim to have found a deposit of copper was "fabulous," designed to "raise himself in importance with the French government."[57]

Le Sueur provided little information on the actual process of mining for the blue earth, the ostensible purpose of his visit to the area. He did, however, give many seemingly random details about the country and the resources the Dakota used, especially if there was some possible connection to minerals. Le Sueur noted that fifteen leagues, or as much as forty-five miles, above the mouth of the Blue Earth River was another river that flowed into the right bank, where the earth was yellow and where there was a stone that resembled glass and crystal. He gave the Dakota name for the river, "ouaqu aujoidebas," which resembles the Dakota name for the Cottonwood River, Waġa Ożu Wakpa, although the reference to yellow earth suggests Le Sueur might have confounded this river with the Yellow Medicine River.[58]

Le Sueur's narrative and those of his companions contain a number of references to bear. André-Joseph Penigault (sometimes Penicaut), a Frenchman traveling with Le Sueur, stated that the Dakota hunted bear extensively, supplying their skins to French traders. Le Sueur himself noted, after leaving Lake Pepin and just before reaching the site of his 1795 fort, that west of the lake was a chain of rocks one-half league in length, within which were many caves where bear hibernated. The caves, three or four feet in height, were dangerous to enter even in the summer because serpents—described in a way that suggested rattlesnakes—lived in them. Later Le Sueur indicated that in the Upper Mississippi were bear with red fur, of very large stature, with claws almost as long as a man's hand. "A Single man did not dear attack them," he wrote. "The Sioux feared them as much as their enemies." A number of other sources provide information on Dakota ceremonies involving bear, and several archaeological sites at Mille Lacs included hundreds of black bear skulls and fragments arranged in a meaningful way.[59]

In the spring of 1701, Le Sueur and some of his men left the Blue Earth River post to travel south the entire length of the Mississippi, carrying with them the supposed copper ore as well as the furs given by the Dakota. Although he left behind a group of men to carry on at the post, they only lasted another year. Le Sueur returned to France, but on a trip to Louisiana in 1704 he died in Havana, Cuba.

LE SUEUR'S MAPS

While in France, Le Sueur provided additional information to Claude Delisle, including place names and ethnographic details about the Dakota on the Upper Mississippi and Minnesota rivers. In 1702 Guillaume Delisle created another map, similar to Franquelin's, showing the region's geography. The two maps, along with Le Sueur's various accounts, provide a rich assortment of information.

Franquelin's 1697 map of the Upper Mississippi names numerous Dakota groups described by the French term *nations*. The use of the word has caused some confusion. Le Sueur himself only applied it to larger groups such as the Maha or the Octota. For the subdivisions of the Dakota, Le Sueur used the term *village*. He made the point in speaking with Claude Delisle in 1699 that the Dakota suffix "-ton" signified village, so that the name "Quiocpeton" meant "village of the Quiocpé."[60]

Le Sueur's understanding of these names, while flawed, was certainly closer to Dakota meanings than some of the information provided on Franquelin's map, which Le Sueur told the Delisles had come from other sources. Nonetheless, the Le Sueur narratives show that the various bands he listed, many of which appeared on the Franquelin and Delisle maps, were not nations but rather Dakota subgroups living at villages whose names were mostly associated with the region's specific geography. This usage is most evident in the Mille Lacs area. Franquelin's map places the "Mendaoucanton," or Bdewakaŋtuŋwaŋ, at the eastern edge of the lake, near the headwaters of the Snake River. It also shows the Mantantons, or "the people of the large rock," near a rock marked on the western or southwestern side of the lake. The Mantantons were also called "the people of a large lake that flows into a smaller one," which may refer to the outlet of Mille Lacs through present-day lakes Ogechie, Shako-pee, and Onamia, at the headwaters of the Rum River. In between them, on a peninsula which seems to stretch out into the lake, Franquelin identified the "Quiocpeton" or "nation enfermé," meaning enclosed in some way. According to Le Sueur they were also known as the village of "the discharge of a lake into a river." Mille Lacs does have several peninsulas along the south and west shores that were the locations of Ojibwe villages in the nineteenth century, including Mozomonie Point, which is located close to Lake Onamia, from which the Rum River flows. Archaeological excavations of sites in this region have located evidence of fortified villages on Lake Ogechie dating as far back as a thousand years.[61]

All these places have been the site of important archaeological discoveries from the Dakota era at Mille Lacs and have also been associated with later Ojibwe villages. It would make sense if the distribution of Ojibwe at Mille Lacs mirrored those of earlier Dakota. Hennepin stated that when the Issatis left Mille Lacs to hunt buffalo to the south, there were eighty houses of people, suggesting a population over one thousand strong. He implied that they all

Otuŋwe Wakpadaŋ / Rice Creek, Anoka and Ramsey Counties

Rice Creek rises in the area around Forest Lake, flowing through marshy areas of Anoka and Ramsey counties via a series of lakes from Mud and Clear lakes in Anoka's Columbus Township to Long Lake in northwestern Ramsey County before reaching the Mississippi River. One of the lakes along the way is named Rice Lake, although wild rice was found in most of the lakes in the area. Place-name historian Paul Durand recorded the Dakota name Otuŋwe Wakpadaŋ, stating that it means a village on a small river. Joseph Nicollet mapped this creek as the Ottonwey River. In addition, Nicollet recorded on his 1843 map the name MdeWakanton Lake for a body of water adjacent to Rice Creek, likely present-day Long Lake in Arden Hills, northwestern Ramsey County.[iii]

Rice Creek was part of an important travel route for Dakota and other native people. Its headwaters, on the border of Chisago and Washington counties, were adjacent to those of the Sunrise River, which flowed north into the St. Croix near the present-day town of Sunrise. The Rice Creek–Sunrise River corridors provided a much shorter passage between the two rivers than traveling south to the mouth and then up the St. Croix. As will be discussed in later chapters, the site mentioned in the 1825 treaty as "the place where they buried the eagles" would have been close to the portage between Rice Creek and the Sunrise River. This may provide further clues about the meaning of these places for the Dakota and for their relationship with the Ojibwe.

Rice Creek is likely the same waterway identified on Guillaume Delisle's 1702 map of the Upper Mississippi as Medepsinou, possibly from bde, "lake" and psiŋ, "rice." Extensive mounds and archaeological sites are found along the creek and its tributary lakes. One of the richest sites excavated, at Howard Lake near the town of Forest Lake, is within an archaeological district placed on the National Register of Historic Places. University of Minnesota archaeologist Lloyd Wilford excavated a number of sites there in the 1950s, finding evidence of Middle and Late Woodland artifacts associated with the ancestors of the present-day Dakota.[iv]

An 1851 article in the missionary journal the *Dakota Friend* argued that Rice Creek was not the site lived in one great village there, but more likely they encompassed a number of settlements at Mille Lacs and in the surrounding region. Like the later Ojibwe, Dakota bands or villages, according to the Franquelin and Delisle maps, were distributed throughout the Upper Mississippi and St. Croix rivers. Among them were the Oudebaton, the "nation of the river"(that is, the Wakpapetuŋ), which Franquelin located north of Mille Lacs, though various later sources support the idea that they were associated with the St. Croix and its tributaries.

Other groups Franquelin placed north of Mille Lacs were the Ocatameneton, the "nation of the lakes" or "nation that resides on the point of a lake," and the Tangaps sinton, "the nation of the large wild rice." Franquelin located the Ouiatspouiton, the nation du foyer, "nation of the home or hearth," later described as a nation that traveled in small bands, west of Mille Lacs, though Le Sueur encountered them on the Minnesota River in 1700.[62]

Further work must be done to decipher the exact Dakota words on which Le Sueur and the mapmakers based these names. It may be impossible to know the precise locations of these bands and what happened to them in later years. It

of Dakota villages at the time of French contact but was inhabited later by the Bdewakaŋtuŋwaŋ in their migration south to their nineteenth-century settlements, after which time they broke into a number of smaller villages along the Minnesota and Mississippi rivers:

> The country along Rice Creek being not inferior to that about Mille Lac, as regards rice, but little was wanting to draw the Mde-wa-kan-ton-wans from the latter place southward, to O-ton-we-kpa-dan (Rice Creek) where it appears they first erected such summer dwellings as they now inhabit, and planted corn.[v]

This and other articles in the *Dakota Friend* were said to be based on the "traditionary history of the Mdewakantonwan Dakotas," suggesting this information was obtained in conversations with Dakota people themselves. The article further stated that the Dakota had migrated into this region to be close to French trading posts, erecting their first villages along the Minnesota and Mississippi rivers. In September they would return to Rice Creek to harvest

wild rice, "Hence the country along Rice Creek became a common center for their division of the Dakota tribe." However, the name of the site, meaning Rice Lake, on Delisle's 1702 map suggests this area could have been an ongoing location for wild rice harvest long before the arrival of the French.

For early settlers of St. Paul, Rice Creek was known as a choice location to hunt the migratory ducks and geese attracted to the abundant rice every fall. In January 1855 the Dakota, by then officially confined to the Upper Minnesota River, were allowed by Governor Willis Gorman, the de facto superintendent of Indian affairs in the territory, to hunt deer along Rice Creek and at Rice Lake. The *St. Paul Daily Democrat* reported on January 27, 1855, that the Dakota had "killed five hundred deer, in addition to a large amount of smaller game." As late as 1881, a local history of Washington County reported that a group of Dakota from Mendota continued to go ricing in a small lake in present-day Hugo Township that flowed into the Rice Creek corridor through present-day Hardwood Creek and Peltier Lake at Centreville.[vi] ■

is likely that as the northernmost Dakota migrated to the south, they coalesced with other groups or took on other names related to events or geography. In particular, many of those who had been located near Mille Lacs came to be called Bdewakaŋtuŋwaŋ when they moved to the region of the Mississippi River, after which specific village bands took on other names.

The records of Le Sueur's time in the Minnesota region, despite their flaws, provide strong evidence associating the Dakota with the entire territory they occupied in the nineteenth century, prior to the arrival of Ojibwe bands. Le Sueur's work, enhanced by knowledge shared by Dakota people themselves, provided more information about them than was recorded until the nineteenth century.

THE DAKOTA IN THE EIGHTEENTH CENTURY

Information on the Dakota is limited for the first several decades of the eighteenth century. Mention is made in the legal records of a Montreal notary documenting French traders operating among the Dakota on the Snake River in 1714, although his note provides no information about the Dakota themselves. A French record of the Dakota is found in a government document entitled "Sioux or Nadouesis" by an unknown author, now preserved in French Colonial Archives. Dating from around 1720, the short document contains a cultural description of the Dakota of the Minnesota region, including their marriage customs, their religious beliefs, their social organization, and their geographic distribution.[63]

Some of the information corresponds well with Le Sueur's and other early accounts, while some of it seems confused. According to the French account, five groups of Sioux inhabited twenty to twenty-six villages. The names of the groups were similar to those given by Le Sueur, and the record divides them into the Sioux of the River or Lakes and the Sioux of the Prairies. Among them were the Outabatonha—Le Sueur's Oudebaton or River Sioux—a group said to live on the St. Croix River at Wild Rice Lake, "which is below and at 15 leagues from the Snake River," which would place it along the lower St. Croix River. It is not clear which lake this would be, although in later years the French called the entire St. Croix, and the region around it, the Folle Avoine, literally "wild oats," for the term they applied to wild rice. The location could also have been along present-day Rice Creek, which was connected by portage to the St. Croix through the Sunrise River.

Another familiar group in the French account were the Mensouhakatoha, or Meneouhakatoha, probably a version of the name of the Bdewakaŋtuŋwaŋ, described here as the Sioux of the Lakes. Also listed were the Matatoha, called the Sioux of the Prairies—though very likely they were the Mantantons (or perhaps Maŋtaŋtuŋwaŋ, which might have been pronounced the way the French transcribed it) associated earlier with Mille Lacs as well as the mouth of the Minnesota River. However if the group was spending more time on the Minnesota, that shift may explain the designation.

Sharing the label of Sioux of the Prairies were the Titoha—a recognizable version of the name Tituŋwaŋ or Teton. Finally, the list included the Hictohan, the Sioux of the Hunt. The name appears to be a variation on Ihaŋktuŋwaŋ, or Yanktons. Aside from the Sioux of the River, the only group located precisely in the document were the Titoha, who were said to live eighty leagues to the west of the Falls of St. Anthony.

The account implied that, aside from the Titoha, the other groups—who were likely located east of them—subsisted on meat, fish, and wild rice. It describes in familiar detail the process of tying wild rice in bunches while it ripened, then harvesting, drying, and winnowing the rice. More confusing was the suggestion that these various groups of Sioux, as well as all other American Indian groups, had animal "signs" representing their nations and their bands. The author claimed the River Sioux were represented by the sign of a "bear wounded in the neck," the Lake Sioux by an "eagle holding its prey in its claws," the Matatoha by a "fox holding an arrow in its jaws," the Sioux of the Hunt by an elk, and the Titoha by a "buck carrying a bow on its horns." Some believe this list indicates the Dakota at this time had animal-named clans, like their neighbors the Ojibwe. Little written historical evidence has been found to support this suggestion, and these symbols may simply represent the names of the bands' Dakota leaders or some other characteristic of the bands.[64]

The account includes some interesting references to spiritual beliefs and the oral tradition, providing the earliest written record of the significance of the area around Bdote, the mouth of the Minnesota River. In the midst of an account about the use of plants in curing wounds, the author noted that the Dakota had "no knowledge of the flood and they say that the first Sioux and the first woman came out of the ground which produced them in a prairie below the falls of St. Anthony and that the earth was formed by the turtle, for which they give no beginning."[65]

The information in this account is compressed and communicated casually with no sense of context. On the one hand, some may be a mixture of beliefs from various native groups, such as the reference to the turtle. The idea that the Dakota had no knowledge of "the flood" overlooks their many flood stories, especially those associated with the Wakaŋ Waçipi or medicine ceremony. On the other hand, the statement about the origin of the first Dakota people relates closely to later accounts of Dakota traditions about Bdote and may have been a part of a longer narrative heard by the French person who recorded the information. But as is the case in many non-Dakota sources, the author only wrote down what interested him, without regard for the meaning and context of the information for the Dakota people.[66]

1727

The French government establishes a "Sioux Post" on Lake Pepin to encourage trade with the Dakota. The post lasts only until September 1728 because of conflict among neighboring tribes.

In the early 1700s official French posts in the western Great Lakes were opened and closed based on wars and diplomacy among the native nations and European powers. In 1727 the French government decided to establish a post along the Mississippi River, among the Dakota, to counter the influence of the Fox in Wisconsin and to discourage the Dakota from going to war against the Illinois, as well as to counter the British at Hudson Bay. Such posts involved a military officer and franchised traders. A French trading company was established with the right to trade only with the Dakota, instructed to avoid trade at Chequamegon or in the area of the Wisconsin River. Trading was supposed to take place only at the post, not in the Dakota hunting grounds.[67]

Several Jesuit missionaries were also sent to the Sioux Post. Father Michel Guignas wrote an account of his first year at the post in May 1728. The French had left Montreal in June 1727 under the command of René Boucher de La Perrière, assisted by his nephew Pierre Boucher de Boucherville. They arrived at Lake Pepin on September 17, 1727, and proceeded to establish a fort at a point along the shore, located, according to varying interpretations of Guignas's narrative, either near present-day Frontenac, Minnesota, or Stockholm, Wisconsin. It turned out to be a good location except during spring flooding, and the fort was abandoned for several weeks the following April.[68]

As soon as the French arrived, Dakota assembled near the post, including ninety-five cabanes, or tepees, containing a hundred fifty men. They departed in late November "for winter quarters." Exactly where they went is not recorded, but Guignas said they were never very far and "there were always some to be seen during the winter," which could have put them in winter hunting bands throughout the many river valleys on either side of the Mississippi. These Dakota would likely have been eastern Dakota bands, but in late February a group of sixty men of the Sioux of the Prairies appeared at the post. In April more Dakota, probably eastern bands, came on their way for spring hunting, but when Guignas wrote his account in late May, they had not been seen since.

Details on the post are sparse after that. René Boucher de La Perrière left the post in the spring of 1728, replaced by his nephew, who remained there until the fall. Boucher gave a short account of his observations, stating that the Dakota had ten villages "very far apart," consisting of the Sioux of the Prairies and the Sioux of the Rivers. He had little opportunity to meet the people since they were always engaged in hunting.

In September 1728 the French, under the command of Constant Le Marchand de Lignery, destroyed a number of Fox villages along the Wisconsin River. The Fox were dispersed throughout the region, some seeking protection from the Dakota. Lignery sent men to Lake Pepin, and from there Boucherville dispatched them with his own men to meet at the Falls of St. Anthony with a group of Dakota, possibly from the nearby Rice Creek village. They returned with Ouacautapé, another version of the name of the Mantanton leader Wakaŋtoŋpi who met Le Sueur in 1700. It is not known if it is the same man or a descendant known by the same name, though this individual appears to have been as powerful a leader as the man Le Sueur met.[69]

Despite assurances from Wakaŋtoŋpi that the Fox would not be able to take refuge among the Dakota, and also fearing a food shortage, Boucherville, Guignas, and others decided to leave Lake Pepin. The nearby Dakota had reportedly not returned to the post because while in their hunting grounds they had encountered Prairie Dakota who induced them to go to war against the Omaha. However, some French traders stayed on at the post into the following year. They were said to have been treated well by the Dakota, who protected them from the Fox. Among the Frenchmen who remained at Lake Pepin was the officer Christophe Dufrost de la Jemerais. He later accompanied some Fox chiefs who wished to make peace with the French to the post at the River St. Joseph on Lake Michigan. During the summer he returned to Montreal, where he provided information to Governor General Beauharnois about conditions in the western Great Lakes. Beauharnois wrote to officials in France stating that Montreal merchants wanted to continue to supply the Dakota at Lake Pepin and that it would be good policy to maintain the post.[70]

French traders had remained active among the Dakota, but the French government did not reestablish the Sioux Post at Lake Pepin until 1731, under the leadership of Louis-René Godefroy de Linctot. The French arrived too late in the fall to reach Lake Pepin, instead setting up camp at Trempealeau. They were unable to obtain adequate provisions, so Linctot sent his men to live among the nearby Dakota, who numbered sixty-two cabanes. Jacques Legardeur de Saint-Pierre was in charge of the Sioux Post from 1734 to 1737. Details on post activities are sparse, but a report from 1735 suggests it was providing a good return of furs. In the fall of 1736 a trader named Jean Giasson who operated at the Sioux Post recorded selling six packs of 480 pounds of beaver in Montreal.[71]

Two versions of a census of tribes from 1736 are known. One lists the Sioux of the Lakes, the Woods, and the Prairies in the region south of the head of Lake Superior as two thousand warriors, stating that the Sioux of the Woods were "at the post of the French." The other indicates the Sioux "in the woods and along the lakes, although dispersed, have the count of three hundred men." As for the Sioux of the Prairies, "voyageurs" judged them to consist of two thousand men. Both documents also state that the "coats of arms" [armoiries] of the Sioux included the Buffalo, the Black Dog, and the Otter. The disproportionate number of Sioux of the Prairies suggests the various groups associated with Mille Lacs may have been classified by the French with so-called Prairie

1730s

The French re-establish the Sioux Post and continue to supply it for trade.

An engraving based on a painting by Seth Eastman from the 1840s shows a Dakota leader addressing members of his village at a camping place.

groups. Discussion of the "armorial" symbols is confusing, though Black Dog was the name of a later Dakota leader.[72]

Relations between Dakota and Ojibwe worsened in June 1736, when the Sioux of the Woods, accompanied by some Sioux of the Prairies, attacked and killed twenty-one Frenchmen at Lake of the Woods in retaliation for Jean-Baptiste Gaultier de la Vérendrye's participation in a war party of tribes allied with the Ojibwe against these Dakota. In September 1736 a group of Dakota leaders came to the Lake Pepin post to report they had not taken part in the attack and to ask the French to continue trading with them. However, the French were suspicious, and relations between the Dakota and French deteriorated when the French burned an adjacent fort set up by the Puants (Winnebago or Ho-Chunk). Saint-Pierre referred to a conversation with Wakaŋtoŋpi, who informed him that the burning of the Ho-Chunk fort had been done "after reflection." Later some Dakota returned to the post and attempted to trade, but the presence of a group of Ojibwe, one of whom spoke Dakota, made exchange of goods difficult. Every day the traders and Father Guignas feared an attack by the Dakota, although Saint-Pierre did not. Still, accepting the advice given him, Saint-Pierre decided to abandon the post on May 30, 1737. The full nature of the interactions is hard to determine from the French accounts, but it does appear that French reluctance to trade with the Dakota and the difficult relations with the Ojibwe contributed to the problems.[73]

Despite their own involvement in aggravating relations between Ojibwe and Dakota, the French attempted to mediate. On December 31, 1738, French official Paul Marin de la Malgue met with two Dakota leaders at "the River of the Swan on the Mississippi"—possibly either the Swan River of central Minnesota or the Wapsipinicon River located in northwestern Iowa—accompanied by twelve "other warriors of this nation." The two leaders were Wakaŋtoŋpi (Ouakantapé) and Pouaitonga. Wakaŋtoŋpi was Mantanton, a band classified as part of the Sioux of the Lakes or River. Later evidence suggests that Pouaitonga may have been part of the western group, possibly Waȟpetuŋwaŋ. They said they represented the chiefs of six villages and asked for forgiveness for their warriors' actions. Marin took two chiefs back with him to Montreal.[74]

Some sources suggest that a chief named "8abachas" (Ouabachas)—perhaps the first reference to the various leaders named Wapahaṡa, or Wabasha—was one of the men who went to Montreal. In a speech there in 1742, Dakota leaders recalled that after Marin had smoked their pipe in 1738, they had sent with him "two of our young men, 8abacha and Sintez." The name Sintez has not been translated. In March 1740, after the two men returned to Dakota country, Marin met Ouabachas and a leader named "Ninsotin or Two Hearts" at the Rock River, where Marin was stationed. The two sought to explain why their people had attacked some Odawa the previous year for saying that the two Dakota men taken to Montreal had been killed there. In a speech on this occasion, the two leaders give no indication that they were the ones in Montreal, though obviously if they were, Marin would have known it.[75]

The identification of one of the two leaders as Ninsotin or Two Hearts raises interesting questions about intermarriage between Dakota and Ojibwe around this time. The name bears no resemblance to the Dakota words for two hearts, but it does resemble the Ojibwe name Niizhode, for niizh, "two," and ode, "heart," which can also translate as "twin." It may be that the chief was Dakota with Ojibwe ancestry. In fact, Ojibwe accounts state that the first Wabasha—who would have been born in the early 1700s—was the son of a Dakota man and an Ojibwe woman.[76]

In 1742, as mentioned above, the leaders Wakaŋtoŋpi and Wazikute (spelled Wasikoute) went to see Governor General Beauharnois in Montreal. Some of the French records describe them as Sioux of the Lakes. In their speeches the Dakota leaders presented a pipe to smoke with him. They pointed out that 160 of their men, not including women and children, had been killed by other tribes and that their young men did not always obey them. They asked for "an

June 1736
Sioux of the Woods, accompanied by some Sioux of the Prairies, attack and kill twenty-one Frenchmen at Lake of the Woods in retaliation for their participation in a war party of tribes allied with the Ojibwe against the Dakota, causing deterioration in relations between Dakota and Ojibwe and the termination of the Sioux Post in May 1737.

1739
French representative Paul Marin de la Malgue takes two chiefs to Montreal, including "8abachas" or Wabasha.

1742
Dakota leaders Wakaŋtoŋpi and Wazikute go to Montreal to see Charles de la Boische, Marquis de Beauharnois, governor general of New France.

officer in our villages, to give us sense," but also probably because his presence would mean the return of French trade. Beauharnois accepted their pipe and stated that the chiefs' promises had not been kept because Wabasha himself had killed a Frenchman on the Illinois River. It would have been better for the elder chiefs to have come than to send young men, he felt. He acknowledged the blows struck against them and thanked them for making peace with the Ojibwe of Chequamegon. He concluded by giving them presents, including alcohol, to take home. Two of their people taken hostage by another tribe were returned to them.[77]

In September 1742, Beauharnois praised Marin for all the mediation he had done with the Dakota and other tribes. He also reported that Marin had written that during the return from Montreal an unidentified Dakota had been killed by Odawa and Ojibwe from Sault Ste. Marie. In November 1742 Wakaŋtoŋpi and a number of other Dakota chiefs, including some representing the Sioux of the Prairies, met with Marin, possibly at Green Bay or on the Mississippi River, to thank him for the treatment their leaders had received in Montreal and for their safe return. They pledged continued peaceful behavior and asked for "pity," the terminology often used to seek a continuing relationship with the French, including ongoing trade.[78]

In March 1743, the leaders of the Sioux of the Prairies met with Marin again and told him they were resolved not to attack any of the French leader's children. They acknowledged a request to go to Montreal to receive the same "grace" the French leader had accorded "our brothers the Sioux of the Lakes." The next month the leaders of the Sioux of the Lakes met with Marin, this time to tell him they had held their warriors back from attacks on other tribes. However, ten men of the Sioux of the Lakes villages had been killed by the Saulteurs. They complained about "French chiefs," meaning officers, in the Ojibwe villages that had attacked them. They asked for the protection and pity of the governor general. On the same day the leaders of the Sioux of the Prairies told Marin they would not be able to go to Montreal that year as requested, though they might be able to the following spring.[79]

The record of these various "paroles," or speeches, given by band spokespersons provides useful information about the leaders of Dakota groups at the time. They included four Sioux of the Prairies and, in addition to Wazikute, three other chiefs of the Sioux of the Lakes. While it is not always clear how to spell these names in Dakota orthography, one stands out, that of Chonkasaba, that is, Šuŋka Sapa, or Black Dog. In the nineteenth century, Black Dog village was the closest to Fort Snelling. Its chiefs were not named Black Dog but were often called "the Black Dog chief." The individual mentioned in this 1743 source may well be one of the first of the Black Dog chiefs, the one who gave the village its name. The varying references to a person of this name and the use of the black dog as an "armorial device" suggests the village existed or would soon exist in this region.

Despite the entreaties of Dakota chiefs in the early 1740s, official trade does not appear to have resumed for the next few years, though French officials and traders did visit the Dakota. Paul-Louis Dazemard, Sieur Lusignan, who was in charge of the Green Bay post, visited in 1746, wintering with them according to one source. Lusignan convinced four Dakota chiefs of the "Sioux of the Lakes and the prairies" to go back with him to Montreal, where they pleaded unsuccessfully for a post.[80]

"THE MARKS OF OUR BONES": DEFINING THE DAKOTA HOMELANDS

In 1749 the Dakota made an "urgent" request of Paul Marin that a post be re-established in their country, which Marin recommended because the Dakota were "very powerful" and had "a great inclination for the French." In response the new Governor General, Jacques-Pierre de Taffanel, Marquis de la Jonquière, raised the possibility of a new Sioux Post with French government officials and took steps toward establishing it, despite suggestions that he was acting too hastily. He sent Marin in early June, first to the Green Bay post and then to the country of the Dakota, to erect a stone fort to be used for a garrison and for trade. Marin was given presents to distribute and medals to award the chiefs who were most influential and supportive of the French. Jonquière also ordered Marin to explore the Upper Mississippi and to look for a route to the Western Sea, which many of the French sought in this period.[81]

While Marin was on his way west in 1749, several Dakota leaders, identified as Sioux of the Lakes, were headed to Montreal to meet with Jonquière. Among them was Le Petit Corbeau, Little Crow, described as a chief of the Matantons—apparently the earliest written reference to a leader of this name. He may be an ancestor of the Little Crow called Çetaŋ Wakuwa Mani, who signed Pike's Treaty of 1805, and the two successors who also took that name. In their speeches the chiefs greeted the new French leader, offered their respect, and asked for supplies and merchandise, including two canoes to go to Michilimackinac.[82]

Chiefs of the Chequamegon Ojibwe were in Montreal at the same time. In their speeches they complained about the Dakota, stating that a recent attack on some Frenchmen was not done by the Ojibwe but by Dakota, "by men of the Wild Rice and of the Snake River, their neighbors." Often such references to "wild rice people" indicate the Menominee, whose name meant "wild rice." However, in this case, it appears to refer to Dakota living on the portion of the Upper St. Croix known for ricing and "their neighbors" living on the Snake River. This detail would confirm that the Dakota were still inhabiting these regions at the time, though the chiefs in Montreal denied that their people had

1749
Paul Marin is sent west to reestablish trade with the Dakota. At the same time several Dakota leaders, including Le Petit Corbeau or Little Crow, go to Montreal to meet with French officials.

done the deed. Le Petit Corbeau made no mention of the event in his speech but did refer to a wampum belt received from the Chequamegon Ojibwe, noting that it represented the fact that the Chequamegon village and his own now were one.[83]

When Paul Marin reached Green Bay, he found relations among various tribes in great turmoil. A rumor was spread that the Dakota chiefs sent to Montreal had been detained there and would be put to death. As a result Marin was required to stay until they returned, and he got a late start in traveling to the Mississippi. Ice had formed on the river by the time he reached Lake Pepin, preventing him from proceeding farther north.[84]

In 1752 Marin was placed in charge of French forces in the Ohio Valley as they fought the British. The following year his son, Joseph Marin de la Malgue, who had been second in command at the Chequamegon post, was sent to take charge of diplomacy and trade in the Upper Mississippi Valley. From September 1753 to May 1754 he recorded his activities in a journal that provides some important information on the Dakota. During the fall of 1753 he oversaw the construction of Fort Vaudreuil, between the mouths of the Turkey and Wisconsin rivers, while sending agents to various Dakota groups farther up the Mississippi. The closest tribes were the Sac and the Fox, both allies of the Dakota.[85]

1753–54

Paul Marin's son Joseph constructs the French Fort Vaudreuil on the Mississippi River, between the Turkey and Wisconsin rivers.

In September Joseph Marin sent Paul Lacroix to the source of the Mississippi River to continue the search for the Western Sea. At the same time he sent a man named Hout to "go to the Sioux" on behalf of the French king and his representative, the governor general of Canada, "with the gifts they normally give on behalf of the general their father." Evidence suggests this group visited the Sioux of the Lakes, located for the winter around Lake Pepin. Marin added that if the Sioux did not want to come to the headwaters of the Mississippi, Hout was to leave a representative behind with them and take a boatload of trade goods to the mouth of the Crow Wing River—known to the Dakota as the Pine River—to meet with the Anctons, the Ihaŋktuŋwaŋ or Yankton Dakota, who were willing to arrange a treaty with the Cree.[86]

On October 13, by prearrangement with Sac leader Pemian, Marin met at the Wisconsin River with Sioux of the Lakes, who greeted him with pipes to smoke. In November, Marin was back at Fort Vaudreuil when he received word about difficulties involving Louis-Joseph Gaultier de la Vérendrye—another son of the famed explorer—who was operating the French post at Chequamegon. The posts' territories were not supposed to overlap, but La Vérendrye had sent traders into regions occupied by Dakota at the same time that he encouraged Ojibwe to hunt in Dakota regions regardless of the Dakota's wishes. A trader was sent to the Soleil Levant, or Sunrise River, where he traded with the Ouadebaton or Wakpapetuŋ Dakota. Marin noted, "This was a consider-

able loss to me as he had there the whole trade for the Ouadebaton Sioux who number about 40 houses. And when we got to Missilimackinac his orders read just to the Serpent [Snake] River." Marin does not say where the Wakpapetuŋ were located, but since the headwaters of the Sunrise River were connected by portage to the Rice Creek corridor and all the way to the Mississippi River, the band could have included Dakota throughout the region.[87]

In December four "Saisaitons," or Sisituŋwaŋ, arrived, the first of a much larger group of Sisituŋwaŋ who came to Marin's fort during the winter. These Sisituŋwaŋ brought news that the 160 houses of Ihaŋktuŋwaŋ, who were to meet on the Pine River with the French to make peace with the Cree, had learned of La Vérendrye's efforts to encourage the Ojibwe to hunt on Dakota territory. They feared a trap and so "returned at once to the prairies," reportedly all the way to the Missouri River. Similarly, later in the month Pemian arrived to say he had learned of another remote village of Dakota consisting of two hundred houses. He would have brought them with him but the Dakota had been warned by the Ihaŋktuŋwaŋ not to come "to the edge of the Mississippi." More Sisituŋwaŋ, numbering eighty cabanes, came to Marin's post a week later,

Dakota men and women often played Takapsiçapi or ball play (lacrosse), on ice in the winter as well as on the prairie during the summer. In 1835 it was reported that Dakota and Ojibwe were at the falls of the St. Croix River, "playing Ball & feasting together," activities which may have occurred on the river or a nearby lake.

but they informed him they had heard "that this French chief wanted to join up with the Cristinaux and the Sauteux to kill them." Marin did his best over the next few weeks to allay their fears. On December 22 the Dakota played ball with the nearby Sac and Fox. The games continued for several days.[88]

In mid-January eighty Sisituŋwaŋ, of the Sioux of the Prairies, left the post to hunt. Twenty Sisituŋwaŋ led by a chief named, in French, Porcupine came in mid-February to learn the latest news. Marin spoke to them of his plans to bring about a treaty between the Illinois and the Sac and Fox and other tribes. A war party of fifty Dakota men came through in mid-April with their chief named La Boule ("the ball"). Some of the Sioux of the Lakes, probably those from around Lake Pepin, arrived shortly after, along with the French trader who had wintered with them. On April 21 all the Dakota chiefs gathered with Marin to discuss their concerns about the Cree and Ojibwe: they feared the Ojibwe, encouraged by La Vérendrye, were attempting to take away Dakota territories. Marin recorded their statement in detail, including an eloquent account of the Dakota people's connection to their homelands:

> We also bring suit, my father, concerning the fact that the Sauteux want to take our territory. Here is a map of the Mississippi. No one could be unaware that from the mouth of the Wisconsin to Leech Lake, these territories belong to us. On all the points and in the little rivers we have had villages. One can still see the marks of our bones which are still there, which are the remains from the Cristinaux and the Sauteux having killed us. But they never drove us away. These are territories that we hold from no one except the Master of Life who gave them to us. And although we have been at war against all the nations, we never abandoned them. They attacked us, my father, a total of twenty-eight times. But that, my father did not keep us from making peace with the Sauteux when you ordered us to. We did that and we allowed them to hunt in our territories . . . And today the Sauteux want to take our territories and chase us away.

The chiefs noted that following long practice they had given permission to the Ojibwe to hunt in the territory around the Pine River for a single year, three years before, in response to Ojibwe gifts and entreaties. But now the Ojibwe wanted to claim the territory for themselves on the basis of that year-long grant.[89]

In late April Hout arrived. He had gone to the "Eau de Vie," now Rum River, in late winter to find a group of Dakota in the place where they gathered wild rice, possibly a reference to the region of the Upper Rum near Mille Lacs, which would also have been an important location for muskrat hunting at that time of year. They consisted, he said, of four cabanes of "demi-Sioux et demi-Sauteux," meaning "half-Dakota, half-Ojibwe." Marin does not explain the identification of the group, but the intermarriage between Dakota and Ojibwe makes plain the possibilities. Hout aided the group by giving them some needed supplies. He also encountered two Frenchmen and ten Ojibwe, whom he believed La Vérendrye had sent to pillage him. They had already stolen a package he had left in a cache at the mouth of the Rum River.[90]

On May 10 various nations, including the bands of Dakota, arrived to gather in Marin's tent and "smoke all together in the same calumet of peace, making peace in their fashion." Later in the month Marin set off for Green Bay. In early June 1754, he wrote a letter to Governor General Jonquière communicating some of the Dakota's grievances. At the same time he mentioned the names of several Dakota leaders and the groups they represented. These included chiefs of the Mineouakantons, a version of Bdewakaŋtuŋwaŋ, the Mataton or Mantantons, and a band known as that of "the bouef," the French term sometimes used for buffalo. The latter may be a reference to Tantagamamy, or Tataŋkamani, Walking Buffalo, the chief of the Sioux of the Lakes in 1742. Lieutenant Zebulon Pike and Indian agent Lawrence Taliaferro would later meet a chief of this name, the leader of the Red Wing village on the Mississippi. Marin's journal also says that one of the Mantanton chiefs, Outape, was Wakaŋtoŋpi's nephew, stating that the younger man would be bringing his uncle's medal "to get a bigger one as the late Marquis de la Jonquière promised him." It is not known when Wakaŋtoŋpi would have met Jonquière, though it could have been on the chiefs' visits in 1746 or 1750. In any case it seems possible that Wakaŋtoŋpi had since died, to be replaced in leadership by his nephew.[91]

Marin's journal documents a key period in Dakota history and their interactions with the Ojibwe, former allies who were increasingly becoming enemies. The rivalry between Marin and the La Vérendryes helped aggravate the strife between tribes. Thus the presence and intervention of the French and other Europeans in intertribal interactions must be factored into any interpretation of Dakota-Ojibwe relations.[92]

Aside from Marin's journal, details of the Dakota's relationship to the land in the Minnesota region are lacking for the rest of the 1750s, during which time the French were distracted by their conflicts with the British. Among the few other sources is a short description by Michel Chartier de Lotbinière, First Marquis de Lotbinière, who led a reconnaissance mission to the Michilimackinac region and west in 1749. He later wrote of the Upper Mississippi and noted the location of two Dakota villages. One, in the headwaters of the Minnesota River, could produce "1500 combatants"; he noted that the people hunted buffalo with arrows and that the women wore buffalo skins and the men were constantly nude. He also spoke of their cone-shaped houses made of buffalo skins.[93]

The other village was three leagues from the portage around the Falls of St. Anthony, a community of Dakota called "the people of the lakes" who lived in a region filled with a great number of little lakes, called therefore mille lacs, or

1758
Cree history records Dakota raids against the Cree and Assiniboine along the Ballantyne River, known as Puatsipi or Dakota River.

"a thousand lakes," who harvested wild rice, hunted, and fished. The geographical description resembles that given by Nicolas Perrot almost a hundred years before and could apply to the entire area between St. Anthony Falls and Mille Lacs Lake. Similarly, like the 1728 Boucherville account of a visit by the French to Dakota in the St. Anthony Falls area, this mention of a village close to the falls may be a reference to Dakota presence along Rice Creek.

THE DAKOTA AND THE BRITISH

A traditional account recorded in the *Dakota Friend* tells how Wabasha and other Dakota traveled to Quebec to meet with the British after the French were defeated by the British in the French and Indian War in 1759. A British trader had reportedly been murdered by a Dakota man near present-day Mendota, and as a result the British ended their dealings with the Dakota, depriving them of tobacco, traps, blankets, and ammunition. A large group of Dakota set off to see the British in Canada and ask for the traders' return, but because of the distance many turned back. In the end only Wabasha and a few others arrived to make their case: "He represented the Dakotas as living in seven bands, and received a like number of chief's medals; one of which was hung about his own neck, and the remaining six to be given, one to each of the chief men of the other bands." According to the story, the seven bands were the Oçeti Šakowiŋ, including the Bdewakaŋtuŋwaŋ, Waȟpekute, Waȟpetuŋwaŋ, Sisituŋwaŋ, Ihaŋktuŋwaŋ, Ihaŋktuŋwaŋa, and Tituŋwaŋ.

As shown in French records, Wabasha was in Montreal during the 1740s and 1750s, but it was during the 1760s that the British sought to reestablish trade in the former French territory. The Ojibwe who had been allied with the French were initially hostile to the British, preventing the full resumption of trade west of Michilimackinac until the mid-1760s. Early British accounts describe several cases of traders being pillaged, though more often by the Ojibwe than the Dakota.[94]

In June 1762 Captain Donald Campbell at Detroit wrote to Sir William Johnson, British superintendent of Indian affairs, that he had received word that "some Canoes that came from Montreal (before we took Possession of the Posts) and went to trade with the Sioux, a numerous nation that inhabit the heads of the Mississippi, had been pillaged by them and some of the men killed and taken Prisoners." Exactly why this happened is not clear, but native groups would sometimes harass traders who were new to a region or who did not take the trouble to establish relationships through rituals, ceremonies, and gifts.[95]

continued on page 75

1760
After seven years of war between the French and British, the French surrender New France. French posts in the western Great Lakes come under British control over the next few years.

Hoġaŋ Waŋke Kiŋ / "Where the Fish Lies" (St. Croix River)

The St. Croix River, the lower portion known as Lake St. Croix, and a prominent sandbar opposite the present-day town of Afton, Minnesota, all shared various versions of a name that translates as "the place where the fish lies," from the Dakota hoġaŋ, fish, and waŋka, lie. The earliest, garbled though recognizable, written record of the name—Ohanonghetaouateba—is in the papers of Pierre Le Sueur, dating from around 1700. Similarly, Jonathan Carver recorded a version of the name—Nehogotowannah—in his 1766 journal. The names derive from a legend, recounted by a number of Dakota groups and also some Ojibwe, of two young men traveling through the area, one of whom turns into a giant fish and in turn becomes the sandbar. Another recorded legend tells of a giant fish blocking the mouth of the river. These Dakota stories are reflected in both the Dakota name for the river and in the landscape itself.[vii]

In most of the stories about the sandbar, known in English as Catfish Bar or Pike Bar, the fish in question is described as either a catfish or a pike, although the largest fish found in abundance on the St. Croix was the sturgeon, which could reach the size of a man. Dakota tradition, however, sometimes sees a horned serpent as the visible form of Uŋkteĥi or Ṭaku Wakaŋ, an underwater being associated with the origins of the Wakaŋ Waċipi, or medicine ceremony. Uŋkteĥi also figured in one of the Dakota creation stories. The association of the place "where the fish lies" might also have to do with Uŋkteĥi.[viii]

A January 1851 article in the *Dakota Friend* tells a story in which one of two Dakota hunters traveling together could eat only flesh that had not touched water. Although he was hungry, he could not eat the meat of a crane, because cranes stood in the water. Finally he was so hungry that he ate a fish, which made him so thirsty that he drank and drank until he lay down in the water and turned into a fish: "This, tradition says, is the origin of 'Pike Bar,' which stretches across the middle of the lake." The author

also argued that the French name St. Croix was derived from the belief that the sandbar "forms a cross with the lake" and that the Dakota viewed the story and the area it adhered to as wakaŋ, mysterious and sacred. He concluded, "Is it not probable that [the French] translated the Dakota idea of Hogan wanke, that is the legend of the giant fish—and so we have the name Saint Croix, or SACRED CROSS!"[ix]

The explanation for the man's transformation into a fish, given in the story recorded in the *Dakota Friend*, involved the individual's violation of a prohibition against eating any food that had touched water. Other versions of the story give other explanations, but most versions take place at the same location on the St. Croix River. The association between the historical presence of the Dakota in this area of the St. Croix and the legend that provided their name for the river is all the more significant given that there was an effigy mound located at Afton, on the bank opposite Catfish Bar a few hundred yards from the river. Archaeologist Newton Winchell referred to this mound as being shaped like a serpent. However, the mound's location and the legend associated with the site suggests instead that it is intended to represent a powerful underwater animal, such as those recorded in many Dakota and Ojibwe myths and legends. According to modern Dakota sources, snakes were associated with Uŋkteĥi, the powerful underwater spirit.[x]

Still other versions of the giant fish story are linked not with present-day Catfish Bar but with Point Douglas, a landform deriving from an ancient sandbar which almost completely blocks the mouth of the St. Croix. One rendition of the story, recorded and translated by Julia Ann LaFramboise and published in 1884 in *Iyape Oaye, the Word Carrier*, a journal of the Yankton mission, describes the man who became the fish turning into "the sandbar across the mouth of the St. Croix where the steamboats are sometimes stranded." Similarly, Alexander Ramsey, in a speech to an early meeting of the Minnesota Historical Society in 1851, referred to >>

>> the "elaborately constructed legends" of the Dakota and, in particular, to one concerning "a huge man-fish which spanned the mouth of the St. Croix and dammed its waters." Significantly, long, almost serpentine mounds on the bluffs above Point Douglas were recorded by the Northwest Archaeological Survey. The Wisconsin side of the river was also covered with a number of mound groups, though most have been destroyed.[xi]

It is interesting to note that the sandbar at the mouth of the St. Croix River was the location where, according to Pierre Le Sueur in the information recorded from his 1700 visit to the region, a man named St. Croix was shipwrecked, providing, he said, the source of the river's French name. Le Sueur's account has been repeated in many other sources without any further explanation. Presumably the man St. Croix was drowned at this sandbar, a fact which does connect, tangentially, with the Dakota story of the man who drank too much water, turned into a fish, and then became a sandbar.[xii] ▪

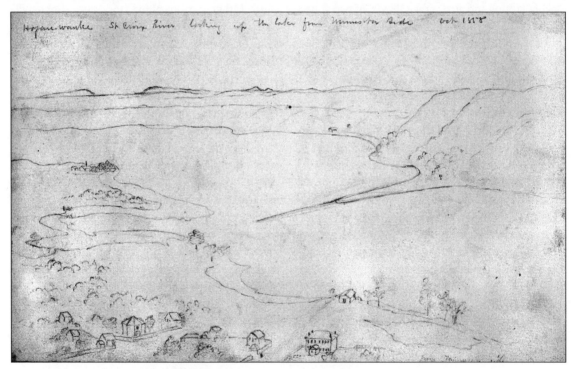

In the 1850s Minnesota artist Robert O. Sweeny drew Catfish Bar on the St. Croix River at present-day Afton, the main location of a Dakota legend about a man who turned into a fish.

continued from page 72

JONATHAN CARVER

The first detailed account of the Dakota from this period comes from explorer Jonathan Carver, covering the years 1766–67. Carver's account was recorded both in a journal and in a book first published in English in 1778 and reprinted and translated many times in the following years. Like many early European visitors, Carver entered the region from the south, traveling up the Mississippi. He arrived at Lake Pepin on November 1, 1766, and noted the remains of a French post below the lake, stating that it had belonged to Captain St. Pierre, perhaps a reference to Legarder de St. Pierre or even Pierre Le Sueur. Carver's first reference to the Dakota describes meeting, along the Mississippi below Lake Pepin, forty warriors and family members of a band of Mawtawbautowahs, possibly his version of the name of the Mantantons. Farther along, he noted three bands of "Nawdoessie, called the River Bands" residing at the St. Croix River. In his journal he mentioned meeting members of the St. Croix band, called the Nehogotowannah—a name similar to Le Sueur's Ohanonghetaouateba, for the St. Croix River, containing a version of the Dakota word hoġaŋ, or fish—though Carver did not record the legend of the giant fish. Carver presented a belt of wampum and some tobacco to these Dakota.[96]

After passing the mouth of the St. Croix, Carver traveled up the Mississippi and came to "a remarkable cave" that he called Wakon-teebe [Wakaŋ Tipi], "dwelling of the Great Spirit," and that contained many drawings "which appeared very ancient." This cave, in present-day St. Paul, came to be called Carver's Cave. Carver noted a burial site nearby where Dakota bands, despite their extensive travels, always brought "the bones of their dead." In his journal he called it "the burying place of the Mottobautonway band." It was also a place where chiefs met to hold councils in the summer.[97]

Carver's narrative is the source for some of the earliest documentation of Dakota participation in ceremonies and rituals, such as those that took place at Wakaŋ Tipi. He also gave details about ceremonies using the pipe he called "shandnuapaw," a version of the Dakota word çaŋduhupa. Carver was one of the first to describe the Wakaŋ Waçipi, or medicine ceremony, the healing ritual the Dakota as well as many other midwestern tribes practiced.[98]

On November 14 Carver reached the mouth of the Minnesota River, which he called Waddapawmenesotor (Mini Sota Wakpa). The river was freezing over, so he decided not to travel any farther, except for a brief visit to the Falls of St. Anthony. There he encountered a Winnebago or Ho-Chunk "prince" on his way to visit various Dakota bands. The prince addressed the falls in the same way Pierre Le Sueur reported the Dakota had, calling it a Great Spirit and throwing

1766–67
Jonathan Carver is sent by British officials to explore the Upper Mississippi River valley. He spends the winter on the Minnesota River and documents Wakaŋ Tipi as the "dwelling of the Great Spirit."

his pipe, tobacco, and jewelry into the falls while asking for protection in his travels. Carver would later note that the Dakota "esteem all extraordinaries in nature as gods, viz., the sun and moon, the earth in general, the greatest of rivers such as the Mississippi, the largest lakes, cataracks, mountains, rocks, or stones that by any means resemble in shape either man or beasts." To these they paid homage with tobacco, beads, and wampum.[99]

In his book Carver stated that he went on to the Rum River, although this excursion was not mentioned in his journals, which suggests he was padding the narrative. He appears to have started up the Minnesota River, arriving at a "Grand Encampment" consisting of five bands of Dakota. The exact location and the purpose of the gathering are not clear. Carver spoke to the Dakota and gave them powder, ball, shot, vermillion, knives, and other items.[100]

Exactly how far up the Minnesota River Carver went is not certain. Later sources suggested that he traveled less than a day's journey. He wrote of reaching the river's headwaters, though this claim appears suspect given the time of year he began. In any case, Carver spent the winter somewhere in the region, during which he said he learned the language and became somewhat familiar with the Dakota. According to his book the people he met were part of the eight bands of the "Naudowessies of the Plains," including the Wapeentowahs (Waȟpetuŋwaŋ), the Tintons (Tituŋwaŋ), the Afracootans (?), the Mawhaws (Omaha), and the Shians (Cheyenne). The list of names, though it sometimes appears to confuse the Dakota with other tribes, shows some familiarity either with the Dakota or with records left by other travelers in the region.[101]

Perhaps the most interesting fact about Carver's accounts is that, despite some confusion, it corresponds to the earlier French description of the Dakota of the Minnesota River as being Dakota of the Plains or Prairies. As such it included Waȟpetuŋwaŋ and Waȟpekute, not just the Tituŋwaŋ. However, except for the St. Croix River bands, Carver gives no real sense of the locations where the eastern Dakota, those of the River or Lakes, resided. The fact that the Ho-Chunk prince was traveling north beyond the Falls of St. Anthony to visit some of the Dakota suggests a good portion of them may still have lived in the Mille Lacs region.

In the spring of 1767 Carver traveled down the Minnesota River with three hundred Dakota who were headed to Wakaŋ Tipi for a council with other bands. Carver took the opportunity to ask for their loyalty to the king of England, to whom he said they pledged peace. In addition to other topics, Carver's account gives some information about hunting and other subsistence practices. He repeated details found in other reports about the role wild rice played in the Dakota diet, noting that wild rice beds were located all along the Minnesota River. He was among the first Europeans to notice that ricing was carried on by women, even noting that rice was "esteemd a sort of female food which they more commonly eat than the men, and another reason is its being a sort of provision they more particularly have the charge of gathering and preparing than they do any other sort."[102]

Another fairly detailed account of the Dakota in this period comes from the narrative of Peter Pond, a trader from Connecticut whose writing style was even more haphazard than Carver's. Pond spent the years 1773–75 on the Upper Minnesota River. He passed by the house where Carver had stayed, making note that Carver had only traveled about fourteen miles up the Minnesota River from its mouth: "this was the whole Exstent of his travels his Hole toure."[103]

Pond was not clear about exactly which bands of "Nattawasease" he interacted with initially, but in the second year he went farther upriver to trade with some "Yanktonoes," Ihaŋktuŋwaŋ, or Yanktons at the head of the Minnesota River. He stated that these Ihaŋktuŋwaŋ were divided into six bands, including the band of the Leaves, the band of the West, and the band of the Stone House, as well as the Assiniboines and a group called the Dog Ribs, which he said originally made up one nation. According to Pond these people had now obtained horses—not previously mentioned in any sources—and used them and dogs to carry their baggage across the plains. Pond also mentioned the Dakota who lived near the mouth of the Minnesota River growing corn, stating, "the Natives near the Mouth of the River Rase Plentey of Corn for thare one [own] Concumtion," a further random indication of the use of this grain by the Dakota before the nineteenth century.[104]

Two years after Pond's departure, in the fall of 1777, a Frenchman named Charles Gautier was sent by the British government to obtain the support of the Dakota and other tribes in the war then under way with the American colonies. He left a short account of visiting the Upper Mississippi and St. Croix rivers, noting that some of the Dakota lived on the upper part of the St. Croix along with a group of Ojibwe called the "Manominikan," a version of the Ojibwe name of the "wild rice" bands of Ojibwe, who lived at the river's headwaters in a region known for its plentiful wild rice—an indication of the Ojibwe's increasing presence in some areas previously occupied by the Dakota. Beginning around this time, traders referred to this trade region as the Folle Avoine district, using the French term for wild rice.[105]

Gautier encountered Chief Wabasha, now described as "a great Scioux chief," although the location of his village was not made clear. Gautier also heard rumors that the Sioux of the Minnesota River were assembling to go to war against the Ojibwe. In April 1778 Gautier went to the Minnesota River, where he met some "8arpeton" (Waȟpetuŋwaŋ) who appear to have been associated with that region. In June 1778 he traveled to Michilimackinac, bringing with him some Dakota, including a chief named Oushkaté, whose name is similar

1773–75
Peter Pond, a trader from Connecticut, operates trading posts at various locations on the Minnesota River and reports Dakota are using horses and dogs to carry their baggage.

1778
Charles Gautier is sent by the British government to obtain support from the Dakota and other tribes in the war then under way with the American colonies.

in sound to that of Tioścaté, the Dakota leader who had gone to Montreal more than eighty years before.[106]

The trader Amable Curot, writing to Captain Daniel Robertson, commandant at Michilimackinac in 1783, referred to Wabasha as one of the Sioux "of the lands." He also mentioned a Dakota chief named Red Thunder (possibly an early reference to Wakiŋyaŋ duta, a Sisituŋwaŋ leader from Lake Traverse) who had gone to war on the Missouri River.

Another trader, Jean Baptiste Perrault, provides further suggestions about Wabasha's location. He wrote that in 1787 men of "La Feuille," or the Leaf, from the Minnesota River formed a party to go to the St. Croix River to make war against the "wild rice" Ojibwe. The name the Leaf was sometimes used to describe the Dakota leader Wabasha, but in this case it may have been meant to apply to the Waḣpetuŋwaŋ, who were called "the people of the leaf" and who were located on the Minnesota River. The following winter Perrault stayed on the Upper Red Cedar River, bringing with him some Menominee as hunters because of their neutral status with both the Dakota and Ojibwe. Ojibwe from Lac Courte Oreilles came to trade at his post, as did members of the "La Feuille" band. Later, Perrault also received a visit from twenty-eight people of Le Petit Corbeau (Little Crow) band, along with their leader, who was likely Çetaŋ Wakuwa Mani (Hawk that Hunts Walking), signer of the Treaty of 1805. Perrault said the Dakota had come to trade with him, defaulting on credit given them by an unnamed trader on the Mississippi. They considered his trading post to be within their hunting area, which extended up to the vaguely defined border with the Ojibwe. The Dakota and Ojibwe agreed to share the territory without fighting, though later a quarrel occurred in which one of the Ojibwe was shot and after which the Dakota departed. The events provide evidence of a pattern of seasonal peace treaties for the purpose of trade along the developing border between Dakota and Ojibwe in the region.[107]

In the next twenty years, relations between the Dakota and Ojibwe shifted as the Dakota began to spend a greater part of the year along the Mississippi and Minnesota rivers and Ojibwe occupied former Dakota villages farther north. Americans claimed the region of the Upper Mississippi after the American Revolution, though they did not make their appearance in the region for many years. Traders continued to come from Montreal through Michilimackinac, bringing British goods. It was not until the first decade of the 1800s that things began to change.

1783
Tensions grow between the Dakota and the Ojibwe who encroach upon their territory, including the area of the St. Croix River. That same year the second Treaty of Paris ends the American Revolution.

THE DAKOTA PRESENCE IN MINNESOTA
IN THE SEVENTEENTH AND EIGHTEENTH CENTURIES

European descriptions of where the Dakota lived, their culture, and their way of life were haphazard, as the varied sources demonstrate, although war between the Dakota and other groups was often described in great detail. These sources illustrate the tenuous nature of this information, especially if the traditional history and knowledge of the Dakota themselves is not factored in.

Still, these European sources show the Dakota living throughout the region of present-day Minnesota and in portions of Wisconsin, Iowa, and the Dakotas, including the areas around the Mississippi and Minnesota rivers that they would continue to inhabit in the nineteenth century. This geographical information is indicated by specific statements made by Europeans about where the Dakota were located and by other details only suggested and implied.

Hidden within the French and British written sources are clues to a parallel but largely unwritten narrative recording the long cultural tradition of the Dakota in the region of Minnesota. The place names mentioned by Hennepin, Dulhut, Le Sueur, and others are records of a people who knew these places well. The continuity in Dakota names Le Sueur recorded for the Zumbro, Cannon, and St. Croix rivers demonstrate a rich Dakota knowledge of the region. Le Sueur's report from 1700 of a place on the Minnesota River where the Dakota had ceremonies to mark the discovery of this place by their ancestors reflects a traditional knowledge that contradicts many historians' assumptions that the Dakota did not reach the Minnesota River until the eighteenth century. Mni Sota Makoce was a Dakota place when the French first arrived, and it continued to be for the next two hundred years, until the exile of 1863, and beyond.

CHAPTER THREE

Dakota Landscape *in the* Nineteenth Century

The Dakota knew Mni Sota Makoce as a network of connected places, each defined in specific ways. They followed a seasonal way of life, hunting game in the woods in winter, pursuing buffalo on the plains in summer, gathering edible plants in the woods and wetlands, fishing in the rivers and lakes, ricing and growing gardens on the lakeshores and riverbanks. Similarly, ritual use of sacred places for burials, ceremonies, and gatherings drew Dakota together at various times of year. Europeans were not present to observe the full seasonal patterns that linked Dakota places. As a result, they often made the mistake of thinking the Dakota were nomads who wandered aimlessly throughout the region. Occasionally they heard Dakota stories connected to places but had little understanding of what those stories and those places actually meant.

DAKOTA ON THE LAND
IN THE EARLY NINETEENTH CENTURY

Dakota bands and the villages in which they lived are an important part of the geographic network for the Dakota people in Minnesota. The names of the bands, their villages, and their chiefs are recorded in the narratives of early travelers and in the records of government agents and missionaries, although spellings and translations vary a great deal. Still, the available nineteenth-century records include a more complete picture of the Dakota throughout the cycle of their seasons than is found in earlier documents. As in the earlier British and French accounts, reading between the lines is important.

By the late 1780s trade between the Dakota and Europeans was stabilizing, with fewer interruptions from war and politics. Traders appeared along the Mississippi and Minnesota rivers on a regular basis, supplying the Dakota with goods and encouraging them to hunt and trap. Many of the traders were French or British and were supplied by British companies. They reached the region through Michilimackinac, which was still controlled by the British government, despite the Treaty of Paris, which in 1783 declared it U.S. territory. Following Jay's Treaty of 1794, Americans occupied the British fort on Mackinac Island but British traders continued to work in the Lake Superior and Upper Mississippi region.[1]

1794

Jay's Treaty, between the United States and Great Britain, resolves issues remaining from the second Treaty of Paris, including boundaries in the Upper Mississippi and Lake Superior regions.

Both the European traders and the Dakota themselves sought to survive in this changing political environment. In the spring of 1805 British traders Robert Dickson and Rexford Crawford, intending to continue their own trade in the region, took a party of Dakota led by four chiefs, including Wabasha, to St. Louis to meet with Pierre Chouteau, a trader who was also the Indian agent for tribes west of the Mississippi River.[2]

As a result of this meeting, General James Wilkinson, the new governor of Louisiana, sent Lieutenant Zebulon Pike to the Upper Mississippi to "ascertain the most commanding Sites for Military Posts and to obtain permission for their Establishment in the Spring early," and to gather knowledge about commerce, waterways, the quality of the soil and timber, and "whatever else may be deemed worthy of Note." By late August Pike's party reached the southern limits of Dakota land. He was accompanied by traders long familiar with the Dakota, including Joseph Renville, who was married to a Dakota woman from Kap'oża (or Kaposia), near present-day St. Paul. In the following days Pike visited Wabasha's village, located on the Upper Iowa River near its mouth; Red Wing village, sited near the mouth of the Cannon River; and the Kap'oża village, then located near present-day Mounds Park in St. Paul. Pike reported the inhabitants of Kap'oża were absent because they were "out in the Land" harvesting wild rice.[3]

Reaching the island at the mouth of the Minnesota River now named for him, Pike observed a burial scaffold supporting four bodies, "two enclosed in boards and two in bark." The dead were wrapped in new blankets. He learned that they had been brought from the Minnesota River and from the St. Croix to be buried there. The site could have been Pilot Knob (Oheyawahi), which rises up above the mouth of the Minnesota River. Near Bdote, the mouth of the Minnesota River, Pike was greeted by Çetaŋ Wakuwa Mani (Petit Corbeau, or Little Crow) with one hundred fifty warriors. They climbed a hill "in the point between the Mississippi and Saint Peters" and saluted Pike and his party by firing off their guns. The next day Pike met with Little Crow and six other chiefs. He gave a speech asking for a grant of land and requesting that the Dakota make peace with the Ojibwe.[4]

After discussion between Pike and the assembled leaders, an agreement was signed on September 23, 1805. The document (discussed in more detail in Chapter 4) was a treaty with the "Sioux Nation of Indians," a term used to refer to the Očeti Šakowiŋ or Seven Fires of the Dakota. The only Dakota signers were Little Crow and "Way Aga Enogee" (Waŋyaga Inaźiŋ, He Sees Standing Up), the chief known as Fils de Penishon. His village, later called Penichon's or Penishon's village, was located on the lower Minnesota River. Shortly after the treaty signing, Pike set off up the Mississippi to spend the winter among various Ojibwe bands. On April 11, 1806, on his return trip, Pike encountered a village of one hundred lodges and six hundred people at the mouth of the Minnesota River. He met with Little Crow at the mouth of the St. Croix, and on April 13 he gathered with other leaders at the Red Wing village. Farther downriver, on April 21 he met Wabasha and Red Thunder (Wakiŋyaŋ Duta), a Sisituŋwaŋ leader from Lake Traverse.[5]

In May 1806 four Dakota chiefs and a number of warriors went to St. Louis to meet with General Wilkinson, seeking to cement a relationship with the Americans. Wilkinson tried unsuccessfully to persuade them to go visit with the president in Washington. He wrote to Secretary of War Henry Dearborn that the Dakota had "strong claims to our attentions and courtesy," but it would be many years before U.S. officials either built upon this relationship or built a fort based on the 1805 agreement.[6]

The British government and British traders continued to operate unchecked in this part of American territory until after the War of 1812. Fur trader Thomas G. Anderson, who worked in the region both before and after Pike's visit, kept a record and later wrote a narrative that provides some information on the Dakota. In 1806–7 Anderson wintered about fifty miles above the mouth of the Minnesota, building a post in a strip of timber which he said in some places stretched a mile out from the river. The distance from the river's mouth would place him near several Waḣpetuŋwaŋ villages, including the Little Rapids village, although Anderson does not identify the Dakota either by village or chief. Game was plentiful in the region that year. The local Dakota were in their hunting grounds most of the winter, returning to the river in March to pay off the credit Anderson had given them in the fall.

The following year Anderson returned to the same location on the Minnesota River, though to very different conditions. It was a mild winter, and deer were hard to track on the bare ground. The nearest Dakota, he said, were fifty or sixty miles away, attempting to hunt for buffalo, which were not plentiful

1805
Lieutenant Zebulon Pike, sent by the governor of Louisiana Territory, signs a treaty with two Dakota leaders, Cetaŋ Wakuwa Mani (Little Crow) and Wanyaga Inaźiŋ (He Sees Standing Up), for the purpose of building military posts.

May 1806
Four Dakota chiefs and a number of warriors go to St. Louis to meet with General James Wilkinson, seeking to cement a relationship with the Americans.

either. Many people were starving. Anderson reported that some had tried to find turtles and other food under the ice in a small lake but had drowned because they were too weak to climb out of the cold water.[7]

In 1809 Anderson went farther up the Minnesota River to Lac qui Parle, apparently among the Sisituŋwaŋ and Ihaŋktuŋwan. Arriving early in the fall, he joined in a buffalo hunt at Big Stone Lake, where many buffalo were killed. Anderson said little about what happened during the winter but noted that in the spring the Dakota he described as "my hunters" informed him they were not coming to the post to pay off their credits but were traveling two days to the south "on the road to Santa Fe" to trade for horses. Anderson was able to get three-quarters of what he said was due him before they left.[8]

The next year Anderson returned to Lac qui Parle, where he ran into difficulties because he refused credit to those who had gone for horses in the spring. In the end he would only give them ammunition for hunting, not the other items of trade they were accustomed to receiving in the fall. It was another difficult winter for Anderson because of a shortage of food, perhaps because the Dakota with whom he traded had chosen not to supply him with game. During the course of the season Anderson received visits from the Sisituŋwaŋ leader Red Thunder and another chief named Broken Leg, of the Gens de Perche (People of the Pole) band, probably of the Ihaŋktuŋwaŋ.[9]

In later years Anderson traded among what he called the Lower Sioux, which he said at this time consisted of six bands, including those of Wabasha, Red Wing, Red Whale, the Six, Little Crow, and Thunder or Red Thunder. Anderson added that Red Thunder was not considered to be attached to any band, which may explain why he included this Sisituŋwaŋ leader among the Lower Sioux. In 1810–11 Anderson had his post on Lake St. Croix. One summer, Anderson stayed at his trading post while his partners went east to Michilimackinac with their packs of furs. During that time Anderson reported the Dakota "were away at their summer villages," though he provided no other information about them. Later he accompanied an entire Dakota village on a summer hunt on the Upper Mississippi River. Anderson noted that in the fringe of timber above the mouths of the Rum and Crow rivers, the deer would "retire from the scorching sun of summer; and if the mosquitoes are troublesome the pestered animals plunge into the river." According to Anderson's account, the men hunted deer while woman and children stopped to pick berries and stretch and dry the skins. Traps were also set for small animals.[10]

The party soon reached "the borders of their Chippewa enemies," although Anderson does not say exactly where this was. Though certainly not the usual summer war party, which would not have included women and children, the group prepared for the possibility of hostilities, but none occurred and the party turned back. Later that summer Anderson also described going west with two canoes of hunters to pursue buffalo at Big Stone Lake but added few details about those he accompanied.[11]

Anderson was involved in fighting against the Americans during the War of 1812, along with other British traders of the region and a number of Dakota, including Wabasha and Red Thunder. Another chief, Taṭaŋkamani, or Walking Buffalo, chief of the Red Wing village, opposed this involvement. Other chiefs remained neutral.[12]

Following the war, Americans sought to reestablish relations with the Dakota. On July 19, 1815, government officials signed a treaty of peace and friendship with the "Sioux of the Lakes" (Bdewakaŋtuŋwaŋ) at Portage des Sioux, near the mouth of the Missouri River. The Dakota were brought to the treaty by Nicolas Boilvin, U.S. Indian agent at Prairie du Chien. The treaty stipulated that the signers "acknowledge themselves and their aforesaid tribe to be under the protection of the United States, and of no other nation, power, or sovereign, whatsoever." The best known of the signers was Taṭaŋkamani. The same day a similar treaty was signed with the "Sioux of St. Peter's River." The following year, on June 1 in St. Louis, a treaty was signed with the "Siouxs of the Leaf [Waḣpetuŋwaŋ, the Siouxs of the Broad Leaf [?], and the Siouxs who shoot in the Pine Tops [Wazikute or Waḣpekute]." Signers of the last treaty, forty-one in all, included some who had signed the other two treaties, including Tatangamarnee (Taṭaŋkamani). The terminology used to describe these groups was garbled, as were the names of many of the signers, making it difficult to identify the Dakota involved.[13]

It was not until the summer of 1819, when representatives of the U.S. Army under Lieutenant Colonel Henry Leavenworth appeared at the mouth of the Minnesota River to build a fort, that U.S. government representatives began to have regular contact with the various Dakota bands and villages in the region.

DAKOTA SEASONAL PATTERNS
IN THE LATE EIGHTEENTH AND EARLY NINETEENTH CENTURIES

In the 1820s and 1830s seven Bdewakaŋtuŋwaŋ villages were located along the Minnesota and Mississippi rivers. Above Ṡakpe's village on the Minnesota were a number of Sisituŋwaŋ and Waḣpetuŋwaŋ villages, continuing all the way to the headwaters. The Waḣpekute did not usually have fixed village sites but used the region between the Minnesota and Mississippi, along the course of the Cannon River, and the area to the south. Dakota villages were, in effect, summer villages, occupied not year round, but at particular times in the warm months. They were located in the river bottoms, in areas that might be subject

continued on page 89

1814
The Treaty of Ghent ends the War of 1812, and the U.S. claim to the Minnesota region is fully recognized.

1819-20
The American military arrives at the mouth of the Minnesota River to begin construction of a military post.

Lawrence Taliaferro: Indian Agent

[THOMAS G. SHAW] **Perhaps the richest** written source of information about the Dakota in the early nineteenth century are the journals and letters of Lawrence Taliaferro, who acted as Indian agent for the Upper Mississippi Dakota at Fort Snelling from 1820 to 1839. Taliaferro's journal provides information on Dakota leaders, Dakota villages, and the patterns in which Dakota people lived on the land.

Lawrence Taliaferro (1794–1871) was born into a wealthy land- and slave-owning eastern Virginia family. He served as an officer in the First Regiment of U.S. Infantry during the War of 1812. Following the war he secured a post as a U.S. Indian agent through the patronage of family friend James Monroe. Like all Indian agents, he was invested with the rank of major, although he did not hold a commission in the army. Taliaferro had no qualifications apart from his experience as an army officer and the common presumption within the U.S. ruling class that gentlemen of proper birth and breeding were natural leaders.

Taliaferro arrived at the new military post at St. Peters, at the mouth of the Minnesota River, in the summer of 1820. The post was known to Americans as St. Peters. He remained as agent for both the Dakota and western Ojibwe until 1826 and thereafter solely for the Dakota until he resigned in November 1839.

During his almost twenty years of association with the Dakota, Major Taliaferro kept a daily journal. He developed close relationships with a number of Dakota during his residence. He provided European-style wooden coffins to grieving families as a measure of his regard and their standing and even allowed a number of Dakota to be buried in a small cemetery behind his house. Over the years he frequently referred to the Dakota both collectively and individually as his "friends." Perhaps most crucially, he had a relationship with Aŋpetu Inażiŋwiŋ, the Day Sets, daughter of Maȟpiya Wiċaṡṭa, or Cloud Man. The nature and longevity of this relationship is not made clear in the journal, but there are references to their daughter, Mary,

mostly after 1835, when she began attending the mission school at Lake Harriet. Despite these relationships, Taliaferro never became proficient in the Dakota language and never rid himself of his biases regarding Dakota culture.[i]

The journals, which are unique for this period, contain an amazing depth and variety of information. The relationships Taliaferro built with Dakota people over almost twenty years are significant in themselves, allowing the reader and researcher to see patterns develop over time. We witness the maturation of these relationships and how they were affected by events and in turn effected events themselves.

The journals are a particularly rich source of information on Dakota lands and land use. They document when particular bands left the vicinity of the agency for hunting, ricing, sugaring, and war, providing firsthand information on the seasonal subsistence cycle. Numerous direct references to places and their significance include camping sites, villages, hunting lands, ricing lakes, and geographical features. Taliaferro did not often have a firm grasp of Dakota understanding, and the factual information is frequently accompanied with misinformed editorializing.

Taliaferro made frequent reference to Dakota agricultural, hunting, and food-gathering practices. He was committed to teaching the Dakota European-style deep-plow farming, believing they could regularize their diets by producing agricultural surpluses in the manner of European farmers. In many cases he misunderstood what he was seeing and the long-standing logic behind traditional practices. Nonetheless, his observations provide the historian with information that is not available in other sources.

Of special significance are numerous transcriptions of Dakota "talks," or speeches. While Taliaferro's reasons for recording them were probably self-serving, these are essentially oral history transcriptions. He was not fluent in Dakota, so the translated text probably came from Dakota interpreter Scott Campbell. Many of the talks are words spoken in formal councils with the attendant ceremony— words calculated for public effect. Many times the scene and the speaker's gestures are described as well. As such, these records are tangible remainders of Dakota oratory. Generally they are recorded word for word. Most have government policy or intertribal relations as their topic.

Other talks were much less formal. Many times they were recorded in the agent's office with only the interpreter and a few other Dakota as witnesses. These can be best characterized as conversations with more personal and local issues as the subject. Sometimes they were set down word for word; in other cases they were paraphrased. Both formal and informal talks record the words of specific Dakota, however, and through them the reader hears contemporary people speak about contemporary issues. The informal dialogues provide much less self-conscious information. The reader learns about burial places, travel routes, hunting grounds, places of spiritual importance, and locations of seasonal food and materials. Because of Taliaferro's long tenure, he was able to record the changes in Dakota culture and living patterns as the Dakota struggled to accommodate and mitigate increased Ojibwe and American pressure on their resources.

Taliaferro seldom ventured far from the agency adjacent to Fort Snelling, though he was responsible for all the Dakota, not just the neighboring Bdewakaŋtuŋwaŋ. He viewed the military reservation as the crucial center of the region and reasoned that visiting Dakota expected to find him at the agency. Consequently, his best information was local. He knew the people of nearby villages far better than those to the west beyond Little Rapids. Much of his intelligence concerning events in this region was obtained through conversations with missionaries, traders, and visiting Dakota rather than by direct observation and experience.

Despite their removal from his jurisdiction in 1826, the Upper Mississippi Ojibwe continued to visit the St. Peters Agency, placing themselves in direct contact with local and visiting Dakota. Taliaferro designated a particular camping area near Coldwater Spring for the Ojibwe. The comings and goings of these people and their interactions with the Dakota gave him opportunities to observe and describe councils, dances, games, and feasts, as well as warfare. Despite his obvious cultural biases and with the benefit of historical distance and clearer cultural understanding, Taliaferro's journals provide much information and many intriguing clues about how the Dakota viewed and interacted with the physical and spiritual world. ∎

Joseph N. Nicollet, Mapmaker and Ethnographer

Before the nineteenth century, the details of Dakota seasonal patterns and the locations in which they took place were described haphazardly. This changed with the arrival of French geographer Joseph N. Nicollet, who came to the Upper Mississippi River in 1836 and compiled a detailed map of the entire region, published by the U.S. government in 1843. Perhaps the most important surviving record of Dakota geography and place names in the nineteenth century, Nicollet's map was the first real attempt to produce an accurate accounting of the region and the first attempt by anyone after Pierre Le Sueur in 1700 to record native place names for local sites. While compiling this geographical record, Nicollet kept journals—not published until the 1970s—recording the meanings of place names, the relationships between peoples and places in the region, and important cultural information about the Dakota and the Ojibwe of Minnesota. Nicollet recorded this information without the prejudices of the missionaries or the government agents, always seeming to show a sympathy and respect for native cultures.[ii] ▪

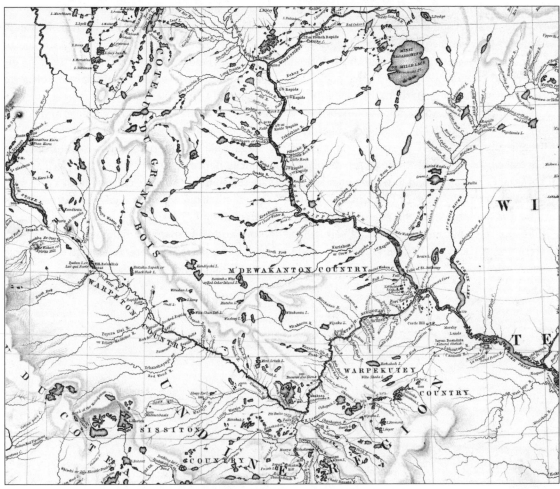

Joseph Nicollet's 1843 map of the Upper Mississippi, including many Dakota and Ojibwe names, was the most detailed map of the region after those done 140 years earlier based on information supplied by Pierre Le Sueur.

continued from page 85

to flooding in the spring. Their location reflected a way of life heavily dependent on the river for transportation. The Dakota had horses but continued to
rely on dogs and canoes, both dugout and birch bark. The summer village sites
were bases of operations occupied sporadically, starting after the rivers had
subsided in the spring and continuing until the fall, when the inhabitants left
the rivers to hunt for deer.[14]

As Stephen R. Riggs noted, the Dakota divide the year differently than
Europeans do. He reported that, while the Dakota have twelve moons or
months to which they give meaningful names, "five moons are usually counted
to the winter, and five to the summer, leaving only one each to the spring
and autumn." The two transitional moons corresponded more or less to April
and October. Present-day Minnesotans will recognize the logic of the abrupt
transition from winter to summer and summer to winter. And like present-day
Minnesotans, the Dakota in the nineteenth century "had very warm debates,
especially towards the close of winter," about whether spring had finally come.[15]

The Dakota use of the land related not only to daily subsistence but also to
their beliefs and rituals and the meaning they attached to particular places in
the region. Medicine ceremonies, feasts, and Dakota ball games were held at
village sites at various times of year. Prominent locations such as Wakaŋ Tipi
(Carver's Cave), Mounds Park, and Oheyawahi (Pilot Knob) were used for
burial and ceremonial purposes.

A regular pattern of resources was available in the country of the Dakota,
but the changeable weather of every season and every year meant that all resources did not have good years at the same time. In some years the wild rice
crop or the corn crop failed. Game was scarce in some places in some years.
Through their knowledge of the region, the Dakota were able to harvest some
crops or resources more intensively when others failed. For example, it seems
the Dakota may have preferred eating meat to fish, but they fished when they
needed to.[16]

To understand Dakota life it is necessary to understand the pattern of seasonal subsistence activities. As will be seen, the Dakota names for the seasons
related to the land: winter moons or months connected to animals, while the
names for the summer months described horticultural or gathering activities.[17]

FALL AND WINTER HUNTING

November is Takiyuȟa-wi, "the deer-rutting moon." Missionary Samuel Pond
stated that in October, after receiving supplies of trade goods, larger bands
broke into smaller ones and set off for the deer hunt. Pond himself spent several
deer hunting seasons with Dakota communities—to learn about the people
and their language. He later wrote that in the fall of 1835, "I went off with the

Indians on a hunting expedition. The Language however was the game I went to hunt, and I was as eager in pursuit of that as the Indians were of deer." In the process, Pond had a unique opportunity to be a participant-observer, in the anthropological sense, of Dakota life, beliefs, and social organization.[18]

Deer hunting took place in backwater regions, up small streams and valleys away from the Mississippi and Minnesota rivers. The Dakota living in what is now the Twin Cities area did most of their hunting on the Sauk River, the Rum River, the St. Croix River, and Rice Creek. This territory was part of a productive area where the Ojibwe, former allies and sometime enemies of the Dakota, occasionally ventured. The region stretched diagonally across the present state of Minnesota north of the Twin Cities. Local Indian agents Lawrence Taliaferro and Henry Schoolcraft and tribal members themselves referred to it as "the middle ground." On August 18, 1836, Taliaferro met with Ojibwe chief Bagone-giizhig (Hole-in-the-Day), who in a conversation at the agency with Dakota chief Wakiŋyaŋ Taŋka (Big Thunder, known as Little Crow) spoke about the need to share this space: "Let us, said he, to the Sioux, —keep our middle ground clear," Taliaferro wrote. Keeping it clear meant keeping the peace, since this was a contested zone, a region where Dakota and Ojibwe battled in summer but which they shared in winter, a season when they rarely fought.[19]

1820
Lawrence Taliaferro begins work as Indian agent at Fort Snelling.

Dakota bands departed the rivers to go to their hunting grounds in September or October, after ricing had been completed, not returning until after the first of the new year. On October 31, 1830, Taliaferro reported that he held a council with the Dakota and Ojibwe "to settle their differences for the winter." They left the next day to "go off on their hunts." He added, "Nothing I hope will disturb their mutual intentions for the winter."[20]

A few hunting locations were associated with particular Dakota villages. The Kap'oża village usually hunted along the St. Croix River, sometimes going as far north as St. Croix Falls. The area was more easily accessible to them by overland travel than through the circuitous water route down the Mississippi to the mouth of the St. Croix. In December 1835, translator Scott Campbell returned to Fort Snelling from the St. Croix River, reporting to the agent that "The Sioux & Chippeways were below the falls of St. Croix—on the Chip Land by invitation—Dancing—playing Ball & feasting together."[21]

Waȟpetuŋwaŋs from the Little Rapids village of Mazamani were reported in 1828 hunting on a small lake near the head of the Sauk River. In 1831 they hunted between the Crow and Sauk rivers, reaching an agreement with the Sandy Lake Ojibwe for the winter. The Black Dog village and Cloud Man's village usually hunted along the Rum River, making arrangements with the Rum River and Mille Lacs Ojibwe. Samuel Pond accompanied a hunting party from Cloud Man's village in the winter of 1836 that traveled along the Rum River.[22]

continued on page 94

The Dakota and Ojibwe people had seasonal peace treaties to minimize conflict in their shared lands. Although they had made treaties prior to the construction of Fort Snelling and arrival of the U.S. Indian agent, Lawrence Taliaferro's presence facilitated the process. His efforts began in 1820, in collaboration with the first commander at St. Peters, Lieutenant Colonel Henry Leavenworth, who negotiated a treaty with the Dakota that year that was never ratified. Meetings with the Dakota occurred both at the site of the first military encampment, Cantonment New Hope, located at the mouth of the Minnesota River, and at Coldwater Spring, which was first occupied by U.S. officials during the summer of 1820. Taliaferro arrived that summer. He did not record a narrative of what occurred, but he did leave lists of presents given to Dakota leaders starting in June 1820.[iii]

Throughout his journals Taliaferro mentions renewals of such treaties of "Peace and Friendship." By 1831, Taliaferro stated, "I have held more than 200 councils since July 1820—between these old enemies—& have been instrumental in doing some good so they say to me & to each other."[iv]

These treaties often involved songs and ceremonies. Taliaferro described one such event in June 1823 at the mouth of the Minnesota River:

> Meeting of the Sioux & Chippeways—June 1823 at the Entry of the St. Peters West of the Mississippi River in View of the Agency House

> 211 Chippeway—342 Sioux from Several Bands. The Sioux were drawn up in line 150 yards from the Chippeways with 4 Flags unfurled—Singing the Peace Song.

> The Chippeways also in line parallel with the St Peters. The Braves of both nations then advanced to the number of about 40, 20 of a side with their Arms & War implements. When at the distance of ten paces—the parties halted for a moment—then advanced singing the Braves Song and gently but Quickly pressed each others Sides above the hips—Shook hands—When the Combined Sioux & Chippeways—fired general Salute—after which Pipes of peace passed as a renewal and Confirmation of their General Peace in the Month of July 1821.[v]

Among the Dakota and Ojibwe leaders most supportive of peace were the bands closest to each other, including the Mille Lacs, Rum River, and St. Croix Ojibwe and the Bdewakaŋtuŋwaŋ from Kap'oža, Black Dog, and Penichon villages. In 1836 Taliaferro noted that Piajick (Bayezhig) or Lone Man, the Ojibwe war leader for a St. Croix band, "was the first to step forward in 1821—to assist me in forming & confirming a peace between the Chipp[e]ways of the St Croix and the Sioux of the Mississippi." Many local Ojibwe were members of the Maingan or Wolf clan, descended from intermarriage between Dakota men and Ojibwe women in the St. Croix River region decades earlier.[vi]

In 1825, as will be discussed in the next chapter, Taliaferro was instrumental in bringing about the Treaty of Prairie du Chien, which sorted out the boundaries between tribes, drawing lines between tribal territories, even in areas where hunting land was actually shared. Because the region had never been surveyed by the government, the agreed-upon line made use of geographic sites known to both tribes—sites which probably had cultural significance, although their meaning is not explained in the treaty. They include such locations as "the standing cedar" on the St. Croix, two lakes known to the Ojibwe as the "Green Lakes" and to the Dakota as "the lakes they bury the Eagles in," and "the standing cedar that 'the Sioux Split'" near the Rum River. In 1835 Major Jonathan Bean, an Indian agent on the Missouri River, surveyed the line between the Dakota and Ojibwe from the Eau Claire River northwest across Wisconsin and Minnesota, though neither side could agree on the exact course it should take.[vii]

Less formal ceremonies occurred on many other occasions. Sometimes Dakota traded with visiting Ojibwe for maple sugar and birch-bark canoes, which they used for ricing. According to Taliaferro, ⟩⟩

>> the Dakota provided blankets, guns, and traps in exchange. Trading such items—which might otherwise have been provided by the Indian agent—may have been especially important for the Ojibwe during the period after 1827, when Taliaferro was instructed by superiors to send them to their designated agent, Henry Schoolcraft at Sault Ste. Marie, or subagent, George Johnston at La Pointe. The distance of the Lake Superior agents and the nearness of Taliaferro to Ojibwe villages on the Upper Mississippi and St. Croix rivers led the local Ojibwe to continue coming to Fort Snelling.[viii]

During such visits the Ojibwe usually camped near Coldwater Spring, which for a while was the location of a trading post run by Benjamin F. Baker, who operated among both the Ojibwe and the Dakota. Representatives of the tribes would take turns dancing at each other's camps. The Ojibwe's landing place on the Mississippi was named Chippewa Point by agency employees.[ix] ■

Ṭaḳu Wakaŋ Tipi / Morgan's Mound and Mni Sni / Coldwater Spring

Ṭaḳu Wakaŋ Tipi is known to the Dakota people as "the dwelling place of the gods." Place-name historian Paul Durand described the location as "a small hill over-looking the Fort Snelling prairie located between the VA Hospital and Naval Air Station." Missionary Samuel Pond learned from Dakota elders that this was the dwelling place of Uŋkteḣi, a powerful underwater spirit, also known as Ṭaḳu Wakaŋ, who inhabited springs, waterways, and locations such as the Falls of St. Anthony. A tunnel was said to lead from this site to the Minnesota River, permitting the spirit easy passage. The soldiers at Fort Snelling named it Morgan's Mound or Hill in the 1820s.[x]

Exactly what constitutes the boundaries of this hill and the boundaries of the sacred site are matters of discussion. Early maps provide varying details. Government agencies like to insist that the Dakota people document every single place a square inch at a time, but Dakota places are often linked by cultural connections that transcend physical borders. Given the recorded Dakota beliefs about a water passage to adjacent rivers, it is clear the "dwelling place of the gods" included nearby Mni Sni (Coldwater Spring), which comes out of the ground just below the lowest part of Morgan's Mound. Dakota elder and minister Gary Cavender made this point in 1999 at a time when the spring was endangered by highway construction: "There is that sacred spring that is in negotiation, that sacred spring is the dwelling place of Uŋkteḣi, the God of the Waters, and in that spring there is an underground river that goes into the big river, and that is his passageway to get out into the world. To block the sacred passageway would be courting with drought and things of that nature that have to do with water, because after all, this is the God of the water."[xi]

The spring has been described as a manifestation of Uŋkteḣi, as are all bubbling springs. Coldwater Spring was also important in the history of Fort Snelling. The soldiers who came to build the fort camped here in the summer of 1820 and Lawrence Taliaferro began his work as Indian agent here that same year. Adjacent to Coldwater Spring was the habitual camping place of the Ojibwe who came to visit Fort Snelling, the Indian agency, and the nearby Dakota communities. The Indian agent's efforts to mediate between the Dakota and Ojibwe began here in the summer of 1820, when the military encampment was moved from Cantonment New Hope to Coldwater Spring.[xii]

At that time a group of Dakota leaders decided

to invite Ojibwe leaders to come to Bdote, the mouth of the Minnesota River, to meet with them to make peace. They left a message on birch bark for the Ojibwe on the Sauk River. Henry Schoolcraft, who visited the area with the expedition of Michigan Territorial Governor Lewis Cass, described this message and later took it back with him to Washington. Schoolcraft stated that the message included images representing Colonel Henry Leavenworth and the Dakota leaders Ṣakpe, Wambdi Taŋka (Big Eagle) of Black Dog village, and another chief whose name was not known to the Americans. The Dakota leaders issued the invitation, and Leavenworth was to mediate the meeting. Another symbol indicated the military cantonment, "then recently established at Cold Spring on the western side of the bluffs above the influx of the St. Peters," which was to be the meeting's location. According to Schoolcraft, "The frame, or crossed poles of the entire 50 lodges composing this party, had been left standing on the high, open prairie on the west bank of the Mississippi above Sauk River, and immediately opposite the point of Hornblende Rocks."[xiii]

As a result of this effort, preliminary meetings occurred between the Dakota and Ojibwe at Coldwater Spring in the summer of 1820. Taliaferro arranged for the Dakota and Ojibwe to meet again in July 1821 to sign a treaty. Anthropologist Ruth Landes, in her work on the Prairie Island Dakota, records a traditional account of a peace ceremony said to have occurred between the Dakota and Ojibwe. The story relates that the Dakota chief was named "Shakopee" and had a village in an area near the former Ford factory in St. Paul and near Minnehaha Falls in Minneapolis, a place which may have been at or near Coldwater. But the story also says

that the event took place at the town of Shakopee, which may be the result of confusion in translation or in remembering the tradition. After a pipe ceremony involving the Dakota and Ojibwe leaders there was a feast, dancing, and other celebrations lasting through the night. Everyone was happy when peace was restored. Landes noted that even in 1935 the Dakota and Ojibwe still talked of being enemies, yet "these people made peace, probably as often as they made war."[xiv]

In 1999 Ojibwe religious leader and educator Edward Benton-Banai recounted other aspects of the Ojibwe and Dakota meetings at the spring. The site was part of "a neutral place for many nations to come, and that further geographically defines the confluence of the three rivers, which is actually the two rivers, that point likewise was a neutral place. And somewhere between that point and the falls, there were sacred grounds that were mutually held to be a sacred place. And the spring from which the sacred water should be drawn was not very far, and I've never heard any direction from which I could pinpoint, but there's a spring near the [medicine] lodge that all nations used to draw the sacred water for the ceremonies." He remembered that his grandfather, who died in 1942 at the age of 108, often recalled that his family "traveled by foot, by horse, by canoe to this great place to where there would be these great religious spiritual events, and that they always camped between the falls and the sacred water place. Those are his words." Benton-Banai went on to say that he had many discussions with Dakota spiritual leader Amos Owen of Prairie Island about the importance of Coldwater Spring to both the Dakota and Ojibwe.[xv] ■

continued from page 90

The people of Wabasha and Red Wing villages usually hunted inland, either to the north in the area of present-day Wisconsin along the Red Cedar and Chippewa rivers or west in the rich region of present-day southeastern Minnesota, along the headwaters of the Cannon, Zumbro, Root, Blue Earth, and Des Moines rivers, an area known as Waȟpekute territory but shared with other Dakota bands. According to Joseph Nicollet, the convergence of the Des Moines and Blue Earth rivers was known as Mni Akipam Kaduza, meaning "water running to opposite sides." Throughout this region Dakota might encounter the Sac and Fox, with whom they were sometimes at war. Here too, Lawrence Taliaferro attempted to reduce friction between groups in an intertribal area known as the "neutral ground." Ultimately several treaties were required to sort out tribal claims, but the uncertainties there, as with the area between the Dakota and Ojibwe, reduced access and increased game populations, which made the area desirable for hunting.[23]

Dakota bands traveled through their hunting grounds regularly, never returning to an area more than every two or three years, according to Samuel Pond. Whole communities of men, women, and children traveled together in these hunting parties, covering a short distance each day. Travel was on foot, with horses—if the community had them—pulling travois frameworks carrying the heaviest loads. Hunters forged ahead looking for game, while the rest of the party followed, taking down the tepees and setting them up in a new place. The social organization of the deer hunt, as described by Samuel Pond, resembled the complex organization of buffalo hunting for Dakota on the prairies: "The movements of a hunting party were regulated by orders issued by the chiefs, or, if no chief were present, by one of the principal men of the party. These orders were given out after the wishes of a majority of the party had been ascertained by consultation, and were commonly proclaimed by a herald in the morning or evening, the only time when the hunters were likely to be all at home." To make sure the whole community was fed, special rules applied to what happened to the deer that were killed. Game was divided among all hunters who claimed a portion even if they did not shoot the deer, though the hunter who killed the deer was always allowed to keep the skin.[24]

During some years in both winter and summer, people from Black Dog village hunted to the south in the region of the Waȟpekute, which bordered the territory of the Sac and Fox, sometimes subjecting them to the threat of warfare. Although the herds of buffalo had receded to the west since the beginning of the nineteenth century, there were years when buffalo were still seen in this region. In June 1827, Wambdi Taŋka (Big Eagle), chief of Black Dog village, left with Wabasha's son-in-law, who had some connection to the village, to hunt on the Des Moines River. Later in the summer Taliaferro reported that the

Black Dog chief, with seven lodges of his band, was still on the plains and was rumored to be going as far as the Coteau de Prairie, though he might return in the fall to gather rice on the Cannon River. Cloud Man, or Maȟpiya Wiçaṡṭa, the Black Dog war chief, was on his way back to the village on the Minnesota River with three lodges. On his return he gave Taliaferro an account of what had occurred during the summer hunt, although Taliaferro recorded no details.[25]

On May 6, 1829, Wambdi Taŋka returned with his followers "from his hunt on the Des Moines River," where they appear to have spent the whole winter. In September 1835 Wambdi Taŋka's son Maza Ḣota (Gray Iron) visited the agent prior to departing for the same region. Taliaferro asked him to transmit a message of peace if he encountered Sisituŋwaŋ and Waȟpetuŋwaŋ people during the winter.[26]

This may have been the hunting trip recorded in the life story of Joseph Jack Frazer or Ite Maza (Iron Face), the son of a white trader and a Dakota woman whose name is recorded as "Ha-zo-do-win," a daughter of Tataŋkamani (Walking Buffalo), the chief of the Red Wing village. Frazer grew up with his mother's family and as an adult remained part of his grandfather's band but was married to a daughter of Maza Ḣota, by then chief of Black Dog village. According the narrative of Frazer's life recorded by Henry H. Sibley, one winter in the 1830s when Frazer and his uncle Wakute wintered on the headwaters of the Root and Whitewater rivers, they were joined by Maza Ḣota. When the Black Dog leader set off to return in the spring, Frazer accompanied him as far as Pine Island on the headwaters of the Zumbro River. There he also met his friend Ta Oyate Duta, son of Wakiŋyaŋ Taŋka, who had by then succeeded his father, Çetaŋ Wakuwa Mani, in the leadership of the Kap'oża band. The two men hunted for several weeks before Frazer and his wife returned to the Root River.[27]

The chief of Penichon's village also hunted in the region of the Des Moines River. In July 1831 Taliaferrro wrote in his diary that he would "send Penition Chief to hunt with the Sioux on the Des Moines this fall and all winter until spring—so as my councils may be continually repeated," a reference to his attempts to foster peace with the Sac and Fox.[28]

Taliaferro's journal mentions the killing of other game in the fall. In August 1835 several bear were spotted on the "9 mile ridge creek [possibly at Kap'oża] within a few days past which fact seems to revive the drooping spirits of our neighboring Indians as Game has been considered scarce this season." The next month ten bear were killed in the cornfields at Cloud Man's village on Lake Calhoun. Taliaferro reported, "This put the Indians in fine spirits—& their Corn was gatherd the faster & with more pleasure." At the same time he noted that "the high winds has blown down the wild rice—unlucky." Taliaferro explained the presence of so many bear by a lack of food farther north. He also noted that raccoons were overrunning the agency gardens.[29]

Muskrat hunting was mainly a spring activity, although sometimes the animal was hunted in the fall. In 1835, when muskrats were "unusually abundant," people killed "40 to 60 per diem." There are only a few references to buffalo hunting, usually by Dakota bands farther west. On March 3, 1828, the Odawa and French trader Joseph LaFramboise arrived at Fort Snelling, reporting hard winter conditions along the Sheyenne River, in present-day North Dakota. He stated that ten lodges containing fifty people had died, probably from lack of food, "the snow being so deep that they could not pursue the Buffalo."[30]

During the winter, chiefs sometimes returned to Fort Snelling to meet with the agent and the traders and pay for the credits of trade goods given them in the fall. In some cases the elderly and infirm were left by their bands near the Indian agency so they could receive aid from the agent when necessary. Toward the end of his time at Fort Snelling, Taliaferro stated that over the years he had aided thousands of Dakota and Ojibwe, at his own expense. For example, in March 1836, with the temperature at twelve and a half degrees below zero, Taliaferro received a visit from a Waȟpekute woman whose name he did not know, along with her children and others in need. The woman presented him with a pipe and spoke about her relationship to two prominent Waȟpekute leaders:

> My Father—I have called to see you with my family & friends to shake hands with you. my child[re]n shake ha[n]ds with your Father—I am connected with the Chief Tah saugah [Çaŋ Sagye, or Cane] of the Wah paa kootas [Waȟpekute] & also with Wah maa de sappah [Wambdi Sapa, or Black Eagle], you see me poor and miserable my friend gone by the hands of his enemies and his children left for me to provide for. We are without a Blanket. Scarcely a petty coat and as you see dirty and in great want.

Taliaferro gave "this family 6 or 8" rations of beef and pork, along with tobacco and four bars of lead for making ammunition. He said it was all he could spare.[31]

In some cases, however, staying near the fort could be a problem, especially for women, who might be molested by soldiers. In December 1827 Taliaferro wrote that the soldiers were "troublesome to the Indian women who are encamped near the Agency—their husbands & friends being out hunting." Taliaferro aided them by driving the soldiers away. Generally, he advised the visiting Dakota to stay away from the garrison at the fort.[32]

SPRING SUBSISTENCE

The deer hunting season continued through November and December and into January. At that point, if the hunt had gone well the community would usually have a large surplus of dried meat. At this time of year deer were becoming lean, so bands left the hunting grounds and moved closer to the summer villages, where they set up tepees in a sheltered area.[33]

Now was the time for fishing or spearing through holes in the ice for "Pike,

Pickerel, Black bass, & Sun fish in all their varieties," according to Taliaferro. Dakota who lived along the rivers, such as the Black Dog and Kapʼoża villages, fished and speared in the lakes in the floodplain—or "ponds," as Taliaferro called them. In late March 1836, Taliaferro noted he saw Dakota fishing in "adjacent ponds in groups of 8 & 15—cutting from the ice, fine pike, pickerel, sun fish, &c &c." From the agency he could have seen Snelling Lake, just below the bluff; across the Minnesota River to what was then known as Prescott's Pond (destroyed by a new river channel in modern times); and upriver toward what are now called Gun Club and Long Meadow lakes. The blacksmith at the Indian agency often supplied spears or repaired them for the Dakota.[34]

Samuel Pond wrote that this was a season of rest, assuming the deer hunt had been successful. It ended in March when the Dakota went to hunt or spear muskrats and make maple sugar. These activities required members of the community to split up because the muskrats and the maple trees were located far apart. Pond wrote, "A few of the women accompanied the men to the hunting ground, and a few of the men staid with the women at the sugar bush, but the men were the fur-hunters and the women were the sugar-makers."[35]

Conflicts over the use of maple sugaring sites occurred during the 1820s and 1830s as demand for firewood expanded from the area close to Fort Snelling. Soldiers apparently sometimes tapped the trees themselves as well. In March 1829, one Dakota leader stated in a discourse with Taliaferro,

> My Father
> We are poor people raised in the woods. We have no rights perhaps—but what we think ours we hope will not be taken away from us without our consent. The Other War Chief (Col Snelling) and you my Father promised not to let any person interfere with a Small piece of ground where our women go sometimes make a little Sugar. You promised us this when the Soldiers made Vinegar on it one year.

A few days later the family of Dakota interpreter Scott Campbell returned from a sugar camp to say they had been "ordered off by the Soldiers of Lieut. Jouetes Company." Taliaferro reflected in his journal on the difficulty of sorting out the laws when public officials were involved.[36]

Not all of the locations where Dakota went sugaring have been recorded. One known site was Nicollet Island just above the Falls of St. Anthony in Minneapolis. A Hennepin County history describing the area in 1842 states that the island was "covered with magnificent maple trees," supplying three or four sugar camps for Dakota people, including those from the Cloud Man and the Penichon (Good Road) villages. Location on an island was said to provide "plenty of moisture" for the trees, making the sap abundant. Later, army officer Seth Eastman painted a view of Dakota women at a sugaring site, perhaps on Nicollet Island. Lieutenant James Thompson's 1839 map of the Fort Snelling reservation marks one "sugar orchard" along the west bank of the Mississippi River below St. Anthony Falls, possibly near the present location of the University of Minnesota. According to Taliaferro, there was also a maple grove near Minnehaha Falls, which was known at the time as Little Falls, and the area around Wakaŋ Tipi (Carver's Cave), near the Kapʼoża village, had a "sugar forrest." Waḣpetuŋwaŋ from Little Rapids may have gathered sugar in the area between the Sauk and Crow rivers, where they also sometimes hunted in winter. Several early settlers of Wright County, in Maple Lake and Albio townships, recall visits from groups of Dakota who gathered sugar on the settlers' claims in the 1850s. Likely many other locations were used by the Dakota for sugaring in the mixed woodland areas around the Twin Cities and throughout the Minnesota and Mississippi river valleys.[37]

While the women gathered the sugar, the men hunted muskrats, the staple of the Dakota fur trade in the nineteenth century. The Minnesota River valley was well populated with muskrats, even while beaver were in decline. Many Dakota traveled long distances for the hunt. Indians living in the area of Bdote might travel hundreds of miles to go and return from the Upper Minnesota River. As Pond wrote, spring was the best time of year to hunt muskrats because as the sun melted the snow and ice, muskrat houses thawed out more quickly than the surrounding areas because of their dark color, making them easy to find. To kill muskrats the Dakota used axes to break open the muskrat lodges and barbed spears as well as traps and guns to kill the inhabitants. Pond wrote that many of those seeking muskrats survived on muskrat meat during this season of the year. He noted that the meat was edible in small quantities during cool weather but spoiled quickly in warm weather and that the carcasses gave off a rank, musky odor.[38]

Pond stated that even if the Dakota had the opportunity to hunt waterfowl at this season of the year, ammunition was often too precious, because the Dakota depended on muskrat furs for much of their trade. Taliaferro mentions the Dakota hunting geese and ducks, especially in areas he could see nearby, such as "the pond near the fort," probably a reference to Snelling Lake. In March 1828, Taliaferro wrote that he saw the first geese that morning and that "the Indians ran out of their Lodges in every direction expressing their delight at the occurrence this early."[39]

For Taliaferro, as well as the Dakota, the appearance of migrating waterfowl was a signal of transition, the coming of spring or the nearness of winter. In March 1828, he wrote of seeing geese: "Indians from all the Lodges within the Vicinity of my house ran out to express their delight at the certain omen of a Speedy Spring—or rather b[r]eaking up of the Ice on the Rivers." On April 4, 1836, Taliaferro wrote,

This day is so fine that the Inhabitants & military are like the Bees, & ants b[u]sy flying about & others sunning and thawing out after a long & tedious winter.

Many stragling Indians also to be seen who are smiling at the prospect of spring—& the appearance of wild geese Ducks &c &c[40]

On March 22, 1828, Taliaferro stated, with a typical lack of understanding, that Dakota people who had just carried out a "Medicine feast" presented him with the first goose killed that month: "This is one of their many Superstitions always to make a feast of the first Animal Killed at the commencement of each Season." Other early observers noted that the Dakota held such feasts for the first corn and wild rice, celebrating the arrival of each season's resources.[41]

The inhabitants of the settlement closest to the fort, Black Dog village, were known as Marhayouteshni (Maǧa yuṭe śni), "those who do not eat geese," a possible reference to the fact that even though they lived in an area known for massive migrations of waterfowl, they did not eat them, but reserved them instead for trade with the officers at Fort Snelling. On March 28, 1828, Talia-ferro wrote of a late snowstorm, mentioning "frequent changes in the weather" and "Ducks—Geese &c in great abundance brought in this day by the Indi-ans." The next year, on April 10, he wrote, "Mild and pleasant weather this morn[in]g—Indians commence to Kill wild geese." A few days later he noted that "Fish—Geese—Ducks are brought in by the Indians to trade at the Fort." The presence of the chief Kaḣboka, from Black Dog village, provides a clue to which bands were killing and trading ducks and geese.[42]

Dakota communities more distant from the agency also hunted waterfowl in spring or fall. While traveling down the Mississippi in October 1821, Talia-ferro noted he "Passed the Band of Chief Warbeshas—on an Island engaged in putting up their tents—with a view to hunt Ducks Geese Deer &c for a short time."[43]

Spring hunting and trapping for furs did not occur in winter hunting ar-eas but along river valleys, sometimes to the west. During one productive season, in May 1836, Taliaferro reported that Maḣpiya Wiçaśṭa (Cloud Man) had returned with several others "from the plains" with eight hundred to five thousand muskrats between them.[44]

On their return to the area of their summer villages in the spring, Dakota people held medicine dances. Joseph Nicollet described such an event in frigid conditions on Pilot Knob on February 15, 1837; Taliaferro recorded these ceremo-nies occurring in February and at other times of the year. On some occasions the Dakota welcomed observers from the fort at locations including Pilot Knob, Carver's Cave, Lake Calhoun, Lands End (near the present-day entrance to Fort Snelling State Park), Pike Island, and other sites "near the agency."[45]

1836–39

French geographer Joseph Nicollet explores the Upper Mississippi region, later producing a comprehensive 1843 map of the region.

The Dakota medicine ceremony, the Wakaŋ Waçipi, was similar in many ways to that of other midwestern tribes. On June 12, 1834, Taliaferro reported, "A large body of Sioux have a medicine ceremony and dance at Lake Calhoun this day. Some Chippeways were invited and attended." In addition to medicine ceremonies, Taliaferro refers in his journal to many dances and ceremonies, often given in front of the agency house for assembled visitors. Yet, Taliaferro provides little specific information. Though he was a keen observer of Dakota customs, his knowledge of their ceremonial life was not sophisticated.

Another important marker of spring's coming was the breakup of ice on the rivers, especially because rising water could flood the sites of summer villages. One particularly bad year was 1826, when in April, as the ice melted, the waters on the Mississippi and Minnesota rivers rose as much as twenty feet above normal, covering most of the houses and government buildings near Fort Snelling on the river flats, including the trading post run by Jean-Baptiste Faribault on Pike Island.[46]

According to Taliaferro, the 1826 flooding also swept away the Penichon, Black Dog, and Shakopee villages. This may explain why, when the river started rising in March 1828, local Dakota were "busily engaged in moving their Lodges from the banks of the River St. Peters upon the contiguous Bluffs—it being rapidly on the rise," even though ice on the two rivers was still firm.[47]

Another regular spring occurrence was the burning of the prairies. In April 1828 Taliaferro reported "Extensive fires in every direction. The Pra[i]ries are and will be burnt over—much damage to the under growth & trees. The fact of the origin of the extensive plains in the north and west may be ascribed to the yearly inroads made by fire on the wood Lands." The previous year he had noted that native people employed fires to aid in hunting, writing, "The moment they Start upon their Winter or fall hunt, they set fire to the Prairies—which starts off the *Game* in every direction, to avoid otherwise certain destruction."[48]

On other occasions Taliaferro suggested burning was practiced by both the Indians and the military. The soldiers may have intended to improve grazing areas and make the land easier to plow in the open prairie west of the fort. On October 11, 1835, Taliaferro wrote that the commander of Fort Snelling, Major John Bliss, had set out at sunrise "with 50 or 60 men to set fire to the Pra[i]rie. Rather wet for fire at this hour. The policy of Pra[i]rie burning may be questioned, at any rate I have order[e]d the Indians in the most positive manner not to set fire or permit their children to fire the Pra[i] rie on any account—for it is sure to burn up the fenceing, wood choppings— Hay stacks & again the Cattle suffer & horses, and the game is at once driven off to a great distance."

The platforms used for beds inside the bark houses of a Dakota summer village were recorded by Robert O. Sweeny in the 1850s.

SUMMER JOURNEYS AND FALL HARVEST

In May the sugar makers and the muskrat hunters finally returned to the villages along the rivers and began to live in summer houses, which consisted of gabled structures made of a pole framework covered with elm bark. These houses had a built-in platform at bed height all around the perimeter of the structure.[49]

For the next few months, meat resources were scarce. Summer hunting was shorter and more sporadic than in winter, though it sometimes covered the same territory. On June 19, 1827, Taliaferro stated, "The Sioux Bands near this Post have generally left for their Summers hunt.—and will remain some thirty or forty days. Some of them will go in the direction of the Chippeways frontier, may expect to loose their Scalps." Hunting in the summer was more dangerous because it was frequently a time for war parties. In July 1817 explorer Stephen Long noted the residents of Cetaŋ Wakuwa Maŋi's Kap'oża village were absent on a hunting party up the St. Croix River. Given the season, there could have been many other possibilities. In July 1823, William H. Keating, a member of Long's second expedition, stated that the Kap'oża village was "abandoned for the season," giving no other details. The people from Kap'oża hunted on the Crow River in the summer of 1834. In June 1829 Kaȟboka of Black Dog village hunted on the Sauk River, while Wambdi Taŋka, Big Eagle, hunted on the St. Peters River.[50]

In July 1827 Taliaferro noted that the chief of Penichon's village and others of his band were "on the plains in pursuit of subsistence." Traveling up the Minnesota River in mid-July 1823, Long's expedition encountered the chief of Black Dog village not at his home but with family members over a hundred miles away, close to the Cottonwood River near present-day New Ulm. In September 1835 British geologist George William Featherstonhaugh stated that the members of Black Dog village were "on the prairies hunting buffalo."[51]

In some cases men could not get ammunition to hunt in the summer because traders were unwilling to supply it until the time of year when animal furs were thickest. In June 1827 Taliaferro stated that some families had little to eat during the summer until corn ripened in August, unless they obtained wild plant foods. Starting in the 1830s the Dakota were promised the payment of treaty annuities, which persuaded them to camp near Fort Snelling rather than go out hunting. Delays in payment led to summer scarcities. At such times and at other occasions during the year, the Indian agency supplied food, ammunition, and other provisions, such as fish hooks and lines and spears.[52]

For the Dakota, June is Wažušteçaśa-wi, "the moon when the strawberries are red," while one name for July is Çaŋpasapa-wi, "the moon when the chokecherries are ripe." In addition to berries and fruits, many wild plant foods became available in the spring and summer, including tipsiŋna or wild turnips, and mdo, a kind of potato. Other food plants included the pśiŋçiŋça (psinchinca), a round root the size of a hen's egg, and the pśiŋça (psincha), a spherical root an inch in diameter, both of which grew in shallow lakes and marshy ground including the wetlands bordering the Minnesota River. Pond noted that these roots were harvested by women standing in the water: "When a psinchinca is detached from the mud it immediately rises to the surface of the water; but the psincha does not float and must be raised by the foot until it can be reached by the hand, a difficult operation, requiring much dexterity where the water is up to the arms as it often is where they grow." Pond recalled, "scores of women might be seen together in shallow lakes, gathering these treasures of the deep." It appears these roots provided food at various times of year when other resources failed. On April 30, 1829, Taliaferro wrote that "the Indians are now Subsisting entirely on Wild or Marsh Potatoes—without Salt or grease of any Kind whatever—(a poor diet)."[53]

Summer was a time of great sociability among the Dakota, when larger bands were reunited. In earlier eras, going back to the 1600s, the mouth of the Minnesota had been a location where western and eastern Dakota bands met. With the building of Fort Snelling and placement of the Indian agency there, an extra dimension was added to its traditional role. Starting with the first treaties, annuity payments were often made during the summer at the fort, drawing those from all the Dakota bands involved.

The area around the fort was often the site for Dakota ball play, or lacrosse, between Dakota villages and between Dakota and Ojibwe. On July 4, 1835, various Dakota villages played ball on the plain near the fort for the amusement of artist George Catlin, who was visiting the area. Catlin painted portraits of some of the players.[54]

If Dakota villages grew corn, it was planted in June, when strawberries were ripe, usually on ground "where there was a thrifty growth of wild artichokes." Dakota women planted corn in hills, not in rows of plowed fields as whites did. Pond wrote that many Dakota villages did not grow more than enough corn to feed the community for a few weeks. Often they ate all the corn in its "green" state—that is, fresh from the cob, at its sweetest. Some corn was dried and put in bark containers for winter sustenance, but because Dakota made use of many other resources it was not common for villages to store large quantities of corn.[55]

During his time at Fort Snelling, Taliaferro sought to encourage a shift among the Dakota to increased dependence on agriculture—particularly the growing of corn—which he saw as a crucial step in instructing them in what he viewed as "the arts & habits of civilized life." These included the use of plows and men's participation in agricultural activities usually carried on by Dakota women. Taliaferro urged the chief Cloud Man, who had been a member of the Black Dog band, to move to Lake Calhoun and establish an agricultural colony which would grow not only corn but other crops, such as beans and squash.[56]

As a result of Taliaferro's influence, the people of that community appear to have adopted plows in preparing the ground for growing corn, but the work of cultivation was still carried out mainly by the women. Taliaferro himself made use of the agricultural skills of Dakota women, hiring some to work in his garden at the Indian agency. In 1839, the final year Cloud Man's band was at Lake Calhoun, missionary Gideon Pond left a detailed description: "The Ind's at this village plant about 80 acres (I plowed only 15 acres for them this spring) as it has all been planted before it is comparatively easy for them to cultivate it with the hoe." He noted that "the women do mostly some of the men however help their wives through the whole of it (the corn belongs to the women)," making the same point about corn that Jonathan Carver had made about women's harvesting of wild rice seventy years before. Pond noted that in 1839 the village had harvested about 2,300 bushels of corn and two hundred bushels of potatoes. Finally, he wrote, "Each woman has her little field to take care of. The 80 acres which they plant is divided into 50 fields yet all lies or nearly all together." He did not say whether the women at Cloud Man's village grew their corn in hills in the traditional way, but a map of the area drawn by Taliaferro in the 1830s suggests the fields were divided up irregularly rather than in rectilinear plots.[57]

continued on page 108

1829
Cloud Man, or Maȟpiya Wiċaṡta, and other members of the Black Dog village begin agricultural experiment at Lake Calhoun.

Bde Maka Ska / Lake Calhoun, Minneapolis

[KATHERINE BEANE] **As one strolls** along the busy shores of Lake Calhoun—known to the Dakota as Bde Maka Ska ("white banks lake") in reference to the sandy white beaches that enveloped the waters—the true history of this place feels absent. A small monument on the east side of the lake marks a spot that largely goes unseen. This location is now more closely associated with inline skating, dog walking, jogging, and summer fun, but it was not always simply a place of leisure. The history of the land and the waters that have protected this space for centuries is a long and contentious one upon which only a small fraction of perspectives have been properly documented.[xvi]

From 1830 to 1839 a small agricultural community of Dakota known as Heyate Otuŋwe, "the village at the side," was located at Lake Calhoun, then a marshy area that had previously served as a place to harvest wild rice, located roughly six miles from Bdote, a site of creation for the Dakota people. The community, which in 1839 had a total population of 207, including 72 men, 54 women, and 81 children, was under the supervision of Indian agent Lawrence Taliaferro. The village of Heyate Otuŋwe came into being in 1829 when Chief Cloud Man, or Maḣpiya Wiċaṡṭa, a member of the Black Dog band of Dakota, decided to try the "white man's way" of farming. He was influenced to do so after surviving a treacherous incident in a snowstorm. Missionary Samuel Pond stated that the chief—who like many Dakota in Minnesota sometimes hunted a great distance from their summer villages—was hunting on the plains near the Missouri River when he and the other members of his party were overtaken by a sudden blizzard.[xvii]

According to Samuel Pond, the storm was so violent that the hunters lay down, each wrapped in his furs. Maḣpiya Wiċaṡṭa could not communicate with his companions and did not know whether they were dead or alive. The men lay there for three days and nights under the snow. During this time Maḣpiya Wiċaṡṭa remembered that Indian agent Taliaferro had urged them to plant crops at Lake Calhoun. When the storm was over, the members of the party found that they were near a "large camp of Indians who came to their assistance." On returning home to Black Dog village, Maḣpiya Wiċaṡṭa persuaded a group of families to accept government assistance to start a new village in which agriculture would be emphasized for subsistence. They were given seed and farm tools, and the colony began in August 1829.[xviii]

Dakota people, historically seen in western anthropological terms as hunters and gatherers, were traditionally not viewed as farmers, though they had always cultivated gardens at village sites. Their way of life did not fit under the term agriculture because they traveled at different times of year and harvested their food from wild and native plants rather than subsisting off of plants that were not indigenous to the area. Another difference from European agriculture was that in Dakota culture it was the women who cultivated crops, not the men.

From Samuel Pond's point of view, Maḣpiya Wiċaṡṭa's decision was "to turn their attention to agriculture and adopt the customs of civilized people." Thus, the Dakota—particularly Dakota men—would spend less time hunting and more time farming: Pond defined the change as "abandoning the chase and cultivating the arts of civilized life." He viewed Maḣpiya Wiċaṡṭa as a "man of superior discernment, and of great prudence and foresight." Pond noted that the chief was "opposed by many of the other chiefs, and none of them entered heartily into his views."[xix]

Maḣpiya Wiċaṡṭa's decision to take up agriculture could be viewed as assimilation to western values and culture. This was Indian agent Taliaferro's understanding: he named the village Eatonville in honor of John Eaton, secretary of war in the administration of President Andrew Jackson, calling the village "my little Colony of Sioux agriculturists." Eatonville was viewed as an experiment to see if the Dakota's lives would be improved by emphasizing agriculture as a way of life. This perspective sees

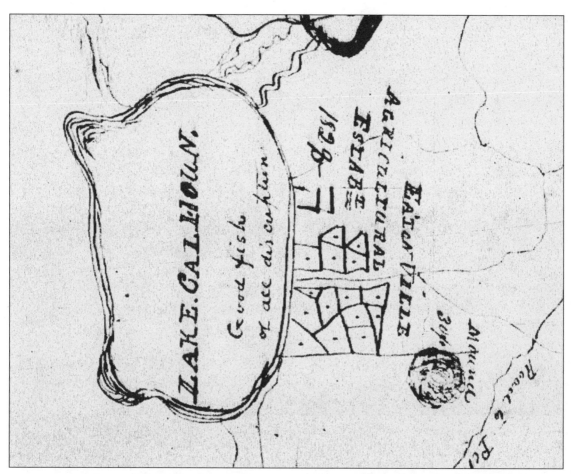

The village of Maḣpiya Wiċaṡṭa, known as Ḣeyate Otuŋwe, "the village at the side," located on the east side of present-day Lake Calhoun in Minneapolis, was recorded in this map by Indian agent Lawrence Taliaferro, who preferred to call the village Eatonville. Here he encouraged Dakota to concentrate more heavily on agriculture, shown in the irregular fields on this map. However, contrary to the male-dominated approach encouraged by Taliaferro, women continued to be the main cultivators of the soil.

Maḣpiya Wiċaṡṭa's and his fellow band members as pawns of civilization, on a "progressive" path to assimilation into European ways. From the chief's perspective, however, he had a decision to make, one supported economically by the local Indian agent and missionaries, which may have had a strong influence. It was a time of transformation for the Dakota. Maḣpiya Wiċaṡṭa's decision was not merely economic or cultural but also political,

a move toward self-sufficiency and independence. Maḣpiya Wiċaṡṭa had a choice to make, and he opted to try another way of life. The traditional ways of the Dakota were becoming less and less viable, especially with the decline of buffalo and its disappearance from the eastern regions of the Dakota homelands.[xx]

Maḣpiya Wiċaṡṭa was not seeking to become something other than a Dakota person. He did not

As the corn in their fields ripened, Dakota women and children sat in scaffolds to prevent birds
from damaging the crop, as shown in an engraving based on a painting by Seth Eastman.

intend to forsake his identity as a Dakota man; he was simply making an honest attempt to adapt to his surroundings, changing with the times as any human being, as well as any community, must in order to live. The change in subsistence patterns did not make the people of this village any less Dakota. Its members not only tried to feed themselves more efficiently but shared their wealth, in a typically Dakota way, with neighboring bands, thus ensuring the survival of even more Dakota people. In September 1835, Taliaferro felt the need to lecture the people of Maḣpiya Wiċaṡṭa's village "to explain fully to the Indians—not to give their corn away to others of

their relations—with other matter of importance to their interests." Despite the fact that the people in this village embraced agriculture, Taliaferro was never able to convince them to stop being Dakota.[xxi]

While the people of the village begun by Maḣpiya Wiċaṡṭa spent more time growing crops than did other villages, he was not the only Dakota leader to turn to farming. Ecological decline had led other nearby Dakota communities to take up agriculture since the 1770s. At the same time, though the members of the village farmed during the summer, they continued to hunt, fish, and gather crops as usual over the course of the year. It was people from Ḣeyate Otuŋwe that Samuel Pond accompanied on a winter hunting trip to the Rum River, hoping to make progress in learning the Dakota language. Ḣeyate Otuŋwe was the place where the Dakota language was first written down in a comprehensive way by the missionaries and the Dakota they taught.[xxii]

Missionaries like Samuel and Gideon Pond, who arrived at Fort Snelling in 1834 and spent twenty years preaching Christianity and documenting the Dakota language, were certain they were working with a dying race of people. They felt it was their duty to record these peoples and to save as many of them as they could. The idea that the Dakota would survive the colonial impact of invasion, or that they had their own spirituality and/or religions that were distinct to them, handed down to them by their own god (Tuŋkaśida), did not seem to pass through their minds. These brothers were, however, among the few whites who came into contact with Dakota people and made any attempt to learn their language. But there was an agenda to their learning the language: in order to convert as many Dakota people as possible, they would need to translate the Bible into Dakota first. Thus language acquisition was a necessary step in order to speed up the conversion process.

In the end, Ḣeyate Otuŋwe was abandoned by Maḣpiya Wiċaṡṭa's band due to fear of retaliation from the Ojibwe following a war between the two nations in 1839. As a result, many have viewed the village at Lake Calhoun as a "failed experiment," ignoring the fact that the villagers continued to emphasize agriculture in the years following, when they were located on the Minnesota River near Bloomington. After the treaties of 1851, Maḣpiya Wiċaṡṭa and his band moved up the river with other Dakota to the area near Yellow Medicine, joining the Hazelwood Republic, a self-governing body of farmer Indians that chose their own officers, advised by the missionary Stephen R. Riggs. According to Pond, Maḣpiya Wiċaṡṭa was among those placed in the concentration camp at Fort Snelling over the winter of 1862–63. He died there and was buried "within sight of the valley he loved so well and not far from where he was born."[xxiii]

From a Dakota point of view, Maḣpiya Wiċaṡṭa's village was not a failure because it insured the survival of his people and his descendants. He could not read the future, but he saw his people hungry and did what he needed to do—and for a period of time it worked. Many Dakota villages were nourished by the crops Ḣeyate Otuŋwe harvested during a time when food was not so readily available to them. The legacy of Maḣpiya Wiċaṡṭa lived on after his death and has served as a source of inspiration to his descendants. He is remembered as a man not afraid to take on a challenge, and he has continued to serve as a source of inspiration for many of his descendants who reside in the Twin Cities area as well as for those who are still living in exile from their home territory of Mni Sota Makoce.[xxiv] ∎

continued from page 103

Dakota who did shift more intensively to growing corn did not abandon hunting or food-gathering. It would have made no sense for people in the Minnesota country to attempt to survive on only a few agricultural resources. Even later white settlers did not try to do so. Pond went hunting with Dakota from Cloud Man's village at Lake Calhoun and wrote that while they waited for their corn to ripen, they could often be found catching bullheads in Mud Lake, now called Lake Hiawatha, along Minnehaha Creek above the famous falls.[58]

During the same period, other bands grew crops as a supplement to hunting and gathering. In 1835, Mazamani of the Little Rapids village asked Taliaferro for aid in getting his lands plowed "as others are." He also asked "for our women a corn Mill as our women find it hard to beat their corn after our fashion," suggesting his band did not intend to change gender roles as urged by the agent. Even Waȟpekute bands, usually described as nomadic, grew some corn, though it is not clear whether this practice was influenced directly by the example of Cloud Man's village. In May 1836, Skush Kah Hah (possibly Škaŋ škaŋ yaŋ, or Moving Shadow) of the Cannon River Waȟpekute visited the Indian Agency at Fort Snelling. Taliaferro wrote, "We had considerable conversation as to his people & his fears of the Sacs & Foxes had induced them to leave the Cannon River for this season only to raise their corn on the St Peters 7 miles up this River & asked for shoes &c." However, the Waȟpekute did not adopt agriculture in the fashion of whites, as an activity for men. The leader told Taliaferro, "My Father—we call for a few hoes to enable our women to break the ground and I hope you will spare us some as we are much in want of such things, we wish also for a few fish spears—& files—& fish hooks & lines if you have any."[59]

Other villages—such as Kap'oża and Black Dog, from which the people of Cloud Man's village had originated—followed the agricultural village's example more directly. In March 1836, Wambdi Taŋka came to see Taliaferro at the agency: "He asked for a plough & chains & harness—to open a farm at his village, his family & friends had (10) horses. His son, & nephew were active men and would attempt to plough themselves if I would start them with the means &c." Taliaferro promised to provide him with a plow and harness.[60]

A similar agricultural experiment was taking place at Lac qui Parle, where the trader Joseph Renville and missionaries Thomas Williamson and Stephen R. Riggs also sought to convince the Waȟpetuŋwaŋ to grow more corn as a way to avoid food shortages. Some of the Waȟpetuŋwaŋ had moved from the villages near Little Rapids to grow corn at Lac qui Parle. However, their experience provided a cautionary tale about the difficulties involved in depending on any single resource in the Minnesota climate when on June 20, 1842, a very late frost killed all the garden crops. Many of those living at Lac qui Parle were forced to move back to the lower Waȟpetuŋwaŋ villages to stay with relatives. The following year a drought made things worse. Williamson, usually stationed at Lac qui Parle, spent part of that time at Fort Snelling. In May 1843 he wrote that more than half the Indian members from the Lac qui Parle church spent half the winter within fifty miles of Fort Snelling. More than a dozen came to his church services from January until April. Many expected to stay in the lower Minnesota River valley and plant that spring. Williamson stated, "One principal object which I had in view in coming here was to procure some aid for those who came in this direction in consequence of the failure of their crops. My success in this respect exceeded my hopes but not their expectations." The government granted them $2,500-worth of blankets, guns, ammunition, and a large surplus of provisions. At the same time Williamson was filling in for the doctor at the fort and was paid sixty dollars per month.[61]

One way or another it was clear farming was not a panacea, and the agricultural way of life was never fully embraced by Dakota communities. In 1839 an elderly Dakota man at Lac qui Parle told missionary Riggs about his recollection that when he was a boy corn was first planted below Fort Snelling on the Minnesota. Generally, "as soon as it was fit to eat they devoured it all." In addition they hunted buffalo and deer and gathered wild rice. According to the account, "they raised no more corn until he was a young man. Then some relatives planted a small patch. The next year his relatives planted a small patch and a number of others planted also. Thus the number who made corn increased every year and their fields were enlarged a little. Other villages along the Saint Peters River, following their example, planted corn." The Treaty of 1837 provided funding to pay for government farms run by government farmers adjacent to many Dakota villages, designed to provide food and to encourage farming by the Dakota. Even among the Dakota who embraced agriculture, however, traditional resources remained important.[62]

Late in the summer was the time for ricing throughout Dakota country. The Dakota equivalent of September is Psiŋhaketu-wi, "the moon when the rice is laid up to dry," while October is Wi-waźupi, "the drying rice moon." The Dakota relied on wild rice as a major resource during the winter. The rice crop was variable, depending on water levels. Many lakes around the Twin Cities, including some in present-day south Minneapolis and along the Minnesota River, had thick beds of wild rice. The Rice Creek corridor in present-day Anoka, Ramsey, and Washington counties provided the Dakota with a great deal of rice. Whole bands went to the ricing places in late August or early September. Dakota people obtained birch-bark canoes in trade from Ojibwe who came to Fort Snelling to visit the Indian agent. Taliaferro noted in his journal on June 10, 1829, "These light canoes are in great demand among the Sioux—who use them in gathering the Wild Rice from the Lakes

Like many Dakota village sites, the one at Lake Traverse recorded in 1823 by Samuel Seymour had burial scaffolds on a nearby hill.

& Ponds adjacent." In August 1827 Taliaferro warned that Dakota who had neglected their corn crops "must look out for rice or starve nearly during the approaching winter."[63]

Cranberries were another important crop in the fall. On October 12, 1835, Taliaferro reported, "Cranberries brought in—high prices paid—by the citizens for transportation to the lower country." In April 1826 he also reported cranberries, possibly dried, being brought to the post. On his departure from the agency in the fall of 1839, Taliaferro included among his effects on board the steamboat *Gypsey* one barrel of cranberries. Later on, during early white settlement, cranberries harvested by Indian people continued to be an export item from the Minnesota region.[64]

Sporadic hunting and fishing also supplemented the gathering of wild plant foods. Spearfishing took place all along the rivers near Fort Snelling. One summer fishing place for the people of Kap'oża was at Grey Cloud Island, near Pine Bend on the Mississippi. In September and October some trapping was done, although it is not described in much detail. Taliaferro in his journal mentioned that the Kap'oża band went above the Falls of St. Anthony to hunt for beaver in late September 1831, intending to stay there until traders arrived with merchandise for credit.[65]

Prior to departing for the winter hunting grounds the Dakota had more ceremonies, though Taliaferro did not always describe them with a great deal of understanding. On October 12, 1835, he gave a puzzled and puzzling account of what he observed by moonlight:

The Indians as late as 7 oclk began Danceing any and [all] kinds of figures of a rude nature—Buffalo—first then—War—Discovery—beg[g]ing and last of all the fence dance—intermixed with Medicine ceremonies—fireing at the Devil—all in great glee—men, boys, women and girls—all by a slight ray of the moons beams. From what I could learn from the speakers remarks alias—captain of the Dance & master of the ceremonies—The Agent is likely to have a general Visit on tomorrow Tuesday.

Some of the dances mentioned, including the buffalo dance, the discovery dance, the war dance, the begging dance, and the medicine ceremony, have been described in various sources, but the reason for the dance taking place in the moonlight and whether it was intended for the benefit of the agent or the soldiers is unclear.[66]

Taliaferro did receive a visit the next day, not from the Dakota but from the fort's commander, Major Bliss, who complained about the Indians' continuing presence around the fort. By late October or early November most of the Dakota villagers had left to go hunting for the winter, not to return until February or March. As Taliaferro put it a few weeks later, on November 4, "Cold rain, and disagreeable weather. The Indians haveing finished their fall hunt—Depart generally for their winter hunt—usually return 1st March—after which the usual spring hunt is commenced. Divided into Fall,—Winter, spring,—summer."[67]

The seasonal cycle never ended, but it did vary from year to year depending on weather, war, and rotation of land use. Managing the cycle required the combined knowledge of many band members, who passed on their experiences through the generations. The record kept by Taliaferro and the missionaries and other whites provides a rich view of the Dakota relationship to the land, as it was then, as it had been, and as it would soon cease to be, in the era after the Dakota land cessions and the devastation of 1862–63.

1839
Lawrence Taliaferro resigns as Indian agent at Fort Snelling.

DAKOTA BALL PLAY

During the summer and at other times of the year Dakota villagers traveled throughout Minnesota to each other's villages to play ball games. These games were associated with many aspect of Dakota culture and highlight their strong connection to the land and the places they lived within it. Views about the ball games varied widely depending on the writer's perspective. Missionaries and government agents saw the game in simplistic terms, often with little sympathy or cultural understanding. Not until Dakota writers such as Charles Eastman gave accounts of the game was it possible for non-Dakota to view it with a fuller cultural understanding.[68]

Dakota ball play, or Takapsiçapi, often called lacrosse, from the French

Robert O. Sweeny made this drawing in the 1850s of Dakota people playing Takapsiçapi or ball play, often known as lacrosse, on Shakopee's Prairie, the earlier location of Śakpe's Village, the present-day site of the town of Shakopee. The Dakota played the game in contests between villages and with other tribes at meeting places.

name for the racket used in the game, was a feature of Dakota life often described by early European visitors and missionaries. Using the takapsiçapi, a hooped ball racket or club, and tapa, the wooden ball, Dakota men and women played energetic games in summer and winter, for their own entertainment and that of visitors. One of the earliest written accounts was given by Joseph Marin, who reported that the Dakota played for several days against the Sac and Fox near his trading post on the Mississippi in December 1753. On his trip down the Mississippi in the spring of 1806, Lieutenant Zebulon Pike stopped at the present site of La Crosse, Wisconsin, the location of a prairie where native people often played the sport. On April 20, 1806, Pike observed a game between the Dakota and the Ho-Chunk and Fox. Pike described the ball as being made of a hard substance "covered with leather." The game was played on the prairie, with goals in the form of a line marked a half mile apart. Pike, like other observers, did not indicate if there were boundaries on the sides of the field, though riverbanks or forests may have created natural boundaries. According to Pike the "parties" wagered "the amount of some thousand Dollars." The object was to carry the ball across the opponent's boundary four times. Players tried to get the ball into their rackets, running with it toward the goal but flinging it great distances when necessary. Pike stated that in the game he witnessed "the Sioux were the conquerors," not for their running ability but "from their superior skill in throwing the Ball."[69]

Many years later the missionary Samuel Pond gave a more detailed account of Dakota ball play. He noted that "all the active and able-bodied men engaged in it," though women also had their own form of the game that was played most often on frozen lakes and rivers. Men wore only breechcloths and moccasins, but they were highly decorated with body paint and ribbons or feathers, "which fluttered like streamers when they ran." The game began when the ball was carried to the center of the ball grounds and tossed into the air, at which time "there was a general rush, followed by a clattering of clubs" by members of the two contesting teams, including, in all, a hundred or more players. The ball could only be touched with the club and the goal was to direct it across two opposite boundaries about a half mile apart, each representing one of the teams. While Pike suggested players could keep the ball "in the air for hours," Pond stated that the net in the hoop of the ball club provided a most precarious surface in which to hold the ball, so that only the most adroit player could balance it there while running toward the goal line. The ball often fell on the ground, and players struggled to get it or direct it through the air as far as possible past the other players, who were scattered throughout the game grounds.[70]

The game required great dexterity, and because men collided, giving and receiving "accidental blows from ball clubs," there were often injuries. The players' endurance was tested, as were their tempers. The inhabitants of two or three villages might watch the game at the borders of the field, "elated or depressed as the ball went this way or that across the playground." Players and spectators bet upon the game's result, often, Pond stated, more than they could afford to pay. Spectators were loud in their applause or "sharp censure" about the course of the game and the actions of individual players.

The game paused after one of the teams scored a point but soon resumed, though unlike Pike, Pond was vague about just how it was determined that a game had ended. He noted, "The game might be soon decided by the defeat of one of the parties, but it was more likely to continue till all were glad to have it end and indeed needed several days of rest."

In writing about Dakota ball play in the 1830s, Pond suggested it was a pure sport, one in which "religious ceremonies were not mingled," and shared many picturesque qualities comparable to the games of ancient Greece. Though "nearly naked," the players were "quite as well clothed as the competitors in the old Grecian games." He noted "this would have been one of the most celebrated games in the world if it had been played by the ancient Greeks and described by Homer."[71]

In later letters, however, Pond gave differing interpretations of the game, presenting the missionaries' prevailing view that it was "heathen" in nature. In August 1835, early on in his residence at Lake Calhoun, Pond wrote about all the events occurring in the community on the Sabbath morning. A man came to borrow an ax, another was chopping wood outside his window, women and children were "screaming to drove the blackbirds from their corn." Then "again I am interrupted by one who tells me that the Indians are going to play ball near our house to-day. Hundreds assemble on such occasions. What a congregation for a minister of Christ to preach to! Alas! As far as I know, the glad tidings of salvation never reached the ears of a Dakota. Yet I cannot hope that some will be gathered into the fold of Christ even from among this wild and savage nation."[72]

Samuel Pond's brother Gideon also wrote disparagingly of Dakota ball play and the contexts in which the Dakota played it. He noted that in 1845 the chief he called Mahkanartahkah, or Ground Kicker, "made a ball-play to the spirit of a child he lost last fall." He bought "$50 or $60 worth of clothing and invited ninety men to play for it, forty-five on a side. Besides this he feasted them all." Gideon Pond compared it to a card game called "game-of-the-departed-spirits," whose object was conciliating the spirits of the dead. He suggested the Dakota believed beautiful weather was evidence of a favorable view. In the case of the ball play, he noted sarcastically that there had been an ensuing snowstorm. "Heathenism is expensive," Gideon Pond wrote.[73]

Other missionaries abhorred the game because it involved gambling and was therefore viewed as a form of "dissipation" that prevented the Dakota from hearing their religious message. Though the missionaries' accounts only vaguely suggested the social context in which games were played, the teams represented the villages from which they came, which meant the games were viewed as tests of the pride and strength of villages and their people. Lawrence Taliaferro, the Indian agent at Fort Snelling in the 1820s and 1830s, provides numerous examples of these contests. Although Taliaferro shared the missionaries' perspective about the need to "civilize" the Dakota, he did not seem to view ball play as interfering with the mission. Instead, he appeared to appreciate it as a picturesque sport which he was eager to show off to visitors, both men and women. Taliaferro also found it useful to encourage ball play as a summer distraction that might prevent young men from going to war. In May 1829 sixty men of the Black Dog band participated in a "Grand Dance" at the council house and other locations. He gave them tobacco and rations of bread and pork, noting "The day was a fine one. This is the season for War & I keep all the Bands amused . . . either playing at Ball, Dancing or some feasting expectation."[74]

In June 1834, two teams of a hundred men each played ball near the agency.

The game was "well contested, with stakes including two horses, six guns, eight kettles, and six blankets." Black Dog village was the winner, though Taliaferro did not state which team they were playing. The following year in July he received a visit from the artist George Catlin, who was touring the Upper Mississippi with his wife. Eager to provide picturesque subjects, Taliaferro arranged for members of Lake Calhoun's Cloud Man village to dance and play ball for him. They assembled "painted and ready for play," but the game was interrupted by a violent storm. Catlin gave them several loaves of bread, and they promised to reappear the next day. Taliaferro noted that "the Ladies were all expectation—but have unluckily been disappointed. I will try again to gratify and amuse them." The next day, July 4, he reported that "the different villages of the Sioux played ball for the amusement" of the Catlins.[75]

Taliaferro also stated that Catlin took "the likeness of two Sioux at Ball Play in the act of doing so." Catlin said that he painted the two men, "Ah-no-je-nahge [Anoka Inażiŋ] (he who stands on both sides), and W-chush-ta-doo-tah (the red man)," possibly both from Cloud Man's village, exactly as they "had struggled in the play," though they posed for him in his "painting room." Catlin noted that the Dakota generally held the club with both hands, unlike the Choctaw, who from Catlin's observation used two clubs. It was much more difficult, he stated, to catch the ball with the hoop of one club than to wedge it between two.[76]

Taliaferro recorded a number of occasions when Dakota played ball with Ojibwe people around Fort Snelling. In July 1835 Ojibwe who often came to the Indian agency at the fort to negotiate short-term treaties with the nearby Dakota danced at the fort and then at the Indian agency council house. The following day they were planning to play ball. Taliaferro wrote, "The Sioux stake Guns & Blankets—Chippeways stake—Bark Canoes, & Sugar." These were the kinds of goods the two tribes generally traded with each other, since the Ojibwe were no longer within the agency's jurisdiction at that time and so could not get the kinds of trade goods the Dakota did. For their part, the Dakota desired birch-bark canoes to use in harvesting wild rice. Later on that same year Taliaferro reported, via interpreter Scott Campbell, that the Dakota and Ojibwe were camped at the falls of the St. Croix River, dancing, playing ball, and feasting together. The Ojibwe had invited them to the area to hunt.[77]

According to Taliaferro, ball play could occur any time throughout the year, often associated with seasonal ceremonies. In February 1836, while the rivers were still frozen and there was snow on the ground, he noted that the Dakota had concluded their medicine ceremonies, ball plays, and other unnamed activities and were going to go on their spring hunts, which would continue into April.[78]

Taliaferro made no references to the Dakota women's version of ball play, but several accounts and visual images exist. In 1835, when descending the Mississippi River from his visit to Fort Snelling, Catlin stopped at Prairie du Chien, where he observed a different kind of ball game played by the women of Wabasha's village, which had come there to receive its annuity payments. The men hung a quantity of ribbons and calicoes from a pole to be stakes in the game. Two balls were attached to a string about a foot and a half long. Each woman had a short stick with which she tried to catch the string and throw the two balls across the goal. According to Catlin, the game was as fiercely contested as those played by men and could go on for hours. Catlin recorded the scene in a painting showing the rushing women at play and the men who cheered them on.[79]

Another portrayal of the women's game was done by Seth Eastman, a military officer stationed at Fort Snelling in the early 1830s and again in the 1840s—an oil painting likely made during his later visit. It shows the women at play on a prairie, probably the area west of Fort Snelling. Eastman's wife, Mary, described a women's game, similar to Catlin's account, in one of the stories in her book *Dahcotah, or Life and Legends of the Sioux*. She told of the women playing a game on the ice during December for the prize of "bright cloths and calicoes" hanging on a pole. However, the game involved the same kind of bat and ball used in the men's version.[80]

Despite curiosity and even interest, it was hard for Europeans to fully grasp all the social and cultural contexts of Dakota ball play and its role in inter-village social relations. Anthropologist Ruth Landes, in interviews with Dakota people at Prairie Island in the 1930s, learned that during the summer months Red Wing villagers were invited to play ball and have other athletic contests with Kap'oża and a village at present-day Mendota. Games were usually played from May to August. Messengers were sent between the villages, a first to tell people to start to train, a second to name the date of the games, "a third to remind the villages of the name and place of the host village and urge all to attend." Bets were put up in advance. According to one of her informants, rivalries between villages were sometimes expressed by the use of "gaming medicines" designed to disrupt opponents, though this more often was done during foot races.[81]

Historian Edward D. Neill wrote that "the last great-ball play" in the present-day Twin Cities area occurred on July 13, 1852, at Oak Grove in Hennepin County, the site to which Samuel and Gideon Pond and the Cloud Man's village band had relocated in 1843. According to Neill, the parties were Šakpe's band playing against the Good Road (Penichon), Sky Man (Cloud Man), and Gray Iron (Black Dog) bands. The game involved two hundred fifty players and lasted for several days "encompassed by a cloud of witnesses." Šakpe's band won the first day, receiving a prize of about two thousand dollars' worth of property. During the next two days Śakpe's band lost three games. Neill reported that a quarrel broke out about some of the prizes, and the Black Dog village band left just as a company from Kap'oża came to reinforce Śakpe's. Throughout these several days, he said, four or five thousand dollars changed hands.[82]

Neill's account made clear the nature of the social relations involved in the game, but with an undertone of sarcasm about the expense involved. However, once again the games' full context was not given from the point of view of the people themselves. Ite Maza (Iron Face), whose English name was Jack Frazer, was a member of the Wakute or Red Wing band of Dakota in the 1820s and 1830s. His account communicated a sense of the excitement that attended Dakota communities gathering in the summer for such games. It told of one occasion when the three most easterly bands—those of Wabasha, Red Wing, and Little Crow—played against "all the other new comers: from other bands." They were encamped near Sand Point at the midpoint of Lake Pepin, in the vicinity of present-day Lake City, and they continued to play for an entire month, with heavy bets of "horses, guns, kettles, silver works and other valuables."[83]

A more detailed account from the Dakota point of view was written by Charles Eastman in his book *Indian Boyhood*, in which he told of a Dakota ball game that occurred when he was a small boy living in a Waȟpetuŋwaŋ village on the Minnesota River. Since Eastman was born in 1858, this event would have occurred after the removal of the various bands to the Upper Minnesota River. Sisituŋwaŋ, Waȟpetuŋwaŋ, and Bdewakaŋtuŋwaŋ bands were located in villages stretching from below Fort Ridgely to the Lower Sioux Agency and beyond, all the way to Lac qui Parle.[84]

Eastman wrote that the events took place at midsummer, after fur hunters had been successful in the spring and the maple harvest had been productive. The women's gardens were already producing corn and potatoes. There was plenty of stored wild rice and dried venison from the winter, as well as "freshly dug turnips, ripe berries, and an abundance of fresh meat." Suggesting the context of the period following the Treaty of 1851, he wrote, "The Waȟpetunwan band of Sioux, the 'Dwellers among the Leaves,' were fully awakened to the fact that it was almost time for the midsummer festivities of the old, wild days." The planned event, he wrote, was something like a present-day midwestern state fair for the Dakota. Invitations in the form of tobacco were sent to the various bands, including the "Light Lodges," or Kap'oża band, the "Dwellers Back from the River," or Cloud Man band, and others from the Blue Earth (Makato) band, a Waȟpetunwan group located close to the Lower Agency.

When the various bands gathered, Makato's tepee was "pitched in a con-spicuous spot, with a picture of a pipe painted above the entrance and opposite, the rising sun, symbolic of welcome and good will to men under the bright sun." There was a meeting to appoint a "medicine man" or spiritual leader to make the balls used in the contest. The task was given to "Chakpee-yuhah, Keeps the Club," who one evening appeared in the circle of tepees to dedicate, in a sense, the coming games. He brought with him a little boy who wore "a bit of swan's down in each ear," referring to the kind of decoration other accounts mention being worn by ball players. Though Eastman wrote the story in the third person, it is evident that the young man was himself. Chakpee-yuhah announced that the game would be between the Kap'oża band—whom, he said, addressing that band, "claim that no one has a lighter foot than you"—and the Waḣpetuŋwaŋs. He brought two balls, a black one representing the Kap'oża band and a red ball for the Waḣpetuŋwaŋs. He announced that if the Waḣpetuŋwaŋs won the game, the young man (Eastman himself), who until now had borne the name Hakadah, which he implied meant "the pitiful last," would then be known as "Ohiyesa, or Winner." If the Kap'oża band won, one of their children could receive the name.[85]

The ground for the game was a narrow strip of land between a lake and the Minnesota River, three-quarters of a mile long and a quarter of a mile in width. Given the general location, the lake could have been an oxbow or backwater of the river. Spectators were arranged along the sides and ends of the grounds. "Soldiers," essentially village policemen on horseback, had the job of keeping order. Eastman noted that "they were so strict in enforcing the laws that no one could venture with safety within a few feet of the limits of the field." Order also required that "if any one bore a grudge against another, he was implored to forget his ill-feeling until the contest be over."

Like outside observers, Eastman described the impressive body paint worn by the players, including images of the rainbow, the sunset sky, the Milky Way, lightning , and "some fleet animal or swift bird." Players were arranged strategically, "as in a basketball game," with the largest men in the middle to receive the ball when it was thrown up in the air at the beginning of the game. Eastman details the precariousness of the racket in holding the ball and the desperate shots across the field, with players clashing to reach it. Though one team or another seemed to get the advantage, the game reached a point when "the herald proclaimed that it was time to change the ball." After a few minutes' rest the red ball was tossed into the game, leading to the resumption of battle, with more than a hundred men scrambling for it. Eventually, a player named Antelope took the sphere and began to run for the goal. Interestingly, Eastman describes the ball being nestled in his palm and him throwing it. It is unclear how this maneuver would have been possible under the rules as described by other accounts, although perhaps there was some provision for it. Despite the valiant efforts of several of the opposing Kap'oża band, Antelope was able to get the ball across the goal. As a result, Eastman received his name, Ohiyesa, at an assembly in which Makato spoke graciously about the opposing Kap'oża band, in the "friendly contest in which each band must assert its prowess."

Given Eastman's age at these events, it is unclear how many details he remembered and how many were based on the stories he heard as he was growing up. In any case, he was able to place ball play in a context far richer and more in keeping with Dakota cultural traditions and values than the accounts of missionaries and other European Americans. For the Dakota, the ball game encapsulated community history and identity and multiple strands of their values and their culture. In telling this story many years later, Eastman described the last days of the Dakota in their homelands of Mni Sota Makoce, before the beginning of their exile.

A TOUR OF DAKOTA SUMMER VILLAGES

In the nineteenth century Dakota summer villages spread across present-day south and central Minnesota from west to east, along the Minnesota and Mississippi rivers from Lake Traverse and Big Stone Lake and through the Twin Cities area to the far southeastern corner of Minnesota. These villages were the base of operations where Dakota communities grew their summer crops and from where they set out for other activities away from the rivers at various times of year.

LAKE TRAVERSE, BIG STONE LAKE, AND LAC QUI PARLE

Bde Hdakiŋyaŋ, "lake lying crosswise," or Lake Traverse, is the southernmost body of water in the river system of the Red River of the North, which flows toward Hudson Bay. A number of Sisituŋwaŋ and Ihaŋktuŋwaŋ or Yankton villages were located around the lake. Hunting buffalo was a primary subsistence activity of Dakota at these villages. In 1839 missionary Stephen R. Riggs visited the village of Sisituŋwaŋ chiefs Maka Ideya (Burning Earth) and Wiċaŋħpi Ite (Star Face). He reported that it was located at the southern end of the lake and had forty houses and ten lodges, perhaps a distinction between summer houses and tepees. Joseph Nicollet wrote around the same time that the people of this village were called "Waziata Sisiton, the Sissitons of the North." Riggs also noted that the village of Wanataŋ, a famous Ihaŋktuŋwaŋ leader sometimes called the Charger, was on the lake and had thirty houses. Two other unidentified villages brought the total of people who lived

Wanataŋ, known to whites as "the Charger," was the leader at Lake Traverse, recorded in 1823 by the artist Samuel Seymour, who traveled through the region on an expedition led by Major Stephen H. Long.

at the lake in the summer to fifteen hundred. Later accounts suggest some villages may have been located on an island at the south end of the lake.[86]

Across the continental divide south of Lake Traverse is Bde Iŋyaŋ Takiŋyaŋyaŋ, Big Stone Lake, a twenty-six-mile-long meandering lake considered the head of the Minnesota River. The lake's Dakota and English names refer to granite outcrops in the region. In 1839 Riggs noted a village with twelve to fifteen houses on an island near the lower end of the lake, perhaps the village of Upi Iyahdeya, or Extended Tail Feathers, the name said to refer to someone who touched the tail of a bird, mentioned by Nicollet in 1838. The same chief was present at the Treaty of 1851 at Traverse des Sioux.[87]

THE UPPER MINNESOTA RIVER

Downriver from Big Stone Lake at Bde Iyedaŋ, or Lac qui Parle, was a Waȟpetuŋwaŋ village. The French name for this lake means "the lake that talks": apparently the French believed this was the meaning of the Dakota name. However, Riggs suggested the name was from bde iyahde, referring to the fact that the Minnesota River was connected to the lake. Another possibility is bde iyahan, which would mean "speaking lake." A Waȟpetuŋwaŋ leader known in English as the Little was associated with this village in the 1820s and 1830s.[88]

The Peẑihutaziziḳ'api ("where they dig the yellow medicine") or Yellow Medicine River flows into the Mississippi southeast of present-day Granite Falls. It was not the site of a Dakota village but in the 1850s the Upper Sioux Agency was located here. The name refers to a plant with a yellow root, possibly the moonseed, which grows in thickets in this region. The Upper Agency was established on the north side of the Yellow Medicine River, one mile west of its mouth. Nicollet visited in 1838 and noted that the Yellow Medicine River and nearby Hawk Creek (on the opposite side of the river) were "very wooded their whole length." He described the Yellow Medicine as three feet deep and sixty feet wide at its mouth, with clear water running "over a bed of sand and pebbles." In the 1850s at the Yellow Medicine's mouth was the village of Waȟpetuŋwaŋ leader Iyangmani (Running Walker). Between 1854 and 1862 Hazel Creek, several miles north of the Yellow Medicine River along the Minnesota, was the location of the Hazelwood Republic mission and agricultural colony, led by missionaries Thomas S. Williamson and Stephen R. Riggs. This is the site of the current Upper Sioux community Pezihutazizi Oyate.[89]

Maple sugaring was an important part of the seasonal round, practiced every spring throughout Dakota country.
When Seth Eastman painted this view of Dakota women, reports suggested that the location was
Nicollet Island, in present-day Minneapolis, which was known for its maple groves. An artist and military officer,
Eastman recorded many aspects of Dakota seasonal life during his time at Fort Snelling, first in the 1830s,
when he had a relationship with the Dakota woman Wakaŋ Inaźiŋ Wiŋ or Stands Sacred, daughter of the leader
Maḣpiya Wiċaṡṭa or Cloud Man, and later during the 1840s, when he returned as commander of the fort.

In a view which suggests the area of the Mississippi River near Fort Snelling,
Seth Eastman recorded a man spearfishing from a canoe.

Spearfishing through the ice was a common source of food for Dakota along the Minnesota and Mississippi rivers in the early nineteenth century. Indian agent Lawrence Taliaferro often supplied them with fish spears or had the blacksmith at the agency repair their spears over the course of the winter.

*Dakota summer villages commonly included bark houses, left permanently
in place for use in the seasons of the year when Dakota people returned to their
villages along the Minnesota and Mississippi rivers.*

The village of Medicine Bottle, Wakaŋ Ozaŋzaŋ, recorded in this
Seth Eastman view from the 1840s was an offshoot of Kapʼoża, located at Pine Bend,
along the Mississippi River south of the present-day Twin Cities.

Seth Eastman's 1840s watercolor view of Fort Snelling from upriver, opposite the site of present-day Hidden Falls Park in St. Paul, shows native people in the foreground and Oheyawahi/Pilot Knob in the distance beyond the fort, at right.

Kap'oża village, near present-day St. Paul, had a number of locations at various times, including the area near today's Mounds Park and downtown St. Paul. After the 1837 treaty which ceded Dakota land east of the Mississippi, residents moved the village to the site of present-day South St. Paul, where Eastman made this painting in the late 1840s.

*A close-up view of the top of Oheyawahi/Pilot Knob, by Seth Eastman
in the 1840s, documented the use of the hill as a burial place.*

*The leader Wapahaša was recorded in this painting
by Henry Inman, based on a view by an earlier artist
during the chief's visit to Washington, DC, in 1825.*

*Çetaŋ Wakuwa Mani, known to whites as Petit Corbeau
or Little Crow, was one of the signers of Pike's 1805 treaty that led
to the construction of Fort Snelling. He was recorded in this
painting by Henry Inman based on an earlier painting or sketch
by an artist during the chief's visit to Washington in 1825.*

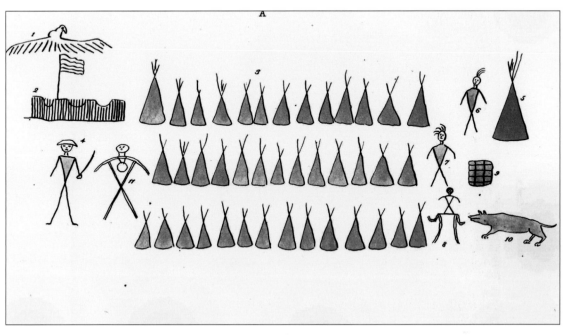

*In 1820 Dakota leaders left a pictographic message on bark along the Sauk River,
inviting Ojibwe leaders to come to Coldwater Spring, where they would agree
to make peace with the aid of American officials. Depicted were the chiefs,
the American military establishment at the spring, and tepees representing the various
Dakota villages. The image was recorded by government officials who found
the message during an expedition through the region.*

*Wambdi Taŋka or Big Eagle, the Dakota leader of the
Black Dog village on the lower Minnesota River, was painted by
the artist George Catlin during his visit to Minnesota in 1835.*

On his visit to Minnesota in 1835, artist George Catlin watched Dakota ball play
near Fort Snelling and recorded some of the participants as they were dressed for
the game. This contest included people of the village of Maḣpiya Wiċaṡṭa or Cloud Man
and others. Among the players was Anoka Inaziŋ, "He who stands on both sides,"
who was a member of Penichon's village on the Minnesota River.

*Ištaȟba or Sleepy Eye, a Sisituŋwaŋ leader from the area around
Traverse des Sioux and Swan Lake, was respected throughout the region.
He played a major role in the negotiations of the 1851 Treaty of
Traverse des Sioux, trying unsuccessfully to secure better terms for the Dakota.*

*The Treaty of Traverse des Sioux, involving the Sisituŋwaŋ and Waḣpetuŋwaŋ Dakota,
was the first of two treaties that year by which the Dakota ceded their land
in southern Minnesota. Frank B. Mayer's color painting provided the basis for another
painting which currently hangs in the Minnesota State Capitol.*

*Burial mounds were a common feature of the Minnesota landscape when whites
arrived on the scene, as in this view by Edwin Whitefield, said to be located in Hennepin County.
Many such mounds were leveled or plowed under in the years that followed.*

The Caŋśayapi or Redwood River flows into the Minnesota at Redwood Falls. The river was an early landmark, though there is no record of a village here. It became the site of the Lower Sioux Agency in the 1850s, the name meaning they paint the trees red at this location. William H. Keating, in his account of Stephen Long's 1823 expedition, noted that where the Redwood and Minnesota river valleys united was a large rock "of an irregular hemispherical form, about forty or fifty feet in circumference." The rock was blackened and "had been cleft" as though by lightning, and nearby trees and bushes appeared to have been burned. The Lower Agency was located roughly eight miles below the mouth of the Redwood River, in the area where the new villages of Dakota leaders Big Eagle, Makato, and Wakute stood in the 1850s. Śakpe's village was located less than a mile north of the junction of Ramsey Creek and the Redwood River, where the township's 1859 survey map showed an Indian village. Nicollet wrote in 1838 that the Redwood River was thirty feet wide, had a strong current, and had "lively and clear" waters.[90]

Birch Coolee, a creek that flows into the Minnesota River opposite the Lower Agency—at Morton in present-day Renville County—was the site of an Indian agency and settlement for remaining and returning Dakota beginning in the 1880s. The creek was said to have been named for the thick presence of paper or canoe birch located there, in the "southwest limit of its geographic range." The creek was named Tampa on Nicollet's 1843 map, from taŋpa, the Dakota word for birch. The present-day Lower Sioux Indian Community is located near the old Lower Agency, approximately two miles south of Morton along the south bank of the Minnesota River.[91]

Near the mouth of the Cottonwood River was Maya Kiçaksa or "village of the cut bank." This was Sleepy Eye's village, the later site of the town of New Ulm. The name refers to a bank cut by the waters of the Minnesota River. The village leader was the Sisituŋwaŋ Iśtaȟba, known as Sleepy Eye. According to Samuel Pond, Sleepy Eye was respected in all the Sisituŋwaŋ villages in the region. When Nicollet visited this village in August 1838, he was served boiled wild rice. He reported that the people were "engaged in collecting their crop of corn, and were much disposed to improve in agriculture." He also noted that his party was entertained with a "grizely bear dance," performed by a band member named Kaŋǧimdoka or Raven Man. Sleepy Eye was often also at Traverse des Sioux but seemed to prefer spending his summers with others of his band at Swan Lake, known to the Dakota as Maǧa Taŋka Ota Bde. The lake was renowned, according to missionary Riggs, for "its ducks and geese, and 'many swans' in former days, with its turtles, its fish, its muskrats, and wild rice."[92]

The Sisituŋwaŋ village Maya Skadaŋ, "little white bluff" (also called White Bluff or White Rock Village), was located on the right bank of the Minnesota

TRAVERSE

Bde Hdakiŋyaŋ
LAKE TRAVERSE

STEVENS

BIG
STONE

**Bde Iŋyaŋ
Takiŋyaŋyaŋ**
BIG STONE LAKE

SWIFT

M I N N E S

MEEKER

Bde Iyedaŋ
LAC QUI PARLE

CHIPPEWA

KANDIYOHI

LAC QUI
PARLE

MINNESOTA

Mni

MC LI

**Pežihutazizik'api
Wakpa**
YELLOW MEDICINE
RIVER

Granite Falls

YELLOW
MEDICINE

RENVILLE

Sota

SOUTH
DAKOTA

LYON

Ċaŋśayapi Wakpa
REDWOOD RIVER

Wakpa

SIB

REDWOOD

RIVER

**Maġa Taŋ
Ota B**
SWAN LA

BROWN

Waġa Ožu Wakpa
COTTONWOOD RIVER

**Maya
Kiċaksa**
SLEEPY EYE
VILLAGE

MURRAY

COTTONWOOD

B

North

0   20   40

scale in miles

I

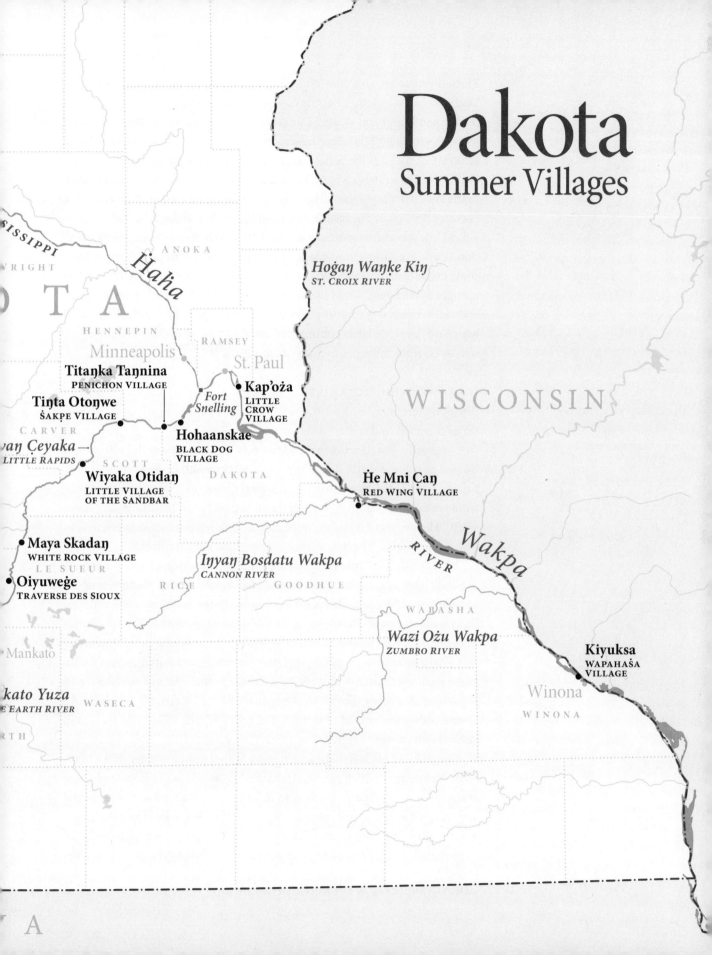

Dakota
Summer Villages

Hoġaŋ Waŋke Kiŋ
ST. CROIX RIVER

ANOKA

Ḣaḣa

HENNEPIN

Minneapolis

RAMSEY

St. Paul

WISCONSIN

Titaŋka Taŋnina
PENICHON VILLAGE

Fort Snelling

Kap'oża
LITTLE CROW VILLAGE

Tiŋta Otoŋwe
ŚAKPE VILLAGE

CARVER

...aŋ Çeyaka —
LITTLE RAPIDS

Hohaanskae
BLACK DOG VILLAGE

SCOTT

DAKOTA

Wiyaka Otidaŋ
LITTLE VILLAGE OF THE SANDBAR

Ḣe Mni Çaŋ
RED WING VILLAGE

River

Wakpa

Maya Skadaŋ
WHITE ROCK VILLAGE

LE SUEUR

Iŋyaŋ Bosdatu Wakpa
CANNON RIVER

Oiyuweġe
TRAVERSE DES SIOUX

RICE

GOODHUE

WABASHA

Mankato

Wazi Ożu Wakpa
ZUMBRO RIVER

Kiyuksa
WAPAHAŚA VILLAGE

...kato Yuza
...E EARTH RIVER

WASECA

Winona

WINONA

...RT

A

River, downstream from the later village at Oiyuweġe, or Traverse des Sioux. Maya Skadaŋ was situated at the eastern end of an overland shortcut across the big southern bend of the Minnesota River at the present site of St. Peter. Nicollet wrote that Maya Skadaŋ was "the rendezvous of all the villages of Sisseton when they left for buffalo hunts or when they went to gather wild rice in the area." It was also where they waited for traders arriving from the east in the fall. In the 1830s the village appears to have relocated across the river to Traverse des Sioux. The Sisituŋwaŋ chief Sleepy Eye, though he had his own village, was sometimes associated with this one. In November 1843 Riggs noted that Sleepy Eye, "the acknowledged chief in this part of the country, who lives some distance above this[,] was here frequently during the rice gathering and brought us ducks etc." Riggs also referred to a chief at this village named "Great Walker," or more accurately Big Walker, Tataŋkamani, "who is next to him, and lives here [and] has lately commenced learning to read himself and promises well to exert his influence in favor of education."[93]

THE LOWER MINNESOTA RIVER

Below Traverse des Sioux were at least three Waȟpetuŋwaŋ villages, all sometimes included under the rubric of the Little Rapids village, which was the farthest north. Traveling down the Minnesota River, the first of the villages was located near present-day Belle Plaine, below the mouth of the Rivière au Bois Franc, "river of the big woods," now Robert Creek. Its leader was Wakaŋhdi, from wakaŋhdi, "lightning," often translated as "vivid lightning," or "lively spirit." He was also known as Broken Arm. Taliaferro sometimes referred to him as the chief of "the Bois village" or the "Bois Franc Indians."[94]

Wiyaka Otidaŋ, "little village of the sandbar," was located near the mouth of Sand Creek as it existed until the late nineteenth century, northwest of the present town of Jordan. This place was known to the French as the Batture au Fièvre, which meant "Rapids of the Fever," referring to the first French traders in the region, who were attacked by fevers when they came here. Downriver was a village at Iŋyaŋ Çeyaka, or Little (now Carver) Rapids. The Dakota name means "the barrier of stone," a reference to the ledges of sandstone and limestone that cross the riverbed a quarter of a mile apart at this location. Together they cause a fall of three feet in the river. The village was located in several spots near the rapids.[95]

The chiefs of Little Rapids, which was a Waȟpetuŋwaŋ village in the 1830s, were Wanakṡante, which Nicollet translated as "Rebounding Iron," and Mazamani, or Iron Walker. According to Taliaferro, Mazamani did most of the speaking when the chiefs came to visit him. He died from smallpox in September 1838. The next month Taliaferro gave his son a condolence gift: "In explenation of the present given yesterday to the Son of the late—war chief

Mooseomone—I remark that his Father belonged to the late delegation to Washington—an old & highly esteemed man of the Wahpeeton Sioux of the Little Rapid on the St Peters—& died of the Small Pox in the early part of September. He was a warm friend of the Agent who was inst[r]umental in saveing his life on his return from the great council of Prarie du chien in 1825. He laid four weeks very ill at the agency." The son took the same name as his father after his father's death.[96]

In the 1820s Taliaferro had dealings with another chief located at or near Little Rapids named Kiŋyaŋ, or Red Eagle. Nicollet stated that the chief had been known as Wambdi Duta, meaning "Red Eagle," but "he is now called Kiya," or "he who flies." Nicollet said that in 1838 the chief was located at a place called Tiŋta Maǧaboȟpa, "the prairie where the swan fell to earth" or "the prairie where he threw the swan to ground," a reference to an incident regarded as miraculous involving a trader named Rocque, which Nicollet did not record. Taliaferro indicated that this prairie was the end of a land route from the mouth of the Minnesota River through the area later known as the Big Woods, a dense forest that followed the east bank of the river. In 1829 Taliaferro referred to a man named Red Eagle as a Waȟpekute chief and stated that he had come from the plains and had "formerly lived ab[o]ve the Little Rapids," though he may have been referring to a different individual.[97]

Both Kiŋyaŋ and Mazamani expressed to Taliaferro their interest in engaging more intensively in agriculture. On August 20, 1827, Taliaferro noted that Kiŋyaŋ intended to go to the Omaha to obtain horses to till his land: "He also applied for some plough & Harness Some Seed potatoes—Corn &c." Similarly, in June 1835 Taliaferro recorded a speech by Mazamani at the agency in which he asked for his lands to be plowed and for a corn mill for the women to use.[98]

The Bdewakaŋtuŋwaŋ village located farthest upstream on the Minnesota River and the one with the largest population in the mid-nineteenth century was Šakpe's village, or village of the Six, located in various places near present-day Shakopee. The Dakota name was Tiŋta Otoŋwe, meaning "village of the prairie," a reference to the unwooded land on the terrace on the river's south side. In 1823 the village was located on the north side of the river, where cornfields and burial scaffolds were found, although explorer Stephen Long may have confused scaffolds for drying corn with those used for burial. At that time a cemetery and a cornfield were also located on the south side of the river. Taliaferro called the village "twenty mile village." Its leader bore the hereditary name Šakpe, the Six (though with one generation it was Šakpedaŋ, Little Six). Another leader of the Shakopee band in the 1830s, whose village was located near the mouth of the Credit River, was known as Ȟuyapa, or Eagle Head.[99]

The bark houses of a permanent Dakota summer village are recorded in this 1850s view by Robert O. Sweeny.

Near the mouth of Nine Mile Creek in present-day Hennepin County was Titaŋka Taŋnina, the village of Penichon (or Penishon, Penetion, and other spellings). The name was said to come from an early chief of the village, known as Fils du Penishon ("son of Penishon"), apparently the descendent of a French trader. Historian Elliot Coues suggests that it is a garbled version of the name given the site of the village, "Taku Kokepeshni Wojupi, the clearing of him who fears nothing." Some have suggested Titaŋka Taŋnina, which means "the old village," shows that it was the first village of the Dakota on the Minnesota River, one that dates back hundreds of years. Nicollet also noted, without explanation, that the band was called Oyateshitsha (Oyate šiça), "the bad band" or "the bad people." The chief of the village in the 1830s was Taçaŋku Wašte, His Good Road, usually Good Road.[100]

The closest village to Fort Snelling was Hohaanskae (Ohaŋska), "the village of the long avenue," or Black Dog village, whose people were sometimes called Maġa Yuṭe Śni (Marhayouteshni), "those who do not eat geese," as explained earlier in this chapter. The village was about four miles above Fort Snelling, near the present site of the Mall of America and below extensive burial mound groups, now almost entirely destroyed. The name "the village of the long avenue" is a reference to the extensive vista of the Minnesota River from its mouth to this village. The Dakota version of this name noted first by Joseph Nicollet is similar to Çokaŋ Haŋska, said to refer to the long bottomland lake parallel to the river in this area, recorded by Frederic W. Pearsall, a local historian whose wife and children were part of the Dakota community at Granite Falls. Taliaferro sometimes called it "four mile village," indicating its distance from Fort Snelling. The earliest published reference to a chief named Black Dog is in a document from November 1742 recording a speech presented to French government official Paul Marin by several Dakota chiefs. Among them was Chonkasaba, that is, Śunḳa Sapa, or Black Dog. Later Dakota chiefs were known as "the Black Dog chief" but had other personal names.[101]

A famous view of what must be a portion of the Black Dog village is found in a watercolor by artist and army officer Seth Eastman, who was in charge of Fort Snelling in the 1840s. Eastman had a relationship with Wakaŋ Inažiŋ Wiŋ (Stands Sacred), the mother of his daughter Nancy Eastman and the daughter of Maḣpiya Wiçaśṭa (Cloud Man). Eastman recorded the area's landscape and the life of Dakota people in a way unmatched by any other early artist. In a view now owned by the Minnesota Historical Society, he depicted two burial scaffolds on a bluff above the Minnesota River at Black Dog. In the background of the painting, in the distance on the left bank of the river, a faint image of Fort Snelling is visible. Opposite it on the right is Oheyawahi or Pilot Knob, also a burial place of the Dakota.[102]

Another historic view of the Black Dog village burial site is found in an engraving published in *Harper's Magazine* in 1853, based on a work by the German artist Adolf Hoeffler, who traveled to the Upper Mississippi that year and recorded his observations and a few images. In his view, Hoeffler showed Dakota summer houses on the lower slopes of the river bank. In the background, higher up, a crude depiction of a burial scaffold appears.[103]

MISSISSIPPI RIVER

Kap'oża, Little Crow's village, was located at various sites near present-day downtown St. Paul. The name Kap'oża meant "those who traveled unencumbered with much baggage," though missionary Thomas Williamson stated that it referred to the skill of the band members at Dakota ball play or lacrosse. In 1805 and 1817 the village was located below Wakaŋ Tipi (the site of Mounds Park and the Bruce Vento Nature Sanctuary in St. Paul) at the Grand Marais, meaning "big swamp," a reference to present-day Pig's Eye Lake, along the Mississippi River. From the 1820s to the mid-1830s Kap'oża was located on the other side of Mounds Park, within present downtown St. Paul, possibly near the mouth of Phalen Creek and at the site where the St. Paul Union Depot was built. After the Treaty of 1837, which transferred Dakota land east of the Mississippi to the United States, the village moved to the South St. Paul side of the river.[104]

At Newport in Washington County is an oval granite boulder, about five feet long, which formerly sat on the east bank of the Mississippi River. The Dakota left offerings at the rock and sometimes painted it. It was a landmark for both the Dakota and early whites. In an account of explorer Stephen Long's 1823 trip in the region, geologist William H. Keating noted it was not surprising that the rock would have been viewed "with some curiosity," considering that its composition differed "so materially from those of the rocks which are found in the neighborhood," largely sandstone and limestone. Keating wrote of the offerings left by Dakota people: "The party found the feather of an eagle, two roots of the 'Pomme de Prairie [prairie turnip],' painted with vermilion; a willow branch, whose stem was painted red, had been stuck into the ground on one side, &c." Unfortunately the "gentlemen" of Long's party, perhaps including Keating himself, "broke off a fragment of this idol to add to the mineralogical collections, taking care, however not to leave any chips, the sight of which would wound the feelings of the devotee, by convincing him that the object of his worship had been violated." A description of the rock from 1888 states, "It is painted in stripes, twelve in number, two inches wide and from two to six inches apart. The north end has a rudely drawn picture of the sun, and a rude face with fifteen rays." In the 1860s the site became a summer location for Methodist camp meetings. In 1964 the rock was moved to the grounds of the Newport United Methodist Church.[xxv] ■

Iŋyaŋ ṡa or Red Rock, located on the bank of the Mississippi River at the present-day town of Newport, was a landmark which the Dakota painted and where they left offerings. An account from 1888—around the time of this photograph—stated that the rock was painted with twelve stripes and had drawings of the sun on the north end.

Today Iŋyaŋ ṡa or Red Rock is located in front of the Newport United Methodist Church, as shown in this 2010 photograph.

The original village was located on both sides of the river and below extensive burial mounds on the bluffs above. Some of these mounds still exist in Mounds Park, described by William H. Keating in 1823 as being "situated at a handsome turn on the river." Indeed, the river here makes a great bend, allowing someone at the site of the mounds or even below them an extensive view both upriver and down. Stephen Long, who visited the site first in 1817, said the village leader, Petit Corbeau (Little Crow)—at this date it was Çetaŋ Wakuwa Mani—claimed this strategic location allowed him "to exercise a command over the passage of the river" and extract tribute from traders who passed.[105]

In May 1829, Indian agent Lawrence Taliaferro, who sometimes called Kap'oża "nine mile village on the Mississippi," referring to its distance from Fort Snelling, wrote that some members wished to form other communities with new chiefs. Taliaferro refused to "countenance" their desire, especially because the "*Seceders*" wished to form "a permane[n]t Camp within Sight of the Garrison of Ft Snelling. But I this day order[e]d them back to their old Village or any other Point the[y] might Select not nearer the Fort than *five miles*." Medicine Bottle, or Wakaŋ Ożaŋżaŋ, whose name was sometimes given as Nasiampah, organized a group from Kap'oża at Pine Bend along the Mississippi River, which rejoined the Kap'oża band in 1836, after Çetaŋ Wakuwa Mani's death.[106]

Farther downriver was the Red Wing village, located near the present-day town of Red Wing. This village was adjacent to the massive landform called Barn Bluff, which rises above the Mississippi just below the mouth of the Wazi Ożu Wakpa (Cannon River). The Dakota name for the village, Ḣe Mni Çaŋ, or "hill water wood," means, essentially, "hill that appears as if it were in the water." German artist Henry Lewis visited the site in the 1850s and said the name Barn Bluff, from the French La Grange, accurately described the massive hill's appearance. He noted that on the top of the bluff was a mound and that the view from there was "indescribably beautiful."[107]

The chief of Red Wing village, known as Tataŋkamani or Walking Buffalo, died on March 4, 1829, at the age of eighty-four. Taliaferro wrote that "during his whole life he was a firm friend of the Whites for the last 30 years more firmly attached to the Americans—and refused utterly to join in the War of 1812 against the arms of the United States." Just before his death he had visited Fort Snelling and made a statement to Taliaferro and Colonel Josiah Snelling: "Among all of My Nation there is not one in it who has held on to the Americans like me and my band—in the worst times. Red Wing never deserted you—this you both well Know to be true. I am the Same Man & have the Same heart for your nation now that I ever had and shall never change."[108]

Wakute became leader of the band after the death of the older chief, who was his uncle. For a time after that he moved with some of the village to live with Wabasha's band at the "Grand Encampment," at the location of the present-day town of Wabasha. In August 1835, Wakute was informed by Taliaferro that as long as he lived with Wabasha's band he would not be considered a chief with whom Taliaferro would deal, since Wabasha's band had been transferred to the supervision of the Indian agent at Prairie du Chien in 1834. If, however, "you return to the Village of your Father at the head of Lake Pepin—you will again be under my care but as you selected 3 years ago Wab[i]shas band as a residence and have been paid upon his pay Roll your annuity since that time of course you must visit Pra[i]rie du Chiens."[109]

Early settlers described various sites around the current town of Red Wing used by Dakota, mentioning a cornfield planted by villagers along Fourth Street and burial scaffolds on College Hill. Dakota often camped northwest of town in the area of Prairie Island, the present location of the Prairie Island Indian Community.[110]

The Bdewakaŋtuŋwaŋ Dakota village found lowest on the Mississippi River was that of the Kiyuksa band, at Wabasha's village or Wapasha's Prairie, now the location of the city of Winona. The name of the band refers to breaking rules and violating customs and was given, according to some sources, "from the intermarrying of relations among them." The band resided part of the year at Wabasha's Prairie, called the prairie aux ailes ("prairie of the wings") by the French. According to place-name historian Paul Durand, the French name described the two bluffs "which stretch like two immense wings" above the prairie. In 1823 Keating stated that the band consisted of two villages, one on Lake Pepin and another on the Upper Iowa River, the latter being where Zebulon Pike encountered them in 1805.[111]

The first Dakota leader of this band recorded in French sources, Wapaháśa, known as Red Standard or Red Leaf, is often called Wabasha. His son was the chief who met Zebulon Pike in 1805. His son, signer of the 1837 treaty, also took the name Wabasha, although he was often listed in government records as "Tah tape saah" (or possibly Tate apa s'a), Upsetting Wind or Whipping Wind.[112]

On May 6, 1836, Taliaferro reported the Kiyuksa band was on the east side of the Mississippi River at "the Foot of the 'Mountain in the Water,'" or Trempealeau, a temporary change brought on by Fox attacks. In the 1850s, before their removal to reservations on the Upper Minnesota River, members of the band still lived in the area of Winona, and settlers described their gardens and burial grounds. John Burns, who built a farm in a valley adjacent to the later town of Winona, received permission to live there from Wabasha's band: "The locality was the special home of Wabasha and his family relatives when living in this vicinity. It was sometimes called Wabasha's garden by the old settlers." Burns's account, recorded by a local historian, continued,

Quite a number of Indian graves were on these grounds. Nearly in front of the farmhouse there were two or three graves of more modern burial lying side by side. These were said to be the last resting-place of some of Wabasha's relatives. The Sioux made a special request of Mr. Burns and his family that these graves should not be disturbed. This Mr. Burns promised, and the little mounds, covered with billets of wood, were never molested, although they were in his garden and not far from his house. For many years they remained as they were left by the Indians, until the wood by which they were covered rotted away entirely. A light frame or fence of poles put there by Mr. Burns always covered the locality during his lifetime.[113]

The locations of Dakota villages and many of the places that made up the landscape of their homelands continued to be known to white Minnesotans for many years after the Dakota were exiled, though the meaning of these places and how they fit together into a coherent relationship with the land was often lost. At the same time, the Dakota were erased from the written history of Minnesota, confined to a kind of prehistoric natural history, in which there was only a vague sense that they had been there at one time before "civilization" transformed the region of Minnesota.

CHAPTER FOUR

Drawing Lines *on* Sacred Land: *The* Dakota Treaties

Mni Sota Makoce is a rich and diverse land that gave birth to the Dakota people eons ago. As the mother and grandmother of the Dakota people, it has sustained them for countless generations. For the Dakota the land was animate, a relative, a mother. When Dakota people greet each other they often say, as Dakota historian Chris Mato Nunpa did at the beginning of a 2006 article, "Hau Mitakuyapi. Owasin cantewasteya nape ciyuzapi do!" This means, "Hello my relatives. With a good heart I greet you all with a handshake." Particularly important in this greeting is the term *mitakuyapi*, or "all my relatives," which acknowledges the central place the Dakota's sense of living in deep and extended kinship with each other has in their culture, a meaning close to their hearts. This kinship leads Dakota to accept the obligation of attending to the well-being of their relations in a way that defines them in their interactions with each other and the land. For them, to carry out this obligation they are called upon to embody wo ohoda (respect) in their actions. This expresses a deep and pervasive sense of respect for the bonds of kinship that starts with the land that gave them birth and is their home. It is in this context that we must understand the way in which the Dakota had their lands taken from them. In the nineteenth century the Dakota were asked to sell the land and make way for its possession by another people. In the process, the deep roots of Dakota identity in Mni Sota Makoce suffered a tragic wound as the Dakota were physically driven from their homelands. This wound is carried by many Dakota people today.[1]

In the nineteenth century a process began through which the Dakota were dispossessed of their Minnesota homelands. Between 1805 and 1858, a period of fifty-three years, twelve treaties were concluded between the Dakota and the United States. These treaties, as understood and acted upon by the United States, had a dramatic impact on the relationship of the Dakota people with their ancestral lands in Minnesota. Where once they had ranged across the entire territory of what would become the state of Minnesota, by 1858 they had been physically confined to a small reservation ten miles wide, running 140 miles along the south shore of the Minnesota River from just east of Lake Traverse to just west of the site of the city of New Ulm.

The negotiation of these treaties was not a clear-cut process or one easily categorized. Collectively these treaties included three great cessions, comprising the Treaties of 1825, 1837, and 1851. But to call these agreements cessions is to privilege the nonindigenous side of the negotiating table. For the Dakota the word *cessions* might well be replaced with *seizures,* because of the stark contrast between the Dakota views of land and that of government negotiators, not to mention the dubious process through which these treaties were written, negotiated, and carried out.

The Dakota people and the government agents who negotiated and signed the treaties had radically different points of view about their meaning. Without understanding these differences, anything said about the treaties can be nothing more than a European projection of a far different story about the land that masks the true identity of the Dakota people. Both the Dakota and the Europeans have an intense and intimate relationship with the land, but that relationship springs from strikingly different sources of understanding. Dakota people view the land as their homeland, their relative, their mother; the Europeans see it as a possession.

Out of these two vastly different understandings have come two equally different *master stories*—the great stories by which a community names and explains itself and its members. The two master stories of the Dakota people and the recent European immigrants to Mni Sota who called themselves "Americans" clashed at the treaty-making table in the nineteenth century, with tragic consequences that continue down to the present day.

In a European American view, the story of the treaties between the United States and the Dakota Oyate or Nation—in individual treaties with various of the Oçeti Ṡakowiŋ, or Seven Fires—is often told as the story of U.S. westward expansion through the extension of American dominion over the Dakota homeland. This is the American story of "how the west was won and held" through warfare and politics and through the spread of European-style agri-

Stories and Master Stories

[HOWARD J. VOGEL] **Why focus on stories?** Because stories are important. People grow up and live their lives hearing and telling stories. Sometimes people find that they are changed by new stories or old stories retold in a new way. Stories are bearers of truth, which is, in the words of Thomas King, "the truth about stories." In hearing and telling stories, human beings participate in an experience that occurs in cultures across the ages, though it varies widely among individuals and peoples. Stories can be entertainment, but they can also tell us who we are—as individuals and as a people—what is true, and what we are called to do in our engagement with the world in which we live.[i]

Master stories are the great stories by which a community names itself and its members. They are the stories through which groups of people come to understand reality and what is of ultimate importance. Master stories often include myths of origin as well as features of individual and community identity. The norms of the community are undergirded by these stories and give them, and the community, shape, meaning, and identity. Master stories are narratives rooted in the historical experience of a people and provide a context for understanding themselves and the world they encounter as well as guidance for how they live their lives. Out of these stories come the distinctive features of individual and collective identity shared by those who are members of a particular culture. The stories both give rise to the norms of the community and provide a resource for their application. These stories are told and retold down through the ages as a central vehicle for cultural transmission and identity. In this dynamic way the master stories are foundational as well as life giving within the tradition that holds them dear.

When two very different peoples meet on the same land, there is always the potential for one master story to become dominant in the relationship that develops between them. And when one people impose their master story on another people in the name of the state, there is the great danger that the subordinated peoples' cultural heritage will be extinguished along with their story. In such situations, the master stories of the other are often obliterated when they come into conflict with the "imperial story" of the dominant culture.

This happens because master stories are not neutral. They embrace and express a particular understanding of reality and are deeply value laden: they can be either "hegemonic tales," enforcing a "colonizing consciousness" designed to erase a peoples' connection to their culture and their communities, or "subversive stories," restoring that connection.[ii]

When such stories come into conflict with the state today, before a court or other governmental decision-making body, the master story of the Dakota that lies at the heart of these conflicts is likely to be given short shrift or ignored altogether, while the American story is likely to dominate the way the dispute is framed for the purpose of governmental decision-making. Thus, an understanding of master stories is especially important when reading and interpreting the meaning of laws and treaties, especially when it relates to ordering the relationship between two different peoples living on the same land. In courts of law and at treaty negotiating tables, these stories can be seen in action, shaping the results and the way those results are carried out. The master stories are both explicit and implicit, underlying the language used, the discourse of those involved, and the actions taken later. Until we consider all the stories, how they clash with one another and how the conflict between them is finally resolved, the story we call "history" is incomplete. ■

culture, forestry, mining, and urban settlement, along with the market-based commercialism that accompanied these activities. The American story also tells how, in the face of this wave of activity breaking over their homelands, Indian people were forced into a smaller and smaller territory and a correspondingly smaller range of activity on the land as they were cut off from the game and plant resources that sustained their traditional way of life. Ultimately, native people were physically separated from their homeland and confined to the small scattered areas chosen by the Europeans and called "reservations."

Often the reservations were marked out on the least desirable land from a European American point of view. These often desolate lands lacked the resources by which the native people could live as they always had and thus compromised not only their sustenance but also their survival as a distinct people. Meanwhile, the European Americans set about to "improve" the rich land which, in their view, had been wasted by the native people. Treaties played a crucial role in the increasing separation of the Dakota from their homeland in the years between 1805 and 1858, leading up to their ultimate expulsion by military force in 1863–64.

DOCTRINE OF DISCOVERY

1493
The year after Columbus "discovered" America, the pope issues the bull entitled *In caetera Divinae*, dividing the continents of the earth between Portugal and Spain, one of a series of Papal bulls creating a European Doctrine of Discovery.

The Americans' exercise of dominion over the Dakota homeland under the treaties concluded in the nineteenth century is both a product and an expression of the European Doctrine of Discovery that goes back to a series of Papal bulls issued by Pope Alexander VI in the late fifteenth century. In 1493, the year after Columbus "discovered" America, the pope issued the bull entitled *In caetera Divinae*, dividing the earth's continents between Portugal and Spain. Under this bull, America was granted to Spain. It was based, in part, on Pope Innocent IV's thirteenth-century legal commentary on an earlier decree by Pope Innocent III justifying the Christian Crusades undertaken between 1096 and 1271. The Discovery Doctrine's foundation, under which dominion of the Christian nations of Europe was extended over the non-Christian nations of Europe and elsewhere, is rooted in the much earlier eleventh-century pronouncements on the crusades which themselves emerged from the imperial church established by Constantine after his *Edict of Milan* tolerating Christianity in 313. The end of persecution of the early Christian movement laid the cornerstone for the imperial church that would eventually usher in the Doctrine of Discovery. It facilitated the spread of European Christian nations' dominion over land where such dominion had not previously existed by laying down the principle that once dominion was established by one Christian nation over such lands no other Christian nation could exercise the same right.[2]

The Discovery Doctrine sparked a race among the Christian nations of Europe to "discover" and "claim" lands over which no Christian nation had previously exercised dominion. Explorers set off across the seas and upon landing in new lands would, Bible in hand, plant the flags of their ruler and claim the lands against any declarations that might be subsequently made by other Christian nations. Understood from a European perspective, the doctrine authorized the "discovering" Christian nations to exercise dominion by virtue of what came to be viewed as the conquest of the non-Christian inhabitants found in the new lands. Discovery and conquest went hand in hand, laying a supposed legal foundation for the spread of European empire upon the distant lands of North America and beyond. The Discovery Doctrine provided the basis for Spanish, French, and English land claims in North America and for carving up the "discovered" land between these three European sovereign powers. Even though it was questioned by the Spanish priest Franciscus de Victoria, who in 1532 challenged the power of the Spanish crown to simply seize the indigenous peoples' land without their consent, the conquering thrust unleashed in the fifteenth century with papal approval continued to inform the Spanish conquest and colonization of America. Eventually the Discovery Doctrine became the source of authority for non-Spanish European colonization of North America, and with the coming of the American Revolution eventually was embraced as legal precedent within the domestic law of the United States.[3]

The first recorded statement of a claim for the Dakota homeland in Minnesota was made under the Doctrine of Discovery in a "Minute of the taking of possession of the country of the Upper Mississippi," to include "the country of the Nadouesioux, the rivers Ste Croix and Ste Peter [later called the Minnesota River] and other places more remote," by Nicolas Perrot on May 8, 1689. Perrot's document was noted in the presence of several witnesses whose names are recorded and includes the fact that he had traveled "to the Country of the Nadouesioux on the border of the River Saint Croix and at the mouth of the River Saint Peter, on the bank of which were the Mantantans [sometimes called the Mdewakaŋtuŋwaŋ], and farther up into the interior to the North east of the Mississippi as far as the Menchokatoux with whom dwell the majority of the Songeskitons and other Nadoussioux, who are to the North east of the Mississippi, to take possession for, and in the name of the King [of France], of the countries and rivers inhabited by the said Tribes and of which they are proprietors."[4]

Perrot's authority for taking possession comes not from any acquiescence on the part of the Dakota or other native peoples but directly and entirely from European law and the Doctrine of Discovery, which justified the occupation of non-Christian lands. After the American Colonies broke from Britain in 1776 and the United States was established as a separate nation in 1781, the Americans increasingly became the successor beneficiaries to the perquisites gained in North America by the European Christian nations of Spain, France,

1532
The Spanish priest Franciscus de Victoria challenges the power of the Spanish crown to simply seize the land of the indigenous peoples without their consent, but his views are largely ignored.

1689
Nicolas Perrot leads a ceremony to take possession, in the name of Louis XIV, of the entire Upper Mississippi region.

1763
The first Treaty of Paris ends the French and Indian War or Seven Years' War, officially transferring French claims to the Upper Mississippi region to the British.

1783
The second Treaty of Paris ends the American Revolutionary War between Great Britain and its former colonies, which become the United States, laying the groundwork for transferring British claims to the Minnesota region.

1789

The U.S. Constitution is ratified; Article 1, Section 8, Clause 3 asserts that Congress has the power to regulate commerce with Indian tribes and that treaties with tribes are the "supreme law of the land."

1803

The Louisiana Territory, including the area of Minnesota west of the Mississippi River, is purchased from France for fifteen million dollars.

and Britain under the Doctrine of Discovery. The doctrine of Manifest Destiny, an American version of the Doctrine of Discovery that envisioned westward expansion across the content, fueled extension of American dominion over indigenous land in the nineteenth century as the frontier of the new nation moved ever westward. Thus the idea that land can and is to be organized under the possession of one owner to the exclusion of all others, an old European idea that now came into American legal usage through English common law, led directly to the Louisiana Purchase of the remaining French territory west of the Mississippi River, including a portion of present-day Minnesota.

The Louisiana Purchase came about through a treaty concluded between France and the United States in Paris on April 30, 1803. By its terms France transferred to the United States 529,911,680 acres in exchange for fifteen million dollars. Following ratification of the treaty, President Thomas Jefferson was duly authorized under the established principles of domestic and international law to take possession of the newly acquired land in the name of the United States and to establish a temporary military government there. On March 10, 1804, formal ownership of Louisiana was transferred from France to the United States at a ceremony conducted in St. Louis. With this transfer the U.S. land mass doubled overnight, with the Dakota nation finding itself, without knowledge or consent, a "captive nation" within the expanded boundaries over which the United States now exercised dominion. Over the next fifty-four years, the U.S. government would negotiate with the Dakota to obtain legal ownership of all of their lands in this region to facilitate its formal transfer, parcel by parcel, to immigrant settlers under the Anglo-American rules of property law.[5]

In this way the United States became the successor to the Europeans who first brought the Discovery Doctrine to North America. Subsequently, this doctrine provided the basis for the U.S. Supreme Court to hold that under American law the land and sovereignty of the indigenous peoples was limited. The court took this position in a series of cases known as the Marshall Trilogy after Chief Justice John Marshall. While native peoples residing on their homelands within the expanding territorial boundaries of the United States had the right to use and occupy these lands, they no longer had the power to convey title to them. That title now rested in the United States and any of its successors to whom the land might be transferred or sold under established principles of real property law imported to the United States from England. In addition, the court held that while the "Indian nations" had some limited sovereignty to govern affairs on the land on which they resided, they did so at the pleasure and subject to the "plenary power" of Congress. Congress could, if it so chose, have the last word on how affairs were to be governed within the communities of Indian nations on their homelands. Indian nations were now defined as "domestic dependent nations," captive within the territorial boundaries of the United States, able to exercise a limited amount of sovereignty with which the individual states could not interfere but which Congress could at any time alter by legislative action.[6]

From this understanding developed the Trust Doctrine, under which the federal government was held to have certain duties toward Indian nations as a guardian does to a ward, the Indian peoples being regarded as in a state of "pupilage." The European master story viewed the indigenous peoples within the United States as defeated nations whose communities were thought to be the diminishing vestiges of a primitive, childlike, savage, warlike, and heathen race that would soon vanish from the face of the earth and/or be fully assimilated into the Christian Euro-American culture that had discovered and conquered them. This master story justified the American nation's claim to dominion over their land, and with it the power to distribute the "free" land to the flood of European immigrants coming to the so-called new world to claim it. The indigenous people would be reduced to a small number, and their culture would disappear through assimilation. Or so it was thought.[7]

But this is not the only way to tell the story, and in fact it is far from complete in many senses, including a legal one. In the first place, the native peoples did not disappear, nor did their culture. Their stories of the land and the language in which those stories were told was severely stressed but not defeated, and they did not vanish as expected. In the second place, the legal assumptions that bolstered the European story were changing. The U.S. Supreme Court developed what are known as the Rules of Sympathetic Construction of Indian Treaties, a protocol for judges who interpret the treaties in cases that come before the courts. These rules recognize the disadvantage of the Indians engaged at the treaty-making table and try to compensate in the judicial interpretation of the treaties. The most important of these rules are that treaties between the United States and the Indian nations are to be (1) liberally construed in favor of the Indians "in a spirit which generously recognizes the full obligation of this nation to protect the interests of a dependent people"; (2) "in accordance with the meaning they were understood to have by the tribal representatives who participated in their negotiation" by "look[ing] beyond the written words to the larger context that frames the Treaty, including the history of the treaty, the negotiations, and the practical construction adopted by the parties"; (3) with ambiguities resolved in favor of the Indians.[8]

Under the Rules of Sympathetic Construction comes to light a Dakota narrative markedly different from the American narrative about the nature and function of land. When both points of view at the treaty table are understood and considered, what emerges is a complex and larger story of the negotiations as a dramatic clash of master stories evolving over the fifty-three-year span of treaty making between the Dakota and the United States, in which contrasting views of land were opposed one to the other.

It should also be noted that there were several distinctive subtexts within each of the master stories. Within the American narrative, the interests of traders, missionaries, government officials, and real-estate speculators became part and parcel of what happened at the treaty table. So did the differing points of view between Dakota traditionalists and those more willing to accept change in reaction to European American patterns of life on the frontier. These subtexts at the treaty table became a source of conflict within each of the narratives themselves. Individuals with vested interests in the treaties, such as fur traders, played prominent roles in preparations leading up to negotiations as well in the negotiations and subsequent ratification process, and the treaties became the source of internal conflicts and double-dealing by many of those involved.

PIKE's TREATY OF 1805 AND ITS LEGACY

In September 1805 Lieutenant Zebulon Pike arrived at the island (later known as Pike Island) at the mouth of the Minnesota River at the place the Dakota called Bdote. Pike was greeted by Çetaŋ Wakuwa Mani, also known as Petit Corbeau or Little Crow, the leader of the Kap'oża village, with a hundred and fifty warriors. The day after he arrived, on September 23, Pike, representing the United States, and the leaders of two local Dakota villages met on the island to conclude a treaty between the United States and the "Nation of Sioux Indians," a term used to refer to the Dakota and other groups making up the Oçeti Śakowiŋ, or Seven Fires.[9]

The Dakota signers were Çetaŋ Wakuwa Mani and Way Aga Enogee, Waŋyaga Inażiŋ (He Sees Standing Up), the chief known as Fils de Penishon, whose village was located on the lower Minnesota River.

By the wording of the treaty, the so-called Sioux Nation granted to the United States "for the purpose of the Establishment of Military Posts" two pieces of land, one at the mouth of the St. Croix River, the other to include land from below the mouth of the St. Peters or Minnesota River to the Falls of St. Anthony. According to Article 1, "the Sioux Nation grants to the United States, the full sovereignty and power over said districts forever, without any let or hindrance whatsoever." As consideration for these grants Pike intended that the United States would pay something, but he left this line blank in the treaty. Additionally, the United States promised "to permit the Sioux to pass, repass, hunt or make other uses of the said districts, as they have formerly done, without any other exception, but those specified in article first." In securing the agreement of the Dakota present at the council to establish military posts, Pike fulfilled specific orders for his expedition.[10]

On the matter of the land's value to the United States omitted in Article 2, Pike noted in his journal that he received on behalf of the United States "about 100,000 Acres (equal to 200,000 Dollars)." Pike also reported that on the day of the council "I gave them presents to the amount of about 200 dollars, and as soon as the Council was over, I suffered the Traders [who, Pike wrote, appeared at the council as "my Gentlemen"] to present them with some liquor, which, with what I myself gave, was equal to 60 gallons."[11]

The Senate did not take up the treaty until it was sent to them by President Thomas Jefferson in 1808, when they filled in the blank of Article 2 with the following language: "The United States shall, prior to taking possession thereof, pay to the Sioux two thousand dollars, or deliver the value thereof in such goods and merchandise as they shall choose." In making this recommendation the Senate was following a committee report that put the amount of land "ceded by the Sioux" at the mouth of the St. Croix at 51,840 acres and that between St. Anthony Falls and the mouth of the Minnesota at 103,680 acres, for a total of 155,520 acres. The report went on to calculate that two thousand dollars amounted to "one cent and twenty-eight mills the acre."[12]

Although President Jefferson sent the treaty to the Senate, once it was ratified he never proclaimed it, the usual final step in the process. Charles J. Kappler, who compiled the definitive collection of all treaties concluded by the United States with the various Indian nations, noted, "examination of the records of the State Department fails to indicate any subsequent action by the President [following Senate approval] in proclaiming the ratification of this treaty; but more than twenty-five years subsequent to its approval by the Senate the correspondence of the War Department speaks of the cessions of land described therein as an accomplished fact."[13]

The documentary record of the 1805 treaty and its subsequent implementation gives some evidence of the clash of master stories at the treaty table, although exactly how Dakota leaders understood the treaty terms has never been completely explained. Did they appreciate the phrase "full sovereignty and power"? How was the word *grant* translated to them? What did they think the treaties were meant to accomplish?

Clues may be found not just in the treaty itself but in accounts of the council that took place to negotiate it and in the words and behavior of the Dakota in the years that followed. In his journal Pike stated that other Sioux chiefs were present at the treaty council, including Le Grand Partisan (possibly Wanataŋ), Le Orignal Levé (Rising or Standing Moose), Le Demi Douzen (Half Dozen or Six, Šakpe), Le Becasse (possibly a mistake for Bras Cassé, Broken Arm), and Le Boeuf qui Marche (Walking Buffalo). Pike stated that "it was somewhat difficult to get them to sign the grant, as they conceived the word of honor should be taken for the Grant, without any mark; but I convinced them that, not on their account but my own I wanted them to sign." Some later Dakota statements about the treaty seem to suggest that the chiefs who did not sign simply did not approve of the treaty, although there is no direct evidence of this.[14]

In an account written on the same date as the treaty, Pike claimed he informed the Dakota that the U.S. government wished to establish military posts on the Upper Mississippi. He echoed the treaty's wording in saying that he wished them to "grant to the United States" two parcels of land and that "as we are a people who are accustomed to have all our acts wrote down, in order to have them handed to our children—I have drawn up a form of agreement." He stated that he would have it "read and interpreted" to them. There is no further discussion of what Pike meant by the term *grant* or how it was translated into Dakota. As will be seen later in relation to the Dakota Treaty of 1851 at Traverse des Sioux, the term *cede* was translated there with a Dakota word meaning to give up or throw away. Given the provision for the continuing use of the land by the Dakota, it is likely that such a word used for *grant* would have made no sense. In any case, the continuing use of the land by the Dakota contradicts the idea of the treaty as involving a sale of land. Further, Pike did go on to explain that this military post would be of benefit to the Dakota who remained around it. He stated that the Dakota's situation would improve "by communication with the whites." He further shared that at these posts, "factories"—usually understood to mean government-run trading posts—would be established where Indian people could get their goods cheaper than they did from their traders.[15]

Another stated purpose of the government-run posts was "to make peace between you and the Chipeway's" through diplomacy. Pike wrote in his journal that he intended to take some Ojibwe and Dakota chiefs with him to St. Louis, where peace could be cemented "under the auspices of your mutual father," meaning General James Wilkinson, then governor of the Louisiana Territory. Pike asked that the Sioux chiefs respect "the flag and protection" Pike would extend to Ojibwe chiefs who came down the river in the spring with him. He would also discourage the traders from Canada who, according to Pike, encouraged the Ojibwe to fight against the Dakota.[16]

In 1816 the War Department developed a plan to establish forts on the northwestern frontier, on the land described in the 1805 treaty. In an 1817 report on an expedition initiated to pursue the War Department's plan, Major Stephen Long recommended constructing a fort at the confluence of the Minnesota and Mississippi rivers. The payment dictated by the U.S. Senate did not arrive in Dakota hands for fourteen years, when in 1819 Major Thomas Forsyth, Indian agent in St. Louis, traveled up the Mississippi River on instructions from the War Department, bringing a quantity of goods worth two thousand dollars, to be delivered "in payment of lands ceded by the Sioux Indians to the late Gen. Pike for the United States." On July 25, 1819, Major Forsyth distributed some of the goods to several Sac and Fox Indians who came to him complaining that one of their brothers had been killed by a white man the previous year. Commencing August 5 at Prairie du Chien in present-day Wisconsin and ending August 26 at the juncture of the Minnesota and Mississippi rivers, Forsyth distributed the remainder of the goods to various Dakota tribal representatives as payment under the terms of the 1805 treaty.[17]

Forsyth's payment was designed to allow the carrying out of an order from Secretary of War John C. Calhoun (after whom Lake Calhoun in Minneapolis was named) directing Colonel Henry Leavenworth to transfer the bulk of his regiment from Detroit to the juncture of the Mississippi and Minnesota rivers, so as to begin construction of a fort there. After wintering on the Mendota side of the Minnesota River, Leavenworth moved his encampment to the north, near the spring at what became known as Camp Coldwater. Later that year construction on Fort St. Anthony, the first name given to Fort Snelling, commenced. Leavenworth himself was not sure about the validity of Pike's treaty, so he negotiated a new one in 1820 to accomplish the same purposes. However, his own treaty was never ratified. In June 1821 Colonel Josiah Snelling succeeded Leavenworth. Snelling redesigned the fort and construction was begun at its present location that fall.[18]

In the years following Fort Snelling's construction, the Treaty of 1805 continued to be discussed in encounters between government agents and Dakota people, each of whom believed for their own reasons that it had been a legitimate treaty. In March 1829 Indian agent Lawrence Taliaferro recorded the comments of Çetaŋ Wakuwa Mani or Little Crow, the only surviving signer of the 1805 treaty: "My Father: Since I was a small boy I have lived upon these Lands near your Fort. I gave this place to your people more than 20 years ago. My Father: I am disposed to be friendly with every body, with your Nation & our neighbours the Chippy. And Sacs & Foxes. It was allways your wish and mine also."[19]

The statements are in keeping with the Dakota idea that they were giving Pike the right to build forts as a means to further the mediation between Dakota and Ojibwe and other groups. Little Crow also mentions the work of Taliaferro, Pike's successor, in that continuing mediation.

At a meeting on June 15, 1829, Little Crow may have repeated his statement about the land on which Fort Snelling stood, because Taliaferro recorded remarks from Kaḣboka, or the Drifter, described as the second chief of the Black Dog band: "My Father I will speak a few words to you. What the Chief the Little Crow said to you this day is all true—he gave you the land on which your Fort now Stands. My Brother was on the spot at the time & knew but he is now no more for he lays among the white people—and I am sorry he did not live longer that you might have know ı him better." Although Little Crow spoke that day, the remarks recorded by Taliaferro do not echo what he had said earlier. However, Taliaferro did record a speech on July 31, 1829, in which the chief stated, "My Father—I gave you the Land on which your fort Stands, if I had not been friendly disposed and wished the white people to settle near me—you would not have gotten an inch of ground from me."[20]

In this period Dakota bands around Fort Snelling were concerned about both the boundaries of the land on which a military post could be built and operated and what rights the military had to the resources within and surrounding those boundaries. In September 1829 Wambdi Taŋka (Big Eagle) of Black Dog village complained to Taliaferro that trees his people needed for fencing and houses were being cut near his village. The following September Wambdi Taŋka returned to see Taliaferro and the fort's commanding officer. Taliaferro wrote, "He wished to know the exact bounds to the U S. reserve—around Fort Snelling—& what we claim as his people wished to be immediately informed."[21]

Taliaferro responded that the military reservation extended from two miles below the fort up to St. Anthony Falls and beyond for nine miles on each side of the Mississippi. This territory would extend just beyond Penichon's village. Taliaferro stated that Henry Leavenworth had misled the Dakota about these boundaries when he negotiated the never-ratified Treaty of 1820, noting that Leavenworth "included by 4½ miles less than Pike—which oversight—has induced the Indians contiguous to this Post to aver that they only gave Pike a mile around the present site of Fort Snelling—or as they say just as far as can be seen around the Fort without elevating the eyes—which would be at the rate of two miles in some places one mile in others—where no promontory intervened it would be the greater distance 2 miles."[22]

In response, Wambdi Taŋka told Taliaferro, "It is a matter of surprize to us that your Nation should come here among us poor Indians—to live hard & suffer upon this barren land. You quit a good country when you have a plenty to eat drink & to wear always with good clothes. This seems Strange to us. When the British used to see us we were better off. Our game was plenty, & our hunts good—they came but few among us—& assisted us much. I do not say this that you are to understand me as dislikeing your Nation—for we do not—but since your Nation has been here, they are catching at every thing, & times are altogether changed."[23]

Taliaferro stated that he knew the chief's feelings. The fort had not been located where it was "to injure any body much less—those whom we feel a disposition to protect." Its purpose was protecting the fur trade and the traders "& to have proper persons in the Country to carry it on also to have a general depot to Store goods—to be divided, & sent out to different Stations for your accommodation & convenience." The Dakota had had "many advantages both

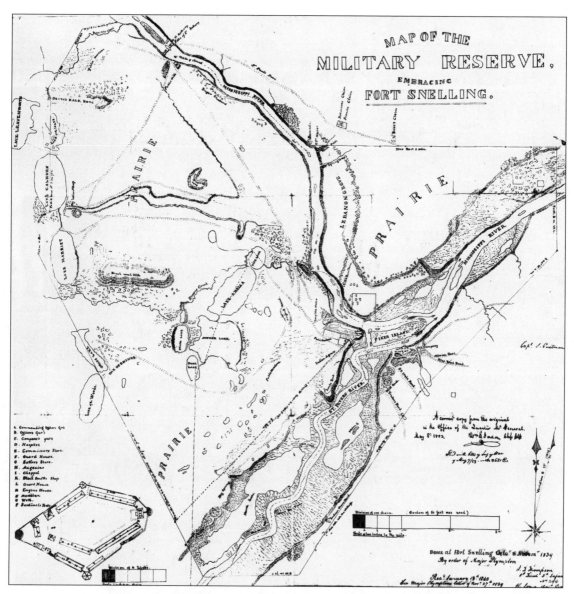

*The first real survey of the Fort Snelling reservation that came into being as a result
of the 1805 treaty was not done until 1839, by Lieutenant James Thompson. As shown
here in a later version of the map redrawn in the 1850s, the reservation was
understood to have included much of the present-day city of Minneapolis as far west as Lakes
Calhoun, Harriet, and Cedar as well as portions of Bloomington and Richfield.*

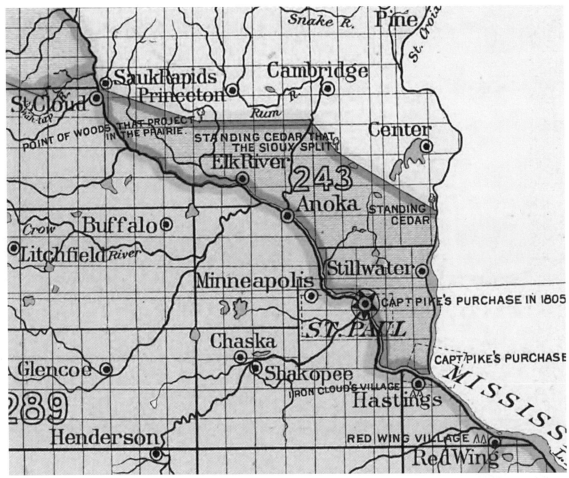

Shown here is a portion of a map drawn by Charles C. Royce
for an 1899 Bureau of American Ethnology report recording the
boundaries for land cessions covered in all of the treaties negotiated
by tribes in Minnesota. The boundary at the top shows the
1825 treaty line between the Dakota and Ojibwe.

yourself & people from our location here. Much bread meat & I am assured in saying much bounty at my hands—all of which you cannot deny—but again I can assure you that we derive neither pleasure or satisfaction from our residence in your Nation, on the contrary such a long Stay has become truly *irksome* & disagreeable and we wish to be away from you—much worse than you do or can possibly suppose."[24]

Questions about the meaning of the Fort Snelling reservation persisted. In June 1835, in a conversation with the American Fur Company trader at Mendota, Henry H. Sibley, Taliaferro referred to Pike's treaty as not a purchase of land but a "perpetual lease." He wrote, "M Sibley—asked how I viewed the reserve at this Post Answer—Here is the Law of June 30 1834—my opinion this rese[r]vation at S Peters is nothing more than a perpetual lease under the convention with Pike. The Treaty of 1825 (August) at Prarie du chiens confirms it. It is taken and deemed to be the Indian country in my view of the case—by the act of the 30 June 1834—as before stated."[25]

This statement implies that the Treaty of 1805 was affirmed by the Treaty of 1825, a reference to Article 10 of the latter treaty which acknowledged "the general controlling power of the United States" and the existence of several reservations made under previous treaties, including one at St. Peters. Nonetheless, the questions relating to the Treaty of 1805 persisted to such an extent that the Dakota would not sign another treaty in 1837 unless a promise was made to pay some of what they considered they were owed for the earlier treaty. A total of four thousand dollars was distributed to five bands of Bdewakaŋtuŋwaŋ Dakota in October 1838.[26]

In 1837 the subject of the treaty's meaning came up in discussions about the nature of the rights the military and civilians had in the Fort Snelling reservation. Fort commander Lieutenant Colonel William Davenport wrote the U.S. adjutant general about attempts to purchase the flour mills built by the military at St. Anthony Falls. Davenport insisted it was not in the public interest to sell the mills. Cattle imported for army use were kept at the mill before slaughter, where there were accommodations for the men who herded them and all the necessary enclosures for the cattle and hay. He interpreted Pike's treaty as simply the Dakota's consent to establish the fort, not a sale of land, so that the Indians never parted with the right in the soil or any other right they previously enjoyed: "Thus we are on Indian land and cannot grant any part of it to a person for private use." Taliaferro's point was that the land was Indian country by definition of federal law, an area where land purchases by private individuals were prohibited.[27]

Even after the Dakota were paid money for Pike's Treaty in 1838 and the new treaty was signed, government correspondence refers to continuing rights under Article 3 of Pike's treaty, "to pass, repass, hunt or make other uses of the said districts, as they have formerly done." On April 23, 1839, Fort Snelling post surgeon John Emerson wrote to Surgeon General Thomas Lawson to complain about the presence of trader Joseph R. Brown selling whiskey within gunshot of the fort. As a solution he suggested extending the military reserve to an area twenty miles square, including the mouth of the St. Croix, "especially as the Indians are allowed by treaty to hunt on it."[28]

Conflicts between the Dakota and other nearby tribes are a subtext within the larger Dakota treaty narrative. The Dakota relationship to the land included sharing that land from time to time with others, in contrast to the European American perspective that the land was a possession and property rights allowed the exclusion of others from the land. The Dakota and other nations moved back and forth through the area of Mni Sota Makoce, which the Dakota considered their sacred homeland, and the idea of drawing a boundary across it would have made little sense to them.

THE TREATY OF 1825

In August 1825, U.S. government officials met at Prairie du Chien to negotiate a "firm and perpetual peace" between the Dakota and the Ojibwe, the Sac and Fox, the Menominee, the Ioway, the Ho-Chunk, and the Odawa. The treaty attempted to establish boundaries between the lands the various nations occupied in the region of the Upper Mississippi River. For the Dakota, this involved a negotiated boundary between them and the Sac and Fox and Ioway to the south and the Ojibwe to the north. Tribes would not hunt on each other's lands without their assent and that of the U.S. government. The various nations acknowledged the general controlling power of the United States and disclaimed all dependence upon and connection with any other power.

In 1823 Lawrence Taliaferro, as Indian agent at St. Peters, proposed that the Dakota and Ojibwe should both send delegates to Washington to negotiate a settlement and draw up a boundary. The following year Taliaferro took a party of Dakota, Ojibwe, and Menominee on the first of a series of trips to Washington, one purpose of which was to give them a chance to see something of the white man's strength and numbers. Although no treaty was signed, the groundwork was laid for a great intertribal council at Prairie du Chien the next year.[29]

Agent Taliaferro gathered a delegation of 385 Dakota and Ojibwe of the Mississippi at Fort Snelling, including interpreters and assistants. They made their way downriver and at length halted at the Painted Rock above Prairie du Chien. After "attending to their toilet and appointment of soldiers to dress the columns of boats, the grand entry was made with drums beating, many flags flying, with incessant discharges of small arms. All Prairie du Chien was drawn out, with other delegations already arrived, to witness the display and landing of this ferocious looking body of true savages."[30]

Twenty-six Dakota leaders, representing the Waȟpekute, Waȟpetuŋwaŋ, Sisituŋwaŋ, and Ihaŋktuŋwaŋ, were present at the treaty negotiation. At the beginning of the treaty council Superintendent of Indian Affairs in St. Louis William Clark told the assembled delegates that the lack of clear boundaries between nations was the cause of hostilities: "Your hostilities have resulted in a great measure from your having no defined boundaries established in your country. Your tribes do not know what belongs to them & your peoples thus follow the game into lands claimed by other tribes. This cause will be removed by the establishment of boundaries which shall be known to you & which boundaries we must establish at the council fire."[31]

In fact the purpose of establishing boundaries may have been as much for facilitating treaties of cession for the lands as for establishing peace. Though the federal policy of relocating Indian tribes west of the Mississippi River was not formally passed by Congress until 1830, the Prairie du Chien treaty prepared the way for removal by establishing boundaries that would be cited in treaties ceding land in the years ahead. In light of ongoing disagreements between tribes, forcing a few tribal leaders to agree to boundaries that might or might not be respected by all tribal members certainly did not guarantee peace.

1825

A treaty between various tribes of the Upper Mississippi valley is signed at Prairie du Chien, laying out boundaries between tribes.

Tribal leaders knew that portions of their territory was shared, and some tried to warn the American officials that they had differing concepts of land ownership. Coramonee, a Ho-Chunk chief, said, "The lands I claim are mine and the nations here know it is not only claimed by us but by our Brothers the Sacs and Foxes, Menominees, Iowas, Mahas, and Sioux. They have held it in common. It would be difficult to divide it. It belongs as much to one as the other . . . My Fathers I did not know that any of my relations had any particular lands. It is true everyone owns his own lodge and the ground he may cultivate. I had thought the Rivers were the common property of all Red Skins and not used exclusively by any particular nation."[32]

Similarly Noodin (the Wind), an Ojibwe leader from the St. Croix–Mille Lacs region, saw a danger in forcing the tribes to agree to a boundary: "I wish to live in peace—But in running marks round our country or in giving it to our enemies it may make new disturbances and breed new wars." A Menominee chief named Grizzly Bear said, "We travel about a great deal and go where there is game among the Nations around who do not restrain us from doing so." Tribal groups often made accommodations with each other and did not require a fixed boundary.[33]

The major disagreements at the council occurred in defining the boundaries between the Dakota, Ojibwe, and Sac and Fox. Leaders from these groups gave detailed descriptions, sometimes with the help of maps, laying out their territories. Only those Dakota leaders whose lands bordered neighboring nations demarcated their territories' relevant boundaries, often not only naming rivers, lakes, and landmarks but noting they were born in or had long connection to these areas. The territories generally corresponded to areas where the Dakota were often described as hunting in the nineteenth century and earlier.

Wabasha, leader of the southernmost Dakota band along the Mississippi, stated that despite his claims he was willing to "relinquish some of my lands for the sake of peace." He noted he had formerly owned the lands at Prairie du Chien but had given them up to the whites. He described a southern boundary for his land extending west of the Mississippi River from below the mouth of the Upper Iowa River to the head of the Raccoon fork of the Upper Cedar River. Beyond that, he said, "I leave for my relations to settle."[34]

Çetaŋ Wakuwa Mani or Little Crow, the surviving 1805 treaty signer, defined boundaries that bordered Ojibwe country in the north, extending from the falls of the Chippewa River to the first river above the falls of the St. Croix and up the St. Croix to Cedar Island, a day's march above the falls at present-day Taylors Falls, Minnesota–St. Croix Falls, Wisconsin. Śakpe's boundary lay west of that described by Little Crow. He stated that he was born on the Minnesota River and that his line "commences at Crow Island and Sandy hills on the East of the Mississippi and runs along where the timber joins the meadow to the Mississippi at the Isle [Aile] de Corbeau [Crow Wing] at the mouth of the Crow Wing River."[35]

A Waȟpetuŋwaŋ leader known as the Little then spoke: "The Band of the lakes have been speaking. I am of the prairie. I claim the land up the River Corbeau [Crow River] to its source & from there to Otter Tail Lake. I can yet show the marks of my lodges there and they will remain as long as the world lasts." Tataŋka Nażiŋ or Standing Buffalo, a Sisituŋwaŋ leader from Lake Traverse and Lac qui Parle, stated that his lands commenced at Ottertail Lake and ran north to Pine Lake and the Pine River, which emptied into the Red River. Wanataŋ, the Ihaŋktuŋwaŋ leader, said, "I am from the plains and it is of that part of our Country of which I speak. My line commences where Thick Wood River empties into Red River thence down Red River to Turtle River—up Turtle River to its source, thence south of the Devils Lake to the Missouri at the Gros Ventre Village."[36]

Çaŋ Sagye or Cane, a Waȟpekute chief whose territory overlapped with Wabasha's on the west, stated, "I will now point out the boundary of the land where I was born. It commences at the raccoon fork of the Des Moines River at the mouth of the Raccoon River, thence up to a small lake, the source of Bear River & thence following Bear River to its entrance into the Missouri a little below Council Bluffs (suppose the Bowyer's [Boyer] river)."[37]

The artist James Otto Lewis recorded the gathering of tribes at Prairie du Chien in 1825, where leaders came to sign a treaty with the U.S. government containing agreements about tribal boundaries.

Among the Ojibwe leaders, two from the Minnesota region delineated land overlapping that of the Dakota, though notably they did not claim birthright for this territory. Pee a jick [Bayezhig], or Single Man, an Ojibwe leader from Mille Lacs who also had Dakota ancestry, gave a southern boundary beginning at the mouth of the Chippewa River and extending to the head of Lake St. Croix, "thence to Green water Lake, thence to the mouth of Rum River," across the Mississippi to the headwaters of the Crow and Sauk rivers. He said, "This is the land I claim for myself & my children hereafter." He presented a birch-bark map showing the area. Kau ta wa be taa (Broken Tooth) of Sandy Lake claimed a line going beyond Pee a jick's through the Crow River, to the Red River and beyond to Devils Lake.[38]

After some discussion, agreement was reached for a boundary between the Dakota and Ojibwe that, as historian Gary Clayton Anderson pointed out, appears to split the overlapping territory in the Minnesota region. The treaty's wording described the boundary in terms of locations known to both nations, though identifying those exact locations today is not always easy. The eastern end of the boundary began

> at the Chippewa River, half a day's march below the falls; and from thence it shall run to Red Cedar River, immediately below the falls; from thence to the St. Croix River, which it strikes at a place called the standing cedar, about a day's paddle in a canoe, above the Lake at the mouth of that river; thence

passing between two lakes called by the Chippewas "Green Lakes," and by the Sioux "the lakes they bury the Eagles in," and from thence to the standing cedar that "the Sioux Split;" thence to Rum River, crossing it at the mouth of a small creek called choaking creek, a long day's march from the Mississippi; thence to a point of woods that projects into the prairie, half a day's march from the Mississippi.

From there the boundary continued in a diagonal line across the present state to the Red River near the mouth of "Outard or Goose creek."[39]

Negotiations between the Dakota and the Sac and Fox were more difficult because of disagreements about the names given to the various forks of the Raccoon River, which involved the Waȟpekute and persisted after the treaty. The treaty also provided for further consultation with the Ihaŋktuŋwaŋ (who had not been fully represented at the negotiation) about the boundary in the area between the Des Moines and Missouri rivers.[40]

At the end of the negotiations, after the treaty was read and "explained to the Indians article by article," William Clark brought out a beaded belt of wampum, such as had been used in negotiations involving Indian people and European governments in North America for hundreds of years, and sought to cast the agreement as a "religious contract between all the tribes," represented in the belt's patterns of beadwork. He pointed out the representation of the Great Father and the "twenty-four great fires" on the belt and offered it to the treaty signers, after which they smoked a pipe. The treaty journal does not record any responses to this aspect of the negotiation.

Although the treaty contains no cessions, it was in effect a cessional treaty for all tribes who gave up claims to land. For the Dakota the line drawn would, for all practical purposes, "cede" the northern portion of their ancestral homeland to the Ojibwe, who had come to dominate it only seventy-five years earlier when the Dakota moved out of the Mille Lacs area. As it turned out, the treaty did not have the desired effect of quelling skirmishes across the line between rival Dakota and Ojibwe bands, but it did "ratify" the Dakota's separation from the northern reaches of their homeland that had come about as a result of the Ojibwe migration to the west. Mni Sota Makoce—the place where the Dakota dwell—had now formally become the place where the Dakota and the Ojibwe dwell.

The treaty was proclaimed by President Martin Van Buren on February 6, 1826: "The negotiations between the Sioux and the Chippewa, with which alone we are concerned, resulted in an agreement on a dividing line between their respective countries, which the Indians solemnly promised would never be crossed by either nation unless on peaceful missions." But the treaty did not transform relations between Dakota and Ojibwe. The Dakota saw the Ojibwe pushing even beyond the agreed-upon boundaries. In June 1829, the chief of Black Dog village complained to Taliaferro, "My Father. We made peace with the Chippeways and gave them up much of our Lands—but it appears they are not satisfied with this but continue to trespass on our Lands which are bad enough & take every thing clean from the Earth as they go." Similarly, in June 1832, Taliaferro heard several Dakota chiefs tell him, in council, "Our lands are destitute of game & our old enemies the Chippeways by constant encroachments—keep our lands so closely to themselves—ever since our treaty at Pra[i]rie du Chien that we suffer more than [can] be well conceived."[41]

The Ojibwe-Dakota boundary was not surveyed until 1835, after repeated requests by the Indians. In Taliaferro's journal for 1835 are twenty-seven entries, beginning June 10 and ending September 23, related to the survey of the "S & C Line" by Major Jonathan L. Bean, whom the Dakota called, according to Taliaferro, "Blue Cloud." While the survey was in progress both Dakota and Ojibwe complained of the location. Taliaferro wrote to Major Bliss, commander of Fort Snelling, on August 30, 1835, that the Ojibwe would not observe the landmarks or survey markers but on the contrary had been throwing them down and attempting to demolish many of them. He predicted occasional bloodshed for the reason that, since their country was "not at all adequate to the support of

---

Bde Wambdi Waȟapi / The Place Where They Buried the Eagles

Bde Wambdi Waȟapi lies somewhere between Green Lake and Forest Lake in present-day Chisago and Washington counties. The exact location of this site and the explanation for the name have not been determined precisely. In the winter of 1828 Indian agent Lawrence Taliaferro noted that a group of Ojibwe from the St. Croix River region "left early this Morning for their Camp near the Sioux—at the Two Lakes called by them—The place they bury Eagles in." It made sense that members of the two sometimes-hostile peoples would meet in this area because they recognized their shared occupation of this place. As a result, the location was along the boundary set by the multi-tribal Treaty of Prairie du Chien in 1825. Article 5 placed the boundary along the St. Croix River on the west, thence passing between two lakes called by the Ojibwe "Green Lakes" and by the Dakota "the lakes they bury the Eagles in," and from thence to the standing cedar that "the Sioux Split," a location along the Rum River which may have specific—though unexplained—cultural meaning.[iii]

On an 1843 map, Joseph Nicollet located Buried Eagle Lake close to the St. Croix River, in the watershed of the present-day Sunrise River north of a lake he calls Green Lake. There is a Green Lake at Chisago City, and it is possible that Buried Eagle Lake is present-day Forest Lake. Archaeological information may shed additional light on the question. Based on information from a late-nineteenth-century survey, Newton Winchell described ten mounds on the northeastern shore of Green Lake, located on a peninsula between that lake and Chisago Lake to the north. Included is an unusual configuration of two mounds connected by a semicircular embankment.[iv] ■

their population," the Ojibwe would force themselves on the Dakota's hunting grounds. A few years later it was reported by a Methodist missionary that boundary mounds constructed by the surveyors "had been destroyed by the Chippewa Indians; and he was under the impression that the Chippewas were opposed to having mounds made in their country." The missionary reported that "Indians greatly prefer natural boundary lines where the situation of the country will permit."[42]

In fact, the government's insistence that the Dakota and Ojibwe reach an agreement about an exact boundary appears to have aggravated the situation between them. Until then, the two peoples would reach yearly agreements about sharing the territory for winter hunting. Such agreements were still necessary despite the definition of the boundary line.

THE 1830 TREATY

Even if the Ojibwe-Dakota boundary had been surveyed immediately after the Treaty of 1825, however, it would probably not have brought about the stability on the frontier that Americans desired. The next attempt to resolve the issue came in 1830, when Congress passed the Removal Act, which attempted to end the ongoing conflict between the indigenous peoples and the immigrant-settlers along the frontier by removing the Indian people from their lands and moving them west. The impact of this law would be felt later in the Minnesota region than in other parts of the United States.

At Prairie du Chien in July 1830, leaders representing the Bdewakaŋtuŋwaŋ, Sisituŋwaŋ, Waȟpetuŋwaŋ, and Waȟpekute signed a treaty ceding a tract of country twenty miles in width, from the Mississippi to the Des Moines River, situated to the north and adjoining the line agreed upon between them and the Sac and Fox in the Treaty of 1825. This was part of a larger agreement, essentially an extension of the 1825 treaty, whereby the Dakota and the other tribes gave up their lands between the Des Moines and the Missouri for the purpose of establishing a neutral "common hunting ground" to be administered by the president of the United States. As stated in the treaty, "it is understood that the lands ceded and relinquished by this Treaty, are to be assigned and allotted under the direction of the President of the United States, to the Tribes now living thereon, or to such other Tribes as the President may locate thereon for hunting, and other purposes." Lawrence Taliaferro took credit for this aspect of the treaty, noting "The purchase of Lands on the disputed line between the Sacs—Foxes—& the Sioux was at my instance." He also urged that a similar agreement be reached between the Dakota and Ojibwe. Waȟpekute leader "Wiash ho ha," who was known at the time as French Crow, stated, "You have asked for a piece of land, but you must give us $3,000 for it, and the privilege of hunting on it, and no white

1830

The Indian Removal Act, passed by Congress, authorizes the president to negotiate with tribes to give up land in the East in exchange for land in the West. A treaty is signed with Dakota and other tribes to settle unsolved questions about the 1825 treaty.

man must come on it." In the end they received only two thousand dollars from the treaty, though with other benefits.[43]

Also at the treaty the Dakota agreed to establish a tract of land for the people of Dakota and European ancestry, beginning at Barn Bluff near Red Wing village, running back fifteen miles from the Mississippi, and then in a parallel line with Lake Pepin and the Mississippi, ending around the Grand Encampment located at one of the Wabasha village sites opposite the mouth of the Buffalo River, to be held by them "in the same manner that other Indian Titles are held." The people to be benefited were sometimes called "half-breeds," and the area set aside was called the "Wabasha Reservation" or the "Half-Breed Tract." The Dakota themselves made no distinctions based on blood quantum, preferring instead to call people of such mixed ancestry with a term usually translated as "our relations"—probably from takuyapi or unkitakuyapi, versions of the word for relatives cited at the beginning of this chapter. The Wabasha Reservation was later abolished and those it was intended to benefit were issued scrip, allowing them to obtain land in other locations.[44]

At the 1830 negotiations Wabasha made clear that as with the neutral ground, he agreed to give up the strip of land for the mixed bloods providing the Dakota would continue to have "the privilege of hunting on it." Other chiefs deferred to Wabasha. Little Crow—still Çetaŋ Wakuwa Mani, the 1805 treaty signer—stated, "We say nothing about the land you spoke of. We leave that all to Wabashaw. But we have brought down a few pipes to smoke with those with whom we have made peace & to the custom of our people." The 1830 treaty was the first treaty after Pike's whereby the Dakota formally ceded any land to the U.S. government and the first to provide yearly payments of money in the form of annuities. The eastern Dakota received two thousand dollars a year for the period of ten years. They also were to be supplied with a blacksmith to work for them, with iron, steel, and tools from the government, as well as tools for agricultural purposes.[45]

THE TREATY OF 1837

The press for "cession" (which could also be called "sale") of land by the indigenous people to the United States became a major theme in the 1830s. The first significant formal cession of Dakota land was undertaken with the Treaty of 1837 in Washington. Despite Taliaferro's high hopes for the 1830 treaty, it did not accomplish what he had expected of it. Relations between the Dakota and the Sac and Fox worsened, as did those with the Ojibwe after the attempt to draw a boundary line in 1835. The answer, it seemed to Taliaferro, lay in another treaty, not merely to try to improve relations between the Dakota and their neighbors but also to cede lands east of the Mississippi for logging, an increasingly important industry in the region.[46]

Taliaferro began to think about such a treaty in late 1835. In a conversation with Major Bliss, commander at Fort Snelling, he suggested that a treaty might involve ceding Dakota lands east of the Mississippi and moving the Ho-Chunk west of the river. He noted that traders, including the American Fur Company, might try to use the agreement to seek repayment of the Dakota's debts, something Taliaferro had successfully opposed in the Treaty of 1830. The trading companies' claims were based on paper debts and not necessarily actual debts because for generations traders had calculated their rates of exchange of furs for merchandise to allow for the variability of fur animal populations and their customers' ability to pay. Some had begun to give out credit to native peoples expecting to be reimbursed by the federal government. Taliaferro believed the traders would oppose the treaty until they could have him removed from his job.[47]

The following spring Taliaferro vowed he would leave his post once he could get such a treaty signed. He continued to write of the "*rascality* & frauds permitted by the treaty making power generally." He wrote, "The Am F Cpy [American Fur Company] I say or many of *its* traders are disposed to stop short of nothing in getting me off from this Agency before the treaties in question are to be commenced with *my Indians*. But I feel doubly strong in my integrity." In July Taliaferro warned that traders threatened or corrupted Indian people into receiving goods, forcing an "acquiescence to their diabolical plans of procuring gold out of their [natives'] hunts and mainly from the proceeds of the sales of their lands to the United States."[48]

Taliaferro submitted a detailed proposal for a treaty to Superintendent William Clark in 1836, receiving a cool reception from Clark and Commissioner of Indian Affairs Elbert Herring. Later in the year, after jurisdiction of the St. Peter Agency was transferred to Governor Henry Dodge of Wisconsin Territory, the treaty was looked upon more favorably. On November 30, 1836, Taliaferro sent a new proposal to Indian Commissioner Carey A. Harris, who appeared to share the enthusiasm. Later, in July 1837, in full view of the Dakota bands, a treaty with the Ojibwe was signed at Fort Snelling, ceding Ojibwe lands east of the Mississippi River and south of the Lake Superior watershed.[49]

The chief negotiator for the Ojibwe treaty was Henry Dodge, who after its completion gave Taliaferro written instruction to organize two delegations of Dakota to go to Washington, one from those who lived along the boundary with the Sac and Fox, "for peace purposes," and the other of Bdewakaŋtuŋwaŋ Dakota "who claim the Lands East of the Mississippi." It was apparent the latter group would be asked to sign a treaty cession for their land, though this plan was apparently not discussed openly and it may be that the Dakota themselves were not aware of it prior to their departure. In early August, Hercules Dousman, agent of the American Fur Company at Prairie du Chien, wrote that the delegations would be going "ostensibly to make peace, but the real object is to get their Lands." Dousman had been shown a copy of Taliaferro's letter and had actively lobbied against the treaty. His efforts were evidence of Taliaferro's fear that the greatest obstacles to completing the treaty would come not from the Dakota but from the American Fur Company. For this reason, officials had decided to hold the treaty negotiations in Washington, despite the logic of having them at Fort Snelling.[50]

Among those with a special interest in the treaty was the Mendota trader Henry H. Sibley, who was present in Washington. Sibley had particular motivation for attempting to influence the treaty negotiations. He had come to the territory in 1834, just in time to cash in at the very end of the successful fur trade and also to experience the difficulties of its decline. He soon became skilled in manipulating the engines of government for his own purposes. Sibley clearly knew of the planned treaty, if only because Taliaferro needed supplies for the delegation going to Washington. On August 16 Taliaferro purchased coats, "laced & garnished," for ten chiefs, and a variety of other cloth, clothing, blankets, and looking glasses. Taliaferro apparently tried to mislead observers into thinking he would be leaving later than he did. Sibley wrote in mid-August to American Fur Company representatives that the delegation would not depart for Washington until September 1, at which point he would follow. Other sources suggest the delegation left around August 18. Historian Edward Neill later wrote that Taliaferro was "keeping his own council." He engaged a steamboat captain to be at the landing at a certain date, and then "to the astonishment of the traders, the Agent, interpreters, and a part of the delegation were quickly on board, and gliding down the river." Stops were made at Kap'oża, Red Wing, and Winona to pick up other delegation members.[51]

Included were at least twenty-six Dakota leaders, numbering among them not only Bdewakaŋtuŋwaŋ and Waȟpekute but also Sisituŋwaŋ and Waȟpetuŋwaŋ, who were not among the twenty-one who ultimately signed the treaty. The explanation for their presence comes from the instructions Taliaferro had received from Governor Dodge to bring delegations both for selling lands east of the Mississippi River and of "the Sioux on the Sac & Fox territory for peace purposes." The various Dakota communities along the Upper Minnesota River all hunted, on occasion, along the line with the Sac and Fox. Though they did not all sign the treaty, some of them participated in its negotiation.[52]

On August 21, Taliaferro and his delegation reached Prairie du Chien. He wrote to Dodge at Mineral Point, stating that he intended to proceed with the delegation by way of the Ohio to Wheeling and thence to Bedford, Pennsylvania, where his wife's family had a hotel, stating that he could "subsist my Delegation for a few days for one half less than in Washington." He planned to wait there until Dodge arrived "with the other tribes," probably meaning the Sac and Fox.[53]

Taliaferro and the delegation reached Washington on September 15, where they were boarded at the Globe Hotel. On September 20, Taliaferro outlined for fellow officials a proposed treaty that would cede all Bdewakaŋtuŋwaŋ Dakota lands east of the Mississippi River between the mouth of the Upper Iowa River and Watab, on the Mississippi River near the present-day town of that name. He advised that one million dollars be paid for the cession. Despite his concerns about fraud on the part of traders, Taliaferro appeared to be open to putting some such provision in the treaty, though he stated that "great care is necessary or extensive frauds will be practiced not only on the Indians but on the government." He suggested that all claims for amounts due from the Bdewakaŋtuŋwaŋ to traders "be laid before the Agent and Sec. of the [treaty] Commission to prevent *frauds*."[54]

On September 21 negotiations began at a Presbyterian church, where those not working for the government were excluded. The record of the treaty meetings provides little evidence of real negotiations. Rather it suggests that government officials had a firm idea of what they wanted based on Taliaferro's suggestions but were unwilling to reveal the terms until well along in the process. Whether designed to keep the Dakota in the dark or to forestall the traders' influence is not clear.[55]

Each day's council was preceded by smoking a pipe passed from the treaty commissioner, Secretary of War Joel R. Poinsett, who was aided in his negotiations by Commissioner of Indian Affairs Carey Harris, to the chiefs. The commissioner began the first session by making clear the negotiations were primarily about the cession of land. He noted that the Dakota had come through "some of our great towns" and had seen "the power of the Nation." This power would never be used to exert evil against them but only to protect them. The purpose of selling their land was to "place the great river between you and the Whites." The hunting grounds west of the river should be sufficient for them. In return for selling their land they would be given money and things they needed. But rather than proposing terms, the commissioner indicated he was ready to receive "any proposition you may be prepared to make for that purpose." It seems the government officials were holding their cards close to the vest, insisting that the Dakota name a price before the officials described the lands they wanted.[56]

The first Dakota leader to speak was Wakiŋyaŋ Taŋka, Big Thunder, son of the recently deceased Little Crow, who would later come to be known by his father's name. He stated, "My Father, we live a great distance in the West, from the rising of the Sun. We have occupied the lands we now live on. We did not come here to learn the strength of your nation. Our friends have been here and have told us of your power." He said they had nothing to say but would be willing to speak the following day.[57]

Subsequent meetings suggest government officials were reluctant to make a full proposal until they had heard what the Dakota wanted. On September 22, Ehake, a leader whose village connection was not named, spoke, stating they had no idea yet of the extent of the lands which government officials wanted. At this point the commissioner stated, "Your father will buy all of your lands East of the Mississippi for what he will pay you, one million dollars as may hereafter be agreed upon." The Dakota responded that they wished to think over the proposition until the next day.[58]

At the meeting on Saturday, September 23, the commissioner began by asking the Dakota if they had an answer to the government's offer. In response Ehake stated that they hoped he would consider that they were "naked, you are rich and well clothed." The amount offered when divided among the Dakota would give "but little to each." The commissioner responded that if he had not considered their needs the amount offered would not be "more than one half of the amount." He stated, "The offer will not be changed."[59]

In response Ehake noted that the recent purchase of Ojibwe lands involved "low and marshy country," while Dakota lands were worth much more. Other leaders representing the various bands spoke, emphasizing in different ways how little the amount offered would give to each Dakota person. It was only after a Sunday break in the meetings that on September 25 the commissioner presented the details of how the one million dollars would be divided in the terms of the treaty. The largest single portion of the money would be invested to pay them a permanent annuity. Other money would be used to pay their trade debts, settle the claims of "the Half Breeds"—or those of Dakota-European ancestry—and pay for agriculture, for blacksmiths, and for presents.[60]

After receiving these terms, the assembled Dakota took the paper describing the division with them and spent until late afternoon discussing it among themselves. They reported they wished to keep considering the matter until they had counseled more. It appears the discussion continued until Wednesday, September 27, when the Dakota indicated they were still not in agreement about the terms. They had hoped for a higher payment but had been told that the "great council now in session" (Congress) would not accept that. The Dakota felt they were in the same situation: they were afraid "our people will not consent." That afternoon, the Dakota leaders returned with their own proposal, apparently changing somewhat the proportions but accepting the total amount of the government's offer. A number of chiefs spoke about their decision, after which the commissioner responded that he felt they had left out "many useful articles that they cannot well do without," such as tobacco, salt, provisions, and stock. He said he would return with his own proposal for dividing the money.[61]

On September 28 several Dakota leaders, speaking in turn, asked for a further change in the provisions to the treaty, concerning the amount set aside for "our relations," that is, the people of Dakota-European ancestry. The leaders asked that the amount be increased to $110,000. Aside from that they accepted the terms offered. Wasu Wiċaṡtaṡni, known as Bad Hail, stated, "I addressed you the other day. I told you that I was a chief and a soldier. My father we are a part of the nation called the Seven Fires. We hope you will consent to our proposition."[62]

The following day, September 29, a number of Dakota chiefs spoke about the treaty and those that preceded it. Among them was Mazamani, the Waḣpetuŋwaŋ leader from the Little Rapids village, who stated, "Since I came here I find that I have no claims to these lands. I thought I had but my friends here say that I have not. I am an old man. I shall not prevent you from buying these lands. [T]hey feel sore about parting with this country. It would bring a great price if you could cut it up and bring it here." Ehake spoke about the land set aside for "some of our relations" in the Treaty of 1830. He pointed out that this land had not been surveyed. He asked if "you will allow us to hunt on the land we now give up to you" and said that they wished "to reserve the islands in the river so that we can go and cut wood." He also asked that when they were paid money it should be in silver pieces. Other chiefs spoke about these and other requests. Maḣpiya Nażiŋhaŋ (Mauc peeah nasiah, Standing Cloud) noted, "We never dreamt of selling you our lands until your agent our Father invited us to come and visit our Great Father. The land that we give up to you is the best that we have. We hope you will allow us to hunt on it."[63]

After the Dakota chiefs finished speaking, the commissioner presented them with the treaty for signing. Some of what they had just requested, including the right to hunt and the ownership of the islands, was not in the treaty. In fact, the treaty specifically included the islands in the land ceded. Article 1 stated that "the chiefs and braves representing the parties having an interest therein cede to the United States all their lands East of the Mississippi River and all their islands in the Said river." From this example it is easy to conclude that the version presented for signing may not have been read or interpreted fully for the Dakota leaders.[64]

IMPLEMENTATION: VARIOUS PERCEPTIONS

Henry Sibley himself did not know the exact nature of the provisions in the treaty until after the signing. Writing to American Fur Company official Ramsay Crooks, he stated, "the whole treaty is but one series of iniquity & wrong and the half breeds here are so exasperated they will not move a step with the

Indians, but will go by themselves. This is the boasted paternal regard for the poor Indians, 'O shame, where is thy blush!'" He noted that part of Article 3, which provided a parcel of land for Taliaferro's interpreter Scott Campbell, had been kept secret. "Not one of our number knew of this provision till the Indians were called upon to sign it after it was read to them." In the end, the grant to Campbell was stricken from the treaty by Congress.[65]

In fact, Sibley's own behavior exemplified the difficulties of getting a fair treaty for the Dakota. Sibley supported the American effort to secure the Dakota land through a cession in the hope that he might then have the Dakota accounts on his trader company books satisfied. On the other hand, Sibley claimed he was concerned about providing for the material well-being of the Dakota, many of whom trusted him and some of whom were related to him through their extended kinship system, based on his relationship with a Dakota woman. By expressing his concern and by actually taking some actions that addressed benefits to the Dakota, Sibley was able to maintain his influence with them and encourage their acquiescence to the cession in the treaty—which of course would secure his own material well-being.

While it is arguably the case that Sibley's efforts had a beneficial effect on the Dakota in terms of their ability to maintain and provide for a decent way of life, the documentary evidence makes clear that his central concern throughout was to maintain his own financial security and also to secure his position in the growing immigrant-settler community. In a letter written to Ramsay Crooks after the treaty was signed, Sibley demonstrated that neither he nor the other traders would be satisfied with what they got out of the treaty for the land east of the Mississippi. He wrote, "The Sioux Indians leave today for home, having come to the conclusion not to treat for the land West of the Miss[issippi], which I am not sorry for, as we can make much better treaties at home than we can here." He was already thinking of the next treaty.[66]

After the treaty signing, Dakota leaders met with Sac and Fox to negotiate for peace and then returned to the Upper Mississippi. Nearly nine months elapsed between the Dakota treaty signing and its formal proclamation, with an additional delay before the promised annuities would begin arriving at the agency. This period was filled with anxiety, fueled in part because even before the treaty was proclaimed white lumbermen, loggers, and settlers had begun to come into the region. Two years after the treaties were signed, the first sawmill on the St. Croix was put in operation at Marine. Five years later, in 1844, lumber manufacture was begun at Stillwater.[67]

In May 1838 Taliaferro noted that several Dakota chiefs came to the agency to report their dissatisfaction, based on "reports all winter unpleasant to the Indians—& calculated to render them suspicious of the government and dissatisfied with their tr[e]aty—& if practicable with their Agent and Interpreters."

1837

Three major treaties signed by the Ojibwe (July 29), Ho-Chunk or Winnebago (November 1), and Dakota (September 29) cede all of their land east of the Mississippi River.

They had been worried "that the treaty would not be fulfilled—that their people thought they would be deceived—with many other idle Stories." He noted, "It is a hard matter for the Agent to disabuse their Ears as to much ridiculous stuff Infused into their minds." Taliaferro tried to quell the rumors they heard, though his task was considerably difficult in the case of the islands, as they had been included in the land cession contrary to Dakota wishes. A few days later Taliaferro wrote that he told visiting chiefs "to say nothing about *Islands* which had been sold nor the land—but leave the whites alone and not seek to disturb Set[t]lers nor to make war on the Chippewas on the Lands which they had sold to the United States."[68]

Some of the annuity goods and money began to be paid in the fall of 1838. However, in the years ahead, the first provision in Article 2 proved to be a more lasting problem. Under the treaty, the U.S. government would "invest the sum of $300,000 (three hundred thousand dollars) in such safe and profitable State stocks as the President may direct, and to pay to the chiefs and braves as aforesaid, annually, forever, an income of not less than five per cent. thereon; a portion of said interest, not exceeding one third, to be applied in such manner as the President may direct, and the residue to be paid in specie, or in such other manner, and for such objects, as the proper authorities of the tribe may designate." Strictly interpreted this clause would have provided the Dakota, apart from any other treaty arrangements, with an annual payment of ten thousand dollars in perpetuity to be divided up by the tribal leadership. Another five thousand dollars would be applied for whatever the president decided. Government officials appear to have assumed the government would spend this money for educational programs, including the missionary schools. Paying this money directly to the Dakota was opposed by missionaries, who felt it would "render them indolent and dissipated," though their point of view was hardly disinterested.[69]

There had been no real discussion of schools in the treaty negotiations. On the second day, Commissioner Harris had noted that with the money received from selling the lands the Dakota could "buy a great many comforts" and could use it to "build churches, to establish schools, to procure blacksmiths." When the first part of Article 2 was initially presented to the Dakota, Harris stated that the interest on the principal, which was then $200,000, "would be sufficient to maintain schools support Blacksmiths and all the necessary articles if given them at once it would be soon lost." At the same time, this first draft of the treaty contained $170,000 for "agricultural purposes, smiths, etc." Throughout the process the Dakota had never mentioned schools. The closest they came to the subject was when Kaȟboka (Koc Mo Ko, the Drifter), the chief from the Black Dog village and later Cloud Man's village, asked for help in teaching them how to plant corn and "cultivate our fields."[70]

Even the ratified treaty did not refer to schools, but it contained in the fifth provision of Article 2 a promise "to expend annually for twenty years, for the benefit of Sioux Indians, parties to this treaty, the sum of $8,250 (eight thousand two hundred and fifty dollars) in the purchase of medicines, agricultural implements and stock, and for the support of a physician, farmers, and blacksmiths, and for other beneficial objects."

The official government journal kept during the 1837 treaty negotiation makes clear the divergence between the recorded statements and conversations of government officials and Indian people and the resulting wording in the treaty. Despite the Dakota's specific requests, language appeared in the treaty that did not follow their wishes. As a result, misunderstandings increased in the years that followed. In particular, Dakota people were not content to have the decision about the school fund left entirely in the hands of government officials. For several years the money was not spent at all, accumulating to the amount of fifty thousand dollars in 1850. This fact would be a bone of contention leading up to the treaty negotiations in 1851.[71]

The misunderstandings that arose both during the negotiations for the Treaty of 1837 and later during its implementation illustrate a number of misconceptions over the terms of the treaty itself that reflect a deeper cultural divergence in the relationship the two peoples at the treaty table had with the land. The Americans assumed the Dakota would be operating out of the American narrative, with its distinctive view of land as subject to possession and therefore sale. The Dakota at this time, however, are unlikely to have embraced this view—or even to have fully comprehended it. They would have had to change the entire self-understanding of their identity and the land in which they lived. The historical record does not support such a conclusion.

THE TREATIES OF TRAVERSE DES SIOUX AND MENDOTA, 1851

By 1840 the population of the western division of Wisconsin Territory, including land between the Mississippi and the St. Croix rivers, was 351 whites. According to historian William W. Folwell, the population of the rest of the region stretching to the Missouri that would become Minnesota Territory, including whites and "half-breeds: living apart from Native people," was likely less than double that number, even counting the garrison at Fort Snelling, the missionaries, and the people at trading posts. In contrast there were as many as thirty thousand native people of various tribes in the same region, most of them consisting of various groups of the Dakota Oçeti Šaƙowiŋ.[72]

In 1841 James Duane Doty, governor of Wisconsin Territory, negotiated a treaty with the Dakota to create an Indian territory in the region west of the

1841

The Dakota sign two treaties with the U.S. government ceding their lands west of the Mississippi River, but the treaties are never ratified.

Mississippi. The 1841 treaty was negotiated by Doty at the instigation of Secretary of War John Bell, a longtime supporter of schemes for the "civilization" of Indian tribes. It provided for the cession of land but at the same time created within the ceded area an Indian territory consisting of much of present-day Minnesota—a northern counterpart of the Oklahoma Indian Territory established in 1834. Indian people and a few government employees and traders would be the only inhabitants. Under the treaty, this territory would be governed by provisions similar to those included in the trade and intercourse laws governing the area defined under federal law as Indian country.[73]

The treaty provided that the ceded area would be allotted for the settlement of Indian tribes for agricultural purposes, "within which no white man shall be allowed to settle or remain except by the permission of the President." The area would be governed by "such government, rules and regulations as shall be established by the government of the United States therein; and a governor or superintendent shall be appointed therefor." Trade in the territory would be strictly controlled, with a representative appointed by the territory's superintendent or governor to trade with each band in the region. These traders would be required to "comply with all the laws for regulation of trade and intercourse with the Indian and for the government of said territory."[74]

Supporters of this agreement saw it as a way of getting around problems with many treaties which, among other things, allowed for "unlimited intercourse with the frontier settlers which . . . brought liquor among the Indians." The treaty would remove the Indians "far into the interior, and beyond the limits of the future State of Iowa, where it would be impossible for the whites to introduce whiskey among them." Doty's treaty aroused a great deal of opposition and was finally rejected by the Senate in August 1842. One of the many criticisms leveled—in particular by powerful Missouri senator Thomas Hart Benton—was that the treaty gave the president and executive branch congressional prerogatives to specify the form of government within the proposed Indian territory. As a result, the Senate did not ratify the treaty.[75]

As loggers and settlers came into the region between the Mississippi and St. Croix rivers during the 1840s, older economic activities such as the fur trade became less important. Traders increasingly sought to position themselves to benefit from the new situation. Men like Henry Sibley were eager for a treaty that would include payments such as those Taliaferro had warned about in 1837, for so-called debts on the part of the Dakota. The traders were prepared to use all their influence to bring about a Dakota treaty that would benefit them.

When Wisconsin became a state in 1848, those living in the residue of Wisconsin Territory west of the St. Croix River sought to organize a new territory under the name *Minnesota*. At a convention in Stillwater in the summer of 1848, Sibley was elected to represent the region as a delegate to Congress. In

December 1848 Sibley went to Washington, where in January he was allowed to take a seat representing Wisconsin Territory. In the next few months a bill to create Minnesota Territory made it through the House and Senate, passing both in March. Soon after, Alexander Ramsey, a thirty-four-year-old Whig politician from Pennsylvania, was appointed territorial governor.[76]

1849

Minnesota Territory is organized, with Alexander Ramsey as the first territorial governor.

Ramsey soon became a chief player in bringing about the cession of the remaining Dakota lands in Minnesota. Almost as soon as he arrived to take office as governor, Ramsey, with the support of many whites in the territory, began urging his superiors to capitalize on what he represented as the Indians' eagerness to sell their lands. Ramsey brought with him an expansionist view of the possibilities for the new territory that permitted him to make common cause with Democrat and trader Henry Sibley. These men, who might be rivals on certain national and local issues, became allies in the effort to acquire the "Suland," as it was called at that time, creating a powerful movement to separate the Dakota from their land. The first attempt at a treaty occurred in 1849, after Commissioner of Indian Affairs Orlando Brown wrote to Secretary of the Interior Thomas Ewing recommending the negotiation of cessions with the Dakota, "in order to make room for the emigrants now going in large numbers to the new Territory of Minnesota." Ewing approved his recommendation and appointed as commissioners to conduct the negotiations Alexander Ramsey and John Chambers, former governor of Iowa. In September Ramsey asked Sibley to send out runners to notify Dakota chiefs to come to Mendota for a treaty council.[77]

Most Dakota had left for their fall hunts, so few came. Among those who did was Chief Wabasha, who spoke about the issues remaining from earlier treaties, particularly the Treaty of 1837. He asked that the so-called school fund left to the discretion of the president be paid. He stated that he did not know the islands were included in the sale of the land. Ramsey responded that these points could be discussed at some future time. He said that presents would be given to make up for their "supposed losses in the matter" of the islands. He stated that the islands were included in the sale "and explained to them what was meant by the term 'Islands,' as the Indians seemed to think there was a distinction between Islands surrounded by water navigable by Steamboats and those which were not." After refusing to negotiate a treaty, Wabasha gave Ramsey a sheet of paper "in the handwriting of Hon. H. H. Sibley." The statement included further discussion of the issues Wabasha raised in the meeting, including an apparent acknowledgment about selling the islands but stating "we did not suppose that advantage would be taken of this, to deprive us of large portions of land because a small stream runs around it, as is now the constriction [sic] of the treaty by the whites."[78]

While Sibley's involvement in helping the Dakota draft a statement appears to suggest sympathy with their concerns, he also had reasons to delay the treaty until he could ensure that its terms would be favorable to his own interests. Sibley had already expressed the belief that Chambers would oppose any effort to get payment for traders under the treaty. It would be better to delay until the right negotiators were appointed. Sibley was prepared to use his influence with both the Dakota and officials in Washington. Writing to another trader in November 1850, Sibley indicated "The Indians are all prepared to make a treaty when we tell them to do so, and such an one as I may dictate," adding that "I think I may safely promise you that no treaty can be made without our claims being first secured."[79]

On his return to Washington as territorial delegate in December 1849, Sibley lobbied for authorization to negotiate a treaty. He and Ramsey addressed a letter to Commissioner Brown with recommendations about how to achieve a treaty with the Dakota. They suggested the Indians would not sit unless assured that they would be permanently located on some portion of the proposed cession. Ramsey suggested they be allowed to remain on the lands north of the Minnesota, above Little Rapids, and that they be further permitted to hunt anywhere on the cession not occupied by whites until the president might direct otherwise. Further, the Indians objected to a limited annuity on the grounds that its expiration would work a hardship on them. A better method, thought both Ramsey and Sibley, was to give them a fixed sum for twenty years, then reduce it if their numbers had diminished, and continue the practice "until the band should become extinct." Finally, the Doty treaties had made the Indians aware of the value placed on their lands by the whites. There was no hope of buying the land for less than ten cents per acre. Buying twenty or twenty-five million acres at this price and deducting the traders' debts would leave a sum sufficient to give each Indian fifteen or sixteen dollars annually, with 5 percent interest on the principal. In September 1850 an Indian appropriation bill was passed that included fifteen thousand dollars for expenses to negotiate a treaty with the Dakota for "the extinguishment of their title to lands in Minnesota territory," but no authorization for negotiating a treaty was issued that fall. In 1851 Ramsey and Luke Lea, the new commissioner of Indian affairs (who was believed to be favorable to the traders), were instructed by Secretary of the Interior Alexander H. H. Stuart to effect a land cession treaty with the Dakota, permitting payment up to ten cents per acre and, if they thought it proper, allowing the Indians to remain on some part of the cession during the pleasure of the president, provided the locations were as remote as possible from the nearest white settlements.[80]

Ramsey and Lea determined to treat first with the "Upper Sioux," the Sisituŋwaŋ and Waȟpetuŋwaŋ Dakota, who were not receiving annuities from earlier treaties and would likely be more eager to sign than would the "Lower

Sioux," or Bdewakaŋtuŋwaŋ. This strategy had already been in place for a year. In September 1850 trader Martin McLeod assured Sibley that the "lower fellows" could only be induced to sign a treaty by first negotiating with upper bands, who were "friendly to us," and that negotiating with them first would bring the other Dakota to terms.[81]

Managing the negotiations in this way was especially important because the traders were attempting to get payments to themselves from the treaty, something Congress had already made illegal. By a resolution of the Senate on March 3, 1843, and reiterated by an Act of Congress on March 3, 1847, all annuities and other moneys and all goods paid under treaties must be divided and paid to heads of families or individuals entitled instead of to chiefs or their assignees, though with the proviso that the "discretion of the president" could make exceptions. As historian William W. Folwell noted, the phrase "transformed the prohibition into a mere piece of advice."[82]

Carefully planned, the subsequent treaties exemplified the theme of many such documents. As historian Roy Meyer has noted, they were sold to the Indians as being in their best interests, but "by a remarkable coincidence, what was deemed best for the Indians was invariably also to the advantage of the government, the traders, and above all, the land-hungry settlers."[83]

TREATY OF TRAVERSE DES SIOUX

On the evening of June 28, 1851, a party including Commissioner Lea, Governor Ramsey, Henry Sibley, and visiting dignitaries set out by steamboat from St. Paul for Traverse des Sioux to negotiate with the Sisituŋwaŋ and Waḣpetuŋwaŋ. Although they would not be signing the treaty negotiated there, Ta Oyate Duta, the third generation of the chiefs known as Little Crow, and members of the Kap'oża band also traveled on the steamboat. The party stopped at Fort Snelling at five o'clock the following morning and arrived at Traverse des Sioux on the morning of June 30. Trader Alexander Faribault and missionary Stephen R. Riggs were present to serve as interpreters. Although missionary Gideon Pond had been picked as one of the interpreters, the steamboat *Fort Snelling* departed before he reached the landing, something Pond himself found to be suspicious.[84]

Only a few of the Sisituŋwaŋ under the leadership of Iṡtaḣba, or Sleepy Eye, the acknowledged elder statesman of the Traverse des Sioux region known to both Dakota and whites, were present when the party arrived. Within a few days some of the Waḣpetuŋwaŋ from Lac qui Parle appeared, but many Sisituŋwaŋ from farther west did not join them for several weeks.

By the time the Dakota people and their representatives gathered for the great conclave, their ability to defend their understanding of their place in Minnesota, their ancestral relationship with the land, had been severely compromised by the region's growing white population, which competed with the Dakota for resources, making it difficult for them to provide for their material well-being over the winter. This was exacerbated by the failure of the United States to live up to its promises under the 1837 treaty, a fact that would be discussed in the treaty negotiations. The actions and words of government officials during the negotiations, repeatedly pressuring the Dakota, suggesting their decision was a simple one, added to the difficulties in which the Dakota found themselves.

For a number of days the commission met each morning with the expectation of further arrivals. Rations were issued to those already there. Finally, on July 18, as the "last of the upper bands of Sioux" appeared, negotiations began with the smoking of a pipe. Governor Ramsey addressed the gathered Dakota about "the distressed condition of yourselves, your wives, and your children" and the desire of the Great Father, "having a warm heart for you all," to do something to "mend your condition." Despite the fact that they had land, they sometimes starved in the summer and froze in the winter. Little or no game remained on their lands, so that the territory was "of little benefit to you." The Great Father did not have enough land for his white children to use but had "plenty of money and goods." His red children had more land than they needed. Thus an exchange could be made for their mutual advantage, Ramsey finished, noting that the Great Father had nothing more "at heart than the prosperity and welfare of the red man equally with the white."[85]

Commissioner Lea then addressed the question of what exactly the Great Father wished from the Dakota. First he noted that he was appointed "to look to the interests of his red children." Nothing he would ask of them would not be for their benefit. The land they had was of comparatively little value to them. He would not ask them to sell it if he thought it was not in their interest to do so. It would be to their advantage to sell all the land they owned as far west as Lake Traverse, up the Red River of the North and down to the western border of Iowa, east to the Mississippi. But it was not his purpose to deprive them of a home, a "comfortable and sufficient home for yourselves and families."[86]

After receiving "full compensation for all the land," the Dakota would be settled on a portion of it for "the future, permanent, and common home of you all." This situation would be better for them than to be "scattered over so large a region poor and often suffering from want of the necessaries of life." If they had a country provided for them high up on the Minnesota River, where they could have farms and improvements, they would be separated from the "bad influence of bad white men." Not only that but the Great Father would give them a great deal in addition, to make them comfortable in the future. Lea offered the example of "many other tribes of red men," though he did not name them, who had given up their large country, had received money and other provisions, and were now "happier and more comfortable and every year growing better and richer." Lea listed the other benefits the Dakota would receive in money and supplies during and after their removal. He concluded by adjourning the negotiations so the chiefs and headmen could talk about what they had heard.[87]

At noon on July 19, the negotiations opened again. The pipe was passed. Commissioner Lea said the Dakota had had time to discuss the proposed land sale. He asked for their response. According to the treaty journal, "Here ensued a long pause. No one appeared ready to speak on the part of the Indians." Then a Sisituŋwaŋ leader named Wiçaŋhpi Ite or Star Face, sometimes called "the Orphan," spoke, noting that not all of his "young men" or band members were present. The commissioner had stated the day before that he was glad to shake their hands, but he had not shaken everyone's hands. Wiçaŋhpi Ite ended by saying, "That is all I have to say."[88]

To this Ramsey responded testily, reminding them of the previous delay: "A man's life in this world is very short and each day should show some works. We have now been here three weeks doing nothing." On arriving at Traverse des Sioux the treaty commission had expected the Dakota to all be there ready to council. The business was of "vital consequence" to the Dakota, "but there must be an end to delay sometime." Provisions were getting low. There was no time to spare. The commissioners were slated to meet with the Bdewakaŋ-tuŋwaŋ and Waȟpekute in Mendota. The question, Ramsey said, was "a simple one, would the Dakota sell all their lands and get in return what would make them comfortable for many years," or would they starve in the midst of a wide country "destitute almost of game"? If they acquiesced to this exchange, the commissioners would surely agree easily upon "the formalities and details of what you should receive." Commissioner Lea added a few words elaborating on Ramsey's points.[89]

Wiçaŋhpi Ite responded that his young men, who had been en route, had met "some persons" apparently sent by the commissioners to tell them to turn back. Ramsey responded in words suggesting that he knew this. He said it was not necessary for all the chief's people or young men to be present for a treaty signing: the government only required chiefs and head men. He added, "by sending notice in time for them to turn back they are at least prevented from suffering" if the food supplies at the negotiation were to run out. After the negotiations were over, the young men could be sent something to satisfy them. They would all benefit from the treaty in any case.[90]

For the Dakota, chiefs acted only with the consent of their people. It was important for their bands to be well represented, so as to develop a consensus. The commissioners' demands interfered with development of that consensus. At this impasse, Sleepy Eye, the elder statesman in the Traverse des Sioux re-

Sioux Evening meal ~ Traverse des Sioux ~ July 20. 1851.

An evening meal among Dakota people gathered for the 1851 treaty negotiation at Traverse des Sioux was recorded by artist Frank B. Mayer on July 20. That day was a Sunday and, according to American custom, the negotiators did not meet.

gion, rose to make a statement: "Your coming and asking me for my country makes me sad; and your saying I am not able to do any thing with my country makes me still more sad. Those who are coming behind are my near relations and I expect certainly to see them here. That is all I have to say. I am going to leave and that is the reason I spoke. (Turning to the other See-see-to-ans he said 'come let us go.')"[91]

It is likely Sleepy Eye's statement was intended to provide a break in the negotiations at an awkward moment—an excuse to defuse the situation. However, at the time the meeting broke up, the commissioners were incensed. Ramsey immediately ordered that no more rations be distributed. Lea announced he would depart down the Minnesota River the next morning. The American flag was "struck and retired from the Council Ground" and plans were made for departure. Toward evening a "committee on the part of the Indians" said they would resume negotiations and disclaimed any intention to show disrespect.[92]

When negotiations continued two days later, on Monday, July 21, after a break on Sunday, when the commissioners would not have met anyway, Sleepy Eye stated, "We only wanted more time to consider. The young men who made a noise were waiting to have a ball play and thinking the Council over arose and as they did so made the disturbance which we were sorry for." Governor Ramsey was mollified. They had "a right for further time," but the manner of their departure "was objected to." He asked to hear anything the chiefs had to say. Upi Iyahdeya, or Extended Tail Feathers, asked "to know exactly the proposition made to us by the commissioners." The "chiefs and people" wanted to see "the particulars of your offer for our lands" in writing. Once they had received this paper they would "sit down on the top of the hill above us, consult among ourselves, come to a conclusion about it, and inform you what it is."[93]

At this point the treaty journal states that Lea "wrote out in detail the terms as verbally given at the previous meeting of the Council." The document contained a slightly more precise proposal, describing the territory to be ceded and the location for lands to be set aside for the Indians. It also gave actual money amounts, stating that "say $25,000 or $30,000" would be paid to them to arrange their affairs, prepare for removal, and subsist them in their new lands for a year. Finally, an annuity of $25,000 to $30,000 would be paid "for many years," part of it in goods and provisions and "other beneficial objects."[94]

Commissioner Lea then stated that though he had written down his proposition, he wished "to know certainly whether they intend to sell this country and have made up their minds to do so" before "we trouble ourselves further in relation to this business."[95]

It is unclear how the Dakota could make up their minds about the sale of their land without a more complete description of the treaty terms. Curly Head responded that they wished to sell "and we will give you our country if we are satisfied with your offers for it." Rather than providing details or the time to review them carefully, Commissioner Lea responded that any treaty "must be done quickly. As men and chiefs, not women and children, they ought to be able to act without delay." The Dakota were expected to give a definite response at the next meeting. Ramsey too seemed to think they ought to respond to what they had heard so far. If they were not satisfied with the terms, they must inform the commissioner about what they did want for their lands. The commissioners would then take the Dakota proposal into consideration.[96]

On July 22, at 7 AM, the negotiations began again, without any of the preliminaries mentioned on earlier days such as the passing of a pipe. Commissioner Lea asked for a response from the chiefs to the government's written proposal. Waȟpetuŋwaŋ leader Iyangmani, Running Walker, rose and handed Lea "a paper containing the terms upon which they would agree to sell." It is unclear what this paper contained, who wrote it, or with whom the Dakota leaders consulted in making it. A similar document, in Henry H. Sibley's handwriting, exists for the later Mendota treaty, which suggests that traders could also have been involved in preparing the one at Traverse des Sioux. In a later summary of the treaty negotiations, Lea and Ramsey stated, "some few of their own number having been taught to read had impressed them with an idea that their country was of immense value and they at first refused to treat unless the sum of six million dollars was paid them." No record of this figure appears in the treaty journal, which suggests that some negotiations were taking place outside the council. Commissioner Lea did not seem to anticipate any difficulty in accepting the terms proposed by the Dakota. He stated that the commissioners would look over the proposal "and as soon as we can draw up the necessary documents we will meet again to complete the work and sign the treaty. We will have our goods and medals ready for those who attend on that occasion and who behave well."[97]

Oddly, Governor Ramsey concluded the day by stating that the Great Father had proposed the treaty "because he is your friend. At any moment, he can have soldiers without number here for the protection of his friends." The final statement suggests the Dakota's proposal contained provisions that not all the leaders had wanted. Ramsey may have been assuring the chiefs they would be protected if they signed a document other Dakota did not like. Perhaps this too was a reflection of outside negotiations and manipulation.[98]

The council resumed at noon the next day. Lea reported the commissioners had accepted the Dakota's proposals and had prepared an English and a Dakota version of the treaty. Specifically, they had drawn up "a paper to be signed by you and ourselves containing the provisions which you have asked us to consent to." Nothing but "our kind feelings toward the Sioux could have induced us to agree to a treaty so favorable to them." Lea ordered the treaty read, in English and then in Dakota, by the missionary Stephen R. Riggs. The Dakota document written by Riggs provides important clues about exactly how the Dakota at Traverse des Sioux would have interpreted the treaty and by extension how the Dakota viewed the idea of the sale of land in general.[99]

Following the readings came a short pause, after which Ramsey and Lea both signed the treaty and asked the Dakota leaders to do the same. At this point Sleepy Eye rose to speak. The treaty journal reports that he "showed a disposition to make a speech and arose for that purpose but Col. Lea reminded him that the council was assembled for business not for talk." There had already been "sufficient time for talk," but they would "hear him briefly." Sleepy Eye began by stating that he hoped the Great Father would furnish the Dakota "some beef" and other provisions, "when the year comes to be white," that is, in the winter. He stated that the "young men" had hoped for a higher price for their land, though he did not mention an amount.

Commissioner Lea's response suggests a great deal more knowledge of Sleepy Eye's complaint than was recorded in the treaty journal. He claimed they had been given a treaty that they wanted and at a price "more than Sleepy Eyes has mentioned." Lea spoke scornfully about the chief, suggesting that "so old a chief as Sleepy Eye who has been to Washington would have understood better what we are paying especially after having had it explained to him so fully. We are paying them in fifty years a great deal more than the amount he

continued on page 180

According to the treaty journal, at a key moment during negotiations at Traverse des Sioux, Commissioner Luke Lea ordered the treaty read aloud in Dakota by the missionary Stephen R. Riggs, who along with the trader Alexander Faribault was an interpreter during the negotiations. The result was a written version of the Dakota version preserved, ever since, in the official treaty record.[v]

Translating any English text into Dakota is fraught with difficulties. The Dakota language scholar Carolynn Schommer stated that "the total language structure is much different from the English and no literal translation can be made from either language into the other." This phenomenon is compounded by the fact that Dakota was an oral language and those who attempted to write it down were, in Schommer's words, "transforming an oral language into written form." The task of writing down the Dakota language constituted a transformation of it by people who were not cognizant of the deep cultural importance of Dakota as it was meant to be spoken. The exchange of one Dakota word for an English word is therefore not a simple literal "translation." This truth becomes even more notable when we consider the text in context of the clashing cultures that encountered each other at the treaty table.[vi]

Samuel and Gideon Pond, the first Protestant missionaries to the Dakota, adapted the English alphabet to Dakota sounds in 1834. This first attempt at writing the Dakota language was hampered in that the Ponds' alphabet was missing a number of the guttural and nasalized sounds common in daily speech. They developed readers and religious teachings and began compiling a dictionary that was the core of what Stephen R. Riggs would publish later. By 1837 many Dakota people were reading and writing in their own language, not only to the missionaries but also to each other.[vii]

Riggs, who had been a missionary among the Dakota since the 1830s, had long been interested in learning the Dakota language and in compiling a dictionary. The year following the Treaty of 1851, Riggs was able to get the first version of his dictionary published by the Smithsonian Institution in Washington, DC. As a missionary, Riggs's purpose was to learn the language to be able to communicate Christian doctrine in Dakota. His task was rooted both theologically and economically in the eradication of Dakota culture and lifeways and the complete assimilation of the Dakota into the European-American agricultural way of life and property ownership.[viii]

In translating Christian concepts into Dakota, Riggs faced many obstacles because of the differences in the belief systems of Europeans and Dakota people. Many words had nuances in English that could not be duplicated in Dakota. For example, he wrote, in regard to the *wiçowoyaķe*, otherwise translated as "declaration, narration, or doctrine," "We have used this word for chapter," meaning the chapter of a book. Similarly, Riggs wrote about the word *wowakaŋ*, which he translated as "something supernatural," a version of the profound Dakota word *wakaŋ*, "We have used this word for holiness." It may have been as close as Riggs could get to the Christian concept, but neither "holiness" nor "supernatural" captured the nuances of the Dakota concept. It appears Riggs was not only a recorder of the Dakota language but a creator of many usages, some of which have persisted after his death.[ix]

Riggs faced the same challenges in translating the 1851 treaty. A simple word, like *article* in reference to a section of the treaty, posed some difficulties. The term Riggs chose, *oehde*, is associated with the physical action of "setting down" something, from the verb *ehde*. In his dictionary Riggs translated the noun as "a setting down; a saying, a verse, a sentence," though here as with other words, he may have sought to add meaning to a Dakota word which did not have the nuances of the English words he wished to attach to it. In other cases he dealt with these challenges by simply leaving out important passages. The language in Article 4 to the effect that $1,360,000 would "remain in trust with the United States, and five per cent interest thereon ››

⟩⟩ to be paid, annually, to said Indians for the period of fifty years, . . . which shall be in full payment of said balance," which in effect meant that the principal would never be paid to them, was simply omitted in the Dakota-language version.[x]

In other cases Riggs made the same kinds of decisions he had in relation to other English words for which there was no Dakota equivalent. A particular problem came from the terms used to refer to the sale of land. Even the Dakota's experience in the fur trade for almost 150 years had not led them to adopt a cash economy, in which everything had a price and everything could be bought and sold—least of all the land. In fact, as many historians have shown, the gift economy of the fur trade represented an adaptation of Europeans to native practices rather than the other way around. Nothing had prepared the Dakota for the idea that lands could be sold. Goods in the fur trade were exchanged through gift, credit, and generalized reciprocity, in which few goods were exchanged one for one, let alone for a sum of money. Only with the first treaties of the 1830s, in which some payments were made in cash, did the Dakota experience the concept of getting and paying for things with money. And in such cases cash was used almost as soon as it was paid, to buy goods from the traders often present at treaty payments. In any case, it is not clear that by the 1850s money was yet understood as something that could measure all things produced with human effort, as well as those things created by the Master of Life.[xi]

Article 2 of the official English version of the treaty stated that the Dakota "agree to cede, and do hereby cede, sell and relinquish to the United States, all their lands in the state of Iowa; and, also all their lands in the territory of Minnesota." The important English words in this passage are "cede, sell, and relinquish." The Dakota words Riggs chose to translate this passage and others relating to ceding and selling failed to capture the cultural nuances of the English words, substituting the entirely different nuances of Dakota words. For the word *cede* Riggs chose *erpe-*

yapi. The word like all those in his treaty version was spelled without diacritical marks or special characters. In his dictionary, the word was *ehpeyapi,* translated by phrases such as to give up, to throw away, to put aside, to leave, to forsake, and to lose, and like many Dakota verbs is dependent upon context for its interpretation. This range of meanings shows in a pronounced way the difficulty of translation.[xii]

What understanding would the Dakota have had of how one might abandon the land considered to be a relative? In the past the Dakota had spoken in diplomacy of sharing land or acquiescing in its occupation by the Ojibwe, but it is hard to imagine a full understanding of how one might throw land away. The difficulty of using the term is further demonstrated by the fact that Riggs also used it in the provision of Article 4 to communicate that $12,000 of the total treaty fund would be dedicated, that is "set aside," and applied to agricultural expenses. Exactly how would the Dakota word contain the meanings of the English word relating to land cessions? More likely, since the English word *cede* is associated inextricably with property rights, it may have been impossible to find a word in Dakota which adequately conveyed its meaning since the Dakota did not recognize the idea of property rights over land.

As for the word *sale,* Riggs chose *wiyopekiya,* spelled the same way in the dictionary, with that meaning. The word was a version of *iyopekiya,* which Riggs translated as meaning "to reprove, chide, to correct, punish, to trade for something else, exchange." Here too it is difficult to recognize the kinds of hands-off economic exchanges that typify the word used in English. Instead it appears to communicate the full range of reciprocal exchanges the Dakota had had with traders for almost two centuries. Such exchanges would have fit within the concept of Anglo-American property law but are distinct from the Anglo-American traditional practice in relating to "real property," that is, land.[xiii]

The confusion about the Dakota terminology for selling and ceding land is shown starkly in a later interpretation of the treaty given by Taŋka Naẑiŋhaŋ (Standing Buffalo), a chief of the Sisituŋwaŋ of Lake Traverse, son of 1851 treaty signer Wiȼaŋħpi Ite (Star Face), and namesake of an earlier Lake Traverse chief. In a statement recorded by a Catholic priest in 1864, Taŋka Naẑiŋhaŋ said, "I loved my lands, it was on them that I had been raised and fed, it was the land of my fathers. I therefore had reason to love it. In the meantime the Americans came and demanded my lands[.] I at once acceded for I loved the Americans[.] I sold my lands for fifty years." Taŋka Naẑiŋhaŋ listed other features of the treaty, suggesting that he had been at the negotiation and was familiar with the contents of the treaty. Fifty years, of course, was the duration of the annuity payments. This suggests, given the difficulty of communicating the very idea of land sale, a reasonable understanding of the treaty as essentially a fifty-year lease—similar in some respects to the earlier view of the Treaty of 1805. Given that the U.S. government planned to keep the principal amount from which the interest was to be paid to the Dakota in annuities, there was a real symmetry of understanding, though one not acknowledged by the white negotiators.[xiv]

Another revealing facet of Riggs's treaty translation concerns the notorious provision in the first phrase of the first provision of Article 4 that set aside $275,000 to allow the Upper bands of Dakota "to enable them to settle their affairs" prior to their removal from the lands ceded. This opening wedge allowed the traders to profit from the treaty despite a law that prevented such payments for trade debts. Riggs rendered the phrase in Dakota as "tuwewe cante en wicayuzapi token owicakiranpi kte cinhan okihiwicaye kta," which would translate into English literally as "whoever they treated badly they will hold them in their hearts" or perhaps "make amends to." It can be seen here that Riggs in trying to communicate the innocuous phrase "settle their affairs" managed to bring in the concept of a debt owed by the Dakota. While it did not refer directly to the traders,

it does in an important sense put back into the treaty the concept of debt that was expressly forbidden by Congress. The fact that Riggs wrote the treaty in this way suggests he cannot have been unfamiliar with the so-called trader's paper that Dakota people were asked to sign after signing the treaty itself. This complicity is something he undoubtedly had in common with most of the other officials present at Traverse des Sioux, who willfully participated in the corruption of the treaty for their own selfish ends. None of them appear to have truly appreciated the Dakota's desire to simply continue to live in their homelands.

In summary, a look at Riggs's translation of the treaty into Dakota raises the question of whether the Dakota, hearing the treaty being read out at Traverse des Sioux, could possibly have understood that it meant they would be totally separated from their ancestral homeland in which was rooted their identity, culture, and language. They certainly understood that the treaty would open the way for a further influx of European settlers, but to suggest, as the idea of "cede" and "sell" do in an English language context that includes Anglo-American real property principles, that possession to the exclusion of all others was fully understood by the Dakota could only have meant that they were severing their relationship with the land to which they were deeply related. The treaty would effect a divorce of the Dakota people and the land that gave them birth and life. Such an understanding is hard to imagine given the expression of deep kinship with the land found in the Dakota language, to say nothing of the fact that the treaty included promises of the Dakota remaining on their homeland, though confined to a narrow reservation along the Minnesota River. Without that provision in Article 3 which promised, in the supplemental Article 3 (see below) in a different form, to reserve a portion of the land they "ceded" for their homes, it is hard to imagine the Dakota would have agreed to the treaty at all, even in the face of the difficult circumstances in which they found themselves at the treaty table.

>>

>>

Printed Treaty Language	Copy, in the Dakota Language, of a Treaty Between the United States of America and the Wah-pay-toan and See-see-toan bands of the Dakota or Sioux Indians. Concluded at Traverse des Sioux. Minnesota Territory July 23d AD. 1851	English Translation of Dakota version
Articles of a treaty made and concluded at Traverse des Sioux, upon the Minnesota River, in the Territory of Minnesota, on the twenty-third day of July, eighteen hundred and fifty-one, between the United States of America, by Luke Lea, Commissioner of Indian Affairs, and Alexander Ramsey, governor and ex-officio superintendent of Indian affairs in said Territory, commissioners duly appointed for that purpose, and See-see-toan and Wah-pay-toan bands of Dakota or Sioux Indians.	Minisota Makoce, Minisota wakpa ohna Oiyuwege eciyapi kin hen, Canpaxa wi anpetu iwikcemna nonpa sanpa yamni, omaka kektopawinge wanjidan sanpa opawinge xahdogan sanpa wikcemna zaptan sam wanjidan, Isantanka Wicaxtayatapi nom, unma Luke Lea eciyapi, Ikcewicaxta oyate kin awanyagkiyapi kin hee, qa unma ix Alexander Ramsey Minisota makoce en Wicaxtayatapi qa Ikcewicaxta en unpi kin atayedan awanwicayake cin, hena oza Isantanka Wicaxtayatapi tanka uwicaxi; hena eepi qa Dakota Warpetonwan oyate Sisitonwan ko mniciyapi qa makoce aiapi, wokiconze kagapi qa tanyan yuxtanpi. Oehde kin hena kaketu.	Minnesota Country, on the Minnesota River at Traverse des Sioux July 23rd, 1851, two United States officials, one called Luke Lea, who looks after the Indian people, and the other Alexander Ramsey, the leader of Minnesota Country and who looks after all of the Indians there, were both asked by the United States government to come, they are here, and the Wahpeton and Sisseton Dakota people also, gathered and spoke about the land, they made an agreement and finished it well. So these are the settlements.

ARTICLE 1.

It is stipulated and solemnly agreed that the peace and friendship now so happily existing between the United States and the aforesaid bands of Indians, shall be perpetual.

Oehde I.

Isantanka Oyate qa Dakota Warpetonwan qa Sisitonwan ewicakiyapi kin hena okiciciyapi qa odakonkiciyapi kin ohinniyan detanhan cantekiciyuzapi kta e nakaha awicakehan wakiconzapi qa yuxtanpi.

Setting Down I.

The people of the United States and the Wahpeton and Sisseton Dakota people, those named, help each other and are allied with each other, earlier this day they purposefully resolved and concluded forever from this time to hold each other's hearts.

ARTICLE 2.

The said See-see-toan and Wah-pay-toan bands of Dakota or Sioux Indians, agree to cede, and do hereby cede, sell, and relinquish to the United States, all their lands in the State of Iowa; and, also all their lands in the Territory of Minnesota, lying east of the following line, to wit: Beginning at the junction of the Buffalo River with the Red River of the North; thence along the western bank of said Red River of the North, to the mouth of the Sioux Wood River; thence along the western bank of said Sioux Wood River to Lake Traverse; thence, along the western shore of said lake, to the southern extremity thereof; thence in a direct line, to the junction of Kampeska Lake with the Tchan-kas-an-data, or Sioux River; thence along the western bank of said river to its point of intersection with the northern line of the State of Iowa; including all the islands in said rivers and lake.

Oehde II.

Dakota Sisitonwan oyate Warpetonwan ko Makoce wiyopekiyapi qa deciyatanhan erpeyapi qa Isantanka Wicaxtayatapi tanki qupi, makoce wan Iowa eciyapi kin tohanyan tawapi hecinhan, qa Minisota makoce kin en, Tatanka kagapi wakpadan mdote kin hetanhan aupi qa Rara ohna tatowam ayapi, Caninkpa wakpa ecen ayapi, qa Mdehdakinyan wiyorpeyatanhan huta kin ecen ayapi, qa Ptansinta etanhan owotanna ayapi ecen Kampeska mde mdote kin hen Wakpa Ipakxan iyorpeyapi, qa wakpa kin he ohn ayapi qa Ipakxan kin hehan aipi; wakpa qa mde kin ohna wita kin hena owasin koya; icagopi kin hetanhan makoce iwiyohiyanpatanhan wanke cin ocowasin kapi.

Setting Down II.

The Sisseton and Wahpeton Dakota people together sell and from this place give up land and give it to the United States government: whatever land in Iowa that is theirs, and the land in Minnesota. They mean all the land continuing eastward from the lines coming from where the mouth of Buffalo effigy creek and the falls upstream go together, along the Woods end river from the western shore of Lake Traverse, going straight from Ottertail, to where the mouth of Kampeska lake and the River of the Bend meet, and on through the river and arrive at the Bend; including all those islands in the rivers and the lakes.

ARTICLE 3.

[This language agreed upon at Traverse des Sioux was stricken by the U.S. Senate.]

In part consideration of the foregoing cession the United States do hereby set apart for the future occupancy and home of the Dakota Indians, parties to this treaty, to be held by them as Indian lands are held, all that tract of country on either side of the Minnesota river, from the western boundary of the lands herein ceded, east to the Tchay-tam-bay river on the north and to the Yellow Medicine river on the south side—to extend on each side a distance of not less than ten miles from the general course of said river: the boundaries of said tract to be marked out by as straight lines as practicable, whenever deemed expedient by the President, and in such manner as he shall direct.

Oehde III.

Dakota makoce tawapi erpeyapi kin heon etanhan makoce onxpa en ounyanpi kta qa ohna tipi maga ko içicagapi kta e Isantanka Wicaxtayatapi tanka wicaqu; Ikcewicaxta makoce yuhapi kin hecen hduhapi kta; wiyorpeyata icagopi kin hetanhan aupi, Wakpa Minisota anokatanhan wiyutapi hanska wikcemna (anokatanhan wiyotanhan imani) hecen aupi qa Pejihutazi qapi mdote kin etanhan wiyutapi wikcemna hen iyorpeyapi; qa unma eciyatanhan Cetanbe wakpa mdote kin etanhan wiyutapi wikcemna hen iyorpeyapi, qa wakpa kin hena ohnahna ayapi qa ecen wakpa Minisota iyahdeyapi kta. Isantanka Wicaxtayatapi tanka kin tohan econpi kta iyecetu dake ça econwicaxi kinhan hecen owotanna iyutapi kta.

Setting Down III.

Because the Dakota give up their land, they will be sent to live on a piece of land that the United States government gives them and they will make houses and fields for themselves. The Indians will keep the lands they have from a western line coming ten miles long on both sides of the Minnesota River (on both sides walking south) they mean ten miles from where they meet at the mouth of the Yellow Medicine; and on the other side ten miles from where they meet at the mouth of the Sparrow hawk river, and where those rivers go together and reach the Minnesota River. When the United States President demands and orders them to do so, then they will measure it straight.

>>

The first page of the Stephen R. Riggs translation of the 1851 Traverse des Sioux treaty begins with the words Mini Sota Makoce, *chosen to translate the phrase* Minnesota Territory.

>> **ARTICLE 4.**

In further and full consideration of said cession, the United States agree to pay to said Indians the sum of one million six hundred and sixty-five thousand dollars ($1,665,000,) at the several times, in the manner and for the purposes following, to wit:

1st. To the chiefs of the said bands, to enable them to settle their affairs and comply with their present just engagement; and in consideration of their removing themselves to the country set apart for them as above, which they agree to do within two years, or sooner, if required by the President, without further cost or expense to the United States, and in consideration of their subsisting themselves the first year after their removal, which they agree to do without further cost or expense on the part of the United States, the sum of two hundred and seventy-five thousand dollars, $275,000):Provided, That said sum shall be paid to the chiefs in such manner as they, hereafter, in open council shall request, and as soon after the removal of said Indians to the home set apart for them, as the necessary appropriation therefor shall be made by Congress.

2d. To be laid out under the direction of the President for the establishment of manual-labor schools; the erection of mills and blacksmith shops, opening farms, fencing and breaking land, and for such other beneficial objects as may be deemed most conducive to the prosperity and happiness of said Indians, thirty thousand dollars, ($30,000.) The balance of said sum of one million six hundred and sixty-five thousand dollars, ($1,665,000,) to wit: one million three hundred and sixty thousand dollars ($1,360,000) to remain in trust with the United States, and five per cent interest thereon to be paid, annually, to said Indians for the period of fifty years, commencing the first day of July, eighteen hundred and fifty-two (1852,) which shall be in full payment of said balance, principal and interest, the said payment to be applied under the direction of the President, as follows, to wit:

Oehde IV.

Hehan makoce erpeyapi kin heon etanhan Isantanka Wicaxtayatapi tanka Dakota kakenken ecawicakicon kta, qa kakenken wicakicicajuju kta.

1. Warpetonwan Sisitonwan ko, Wicaxayatapi wicayuhapi taku econpi kta hecinhan hduxtan wicakiye kta, qa tuwewe cante en wicayuzapi token owicakiranpi kte cinhan okihiwicaye kta; qa makoce wicaqupi kin ekta iyotankapi kta, detanhan waniyetu nonpa qa ix iyokpani, Isantanka Wicaxtayatapi tanka econwicaxi kinhan econpi kta; qa toiçikxupi kin on taku sanpa wokajuju dapi kte xni; qa nakun kta iyotankapi kinhan waniyetu tokaheya on taku yutapi opiçitunpi kta; qa heon taku sanpa wokajuju dapi kte xni; hena owasin okihiwicaye kta e on mazaska kektopawinge ece opawinge nonpa sanpa kektopawinge wikcemna xakowin sanpa kektopawinge zaptan. Tohan Dakota ekta iyotankapi qa mazaska iyog ehnakapi kinhan hehan Wicaxtayatapi wicayuhapi kin hena he wicaqupi kta.

2. Tipi ohna waonspe wicakiyapi kta, wiyutpan tipi, canbasdesdeca tipi, mazakaga tipi ko kagapi kta qa maga wicakicagapi kta, qa token Dakota tanyan unpi kta naceca, on owicakiyapi kta mazaska kektopawinge wikcemna yamni erpeyapi kta.

Setting Down IV.

Then because they gave up the land, the United States government will do this for the Dakota, and will pay them like this:

1. The leaders of the Wahpeton and Sisseton will be allowed to finish up their affairs, and will be able to make amends to whoever was treated badly; and they will go to land they were given in two years or less from now, when the United States government orders them, they will do it; and transport themselves and not demand additional payment; and when they settle there for the first year they will buy their own food; and therefore will not demand any additional payment; to enable them to do all these things, $275,000. When the Dakota settle there and the money is put aside, then the officials will give it to them.

2. For building schools, mill houses, saw mills, and blacksmiths, and for making fields for themselves, and however they might live well, they will be helped, $30,000 will be put aside.

3d. For a general agricultural improvement and civilization fund, the sum of twelve thousand dollars, ($12,000.)

4th. For educational purposes, the sum of six thousand dollars, ($6,000.)

5th. For the purchase of goods and provisions, the sum of ten thousand dollars, ($10,000.)

6th. For money annuity, the sum of forty thousand dollars,($40,000.)

3. Qa nakun makoce on tanyan kajujupi kta, omaka eca kakenken econpi kta ce; Waxunpa wi 1852 hetanhan waniyetu wikcemna zaptan hehanyan.

(A.) Maga ikicanye kin hena, wanuyanpi opetunpi kta, qa taku hecekcen owasin on mazaska kektopawinge akenonpa erpeyapi kta.

(B.) Waonspekiyapi kin on mazaska kektopawinge xakpe

(C.) Woyuha qa taku yutapi opetonpi kta on mazaska kektopawinge wikcemna.

(D.) Mazaska ece omaka eca wicaqupi kta kektopawinge wikcemna topa.

3. And also for the land, they will be paid well every year, from July 1852, for 50 years.

(A.) For buying tame animals and field implements, and all things like that, $12,000 will be put aside.

(B.) For the teachers, $6,000.

(C.) For possessions and food they will buy, $10,000

(D.) Money to give them every year, $40,000.

ARTICLE 5.

The laws of the United States, prohibiting the introduction and sale of spirituous liquors in the Indian country shall be in full force and effect throughout the territory hereby ceded and lying in Minnesota until otherwise directed by Congress or the President of the United States.

Oehde V.

Isantanka wicoope eciyatanhan, Ikcewicaxta tamakoce kin en mini wakan aupi qa wiyopekiyapi kte cin he terindapi ece kin, makoce nakaha opetonpi tinskoya Minisota eciyapi, hinskoya hen hecetu kte; tohanyan Isantanka omniciye tanka qa ix Wicaxtayatapi tanka togye wakiconzapi xni hehanyan.

Setting Down V.

From American laws, selling and bringing liquor into the Indians' land is forbidden, all around these lands newly bought in Minnesota; until Congress or United States officials decide differently.

ARTICLE 6.

Rules and regulations to protect the rights of persons and property among the Indians, parties to this treaty, and adapted to their condition and wants, may be prescribed and enforced in such manner as the President or the Congress of the United States, from time to time, shall direct.

In testimony whereof, the said Commissioners, Luke Lea and Alexander Ramsey, and the undersigned Chiefs and Headmen of the aforesaid See-see-toan and Wah-pay-toan bands of Dakota or Sioux Indians, have hereunto subscribed their names and affixed their seals, in duplicate, at Traverse des Sioux, Territory of Minnesota, this twenty-third day of July, one thousand eight hundred and fifty-one.

Oehde VI.

Qa Dakota tona wowapi kin de yutanpi qa opapi kin hena owasin iye tanatayedan tanyan unpi kta, tawarpaya xuktanka ko tanyan hduhapi kta e heon woope qa wicokiconze, tona on waxteya unpi kta iyececa, hena wicakicagapi kta qa iyecetu wicakiciciyapi kta; Wicaxtayatapi tanka qa omniciye tanka kin tokenken qa tonhanhan eyapi kinhan.

Nakaha wicaunkapi kta e heon Isantanka Wicaxtayatapi, Luke Lea eciyapi qa Alexander Ramsey eciyapi, qa Dakota Warpetonwan qa Sisitowan wicaxtayatapi akicita wicayuhapi ko wowapi kin de yutanpi qa caje içicagapi. Oiyuwege ekta Minisota makoce kin en omaka 1851, Canpaxa wi, anpetu iwikcemna nonpa sanpa yamni.

Setting Down VI.

And those Dakota who honor and follow this treaty, all of them individually will be well taken care of also their belongings and horses laws and rights for taking good care of them will be made good for them, the President and Congress will decide how and for how long those things will be provided and rights will be given.

Now we are all truthful, therefore the United States officials, named Luke Lea and Alexander Ramsey, and Wahpeton and Sisseton Dakota leaders and soldiers also honor this treaty and write their names. At Traverse des Sioux in Minnesota country in the year 1851, the 23rd day of July.

continued from page 172

says the young men want for the land." Governor Ramsey joined in heaping scorn on Sleepy Eye, saying the chief "is not a very good hand to manage the business of his people and if it had not been for other Indians wiser and more vigilant they would not have obtained so much as now will be received by the treaty about to be signed." Insulting Sleepy Eye appears to have been a strategy on Ramsey's part, designed to undermine his standing among the Dakota, but it reflected a general contempt on the part of the officials for all the Dakota.[100]

At this point the chiefs and headmen were called forward to sign the treaty. One of them, Upi Iyahdeya, or Extended Tail Feathers, spoke, saying that contrary to the commissioners' thinking, the government was not offering a great amount for their lands: "All we get for them will at last belong to the white man. The money comes to us but will all go to the white man who trades with us." There was no response to this comment, but the truth of what he said would soon be demonstrated.[101]

According to the language of the treaty, in return for their land cession the Sisituŋwaŋ and Waĥpetuŋwaŋ received a reservation on the Upper Minnesota extending for ten miles on either side of the river and from the western end of the cession down to the Yellow Medicine River. In addition they would receive the equivalent of $1,665,000. Of this, $30,000 was to be spent to establish schools, blacksmith shops, and mills and to open farms on the new reservation. A principal of $1,360,000 was to bear interest at a rate of 5 percent for a period of fifty years, with interest to be used for the benefit of the Indians, who would receive a $40,000 cash annuity and $10,000-worth of goods and provisions annually; $12,000 was to be spent for general agricultural and civilization purposes; $6,000 for education.[102]

Finally, a sum of $275,000 was set aside to pay "to the chiefs of the said bands, to enable them to settle their affairs and comply with their present just engagement; and in consideration of their removing themselves to the country set apart for them as above, which they agree to do within two years, or sooner, if required by the President, without further cost or expense to the United States, and in consideration of their subsisting themselves the first year after their removal, which they agree to do without further cost or expense on the part of the United States." In the original proposal made by the commissioners, the amount to be spent for the purpose of removal had been $25,000 or $30,000: this amount increased tenfold at some unrecorded point in the treaty process.

Despite language suggesting this provision "to settle their affairs"—that is, to pay off supposed debts owed the traders—was designed to benefit the Dakota, it was instead intended to be the trigger that would earn the traders the windfall they had hoped for from the treaty. This was exactly the way it worked.[103]

After signing the treaty, each Dakota leader was led to a nearby barrel on

Treaty Traverse des Sioux

Treaty Traverse des Sioux.

which sat a document prepared by the traders. By its terms, the signatories acknowledged their debts to the traders and "half-breeds" and pledged themselves as representatives of their respective bands to pay those obligations. As Folwell noted, the document had not been read or explained in open council. Many, including white observers at the treaty table, had no idea what the document was. Missionary Thomas Williamson believed it was a third copy of the treaty. At the time the document was signed, it contained no schedule of the debts involved, though this was added shortly after the signing. Initially the amounts claimed added up to over $431,000, but the total was scaled back to $210,000 to fit within the constraints allowed in the treaty. Henry Sibley along with other traders helped prepare the schedule. What it meant was that the amount set aside for the benefit of the Dakota would go directly to the traders.[104]

After praising Dakota leaders for their wisdom and vigilance, the commissioners themselves, who at various points had insisted the issue of debts to be between the Dakota and the traders, allowed the signing of the traders' document to occur. No reference was made to it in the treaty journal. Although the traders later claimed the contents were well known to the Dakota, Indian agent Nathaniel McLean, observing the signing of the document, asked to have it explained but was rebuffed by the commissioners "because it would make a disturbance." The agent believed that had the paper been explained, the Dakota would not have signed it.[105]

During the treaty signing itself, the commissioners exhausted their supply of medals but promised to deliver them to the leaders who did not receive them. A few more remarks were exchanged between the leaders and the commissioners. Curly Head complained about earlier treaties that had allowed a de facto transfer of land from the Dakota to the Ojibwe: "A great deal of our country was sold by the Chippewas without our consent and our Father promised to make an arrangement about it." He added that "the Winnebagoes occupy the country," referring to lands sold by the Ojibwe for the Ho-Chunk reservation on the west bank of the Mississippi River, suggesting the Dakota had not agreed on the boundary between Ojibwe and Dakota there. Ramsey evaded the question, stating that the Dakota had now sold their lands west of the Mississippi. Lea quickly returned to a happier topic, the conclusion of the treaty, which he described as the "good treaty" they had been promised. If the Dakota remained faithful to the treaty, the government would do the same. He had come among them "a stranger and as a friend I leave you with the kindest feelings." He bid them farewell.

1851

Treaties of Traverse des Sioux and Mendota with the Sisseton and Wahpeton and Wahpekute and Mdewakanton, respectively, cede twenty-four million acres in southern Minnesota.

Ramsey concluded by giving a lengthy speech—two pages long in the treaty journal—painting a rosy picture of the Dakota's future, their farms, schools, and the many services they would receive from the treaty. After further discussion, the commissioners left and presents were distributed to the gathered Dakota.

TREATY OF MENDOTA

With the treaty concluded at Traverse des Sioux, the stage was set for replication of its terms with the lower tribes. On July 25 the commissioners arrived in Mendota, lodging at the home of trader Jean-Baptiste Faribault. Negotiations began with Bdewakaŋtuŋwaŋ and Waȟpekute leaders on July 29. A pipe was passed to those gathered in a room of Faribault's house. In addition to Alexander Faribault, Jean-Baptiste's son, now serving as interpreters were Philander Prescott and Gideon Pond, who had not been at Traverse des Sioux. Governor Ramsey began by stating his purpose to advise the Great Father's children "for their good." It was time for his red children to dispose of "the lands you own," so that his agents could transfer them to his white children. These lands had ceased being "of much value" to the Dakota because the game was gone and would be more valuable to the Great Father's white children. Now that the Sisituŋwaŋ and Waȟpetuŋwaŋ had signed the treaty at Traverse des Sioux, if those gathered in Mendota did not sell their lands they would be surrounded by whites. Thus, the negotiations should be of particular interest to them. Ramsey then introduced Commissioner Lea.[106]

Lea began by saying that he was a "friend to the red man," as was the Great Father in Washington. Every year their "white brethren" were "thickening" around them. It would be to their benefit if they were to give "his white children" lands "for their homes." But the Great Father also wanted to provide the Dakota with "a good home." The Dakota now had an opportunity to sell their lands and select a new location on the Minnesota River, between the Yellow Medicine River, where the homes of the Sisituŋwaŋ and Waȟpetuŋwaŋ would begin, and "the Tchaay-tan-bay [Çetaŋbe, Hatching Hawk, now Hawk Creek] and Tchappah [Çapa, or Beaver Creek] Rivers." In addition to providing them with "a comfortable home," the Great Father was willing to supply the Dakota with a large sum of money for their land, Lea said, offering them $800,000 as well as money to assist them when they arrived at their new homes and to pay for schools, mills, blacksmith shops, and farms, as well as other benefits.[107]

Lea would not ask them to sign a treaty if it was not for their own good. He provided evidence from his own life: "I love the home where I was born and spent my boyish days, as much as you do the country where you lived," but he had moved two or three times in his life, each time farther than they were being asked to go. Even if they moved they would still be living on lands "that have for centuries belonged to the great Dakota nation." Lea expected they would want to consider the offer before responding, and he suggested meeting again the next day. The interpreter would hand them the written proposal, although Lea did not state whether it was in Dakota or English.[108]

After Lea had spoken, Chief Wabasha rose and reminded the commissioners of unanswered questions about earlier treaties. As he had stated at the failed treaty negotiations in 1849, there were still "some funds laying back" in the hand of his Great Father, a reference to the so-called educational fund from the Treaty of 1837. The Dakota were anxious to "get that which is due them before they do anything." Lea responded that if they were able to reach agreement about a new treaty, "no doubt all can be satisfied in reference to the back money."[109]

At the end of the meeting Wabasha requested that the next day's council be held outdoors instead of in the stuffy room. A large arbor was constructed on Oheyawahi (Pilot Knob), "immediately above the landing," a location with "a fine view of Fort Snelling and the beautiful surrounding country," on a site which also happened to be culturally important for the Dakota people. The commissioners sat at tables with the chiefs around them in a semicircle, and when the council resumed at three o'clock Commissioner Lea asked for the Dakota's response to the offer. Wabasha stood and said the chiefs, soldiers, women, and children had heard what Lea had said the day before and had considered the proposal. He said, "We . . . now return it. I have nothing more to say." Lea asked for any response from seven or eight other Dakota leaders, "all chiefs of equal rank." The treaty journal reported, "Here there was a long pause and no reply."[110]

At this point Governor Ramsey suggested adjourning the council to give the Dakota further opportunity to discuss the subject. Lea expected them to meet and discuss things and then arrive at a speedy conclusion. He noted that he was a long way from home and was obliged to leave in a few days. He advised them of the importance of making up their minds as soon as practicable. In fact, Lea had been on leave from his work in Washington since early June and did not return to Washington until the end of August. As for Ramsey, he left late in August along with others involved in the Dakota treaties to go to Pembina, on the Red River near the Canadian border, to sign a treaty with the Ojibwe for a land cession in that region.[111]

Wakute responded to Lea's impatience: "Our habits are different from those of the whites and when we have anything to consider it takes us a long time." Lea responded that he understood but that the subject had been "before them a long time" and they were chiefs and men and not women and children. He wished them to be prepared to give an answer the next day.[112]

On July 31 at three o'clock the council resumed with Wabasha indicating that some of the chiefs might have something to say. The journal notes, "Here ensued a long and on the part of the chiefs, apparently constrained silence." Finally Ta Oyate Duta or Little Crow rose and reiterated the questions raised by Wabasha about the fund from the 1837 treaty. Chiefs who were older than he, who had been in Washington at the negotiations for the Treaty of 1837, were promised a settlement but had not received it, he said: "These men sit still and say nothing." They desired to have the money "laid down upon us. It is money due on the old treaty and I think it should be paid and we do not want to talk about a new treaty unless it is all paid."[113]

Commissioner Lea now spoke in detail about the 1837 treaty, stating that government officials had understood the money would be paid "for the benefit of their children" but "the Dakotas thought otherwise"—an unfortunate difference of opinion. The Great Father had not wanted to hold back anything. He regretted the difficulty the Dakota had faced and was anxious "now to make a treaty that will release them from this difficulty." With this new treaty, there would be no difference of opinion. Once they signed, they would be able to "arrange satisfactorily the money matter." Ramsey added that if the treaty were completed then the officials could "be justified in paying you the money, as much of it will be paid down to you as will be equal to your usual cash annuities for three years."[114]

Ramsey hinted that the commission had come with every intention of paying the funds due under the 1837 provision, but they were using them as leverage to pressure the Dakota into making a new treaty. According to Ramsey, "to get the money ready and every thing arranged to pay it will take a good while and we may as well therefore proceed with the treaty." In response, Ta Oyate

Duta—who may not have realized the commissioners actually had the money there, intending to pay if the Dakota signed the treaty—stated that they would "talk of nothing else but money if it is until next spring. That lies in the way of a treaty." In response, Ramsey promised they would be paid as soon as they finished the treaty. If they signed the treaty the next day, they would be paid the following day. He hoped this plan would satisfy them and suggested going back to discussions of the new treaty. The interpreter was asked to explain the treaty provisions. Apparently the offer about the money was acceptable, although no Dakota leader rose to speak. The council was adjourned.[115]

On August 1, the Dakota sent word that they were willing to resume. The council began at four o'clock. Wakute had been appointed to speak for the other leaders, but he declined, asking only to listen. A long silence ensued. Commissioner Lea rose to urge them to discuss the treaty. He reemphasized that the treaty was for their own good and he would not encourage them to make a treaty that was not. He predicted trouble if they did not sign. He would return to Washington, and if trouble occurred he would feel sorry for them, but they would only have themselves to blame for opposing the Great Father's wishes. He repeated earlier statements about the Great Father's desire that they have a "comfortable home" for "themselves and their posterity." Ramsey suggested that while the younger men might not think it so, the elders could see that the treaty was a means of improving their lives. The elders should without hesitation accept the offer. As he had earlier at Traverse des Sioux, Ramsey promised the government would protect the headmen from any consequences they might face in doing anything "to save their tribe from difficulties and to carry out the benevolent wishes of their Great Father." Commissioner Lea interpreted their silence to mean they did not wish to sell their lands. This decision would sadden the heart of their Great Father. The council adjourned.[116]

For several days the council did not meet, while, according to the treaty journal, time was "profitably spent in maturing the terms of a treaty nearly acceptable to both parties." As with the treaty of Traverse des Sioux, the process was not recorded. A one-page document entitled "Proposition of the Mendaywakanton and Wakpakoota Sioux to the U.S. Commissioners," in the handwriting of Henry H. Sibley, suggests that he and other traders were involved in bringing about an agreement. The document contained familiar provisions. One way or another, the process, presumably with private negotiation, resulted in a treaty virtually identical to that signed at Traverse des Sioux. On August 5 the council began with an apparent understanding that the treaty would be signed. However, Taçaŋku Wašte or Good Road indicated that the Dakota wished to discuss certain matters first. Commissioner Lea preempted this request, stating that the treaty had been prepared "in pursuance of the terms agreed upon" and was now ready to be signed. He called for

Oheyawahi, "The Place Much Visited" / Pilot Knob, Mendota Heights

This hill, located opposite Fort Snelling, is a sacred site and an ancient Dakota burial place, possibly the same site mentioned by Zebulon Pike on his arrival at Pike Island in 1805. The hill is considered a sacred place for several reasons, in part because of its associations with the underwater being Uŋkteȟi. According to an account recorded by missionary Samuel Pond, the hill was created when Uŋkteȟi, chasing another creature, plowed into the bank and raised up the hill. The health-giving Wakaŋ Waçipi, or medicine ceremony, was sometimes performed on the hill. Explorer Joseph Nicollet wrote of seeing such a ceremony there in 1837. The ritual teachings of the Wakaŋ Waçipi were said to have come from Uŋkteȟi.[xv]

Seth Eastman, a soldier and an artist, painted at least one view of burial scaffolds on the summit of Pilot Knob in the 1840s as well as an image showing a medicine ceremony that may also have taken place on the hill. The English name refers to the knob-like top, useful for navigation. Many visitors to the hill from the 1820s to 1850s remarked on the extensive and impressive view from its heights, from which the growing downtowns of both Minneapolis and St. Paul were visible. Some early visitors described hearing the rush of water at St. Anthony Falls from the hill.

Located within the sacred district of Bdote, Oheyawahi was not the site of permanent or seasonal villages, though the area was often visited by

Seth Eastman painted the sacred Dakota hill known as Oheyawahi or Pilot Knob, with its burial scaffolds on the top, in a view from below at the mouth of the Minnesota River, which enters at right.

Dakota. According to Dakota elder Ta Šuŋka Wakiŋyaŋ Ohitika Chris Leith, living on a sacred site was not advised. He explained that such places served as cemeteries because they were sacred. There was "a lot of energy in that area . . . There's a vortex energy there, that's why, and the Dakota nation held it sacred." People knew that burials placed in such a sacred space would be left alone. If someone tried to build something there, a housing development for example, it would not last. In a pipe ceremony Leith led with Chief Arvol Looking Horse on the north slope of the hill in March 2004, the hill was given a new name: Wotakuye Paha, "the hill of all the relatives." At the time Leith stated, "We have a lot of relatives buried here. That's why all these years people have prayed. People asked me to come there—to pray for them."[xvi]

Throughout the nineteenth century the hill had a characteristic mound-like top. As far as is known the form was natural. In the late 1920s the designers of Acacia Cemetery, located on a portion of the hill, removed the top twenty feet, so its original form cannot be verified. Between 2003 and 2008, successful efforts were made to preserve another district of the hill as a public park. Efforts are currently under way to restore the native oak savanna. In recent years a number of Dakota events and ceremonies have been celebrated on the hill.[xvii] ■

In 2010, the view from Oheyawahi/Pilot Knob toward the city of Minneapolis, with Fort Snelling in the intervening space, was very different from what would have been seen 150 years before. Today the northern part of the hill has been protected from development and efforts are under way to restore native vegetation.

the treaty to be read by the secretary in English and "explained" in Dakota by Gideon Pond.[117]

Why the document in Dakota was "explained" at this meeting rather than simply read, as had been done with the earlier treaty at Traverse des Sioux, is not clear. It may be that Pond, assuming he was shown the Dakota document written by Riggs, realized that a direct translation would not have adequately conveyed the differences in cultural meaning between the English terms and the Dakota ones, especially in relation to the concept of land sale. Unfortunately, no record of Pond's explanation has survived.

Ramsey asked the chiefs to begin signing the document, but discussion ensued that raises questions about whether the treaty as read had actually been discussed with the chiefs earlier. Wabasha debated whether the treaty provisions were for the good of the Dakota. The statements about farmers, schools, physicians, traders, and "half-breeds" were similar to those in the Treaty of 1837, which had not truly benefited the Dakota. And the place named for their reservation was prairie country, which was not suited to them. He wished to remain in their lands to receive the benefits promised under the previous treaty, until those benefits expired.[118]

In response Commissioner Lea sought to undermine Wabasha in the eyes of his own people. He accused Wabasha of "speaking with a forked tongue" and trying to deceive the other Indians. Lea did not expect to revise the treaty to suit him personally. Was that any way for a chief to act? Ramsey again asked for the chiefs to sign the treaty. Wasu Wiçaśtaśni, known as Bad Hail, and Śakpe requested approval of benefits the chiefs had sought in the 1837 treaty, including the land set aside for Scott Campbell that had been stricken from the treaty by the Senate. Lea responded that the Great Father had instructed his agents not to include benefits to traders and others in treaties, a reference to the rule the traders were actively seeking to undermine both at Traverse des Sioux and Mendota. Lea noted, accurately, that the Dakota could pay benefits to anyone they wanted with the money they would receive from the treaty.[119]

Various chiefs now questioned the reservation's boundaries. Ta Oyate Duta wished it extended down the Minnesota River to Traverse des Sioux. A soldier in Śakpe's band asked that it include Big Lake on Falls Creek, an unidentified location, adding that there were no objections to other parts of the treaty. Ramsey agreed to change the boundary to extend to Little Rock River (now Little Rock Creek in present-day Nicollet County). Wakute made known his fears about how the treaty might be changed after it was signed, recalling that in the earlier treaty good things were altered by Congress after the Dakota returned to Minnesota: it was "very different from what they had been told and all were shamed." He added his preference for the area of Pine Island (Goodhue County) to be included in the reservation, but this sideline allowed Ramsey to ignore concerns about how the treaty might be changed. He did, however, note that they would be allowed to "hunt over the large country you sell just as you hunted before" because whites would not need it for many years. He then drew the discussion to a close: "a great deal could be talked about but it is useless to say more. You must have confidence in us and in your Great Father."[120]

Still, further discussion ensued about the reservation boundaries and the general nature of the treaty. A sticking point appeared to be that the "soldiers," or younger men, were distrustful of the process—based on the Dakota's experience with the Treaty of 1837—which prevented the Dakota from reaching a consensus on signing the treaty. Wabasha rose to speak: "you have said, young men, that the chief who got up first to sign the treaty you would kill. It is this that has caused the difficulty." One of them responded that they had not threatened the chiefs with death but they had heard the chiefs "were making a paper" and "they didn't like it for the land belongs to the braves." But now the younger men had agreed with the sale of the land, and Ramsey asked which of them would be the first to sign.

Medicine Bottle of Kap'oża asked that the signer be one who had not gone to Washington and had no part in the first treaty. He designated Ta Oyate Duta, who once again requested that the reservation be extended to Traverse des Sioux, where "wood was plenty, wild rice &c." Lea responded that they had already extended the line and would extend it no farther. Ramsey added that the Dakota seemed to think the commissioners had come to cheat them: "We have marked out a large piece of land for your home. The soldiers asked for more. We gave it. It is all we can do." Lea declaimed, "No man puts any food in his mouth by long talk but may often get hungry at it." At this, Ta Oyate Duta, who knew how to write his own name, signed his Dakota name rather than the name Little Crow, by which he was known to whites, on "each of the duplicate copies of the treaty." In all, sixty-four chiefs and warriors made their marks.[121]

To resolve the difficulty posed by the Dakota's insistence that they be paid the balance due from the 1837 treaty's education fund, the new treaty included a provision stating that "the entire annuity, provided for in the first section of the second article of the treaty of September twenty-ninth, eighteen hundred and thirty-seven (1837), including an unexpended balance that may be in the Treasury on the first of July, eighteen hundred and fifty-two (1852), shall thereafter be paid in money." In the meantime arrangements were made to pay the past balance due. It is unclear whether the commissioners arrived with the intention of paying that amount. Historian William W. Folwell said "it was probably no accident that the American Fur Company had that amount of specie on hand." The funds were advanced to the Indian agent, who paid out thirty thousand dollars to the Bdewakaŋtuŋwaŋ and Waȟpekute on August 8, 1851. Each of the 2,585 men, women, and children received $10.50 plus 78/100 of a cent of the money.[122]

The process for obtaining the Mendota treaty signers' consent to pay alleged debts to the traders was slightly different from that at Traverse des Sioux. Waȟpekute band leaders signed a document on August 5 promising to pay varying amounts, including $42,000 to interpreter Alexander Faribault and $31,500 to Henry Sibley. No such document was signed by the Bdewakaŋtuŋwaŋ leaders, so other means were found to induce them to hand over $90,000 of the treaty money to the traders.[123]

THE AFTERMATH OF THE 1851 TREATIES

In the months following the 1851 treaties, the primary repercussions related to the extra-legal documents designed to pay the traders. A trader named Madison Sweetser, who represented the interests of the firm of William G. and George W. Ewing, traders who did not benefit from these documents, attempted to create difficulties for the traders who did, hoping to change the situation.[124]

At Sweetser's encouragement, a group of Sisituŋwaŋ and Waȟpetuŋwaŋ leaders came to St. Paul in December 1851 to speak with their agent about the traders' paper. They stated that the document had been obtained by fraud and deceit and that it was not explained to them at the signing. They had thought the document was part of the treaty. They were not against paying their debts but only those proven to be justly due. They presented a protest signed by fifteen of the Traverse des Sioux treaty signers. They also met with Governor Ramsey, who told them they could control the process of payment from the amount set aside by the treaty. The traders' paper was not part of the treaty: it was a "matter entirely between themselves, over which the commissioners would exercise no control." Sweetser, acting as agent for the protesting chiefs, forwarded the document to the Indian office, describing what had happened as a "stupendous fraud."[125]

Meanwhile, the treaties were making their way through the bureaucracy in Washington. The president submitted them to the Senate in February 1852. Southern Senators opposed measures that would facilitate eventual statehood for the region, but the treaties were finally ratified by a narrow margin in June. The treaty Ramsey negotiated with the Ojibwe in Pembina failed to be ratified.[126]

Amendments to the Dakota treaties had been made by Congress, however. Among them was cancellation of the reservations along the Minnesota River, the home for the Dakota the treaty commissioners had spoken of in such glowing terms. Instead the president was authorized to select suitable land outside the ceded territory. The Dakota were to be paid ten cents an acre for the reservation land, with the value, approximately eight thousand dollars, to be added to the trust annuities. Later that summer an Indian appropriation bill was passed by Congress. It dictated that no payments would be made until the Dakota had assented to the treaty amendments and that the money would not be paid to any attorney or agent but directly to the Indians, "unless the imperious interest of the Indian or Indians, or some treaty stipulation, shall require the payment to be made otherwise, under the direction of the President." This bland provision provided more cover for the scheme to intercept the money from the Dakota treaties. Alexander Ramsey was authorized to obtain the Dakota's consent to these amendments, but he contracted with trader Henry M. Rice to do the job. Rice accomplished his mission, inducing Dakota leaders to sign a document authorizing Ramsey to receive the $275,000 set aside in the Traverse des Sioux treaty. In October a draft for over $593,000 was issued to Ramsey by the U.S. Treasury Department for payments to be made under the treaty.[127]

Meanwhile Governor Ramsey, who was then in Washington, was shown the traders' paper. He later claimed to have known nothing of it before, even while at Traverse des Sioux. Now on examining the document, it was later reported, he disingenuously "discovered that while not a power of attorney, it was a most *solemn acknowledgement,* made by the chiefs in open council, of their indebtedness to certain individuals, 'pledging the faith of their tribe' for payment, and requesting, in the words of the treaty, that the United States would pay the individuals named the sums acknowledged to be respectively due them." At the same time Commissioner Lea advised Ramsey that the Dakota should be required to abide by such an agreement, "provided it was fairly and understandingly made." Historian William W. Folwell wrote with irony that "Ramsey at no time contemplated any other procedure." Ramsey had now concluded that the paper was an "irrevocable order to pay the persons named" and that, far from being a private matter between the traders and the Indians, it was an agreement that he as governor would enforce.[128]

In this fashion, Ramsey and Lea provided the necessary mechanism to evade the legal sanction against payments to traders and other individuals and assured that the traders would get their money. Different means were employed to coerce the traders' funds from the Mendota treaty—by individual payments to chiefs, by holding back on their annuity payments, and by detaining five young Dakota men in prison at Fort Snelling for killing some Ojibwe—until Dakota leaders were willing to sign receipts for money they did not receive. In November 1852 Ramsey went to Traverse des Sioux to pay the Sisituŋwaŋ and Waḣpetuŋwaŋ. Though he was armed with the authority of various documents already prepared for him, he sought to secure "cumulative evidence" of those treaty payments, that is, signed documents showing that the chiefs had received the money, even if the money was paid not to them but rather directly to the traders. Many of the chiefs were not cooperative, wanting the money to be paid to them in open council as the treaty provided. Ramsey stated that the document—the traders' paper—signed at Traverse des Sioux was irrevocable and he was authorized to carry it out. But Sisituŋwaŋ Chief Red Iron, or Maza Ṡa, leader of a soldiers' lodge, sought to organize opposition to Ramsey's actions. Ramsey sent for a detachment from Fort Snelling to deal with the situation and then ordered the chief confined. As he had with the Bdewakaŋtuŋwaŋ, he delayed payments for current annuities that were due the Sisituŋwaŋ and Waḣpetuŋwaŋ, forcing eleven chiefs and soldiers to sign a receipt for $250,000 owed to traders and mixed-bloods, which Ramsey was to pay to the private parties listed in the traders' paper. However, in many cases it appears that some of the money went not to those listed in the paper but to others who had facilitated this theft of the money from the treaty.[129]

Even by the standards of the time, this convoluted series of steps that extracted Dakota money appropriated through governmental process—that is, payment due via the treaties—was tainted. A subsequent Senate investigation in the spring of 1853 revealed many irregularities, providing ample evidence of graft and corruption. Nonetheless, the Senate committee, acting in a political fashion to protect its compatriots, concluded that Ramsey's conduct was not only blameless but "highly commendable and meritorious." This decision was widely criticized by Ramsey's political opponents. As for Sibley and his fellow traders, the obstacles to producing the desired result in the treaty process were almost too much to bear. Frederick Sibley, who worked in his brother's business managing the "Sioux Outfit," wrote in July 1853 to Hercules Dousman, "You truly said 'the Sioux treaty will hang like a curse over our heads the balance of our lives.'" Perhaps even they recognized that the means they had used to achieve their ends went well beyond the casual corruption of the time.[130]

Meanwhile, the Dakota had neither their old land nor the new home that had been promised them. Ramsey appealed to Commissioner Lea and the president for permission to allow the Dakota to live in the reservation areas along the Minnesota River that were to be reserved temporarily, pending further action. This compromise was approved by President Franklin Pierce in 1854, though removal of the Dakota to the area had already begun in 1853.

Two treaties in 1858, concluded in Washington, DC, altered the terms of the 1851 treaties by adding the northern shore of the Minnesota River to the lands "ceded" to the United States under the 1851 treaty. This change confined the Dakota people to the southern shore of the Minnesota River. The treaties of 1858 signed by the same groups of Dakota were further clarified by a Senate resolution in 1860 to settle the titles to land of both Dakota and non-Dakota people under the 1858 treaties.[131]

These later modifications of the 1851 treaties effectively removed the Dakota people from all of their ancient homelands in Minnesota except for the narrow ten-mile strip running for 140 miles along the Minnesota River's south

1853

With ratification of the 1851 treaties, removal of Dakota bands to proposed reservations in the Upper Minnesota River valley begins. Settlement encroaches on ceded Dakota lands even before the land is surveyed by the government.

1858

Minnesota becomes a state. Former trader Henry Hastings Sibley is elected the first governor. In June a treaty signed with the Dakota at Washington, DC, cedes one-half of Dakota reservation land on the north shore of the Minnesota River to the United States. The treaty is not ratified until 1860.

Wambdi Taŋka or Big Eagle, a Dakota leader originally from Black Dog village, whose grandfather of the same name was painted by the artist George Catlin in 1835, was photographed by A. Zeno Schindler in Washington, DC, at the time of the Treaty of 1858 negotiations.

shore. Confined to this small area, the Dakota could not possibly maintain their lives according to the hunting and gathering practices they engaged in for centuries before the Europeans' arrival. This dependence was recognized in the 1851 treaties by the obligation of the United States to provide the Dakota people the wherewithal each year to purchase goods to sustain themselves in what proved to be a meager existence at best.

The long-term effects of these federal actions became apparent in summer of 1862, when the shipment of annuities due under previous treaties was delayed. Desperation among the Dakota deepened and in August war broke out in the Minnesota River valley between some of the Dakota and the United States. In less than two months, after much loss of life on all sides, the Dakota

1862

A war between the Dakota and the United States begins in August. On September 9, 1862, Governor Ramsey responds to public discontent and calls for the expulsion and extermination of all Dakota.

Sisituŋwaŋ and Waḣpetuŋwaŋ chiefs gathered in Washington, DC, for a photograph in the studio of Charles DeForest Fredericks in 1858, at the time of the negotiation of their last treaty with the U.S. government. Among them was the Sisituŋwaŋ leader Maza Ša or Red Iron, in the center at back, and Waḣpetuŋwaŋ leaders Mazamani, seated at far left, and Upi Iyahdeya, seated at far right.

were overwhelmed and defeated by the superior forces of the United States. A violent backlash broke out as settlers, new to the region and terrified by the war, demanded that the Dakota be expelled. Governor Ramsey stated in a public message in September 1862 that the "Sioux Indians of Minnesota" must be "exterminated or driven forever beyond the borders of the State."[132]

The furious response was further manifested in bounties offered for Dakota scalps and the fevered pitch of retribution demanded by Minnesota's white citizens. In September, approximately two thousand Dakota people gathered at the Upper Camp near present-day Montevideo to wait for Sibley's arrival. They "surrendered" fully expecting to be treated humanely as prisoners of war, based on Sibley's promise that they would "be protected by me when I arrive." Once there on September 26, he renamed the area "Camp Release." The men were separated from the women and children and tried for their crimes; 303 were condemned to die in Mankato. The remaining seventeen hundred women, children, and elderly, including hundreds of noncombatants, some of whom had protected white settler refugees from the war, were rounded up and force-marched to a concentration camp beneath the bluffs of Fort Snelling, where they were held over the winter of 1862. Several hundred died, and in the spring of 1863 the survivors were sent by steamboat down the Mississippi River and up the Missouri, beyond the borders of their Minnesota homeland. In addition two military columns were organized and rode out to the west under the command of Sibley and General Alfred Sully in a pincer movement to expel the remaining Dakota from the state. They massacred more than three hundred noncombatant Dakota at Whitestone Hill just northwest of Lake Traverse in September 1863.[133]

The Minnesota backlash reached all the way to Washington, DC, where Congress in February and March 1863 passed two statutes, one for the "relief" of settlers harmed by the war and another for the removal of the Dakota. The Relief Act, sometimes called the "Abrogation Act," purported to abrogate all treaties with the Dakota and directed that payments due from the United States to the Dakota would instead be made into a fund to provide relief for settlers harmed by the war. This unilateral action by the United States was not the subject of negotiation in any treaty signed by the Dakota. Even if the war is considered to be a breach of the treaties by some of the Dakota, the treaties contain no language that specifies what the legal remedy might be for such a breach. Instead the United States unilaterally not only decided that its obligations to provide payments to the Dakota under the terms of treaties were no longer in effect but went on to seize the lands of the Dakota. However, it should also be noted that although the act abrogated U.S. obligations toward the Dakota, it gave contradictory evidence of some continuing support, providing sustenance for the Dakota and setting aside other lands for them at an unspecified site beyond Minnesota's borders.[134]

These provisions raise more questions than they answer about the long-held treaty rights of the Dakota people and the federal government's relationship toward them, questions which have yet to be settled by courts of law. When considered in the larger arc of time from 1805 to 1863, the Abrogation Act is an important moment in the long-running clash of master stories that we have seen occurring at the treaty table. And this makes clear that the story of the Dakota, their relationship to the land, and the meaning of the treaties they signed did not end in 1863.

As shown here, government officials and those who worked with them sought to manipulate the treaty processes for their own ends. Regardless of "good intentions" stated by officials who claimed they wanted to preserve a place for the Dakota in their ancient homelands, the Dakota were always at a disadvantage, manipulated by individuals and by the process itself. They did not understand European concepts of land, the very process of treaty making, and the extent of the corruption of officials involved. They often assumed the best of the officials with whom they dealt. As a result they were banished from their homelands at the moment of their last treaty. What happened in 1862 and 1863 was simply the aftermath of actions taken in the treaties that came before.

1863
Treaties with the Dakota are abrogated by Congress. In April and May, the remaining condemned men and the survivors of the Fort Snelling concentration camp are forcibly removed from Minnesota.

CHAPTER FIVE

Reclaiming Minnesota— Mni Sota Makoce

"By putting forth our stories we are exerting this belief in ourselves, in our history, and our ability to transform the world."

Waziyatawiŋ Angela Wilson,
Remember This! Dakota Decolonization
and the Eli Taylor Narratives

The treaties of 1851 marked the beginning of the Dakota's exile from their homelands in Minnesota. The Dakota people were not given a permanent home in which to live, and efforts to confine them to the region of the Upper Minnesota River began before the treaties were even ratified. Willis A. Gorman, who succeeded Alexander Ramsey as governor of Wisconsin Territory in May 1853, took official charge of the removal beginning in August of that year. Although the Dakota did not have full possession of their reservation and preparations to receive them at their new locations were far from complete, Gorman persuaded the Red Wing and Wabasha bands to move as far as Kap'oža in September. By November he had succeeded in getting all but a few of the Bdewakaŋtuŋwaŋ, Sisituŋwaŋ, and Waȟpetuŋwaŋ who lived on the Mississippi and lower Minnesota rivers to move to the Upper Minnesota. Gorman noted, however, that "A portion of Wabasha's band left the Village near Lake Pippin [*sic*] on the Mississippi R and hid themselves in the country on the Red Cedar river near the Iowa line. But every soul of every other have been removed." An agency was established on the south side of the

Minnesota River near the mouth of the Redwood, about fifteen miles above Fort Ridgely, the new military post.[1]

During the removal process, Gorman recognized the difficulty of defining a reservation consisting of ceded land in which the Dakota resided under the sufferance of the president. Writing to the commissioner of Indian affairs, he stated that there were places in the ceded lands the Dakota were leaving that were "quite as much out of the reach of the white settlements as on the purchased reservations," which were actually, by the original terms of the treaty, reserved from the lands ceded. If the reservation was to be open "to all to come and go at pleasure," then there was no way to protect Indian occupancy through the laws generally applied to "Indian country." Gorman declined to authorize extensive improvements on the reservation lands until the matter could be settled. Despite these difficulties, he was determined to keep the Dakota on the reservation.[2]

Plowing and the construction of a few houses for the Bdewakaŋtuŋwaŋ and Waḣpekuṭe bands began in 1854. But supplies and food were lacking, due in part to government appropriations that did not fulfill the 1851 treaty provisions and to continual delays in the delivery of annuities. To support themselves, many Dakota continued to return throughout the 1850s to areas in which they had lived, hunted, and harvested for generations. In January 1855, Gorman allowed Dakota to hunt deer along Rice Creek and at Rice Lake. The *St. Paul Daily Democrat* reported on January 27, 1855, that they had "killed five hundred deer, in addition to a large amount of smaller game." A well-known daguerreotype of tepees adjacent to the John H. Stevens house, in the area of present-day downtown Minneapolis, was probably taken during one of the removed Dakota's return visits. Meanwhile Sisituŋwaŋ and Waḣpetuŋwaŋ bands located farther up the Minnesota River had received very little assistance on their reservation. They continued hunting as a primary form of subsistence during the winter.[3]

Even before ratification of the 1851 treaties and removal of the Dakota from the ceded lands, whites predicted the Dakota would disappear from the landscapes in which they had lived for thousands of years. And, at this point, the Dakota began to disappear from the written history of Minnesota. In February 1853, just before the treaties were proclaimed by the president, Governor Alexander Ramsey, acting as president of the Minnesota Historical Society (which was founded in 1849, within the first months of the territory's existence) wrote a letter, with the historian Edward D. Neill, to the commissioner of Indian affairs in Washington: "The Dakota Indians having ceded their territory on the Mississippi and Minnesota rivers, in a short time the villages of this tribe which greet the eye of the traveler from Galena to Fort Snelling will be obliterated."

Ramsey and Neill noted that ever since the territory's organization, white inhabitants had had "the most friendly relations with this nation." They had

Tepees of Dakota people camped in what would one day be the intersection of Hennepin and Nicollet avenues in downtown Minneapolis, shown in a daguerreotype taken in the 1850s. A portion of the house of city pioneer John H. Stevens is visible in the background. Because of poor food supplies on the reservations created under the Treaty of 1851, Dakota people continued to return to the areas they had ceded, including the Twin Cities.

A Dakota hunter was probably photographed in a St. Paul studio in the 1850s; he may have come to sell his ducks to local grocers.

seen Dakota in the streets of St. Paul and had looked at them as their "new neighbors." They had taken "lively interest in their customs and culture." At the fourth anniversary of the Minnesota Historical Society, held in St. Paul, the organization passed a resolution requesting that a member of the society edit a work on "the early history, customs, and belief of the Dakotas, as a memorial of the people who now dwell where our children will build and plant." They also resolved to ask for the right to use some of the plates prepared for the massive six-volume work on Native American tribes compiled by the former Indian agent Henry Schoolcraft and published at government expense beginning in 1851. That work included the engravings based on the works of Seth Eastman, the military artist and officer stationed at Fort Snelling in the 1830s and 1840s.[4]

Neill, a Presbyterian minister who was the author of the first histories of Minnesota as a territory and a state, had already begun to gather materials about the Dakota, working with some of the missionaries who had arrived in the region in the 1830s. Though the missionaries' purpose was to convert Dakota people to Christianity and to change the Dakota way of life, they made a real effort to record the Dakota language and traditions, not just for their own uses but for what they viewed as posterity, though perhaps a posterity that would give them credit for their work. One motivation was the belief that removal of the Dakota from their earlier band locations after the Treaty of 1851 would mean the earlier history of the places they were leaving would be lost.

The bilingual Dakota-English publication *Dakota Tawaxitku Kin* or *The Dakota Friend*, published by Samuel and Gideon Pond in 1851 and 1852, included a series of articles on the history of the Dakota, gleaned not only from French sources but also from the Dakota language and oral tradition. An issue published in March 1851 included a short article, "Dakota's First History," containing a description of the earliest French commentators on the Dakota. This was just the sort of account one would have expected non-Dakota to view as authoritative. But the same issue contained another article about "hints concerning the traditionary history of the Dakotas."

The author of this and subsequent articles based on Dakota oral tradition, who may have been Gideon Pond, began by suggesting that he had little confidence in Dakota oral tradition, a view the Dakota themselves would not have shared. He gave the opinion that the Dakota did not see any importance in their own history, writing that "a book on this subject is lost in the death of every old man." It was left, he said, for "white men, half-breeds, and educated Indians" to "collect and preserve" Dakota traditions. The author appeared to hope that a person of mixed ancestry, who knew how to read and write, someone like the Ojibwe historian William Warren, would appear among the Dakota. He concluded the first installment by stating, "Is it not the imperative duty of every Dakota, or half-breed Dakota, who can read and write—a duty which he owes to himself, his people, and the world—to commence, without delay, to glean in earnest in this long neglected field, formerly rich in Dakota tradition."[5]

In May 1851 the journal included the first of several of these articles based on oral tradition. The author stated that he wanted to contribute his "mite of Dakota history" in the hopes that it would provoke others to contribute in a similar fashion on the Bdewakaŋtuŋwaŋ Dakota and other groups: "Who will give us the Sisitonwan, Warpetonwan, Ihanktonwan and Titonwan traditions? Who will collect and write out their interesting history, as it has been handed down by themselves?"[6]

In subsequent issues, further articles drew together information from the Dakota oral tradition and from early European sources while also including important accounts of Dakota stories and traditional beliefs such as the Wakaŋ Waçipi or medicine ceremony. Another focus was language, particularly the way in which the names of Dakota bands and villages preserved a piece of their history, a record of where and how they lived in the past. The interest in language was shared by another missionary, Stephen R. Riggs, who wrote in the 1893 version of his *Dakota Grammar,* first published in 1852, that the Dakota people carried with them "to some extent, the history of their removals in the names of the several bands," a point supported by the names recorded by Pierre Le Sueur 150 years before. Dakota names for particular communities recorded where the Dakota had been and where they moved at different points in their history. Village and group names were a link between the written record and the oral tradition.[7]

Though influenced by missionary attitudes and language, these accounts offered a Dakota view of history not as an abstraction but within the context of the world view and values of the people themselves. The *Dakota Friend*'s perspective on the Dakota tradition was more sophisticated than that of other non-Dakota observers, but it did show many biases, in particular in its sense of the precariousness of Dakota knowledge about their ancient homelands, a belief that oral tradition would not be able to survive. If there was any faint truth in these predictions, they might seem eerily prescient when viewed with the knowledge that scarcely ten years from the date of the articles almost all of the Dakota in Minnesota would be driven from their homelands. The precariousness of oral tradition would be an effect of genocide practiced against the Dakota, tearing the people from the places in which that tradition was encoded.

EXILE AND RETURN

Remaining condemned men and the survivors of the Fort Snelling concentration camp are forcibly removed from Minnesota to Crow Creek on the Missouri River. A few hundred Dakota people remain in Minnesota, some providing assistance as scouts and soldiers in battles against their fellow Dakota. After the events of 1862, a small group takes refuge in Mendota and Faribault.

As a result of the Dakota–U.S. War of August and September 1862, there was widespread hatred for the Dakota among whites in Minnesota. All Dakota regardless of their actions were punished. Many became refugees on the prairies to the west and in Canada, the object of military actions by the U.S. Army. Thirty-eight Dakota men were hanged at Mankato in December 1862 and more than 260 others, who had been sentenced to hang but whose sentences were commuted by President Abraham Lincoln, were sent to a prison in Fort Davenport, Iowa, for varying terms. Approximately seventeen hundred Dakota men, women, and children were placed in a concentration camp below Fort Snelling during the winter of 1862, where many died. In May 1863 as many as 1,310 surviving Dakota left Fort Snelling in two steamboats for a site at Crow Creek, near Fort Randall on the Missouri River, Dakota Territory. As historian Roy Meyer put it, never again would the Bdewakaŋtuŋwaŋ, Waḣpekute, Sisituŋwaŋ, and Waḣpetuŋwaŋ Dakota occupy a "single fairly well defined land area." Instead, wrote missionary John P. Williamson, "henceforth they were

A young Dakota girl holding her doll, shown here in a photo from the 1880s or later, was one of the members of the community who survived in Mendota long after the exile of their relatives from the state in 1863.

scattered over states and provinces, with hundreds of miles separating their dispersed settlements and the lands rapidly filling up with white men, who learned eventually to tolerate the Indian, if only to exploit him, but never to accept him as an equal."[8]

After 1862 a few hundred Dakota people remained in Minnesota, some providing assistance as scouts and soldiers in the battles against their fellow Dakota. Some were able to take refuge in Mendota under the protection of Henry Sibley, who at the same time was out on the plains seeking to punish their relatives who had never been captured. Others were protected in Faribault under Alexander Faribault and Bishop Henry Whipple. Some continued to make use of their traditional resources.

Little was done by the federal government to provide for the Dakota who remained in or those who had returned to Minnesota—until the 1880s, when federal appropriations allowed for the purchase of small parcels of land at Hastings, Birch Coulee (near the old Lower Agency), Prior Lake, and Prairie Island. Purchased land was first given in title to individuals and later only to those who had lived in Minnesota before the arbitrary date of May 20, 1886, and who wished to cultivate the land. A January 1889 census of the "Mdewakanton Sioux in Minnesota," compiled by the Birch Coulee agent Robert Henton, enumerated 264 people in eighty family groups, including settlements at Redwood, Prairie Island, Hastings, Bloomington, Prior Lake, and Wabasha and camps at Grey Cloud Island and Mendota. This figure did not include all Bdewakaŋtuŋwaŋ Dakota in Minnesota but rather those living in Dakota communities and considered most in need. A census taken ten years later by U.S. Indian inspector James McLaughlin recorded 903 Dakota people, including those residing in Indian communities as well as many living in white cities and towns.[9]

After 1900 many Dakota continued to live in locations covered by these land purchases, where they were permitted "land assignments" on territory that continued to be held by the federal government. Individual Dakota were not permitted to own this land. Many other Dakota bought their own land or lived in white communities. In the 1930s, under the Indian Reorganization Act, communities were organized under tribal constitutions at Lower Sioux and Prairie Island, while an informal organization was created at Upper Sioux where Sisituŋwaŋ and Waȟpetuŋwaŋ had begun to return in the 1880s. In 1969, the Shakopee community was organized around land purchases at Prior Lake. Despite efforts from members of Lower Sioux and Prairie Island to organize as Mdewakanton Sioux of Minnesota, the federal government insisted arbitrarily on organization based on previous federal land purchases.[10]

<aside>
1880s
Communities of Dakota form in Minnesota at Upper Sioux, Lower Sioux, Prior Lake, Prairie Island, and the nucleus already at Mendota. The federal government begins to purchase small parcels of land for the Dakota.

1934
The Indian Reorganization Act allows communities of Indian people living on trust lands to reorganize under federal oversight.
</aside>

RECLAIMING THE LAND THROUGH STORY

Despite the missionaries' fears about the precariousness of Dakota oral tradition, Dakota people themselves kept the traditional knowledge about Mni Sota Makoce alive. Some Dakota also began to write down stories as a way of preserving them and of spreading the knowledge of Minnesota as a Dakota place. Many of these Dakota writers recounted or translated traditional stories about the origins of the Dakota people and their ties to specific places in the landscape. Frequently published in the past as children's stories or folktales, they serve as a record of culture and history as well as of land tenure, reclaiming in language the land the Dakota were forced to leave. Julia A. LaFramboise and Charles A. Eastman are two of the earliest published Dakota writers born before exile.

Julia A. LaFramboise is often referred to as the first Dakota woman "to translate and record Dakota legends"; her stories appeared in English in *Iapi Oaye*, the Dakota- and English-language newspaper established by Stephen R. Riggs and John P. Williamson in 1871. Her translations of seven Dakota stories

Hoġan Waŋke Kiŋ—The Place Where the Fish Lies

This version of the Hoġan Waŋke Kiŋ / St. Croix sandbar legend (see page 73) was translated by Julia LaFramboise.

Along the banks of the beautiful St. Croix, a party of Dakota warriors were wending their way home from a successful invasion of the country of the enemies. Their war paint and dancing eagle plumes gleamed in the last rays of the setting sun. Toward the right of the main party are a couple of stalwart braves. There is a tenderness in their manner that at once reveals their comradship [sic]. The love of two men for each other that surpasses the love for women.

Many days and nights they had been on the perilous war path, and two days and nights have passed since the last morsel of food had been consumed. Chaske one of the friends, sees a splendid pike on the shore—a fish of fishes in the river.

Now they bivouac for the night. Chaske with eager hands prepared the fish for his friend Hepan, but now that it is prepared in perfect Indian style he refuses to partake of it. In vain Chaske urges it, thinking to overcome his friend's reluctance to share his meal. At length, being unable to resist the pleadings of Chaske, Hepan says: "My friend, I do as you urge; as you love me, as you would save me, don't become weary of bringing me water from the river, this night only." So the two joyfully partook of the fish. The meal was scarcely over before Hepan says, Chaske bring me some water. Chaske joyfully brings his friend water, for any service for him is happiness. Soon the pailful is gone and still his friend is panting for water.

Thinking to allay the painful thirst, Chaske is on the run between the river and his friend. But alas, instead of satisfying it, it becomes more intense. And as the night wore on, the flagging energy of Chaske suggested an easier and surer method of quenching his friend's unaccountable thirst, which was to remove him to the margin of the stream where he might drink his fill. Upon proposing it his friend acquiesced, but at the same time exclaimed! "My friend, you have undone me." Carefully Chaske guided him to the river margin, and there left him to snatch an hour's rest, before dawn should come. Scarcely had he dozed before the voice of his friend says, behold me. When he reached him the upper half of his body had turned into a pike. In distress and anguish Chaske upbraids himself for his friend's misfortune, but all too late, for the fish part was already submerged in the river, and the remainder of the body was following fast, till the last vestige of man had disappeared and a great pike had stretched across the mouth of the river. And as time sped on, the sand washed upon it, and to ordinary observers it seemed but a sandbar.

Yet the daring canoe that came down the river, was invariably wrecked on the big fish. Until one day an Indian maiden, said to be beloved of Hepan, came slowly down the stream in a birch bark canoe, being loaded with beaded moccasins and all kinds of maiden handiwork, dropped them to her lost love, and in token of acceptance the fish retires under the water. Since the arrival of the pale-face, they call it the sandbar across the mouth of the St. Croix, where the steamboats are sometimes stranded.[i] ▪

include "The Orphan Boy," which describes a large Dakota village along the "sea shore" of Lake Superior, and a version of "Hogan wanke kin—The Place Where the Fish Lies," about the sandbar on the St. Croix River.[11]

LaFramboise was born in 1842 into distinguished and influential native families. Her mother was Hapstiŋna (also known as Julia), the third daughter of Ištaliba or Sleepy Eye. Her father was Joseph LaFramboise II, son of the Odawa trader Magdelaine Marcot and her French husband Joseph LaFramboise I. Julia LaFramboise's early education came from missionaries Stephen R. Riggs and Amos Huggins, and she was later sent to the Western Female Seminary in Ohio. She returned to Minnesota in 1860, where she was appointed as a teacher at Lac qui Parle by the Indian agent. A member of the Hazelwood Republic, established by Stephen R. Riggs for Christian Dakota, she remained at U.S.–controlled Camp Release in the 1862 war to serve as an interpreter for Tataŋka Nażiŋ (Standing Buffalo) and other Dakota leaders who corresponded with Sibley. When the majority of the Dakota were removed from Minnesota in 1863, LaFramboise sold her "Half-Breed Scrip" (based on her claim to land set aside for people of mixed Dakota-European ancestry in the Treaty of 1830) in order to fund her continued education at Rockford Seminary in Illinois. In August 1867 she received a teaching certificate granted by the Hennepin County superintendent of schools and was listed as a Minneapolis Public School teacher. She then went to Santee, Nebraska, in the spring of 1869, where she taught the Dakota people to read and write first in their own language and then in English. She died of tuberculosis in 1871.

Charles Eastman became famous as a Dakota writer whose explicit mission was to reclaim Minnesota as a Dakota place. He did so by situating all his books within the Dakota geography of Minnesota, placing actual events in specific Dakota places. Eastman was born in 1858 among the people of Cloud Man's village after their removal to the Upper Minnesota River following the Treaty of 1851. His grandparents were artist Seth Eastman and Wakaŋ Inażiŋ Wiŋ (Stands Sacred), Cloud Man's daughter. Charles Eastman's Dakota family was exiled to Canada in 1862. They lived along the Saskatchewan River in Saskatchewan and Manitoba until being reunited with Eastman's uncle and father, who had been in prison at Fort Davenport. Eastman then lived in South Dakota before attending Knox College in Illinois. He received a teaching certificate from the Hennepin County superintendent of schools in October 1866 and went on to receive an undergraduate degree from Dartmouth and a medical degree from Boston College. He was stationed at Pine Ridge Indian Reservation as a government physician during the Wounded Knee Massacre in 1890.[12]

Eastman would later write extensively about the origins of his family in Minnesota. In his book *Indian Boyhood*, he told of his great-grandfather Cloud Man, "whose original village was on the shores of Lakes Calhoun and Harriet,

Charles Eastman, the great-grandson of Maḣpiya Wiċaṡṭa or Cloud Man, shown in 1897, became widely known in the early twentieth century for his many writings recording the heritage of the Dakota in Minnesota.

now in the suburbs of the city of Minneapolis." He told of the ball game at a Waḣpetuŋwaŋ village on the Minnesota River, when he received his Dakota name, Ohiyesa, meaning the winner (see page 119). In another story Eastman referred to the place where his family went maple sugaring along the Minnesota River, their last Dakota sugar-making before 1862. Other stories about his people's history in Minnesota were relayed to him during his many childhood visits with Dakota elder and historian Smoky Day. Eastman and LaFramboise represent the impact of oral tradition about Dakota connections to Mni Sota Makoce as a bridge between oral history and printed primary sources.[13]

RECLAIMING DAKOTA PLACES IN MINNESOTA

Throughout the 150 years following exile, many Dakota have sought to retain or reclaim the heritage of their homelands, including places which had been part of their history and culture for hundreds of years. A history of Washington County and the St. Croix River region recorded in 1881 that Dakota people continued to make use of the wild rice resources along the Rice Creek corridor in Anoka and adjacent Washington counties. It reported that Rice Lake just east of Hugo "has long been the resort of a band of Indians from Mendota, who go to it every summer, bringing with them from eight to twelve lodges; they gather rice during the summer, which they sell in St. Paul. The lake affords them excellent fishing-ground, containing more pickerel than any other lake in the town. It is fed by springs on the east and west sides in such a quantity as to furnish a steady flow of water into Rice Creek."[14]

Exiled Dakota began returning to Minnesota in the 1870s, often going to places where the Dakota who had remained were still living and to places where they had lived before. Dakota anthropologist Ella Deloria wrote about her conversations with Minnesota Dakota: "Dakota felt pulled to the region where their dead were put to rest. A survivor of the 1862 Minnesota Uprising reported in her interview the following: 'We were driven out of Minnesota wholesale, though the majority of our people were innocent. But we could not stay away so we managed to find our way back, because our makapahas were here.' The term means earth-hills and is the Santee idiom for graves."[15]

Dakota residents of the Mendota area, who lived near the sacred hill of Oheyawahi/ Pilot Knob in the 1890s, were recorded by photographer James Methven.

Like many of the burial mounds that covered lakeshores and river-banks in Minnesota, a large mound at White Bear Lake was "demol-ished" in April 1889 as a result of a road project. These workmen are cut-ting trees in preparation for the destruction.

The attraction of burial sites and culturally important places was noted by whites. The *Hastings Gazette* reported on February 20, 1866, in reference to the Dakota's return to Oheyawahi, the hill opposite Fort Snelling, "The Pilot Knob is an ancient burial place of the Dakota's, and is yearly visited by many of the Indians of that nation." Despite the Dakota people's knowledge about places of importance to them, reclaiming their connection was difficult be-cause of white Minnesotans' residual prejudices against them and the growth and development of cities and towns, especially in the Twin Cities area. Even if knowledge of the importance of places as sacred to Dakota people existed, it was seldom seen as a reason to preserve such places.

As areas along the Minnesota and Mississippi rivers were developed from the late nineteenth century and into the twentieth, destruction of burial mounds was a routine activity. Such mounds were mapped extensively by archaeologists during late-nineteenth-century surveys. Many of these mounds have since disappeared. In a booklet called *Burial Places of the Aborigines of Kaposia*, South St. Paul historian Reinhold Weiner wrote in 1974 of the fate of many burial mounds. Of one mound group located on a bluff above Concord Street, Weiner wrote, "This bluff existed as late as 1885 when excavations be-gan for fill and sand and gravel . . . This was later known as the Stiefel pit." Of another mound he wrote, "In the winter of 1973 I tried to locate this mound but they had already started a sanitary land fill in this area." For a group of eleven mounds, once the "largest recorded burial place in South St. Paul," he noted their destruction through placement of several sandpits as well as street grading and home building: "This must have been a very impressive sight along the brow of this bluff to see those eleven mounds in a row."[16]

Efforts to protect such sites did not begin on a statewide level until the 1960s and 1970s. Archaeologists and Indian people working together helped create laws to protect burial places. But for many more sites, it was already too late.

BLACK DOG VILLAGE AND PROTECTING NATIVE AMERICAN BURIAL SITES

Traditional burial places in Minnesota continued to disappear at the hands of developers well into the twentieth century. After midcentury, however, attempts were made to halt the destruction. In the late nineteenth century a group of 104 mounds had been mapped in the area of Black Dog Village, located on the south side of the Minnesota River in present-day Eagan, then one of the townships of Dakota County. The first recorded excavation of a Black Dog cemetery took place in 1943 when Lloyd Wilford, a University of Minnesota archaeologist, explored a site disturbed by a molding sand pit on Thomas Keneally's farm in Eagan. Wilford found four historic Dakota burials in rough wooden coffins. Included with the burials were a variety of metal trade artifacts, glass and shell beads, and a pipestone pipe.[17]

Excavations of other burial sites in the area by the Science Museum of Minnesota in 1963 and by the Minnesota Historical Society in 1968 took place as a result of highway construction. Some of the remains uncovered were later reburied at the Lower Sioux Community. Another burial site at Black Dog was discovered in January 1977 after a report from a concerned citizen. The site was included in the same quarter-section where the first Black Dog burial was excavated in 1943. It was slated to be used as a borrow pit for gravel for the construction of a new Cedar Avenue Bridge. Although the highway itself did not affect burial sites, the contractor on the project proposed using a nearby property for the borrow pit. The digging was expected to impinge directly on the area where Wilford had found remains in 1943.[18]

In the months that followed, negotiations to save this burial site involved the Minnesota Sioux Inter-Tribal, Inc. (also known as the Sioux InterTribal Council), which represented the Upper Sioux, Lower Sioux, and Prairie Island communities; the Minnesota Indian Affairs Intertribal Board (now the Minnesota Indian Affairs Council); and the Minnesota Historical Society. Dakota representatives were unanimously opposed to any plan to rebury the bodies or further disturb the burial ground. Prior to 1976 there was no specific protection in state law for Indian burial grounds, though there was a rule against destroying tombstones and other features of cemeteries and discharging firearms in such places. This provision was amended in the 1976 legislative session to forbid damage to any "authenticated and identified Indian burial ground." The law provided that Indian cemeteries must be protected from destruction and that the Indian Affairs Board had to give permission to relocate an Indian burial ground, but it offered little instruction on how to "authenticate" and "identify" Indian burial grounds or what specifically could be done to save them from destruction. It was unclear how the various provisions might be applied to burial grounds on private property. There was also no funding mechanism for dealing with remains on private property.[19]

In the case of the Black Dog site in 1977, it did not appear practical to allow the remains to lie undisturbed. The landowner was obstinate in his desire to sell off the fill from his property. Even if the segment of land containing the remains was left untouched, it would be in a precarious position because of all the earth removed around it. And there was no funding available from the federal or state governments to acquire the land in order to protect the remains. The Minnesota Indian Affairs Council came to the conclusion that "the most feasible means of insuring the integrity of any remaining burials would involve the removal and reburial of the remaining burials in a secure location."[20]

The work of removal was delayed due to the continuing problem of finding the money to pay for the removal. Because of the time constraints, the excavation was primarily a salvage operation, not a scholarly one like Wilford's in 1943. Over a three-day period twelve archaeologists carefully removed remains and burial materials. After being inventoried the remains were reburied at Morton, on land belonging to the Lower Sioux Community.[21]

There were many lessons to learn from the events that unfolded at Black Dog in 1977. For Dakota people and native people of other tribes, the experience illustrated the need to strengthen laws to give them more control over what happened to American Indian cemeteries. In October 1977 Don Gurnoe, executive director of the Indian Affairs Intertribal Board, summarized the need to change the law, citing "inequities in current law making it legally impossible to protect Indian burials existing on private lands." The law made the authentication of a burial ground contingent on a request by a political subdivision owning the land. In the case of Black Dog, Gurnoe later wrote, "the only person having title to the land was the unsympathetic [private] landowner." If burials were discovered on private land there was no allocation of money or any procedures to be followed under the law.[22]

As a result of these problems there was a push to change the law. Veteran archaeologist Alan Woolworth, then with the Minnesota Historical Society, worked with Don Gurnoe on a bill submitted at the legislature in 1978 that was passed in early 1980 as Section 307.08 of Minnesota Statutes. Gurnoe noted that the new law looks at the problem of unmarked burials as "an issue of human dignity and treats it cross-culturally." More responsibility was given to the Minnesota Historical Society and the Indian Affairs Intertribal Board. The bill allocated fifteen thousand dollars for the costs of identification, posting, removal, and reburial of remains. One significant change was an amendment giving the Indian affairs board the power to approve any request to relocate authenticated and identified Indian burial grounds. This new provision stated that "if large Indian burial grounds are involved, efforts shall be made by the state to purchase and protect them instead of removing them to another location."[23]

Section 307.08 of Minnesota Statutes still bears the marks of the extensive changes made in the law in 1980. Despite these updates, however, protecting burial sites on private property continues to be a persistent challenge, with no easy solutions.

PROTECTING DAKOTA SACRED SITES

One major challenge for Dakota people today is that despite being able to live within their ancient homelands, they own little of the land and can seldom control what happens to their sacred sites. Even in the case of public lands they often have little influence over the results of decision-making. Perhaps the most contentious issues have occurred within the area known as Bdote, surrounding the mouth of the Minnesota River, the site of some Dakota creation stories and also, coincidentally, within the Fort Snelling military reservation negotiated in Pike's treaty of 1805.

Many areas within Bdote were preserved because of their natural features and their connections to European American history, but until recent years the importance of these places for Dakota people had been little noted. Minnehaha Falls, several miles north of Fort Snelling, was preserved beginning in the 1880s because of its association with the inauthentic Indian legends popularized by Henry Wadsworth Longfellow in *The Song of Hiawatha*. Later the homes of Henry H. Sibley and Jean-Baptiste Faribault in Mendota opposite the fort were preserved through the efforts of the Daughters of the American Revolution. Fort Snelling State Park, including within its boundaries the site of Pike's treaty signing and, unheralded, the concentration camp of 1862–63, came into being in 1962. In the 1950s the remains of Historic Fort Snelling, the original fort built in the 1820s, were saved from highway construction and the Minnesota Historical Society began to reconstruct the fort as it existed in the 1820s. In none of these efforts was the importance of these places to the Dakota a major focus.[24]

In the 1990s, the proposed expansion and reconstruction of Highway 55 from downtown Minneapolis to the Mendota Bridge led to controversy because of its effect on Minnehaha Park and the area to the south around Mni Sni, Coldwater Spring. A coalition of environmentalists and native people fought this construction through protests and by occupying houses, groves of trees, and lands in the highway's path.[25]

Among those opposing the highway was a group known as the Mendota Mdewakanton Dakota community, descendants of Dakota people who intermarried with French Canadian employees of Henry Sibley, including the family of trader Jean-Baptiste Faribault and Hypolite Dupuis, Sibley's bookkeeper. Dupuis was married to Angelique Renville, a cousin of Little Crow, the leader of the Kap'oża band. These families, not among those exiled in 1862–63, continued their association with the area of Mendota throughout the late 1800s and into the twentieth century.[26]

Though they were relatives of Dakota who were members of the federally recognized Dakota communities in Minnesota, the Mendota Dakota were not a federally recognized community. However, their leader, Bob Brown, and other community members felt an obligation to defend sites of importance to Dakota people. Coldwater Spring and other sites in the area were directly endangered because of the effect construction would have on the water and on the landscape around the spring, which was located on property once operated by the Bureau of Mines–Twin Cities Campus, just east of the path of Highway 55.[27]

Making the case for the importance of the spring and the area known as Bdote to the Minnesota Department of Transportation and to the Federal Highway Administration proved problematic. In retrospect it is clear that government administrators' skepticism about the area's cultural importance was not just about the people—a non-federally recognized group of Dakota—bringing the message. It was also about the message itself, that there were now Dakota people making their voices heard in the Fort Snelling area and in larger Minnesota, seeking to reclaim their homelands and be involved in decisions about places of cultural importance to them.

Subsequently a cultural resource firm was hired by the Minnesota Department of Transportation to examine some of the issues associated with the highway construction. While the study found no evidence that the highway would impinge on historical resources, including an arrangement of four oak trees said by some to be culturally important to the Dakota, it compiled evidence that Coldwater Spring could very well be a Traditional Cultural Property, or TCP, under the criteria of the National Register of Historic Places. Designation as a place of traditional cultural importance is one way to protect sites from damage during projects paid for with federal money. The study recommended a full TCP evaluation, including consultation with Dakota and other Indian people

The Sacredness of Coldwater Spring

The Mendota Dakota were not alone in saying Coldwater and Bdote were important. In 1999, Dakota tribal governments in Minnesota passed resolutions in support of preserving Coldwater Spring, and at a press conference Dakota elder Reverend Gary Cavender spoke about the importance of the area for Dakota people:

> We are coming here to talk about sacred land, and especially the sacredness of that place. In our creation story of where we first began as people on this earth, that place was sacred long before anybody from Europe arrived and saw the place. Because of the topography of the land and because of the coming together of two great rivers (Minnesota and Mississippi) it is called "Mdote" or the throat of the waters, and they named a town after it—Mendota—although it is pronounced altogether different.
>
> In our Creation myth we the Dakota, the Seven Fires of the Dakota, came from the belt of Orion—the seven planets of the belt of Orion, the seven stars—and arrived at the convolution of the Minnesota and Mississippi Rivers, and so in some respects it is our Eden, and the land around there is sacred as well. There is that sacred spring that is in negotiation, that sacred spring is the dwelling place of Uŋkteȟi, the God of the Waters, and in that spring there is an underground river that goes into the big river, and that is his passageway to get out into the world. To block the sacred passageway would be courting drought and things of that nature that have to do with water, because after all, this is the God of the water. So when you hear a thunderstorm and it starts to rain, that is the Underwater God having battle with the Sky God and the reason for that battle is so that the rain may come down and replenish the earth, and the Sky God is fighting—throwing down thunderbolts to fertilize the land. That is a scientific fact, and so it is not without reason that this land should be sacred to us, and so the Underwater God lives there. We came there as human beings and so that is our Eden, and the irony of it all is that in 1862–1863 that was almost the end of us as people, because that was the Fort Snelling concentration camp. It may have been a full circle for us—the beginning and the ending, which is sacred in and of itself, but the land is sacred. The high bluffs where we went to trade provisions, the throat of convolution of the two rivers where we got our start and almost where we got our ending. There are bodies there, there is a sacred cemetery there. Maybe all of it is gone but it is still sacred.
>
> We hold our lands sacred, but these lands are more sacred because of the history, because of the myth and what we are pleading for is some understanding. To understand our sense of sacredness of the land. To use our image as the ultimate environmentalists—we may not be, but we have a connection to the land that perhaps you don't understand and so this is more than an argument over a plot of land. It is a debate of two cultures and the understanding of the sacredness and what is sacred. We can't say that the land has nothing on it and disregard the sacredness and go ahead and build on it. Wašicuŋ seem to have the ability to prioritize, and when it comes to progress, spirituality or sacredness takes a back seat to progress. We don't have that understanding, it is not in us, even though we've been in your culture for at least two hundred years now and we've only been citizens of our own land since 1925. So how can we expect you to understand those things when you didn't even recognize us as human beings until the twentieth century. But what we're asking for is the beginning of understanding. Use this sacred place as a neutral ground to start a journey of understanding each other and leave it alone. Our people's beginning spirits are there and our people's ending spirits are there. All of the Gods are there. The Wakaŋ Taŋka is there. The Wakaŋ Taŋka is everywhere and so for us it's only a little patch of land we're asking for. The economy isn't going to collapse. There is an alternative way to solve the problem, but for us it is a great, great sacrifice and we've sacrificed so much for so long. All we're asking for is a little understanding and perhaps respecting what we hold sacred![ii] ■

to examine the question. Referring to places of cultural importance as TCPs was one of several ways tribal groups could seek to have an effect on government actions. Sacred sites were also specifically mentioned in President Bill Clinton's Executive Order No. 13007 of May 24, 1996, relating to Indian sacred sites. However, the order merely required government agencies to accommodate tribes in using the sites and did not offer any real protection for them.[28]

Despite the efforts of highway opponents, Highway 55 was built, although because of a state law its design had to be altered to minimize the impact on the flow of water to Coldwater Spring. In the years that followed the Highway 55 controversy, action was taken on other fronts in the area of Bdote. In 2003, as a result of plans for a 157-unit housing development on Pilot Knob, the hill was nominated to the National Register as a TCP and a place of importance because of its association with the signing of the Treaty of 1851. In 2004 the Keeper of the National Register agreed that the site was eligible, though it could not be listed because of the landowners' objections. In the following years this private land was purchased through a variety of funding agencies and preserved as open space by the City of Mendota Heights, precluding any development.[29]

One of the difficulties in protecting Oheyawahi/Pilot Knob and other Dakota sacred sites has to do with the concept under National Register criteria of "integrity," meaning the degree to which a site preserves the characteristics that make it important. The question of integrity is easier to answer about buildings or archaeological sites than it is about natural sites. Darlene St. Clair, an educator and Lower Sioux community member, noted that in some cases Dakota traditional cultural sites bear the litter of settlement, industrialization, and commercialization of the landscape, including industrial structures and government buildings. Pilot Knob is surrounded by freeways, the Wakaŋ Tipi/Carver's Cave site is on the edge of a railroad yard, and the Coldwater Spring site is filled with crumbling buildings. The question of whether such sites can still be sacred for Dakota people is often raised. But as St. Clair noted, to assume these sites have to be naturally beautiful to be TCPs is to mistake beauty for sacredness. These sites may once have been beautiful and it might be good to protect them from further changes. But even if they lose the natural beauty they once had, their sacredness is not destroyed.[30]

In October 2009 Lakota Chief Arvol Looking Horse participated in a pipe ceremony on Pilot Knob to celebrate the protection of the land on the hill from development, noting that sacred sites are for Dakota, Lakota, and Nakota peoples "power points, the grid" through which people interact with the landscape. From this point of view development, while damaging to the environmental characteristics of sacred places, sometimes reflects the energy and power found there. Chris Leith, the late spiritual leader of the Prairie

Coldwater Spring, like many sites sacred to the Dakota, survived despite the debris of industrial building such as structures south of the basin where the water from the spring is collected. Since this photo was taken in 2011, the National Park Service has removed the buildings and is undertaking re-vegetation of the property.

Island Dakota, also present at the 2009 event, stated in a 2003 interview that Bdote, a site of creation for the Dakota that contains many sacred sites, was a "vortex" in the landscape. The very presence of Fort Snelling, the airport, and the complex freeway system there reflected the site's powerful energy. Leith cautioned, however, that powerful spiritual places should rightly be left alone, not because they would be damaged by what was built upon them but because in the long run the nature of the place would damage what was built there.[31]

Such perspectives are often far from the minds of government agents who make decisions about Dakota sacred sites. In 2005 plans were under way to dispose of the Bureau of Mines site that included Coldwater Spring. As part of an environmental review process, the National Park Service (NPS) hired a cultural resource firm to examine the cultural importance of Coldwater Spring for Dakota and other native groups. Through research and interviews, the firm determined that Coldwater Spring was a TCP for the Dakota people. The report cited the spring "as being significant at a statewide level as a TCP associated with the Dakota communities in Minnesota," involved in Dakota traditional practices and "important for the continued maintenance of their cultural identity." The report also noted, in relation to the traditional cultural property's boundaries, "There is a consensus that the boundaries of Coldwater

Spring include not only where the water flows from the rock wall, but also the source of the spring and the location where the spring water finally deposits into the Mississippi River."[32]

The study's findings were based not just on historical facts about the spring itself but on the fact that springs like this one—its water used in the ini ceremony, also called inipi, or "they sweat"—have been known for many years to be of great significance for Dakota people in Minnesota. In addition, Coldwater Spring was located within not only Bdote but also Ṭaku Wakaŋ Tipi, the place where the water spirit Uŋkteȟi was said to reside. The precarious written record left by whites that the spring was important to Dakota people was not necessary to prove its significance. The traditional accounts given today and the historical records of the importance of springs were enough to show that this spring was a TCP for Dakota people.[33]

Despite this report and the earlier testimony of Dakota people, NPS staff announced publicly in August 2006 that they would not accept the study's findings about Coldwater Spring. By that point the Mississippi National River and Recreation Area superintendent had already written to Dakota communities, stating, "After thoroughly reviewing the evidence provided in the report the National Park Service has concluded that neither the Center nor Coldwater Spring meet the specific criteria in the National Register to designate the area as a TCP." The letter concluded by acknowledging that the spring had "significant contemporary cultural importance to many Indian people" and noting that "the spring is already a contributing element to the Fort Snelling National Historic Landmark and the Fort Snelling National Register of Historic Places District." In recognition of the "contemporary cultural importance" of the site to the Dakota and the significance of the site in Fort Snelling history, protections would be recommended.[34]

The condescending words suggested that although the federal government rejected the Dakota communities' claim to the spring as a historical and cultural feature and in the process rejected the history and cultural traditions on which the claim was based, the park service would try to protect the spring because it was part of a site important for, among other things, its role in colonizing Minnesota and sending the Dakota into exile in 1863. The area's place in Dakota history was not significant; its white history was. A reaction to these offensive comments could be seen in the support among some Dakota people for a movement to tear down Historic Fort Snelling, where interpretation of military history was often the emphasis to the exclusion of its role for the Dakota.[35]

The idea that the spring's cultural and historical importance had to be verified using written historical sources is a problem all too familiar to the Dakota, who in trying to reclaim their homelands are often required to prove, through written sources recorded by white people, the cultural importance of every bit of ground in Minnesota, one square inch at a time.

In fact, the very idea of Traditional Cultural Property was intended in part to avoid requiring written historical evidence produced by non-native people to nominate sites to the National Register. Thomas F. King, who together with Patricia Parker wrote Bulletin 38 of the National Register, which pioneered the concept of the TCP, has written that a people's belief in the sacredness of particular kinds of places within their homeland makes those places important traditionally regardless of the historical record associated with them: "Traditional cultural properties must be respected for their own sakes—regardless of whether they are referred to specifically in oral history." He argues that "traditional cultural properties can legitimately be identified through field inspection by knowledgeable people in the absence of specific association with known traditions, and that whole classes of properties—such as ancestral archeological sites—can be categorically identified as traditional cultural properties."[36]

The criteria of the National Register as interpreted in Bulletin 38 states that a traditional cultural place is eligible for the National Register "because of its association with cultural practices or beliefs of a living community that (a) are rooted in that community's history, and (b) are important in maintaining the continuing cultural identity of the community." King wrote, "if a community traditionally believes that rocks pointed toward the sky are places of communication between this world and the spirit world, and if belief in communication between these worlds is important in maintaining the community's identity, the fact that its members may not know of any pointed rocks in a given area doesn't make such rocks, when discovered in the area, any less recognizable to the community's elders as places of interworld communication, which automatically have cultural significance."[37]

In the case of Coldwater Spring, direct oral tradition is related to the spring, but federal officials declared this to be inadequate. One official lamented the lack of more detailed narratives which would support the spring's significance. Anthropologist John Norder provided an answer to such demands. Norder, whose family is from Spirit Lake, North Dakota, and who has worked in a number of native communities in the Great Lakes region, argued the lack of relevance about the need to prove native connections to particular places—in this case rock art in the border lakes region of northern Minnesota and Ontario—through stories or detailed explanations of their origin and meaning. Landscape itself is perceived by many groups as having its own agency and power with which people today engage, regardless of a relationship proved through narrative. Even if they do not know the "full story" about places of importance, they understand them and know how to act toward them when they see them. In other words, the traditional importance of such places is recorded in behavior, not narrative. Norder noted, "the landscape provides the impetus for stories as much as humans do. Places in the landscape speak, and it is the responsibility of the people inhabiting it to listen and to learn what they must to engage appropriately with it."[38]

Norder's analysis recalls the words of elder Chris Leith, who, during the contentious process which led to the preservation of Oheyawahi/Pilot Knob, was asked repeatedly for a more detailed explanation about the meaning of the hill for Dakota people. Leith stated that the origins of Oheyawahi's sacred character could not be explained by any person: "There are many questions that no human being can answer." When Leith was pressed for details about the connection of the site to Uŋkteħi, he stated,

> I just answered it . . . You asked me something in a different way . . . That's a European concept. If they don't get an answer, well then they'll ask another way. They can't accept what they've been told. They want to change it . . . Our ceremonies come in dreams and visions. Our way of life is conducted under dreams and visions. We don't change it. We don't have that right. It is not of our making.[39]

According to the cultural-resources study that found Coldwater Spring to be a traditional cultural place, the meaning of Coldwater Spring can only be understood within the Dakota's beliefs—ceremonial and cultural—about springs of various kinds. Culturally important places are significant for traditional reasons regardless of whether the particular place has the kinds of specific associations that connect Coldwater Spring to Dakota history and identity. In Charles Eastman's account of his boyhood years in his family's exile in Manitoba, he was asked by elders, as part of his becoming a man, to sacrifice to the Great Mystery that which was most precious to him—his dog. He and his grandmother took the body of the dog and laid it inside a cave located along the Saskatchewan River. The immense cave was located fifty feet above the river, under a cliff. "A little stream of limpid water trickled down from a spring within the cave. The little watercourse served as a sort of natural staircase for the visitors. A cool, pleasant atmosphere exhaled from the mouth of the cavern. Really it was a shrine of nature and it is not strange that it was so regarded by the tribe." They laid down the dog's body, decorated and accompanied by a pipe, within the cave. The boy's grandmother spoke the offering: "O, Great Mystery, we hear thy voice in the rushing waters below us! We hear thy whisper in the great oaks above! Our spirits are refreshed with thy breath from within this cave. O, hear our prayer! Behold this little boy and bless him! Make him a warrior and a hunter as thou didst make his father and grandfather."[40]

Sheldon Peters Wolfchild, a Lower Sioux Indian Community member and activist, commented on this story, noting that Dakota people living so distant

The area known as Wakaŋ Tipi originally consisted of six caves but now includes only two, the largest of which was named after its first European visitor, and an area above on the adjacent bluff which once contained hundreds of burial mounds. In 1766 explorer Jonathan Carver visited the "remarkable cave" which he called Wakon-teebe (Wakaŋ Tipi), "Dwelling of the Great Spirit," noting the cave contained many drawings "which appeared very ancient." Dakota have viewed the site as one related to Uŋkteȟi, indicated by some of the pictographs of snakes—generally associated with the powerful underwater spirit—on its walls. Carver also referred to the burial place above the cave and noted that Dakota bands, despite their extensive travels, always brought "the bones of their dead" to this location. In his journal he called it "the burying place of the Mottobautonway band," a reference to the Bdewakaŋtuŋwaŋ or Mantanton Dakota. He also mentioned that chiefs met there to hold councils in the summer. The next spring Carver described a ceremony involving many Dakota bands at this site.[iii]

Following Carver's published account, widely distributed beginning in 1778, many other visitors came to the cave and explored its interior, although some had trouble finding it, perhaps because of fallen rock blocking its entrance. Later on however, like many important Dakota sites, the area was overcome by development, including the construction of a brewery and then railroads around the cave and a housing development on the bluffs which destroyed many of the burial mounds. Four of the caves were blown up. What is left of both areas has been preserved in Indian Mounds Regional Park, including six mounds on the edge of the park, and in the Bruce Vento Nature Sanctuary, which includes a cave and the former rail yard, which is being restored to native vegetation. The cave's entrance is currently blocked by iron doors, although the spring within continues to flow. A 2003 cultural resource analysis of the history and cultural meaning of the cave found it eligible for nomination to the National Register of Historic Places under several criteria as a Traditional Cultural Property and as a place of importance in non-Dakota history.[iv] ▪

By the end of the nineteenth century, the city of St. Paul set out to preserve the few remaining burial mounds on what was an extensive bluff at Wakaŋ Tipi, now part of Indian Mounds Regional Park.

from their homelands had found places that echoed the importance of those they had known for centuries. This cave bore great similarities to Wakaŋ Tipi/ Carver's Cave, where early European visitors mentioned that the Dakota yearly brought the bodies of their deceased family members for blessing. In finding such locations even in exile, Dakota people made clear the importance of place and the characteristics that made such places sacred, ultimately defining them as traditional cultural places.[41]

Another spring, located near Shakopee and called Boiling Springs, was nominated to and placed on the National Register in 2002 as a TCP, based mainly on an early newspaper article and the testimony of Gary Cavender, a Dakota elder whose traditional accounts were called into question by the NPS when he spoke about Coldwater Spring. The water in this spring was unusual in that it boiled up from the bottom of a deep pool. Given this example, Wolf- child pointed out that the Dakota did not view all springs in the same way. The water from this spring was sacred, according to Dakota elders, but, due to its unusual qualities, was not appropriate for use in ceremonies. Instead, the water of springs like Coldwater—which seeped from between the rocks—was preferred for sweat lodges and other ceremonies.[42]

Despite community members' testimony, agencies such as the National Park Service continue to ask for written verification of a site's importance. Dakota historian Waziyatawiŋ, writing in *Remember This!* noted that verification is a common requirement in white interpretations of oral history and oral tradition, not just in relation to cultural places. She cited Vine Deloria Jr.'s observation that the differences in native and western views include the belief that native people "tend to be excitable, are subjective and not objective, and consequently are unreliable observers" and that all of the evidence their traditions present must be verified. Waziyatawiŋ comments, "This dismissal of Indigenous per- spectives is symptomatic of the relationship of the colonizer to the colonized. Colonial domination can be maintained only if the history of the subjugated is denied and that of the colonizer elevated and glorified."[43]

Dakota views on these questions are borne out in part by NPS actions in relation to the Coldwater/Bureau of Mines property. In 2005 and later, Dakota communities in Minnesota sought to obtain ownership of the site, citing their cultural connection to the spring and to Ṭaḳu Wakaŋ Tipi and Bdote and making reference to the rights retained under Pike's Treaty of 1805, Article 3, which states, "The United States promise on their part to permit the Sioux to pass, repass, hunt or make other uses of the said districts, as they have formerly done, without any other exception, but those specified in article first."[44]

At a contentious meeting in February 2009 at the Minneapolis Veterans Ad- ministration Hospital, which is built on a portion of Ṭaḳu Wakaŋ Tipi/Morgan's Mound, various Dakota people spoke out in favor of Dakota ownership and objected to the NPS's continuing refusal to recognize the importance of the place for the Dakota. In January 2010, at the end of the environmental review process, the National Park Service announced it would retain ownership of the property for itself, to be used as a public park. The park service issued a press release: "The public's interest in this site throughout this process illustrates the great significance that the Dakota and so many others attach to this special place . . . We are excited to be the caretakers, and to work with many partners to tell all the stories associated with this place. There are many layers of history associated with this site, from the Dakota to European settlement to 20th century mining technology." Since the park service had consistently denied any historical or cultural connection of the Dakota to the property, the statement was surprising. Rejecting Dakota traditions and then using them in the agency's historical interpretation appeared to add insult to injury.[45]

The example of Coldwater Spring suggests the Dakota have a long way to go in reclaiming their homelands in Minnesota, whether in achieving protection for their sacred places or in the simplest sense of making Minnesotans aware of their history and contributions. Ignorance and skepticism about their place in the region continues to be widespread. In 2012, when recalling the events of 1862, many remember what happened in August and September of that year. But far fewer remember the words of the Dakota leaders who came to see the French official Joseph Marin in 1754, carrying a map and stating, "No one could be unaware that from the mouth of the Wisconsin to Leech Lake, these territories belong to us. On all the points and in the little rivers we have had villages. One can still see the marks of our bones which are still there . . . These are territories that we hold from no one except the Master of Life who gave them to us. And although we have been at war against all the nations, we never abandoned them."[46]

Reclaiming Our Voices

[ERIN GRIFFIN] **The Dakota people**, and many other nations, have been physically, culturally, and spiritually connected to this land long before their encounter with Europeans. The issue, however, is not black and white: people in history were not simply divided into victims and perpetrators, nor were Dakota people simply removed from the land and from history in one single action. The outcomes have become just as complex as those that created Dakota loss to begin with. In an interview, Dakota historian Waziyatawiŋ said, "Everything about who we are and who we are supposed to be makes sense only in this context, on this land base." The removal of Dakota people from Mni Sota Makoce disrupted access not only to the land itself but also to our sacred places. Such places are essential to our being and our connection to the land. Their loss has consequences for our cultural identity. As anthropologist Keith Basso stated, "What people make of their places is closely connected to what they make of themselves as members of society and inhabitants of the earth, and while the two activities may

>>

>> be separable in principle, they are deeply joined in practice."[v]

As Dakota people, if we are required to gain permission from Minnesota officials or, worse, denied the ability to visit our sacred sites and maintain them in a culturally appropriate way, we are subsequently being denied the ability to maintain our culture and spirituality. Without the ability to contextualize our cultural identity in the physical spaces in which it was created, its continued existence becomes uncertain.

An issue related to the imposed distance between our communities and reservations is the effect it has had on individual Dakota people. In the specific time period surrounding the Dakota–U.S. War of 1862 and Dakota removal, Dakota individuals, families, and bands suffered a range of experiences. Some Dakota left "voluntarily" before the wars, some escaped shortly afterward, and some were forcibly removed from Mni Sota Makoce. Further complicating matters, a few Dakota were allowed to remain under the protection of missionaries, and some Dakota, referred to as "Loyal Mdewakantons," were allowed to return from exile and resettle in Minnesota in 1886 and 1889. This resettlement was a "reward" for the loyalists' perceived alliance with Minnesotans during the war. The displacement of Dakota people did not happen at one time or in one action; it happened in different ways and at different times for different groups. This complexity further complicates how Dakota people perceive our connection to Mni Sota Makoce and Minnesota.[vi]

Interconnected to this invisibility and the partial histories marked on the land is the dismissal of Dakota perspectives, silencing of Dakota voices, and perpetuation of partial histories. If the diverse Dakota perspectives are not acknowledged or accepted as additional truths to the fabric of history, then that history is limited. Finally, whether we are Dakota or Minnesotan, if we continue to accept only partial histories, we will continue to limit our understanding of them and their effects on us. ∎

THE POWER OF PLACE

Human beings have recorded their relationships with places in innumerable ways throughout their existence. They have given descriptive names to special features of the landscape, gathered in powerful areas, and marked their experiences on the land. The power of place is undeniable. Many of us have experienced it in different ways during our lifetimes—returning to ancestral homelands or family burial sites, visiting spectacular places of worship or historic battlefields, or standing in awe of remarkable natural beauty. These places tell us stories and provide us with long-lasting memories. It is through stories and experiences that we understand the power of place.

For Dakota people, this place, Mni Sota Makoce, embodies all of those characteristics. It has been described as our "Garden of Eden," where the first Dakota people—the Wicaŋhpi Oyate—walked upon the land given to them by the Creator, the Maker of All Things. As such, everything is imbued with an element of wakaŋ, or sacredness. In describing the "great mystery," Ohiyesa Charles Eastman observed that sacredness is encountered as it is present in the natural landscape. Those encounters are remembered still today through Dakota place names that tell the stories and histories of our interaction with the land—Minnetonka, Chanhassen, Mahtomedi, Wayzata. And what makes a place sacred is collective memories.[47]

While story and memory form the basis of all our human experience, it is the written record that we have come to rely on as primary evidence of land tenure and possession. However, that "written" proof includes the earliest forms of inscription on rocks and in caves as well as maps drawn on birch bark and wood described by the first European explorers to this region, the French. Their documentation of villages, burial mounds, and names at the beginning of the seventeenth century testify to the importance of this place as the Dakota homeland. In the extended relationships Dakota people developed with the explorers, the French seemed to understand how they valued kinship, not only between human beings but also with the land.

Their relationship with the land was intimate and reverent. The Dakota knew Mni Sota Makoce as an interconnected network for travel and subsistence and followed seasonal rounds of hunting, fishing, gathering, and cultivating. They understood the power of place and gathered together for ceremonies and celebrations, games and feasts, and to bury the dead. As missionaries and traders entered their territories, the Dakota shared their knowledge of the land and its abundant resources. Conflicts were inevitable, but it was inconceivable that Dakota people would ever be separated from the land of their birth.

By 1805 the lines were beginning to be drawn. Not the maps of waterways and centuries-old travel routes, but the demarcation of possession. Mutual hunting and ricing areas shared by the Dakota and Ojibwe were divided in 1835 by the "S & C" line implemented by the U.S. government. Treaty negotiations in 1851 were supplemented by a written Dakota-language version that underscores the differences in understanding about the meaning of land "possession" and the difficulties of translation by a missionary and interpreters. The vast homeland of the Dakota, "from the great forest to the open prairies," was reduced by 1858 to a ten-mile strip running 140 miles on the south side of the Minnesota River from Lake Traverse to just west of present-day New Ulm. And then exile in 1863.

To "reclaim" Minnesota as a Dakota place is to once again interact with what is sacred and to recall its stories. We believe the land remembers, and as we walk near Minneopa Falls or in Blue Mound State Park or around Lake Calhoun, we are surrounded by those memories held in the land. These stories recount Dakota experiences and help us remember beyond the historical record. The collective voices of the earliest inhabitants, the explorers, the missionaries, and the historians of this place tell us unmistakably that this is Mni Sota Makoce—Land of the Dakota.

Contributor Statements
and Acknowledgments

GWEN WESTERMAN

In 1995 my uncle told me that one day I would understand how deeply connected I was to Mankato in particular, and to Minnesota. I have remembered his words and through the years have come to learn what he meant. We are the direct descendants of many figures in nineteenth-century Dakota history: Yajopi, whose village was near what is now North Mankato; Tacaŋdaħupa Hotaŋka, or His Pipe, one of the 303 Dakota men condemned in 1862; Mazamani, killed at the Battle of Wood Lake; Makanahotoŋmani, imprisoned at Davenport after the war; Wakiŋyaŋ Taŋka, known as Big Thunder or Little Crow III; Iśtaħba or Sleepy Eye; Joseph LaFramboise, the Odawa and French trader who married into Iśtaħba's family; and Kaŋǵi Duta, also known as Scarlet Crow. And we know the names of our grandmothers as well. Our roots are deep in the Minnesota River valley, the Big Woods of Minnesota, and the tallgrass prairies of the northern Great Plains.

Years later, my uncle told me about a project he was involved with to produce a history of the relationship of Dakota people with the land. As a founding board member of Two Rivers Community Development Corporation, my uncle—Floyd Westerman—asked me to help lead that project. Especially exciting to me was the goal to use the written historical records and our oral traditions and history. My role was to help conduct the oral histories and collect the stories about our presence in this place, Mni Sota Makoce.

Together with Glenn Wasicuna and Erin Griffin, I traveled to the four Dakota communities in Minnesota, to Nebraska and South Dakota, and to Manitoba to listen to the stories our relatives had to tell—in Dakota and in English—about our land and their lives. Other times, they came to us or we met at community gatherings and powwows. We had a series of interview questions and an approach to conducting the oral histories, but mostly we listened to what our relatives wanted to tell us. They held our hands and recounted their family stories, they cried and laughed about what had been written in books

225

about our Dakota people, and they asked us to come back because they had more to share. In short, they have entrusted us with their words.

More than anything, this project has been a collaborative endeavor. We traveled among the different bands, communities, reservations, reserves, countries, and families to gather this history. We spoke with our relatives in English and in Dakota. We learned that we have only scratched the surface of the vast knowledge that our people hold. This book will be just one among the many more we hope will follow. We have high expectations that it will inspire many more stories, from many more viewpoints, and above all, more sharing of what it means to be a part of this beautiful homeland. I am humbled to have been a small part of the process. Ihuŋ, wopida ye. Henana epe kte. De winuna miye.

BRUCE WHITE

My mother, Helen McCann, was born in Minnesota, and my father, Gilbert White, was born in Shanghai, China, the child of missionaries. I was born in Japan. For a good part of my childhood we lived overseas. During that time my parents insisted on the importance of respect for the people and the cultures of those in whose countries we were guests. When my family returned to live in Minnesota, it made sense to act with the same respect for the original inhabitants of this place, of whom we were guests.

Because my mother was a historian, I met several generations of the state's historians, many connected with the Minnesota Historical Society, when I was a child. I later had the opportunity to work with some of them, including Rhoda Gilman and Alan Woolworth, both of whom have continued to share generously their knowledge and encouragement with me. From such Minnesota historians, I learned something of the skills for which I have always strived, of dogged research and writing and the pursuit of knowledge without prejudice. Without their aid, it would not have been possible for me to do the work I did on this project.

In 2007 Syd Beane and Sheldon Wolfchild asked me to be part of this project. I was happy to accept because the relationship of people to the lands in which they live has always been a strong interest of mine. Perhaps because I lived in so many places as a child, I have come to appreciate what it means to have a homeland. I had also learned something of the Dakota connection to Minnesota beginning in 1999 from the Mendota Mdewakanton Dakota community, whose ancestors have lived at the mouth of the Minnesota River for generations, and who have applied their efforts to protect Dakota sacred sites.

In working on this project, I sought to show that written records could be combined with the Dakota oral tradition to shape new understandings of Dakota history. At project meetings, when someone pointed out, justly, the issue of bias against Dakota cultural understanding in the written records, I tried to counter with the possibilities of seeing Dakota meanings sometimes unconsciously recorded in such documents.

At one of the spirited project meetings, one participant referred to the "stale information" found in many written accounts about the Dakota. It was an important point to make. Many accounts are stale because they are biased, with little attempt to get at Dakota understandings. For many people, history is defined as being based on a written record, often the most biased written records. In this project we have rejected this kind of ethnocentric understanding of the meaning of history.

For me, learning something of Dakota understandings about their homelands has made my perspective of this place much richer because my view of Minnesota now resonates with a sense of the experiences of those who lived here before. As a result of the time spent working on this common topic with the other participants in the project, who are now my friends, I believe our work has not ended. Instead it is just beginning. We have learned a great deal from each other, but we have a lot more to learn. And I know there will be others who carry on after us, telling the story of the Dakota and their homelands.

I would like to thank Kate Regan for aid in writing the project grant proposals, Larry M. Wyckoff for creating the project database and transcribing documents, and Virginia Martin for research and editorial assistance.

GLENN WASICUNA

Ate Wakaŋ Tanka ho hiyuwayaye kiŋhan anayagoptan kte kehe. Ho aŋpetu kiŋ de ho waŋ unsiya hiyuciciye. Mitakuyapi uŋsimadapi kte taku kiksuya unsipi kiŋ hŋan taŋyan weksuye kte.

Great Spirit, you said you will listen if I send my voice to you. Today with a sincere voice I ask our ancestors for compassion in that I remember the accounts of our history correctly.

Being involved with this group of bright, energetic, articulate (I could go on, but I think I am allowed only three adjectives) people to create *Mni Sota Makoce: The Land of the Dakota* greatly contributed to my healing as a Dakota man. My family and tribe were not exiled into what is now Canada but were part of a concerted, well-thought-out plan implemented in the sixteenth and seventeenth centuries by our own people to save "what is Dakota." Our tribe was given the responsibility of preserving the language, traditions, and culture. And they did.

Then with research for *Land of the Dakota,* coupled with personal accounts of events, it all made sense. Only then did I understand what Tuŋwiŋ Molly must have felt when she recounted her memory of being a little girl holding onto a horse's tail—fleeing. And the archeological evidence of Dakota presence uncovered in the far reaches of northern Manitoba where no roads exist even today—the significance of these details became clear. Dakota people approached us wanting to relate information. It is endless. We realized we were just scratching the surface of something so enormous it is beyond comprehension—for now.

We say thank you to all those people who have tried over the years to tell the stories of the Dakota people. Now it is our turn. There are some magnificent young Dakota out there today able to tell who they are without fear or shame. Listen to them this time. At the beginning, we Dakota people held out our hands in friendship, greeting, and willingness to share what we could. History has shown us what took place.

We say thank you to all those who took part in the making of *Mni Sota Makoce*. But most of all, we say thank you, wopida, to all the Dakota people who took part in this project and helped us. Many more Dakota people out there have something to share and tell that will promote understanding.

It is a painful journey. I cannot go to Tiŋta Wiŋta yet because Wakiŋyan Zi Sapa is no longer physically there. He shared with us the history and his knowledge of the people. When we were getting ready to leave, the look on his face said, "There is more, don't go yet. I will see you again." He passed on shortly after that. I will never forget TaŚuŋka Wakiŋyaŋ Ohitika. He led me every step of the way through my first Sun Dance.

Today I am so grateful that I work with Phyllis Redday Roberts at Tiośpa Zina Tribal School in Sisseton, South Dakota. She understands the Dakota ways. She lives the Dakota way. She speaks the Dakota way.

I work with Dakota people of all ages at Tiośpa Zina Tribal School. I see young boys and girls in the hallways, and they say, "uŋkaŋna, hau, toked yauŋ he?" It is not the same as in English, "grandpa, hello, how are you?" They are speaking from their hearts when they speak Dakota—the way the Creator decreed.

So, this *Mni Sota Makoce: The Land of the Dakota* is a blueprint. From it will evolve many more books about Dakota people, from a long time ago, through the years, to today.

KATHERINE BEANE

As a Dakota person I am searching for the truth of what happened to my ancestors and an explanation of why my family was raised outside our homeland of Minnesota, to which we have such strong ties. Throughout this project I have been learning and reflecting upon where these ties come from and where we as a community must go to ensure our knowledge is not lost within a state that holds a name in our very language but whose inhabitants, in large part, have no clue where the meaning lies.

To a large extent the Dakota people were erased from Minnesota history after 1862. Telling our history is part of a quest for full acceptance of Dakota people. It requires a lot of inner strength to dig into the historical archives that contain written records of my people. Those of us who may understand some of the materials on a more personal level and who may carry an indigenous perspective of these archival materials can become quite disenchanted with the work. The use of language that seems derogatory to our ancestors coupled with statements made one hundred–plus years ago by white missionaries that are disrespectful to our traditional spiritual beliefs can and often do still hit a nerve. Living in a colonized society, struggling in our own ancestral homeland, all while fighting to remain indigenous by preserving what we have left of our language and culture can make reading these materials a very emotional experience. This work is not easy.

One of the cruelest barriers Dakota people face in locating their histories is the rate at which the Dakota language is declining. It has been estimated that there are less than ten fluent speakers currently living in the ancestral homeland of Minnesota. Though others live in the diaspora since being exiled, the separation of the people and other colonial forces have caused a fluency loss that is detrimental to Dakota people and to the future existence of the traditional knowledge and stories told in the language.

Yet I have felt very blessed to be a part of this project. The hours I have spent at the Minnesota History Center looking through archives have been significant to me not only as a student but also as a member of my community who is searching for the meaning of my history. Combining my educational training with outside projects such as this one, I really do feel that knowledge and history are being perceived in another light (not a new one, as it is as old as time), and I give thanks, many thanks for the opportunity this project has given me, as a young Dakota scholar, to apply my skills and knowledge to something far greater than my own pursuits. Nina pidamayaye.

KATHERINE BEANE (Flandreau Santee Sioux) is a PhD candidate in American studies at the University of Minnesota, Twin Cities. Her research work focuses on Dakota history and language revitalization, and she is a descendent of Maȟpiya Wiçaṣṭa (Cloud Man).

SYD BEANE

My Bdewakaŋtuŋwaŋ Dakota family was exiled from Minnesota after the 1862 Dakota War. I am a descendant of Waŋyaga Inaźiŋ (He Sees Standing Up), also known as Penichon, one of the Dakota chiefs who signed Pike's Treaty of 1805. One of my grandfathers was the Bdewakaŋtuŋwaŋ Maȟpiya Wiçasta, known by his English name Cloud Man, through his daughter Wakaŋ Inaźiŋ Wiŋ or

Stands Sacred, who married the officer Seth Eastman. Thus I am related to both the original Dakota inhabitants of this region and some of the Americans who colonized Minnesota.

My exiled Dakota family included my grandfather John Eastman, who became a Presbyterian clergyman, and his brother, my great-uncle Charles Alexander Eastman, the internationally known medical doctor and author. Our Dakota family homesteaded near the eastern South Dakota town of Flandreau and was instrumental in establishing the federally recognized Flandreau Santee Sioux Tribe. In this community I was born and raised as a member of the tribe.

One of my earliest memories of the historical and cultural conflicts into which I was thrown as a young boy involved the most traditional and eldest member of our tribe. I recall attending a tribal community gathering where a group of white lawyers in suits and ties were explaining why our tribe should vote in favor of accepting a federal land claim settlement for which they had represented our interests in Washington, DC. One tribal member after another responded that we should accept the financial settlement for lands lost because we needed the money and it would lead to a better life for our families. Suddenly from the back of the room, I heard the growing sound of a thumping cane coming down the aisle to the front. It was the eldest member of our community; he had heard enough and was ready to speak his mind. The crowd became silent as he raised his cane toward the lawyers seated up on the stage and said we should not accept this money because the land cannot be sold and we will no longer be Dakota people. Just as quickly as he had appeared in front of the crowd, he left the room.

The lawyers asked for a vote in favor of accepting the money, and the measure passed without further discussion. This event has stuck with me over the years, and now that I am an elder I understand better both what the old man meant and why the vote was to accept the money. This scene represents the different world views of history and culture which we all find ourselves struggling with, not only from the past but now and in the future. Many years later, after returning to my ancestral home I have found numerous unanswered questions of history and culture related to my Dakota people and our lands in Minnesota. This book has grown out of a history of Dakota and non-Dakota relationships and conflicts which continue to this day.

SYD BEANE, a Flandreau Santee Sioux tribal member, is a professional educator, social worker, documentary filmmaker, and community organizer.

ERIN GRIFFIN

Haŋ mitakuyapi. Erin Griffin emakiyapiye. Sisituwaŋ otuŋwe ed wati. Dakota winyaŋ hemaca ye.

Hello my relatives. My name is Erin Griffin and I live in Sisseton, South Dakota. I am a Dakota woman. I am enrolled with the Sisseton-Wahpeton Oyate and a member of the Ḣeipa District.

I grew up in Mankato, Minnesota. Today I laugh and tell people it was a pretty ironic place for a Dakota person to grow up. I say that as a joke but also with pride. I lived with a lot of confusion, anger, resentment, and sadness in a place where thirty-eight of my ancestors were put on display and executed. I often wondered how many people would drive by that site in a day and not even know what had happened there in 1862. I wondered how many people would care.

In the last ten years, awareness and knowledge of this place has grown. The fact that more people are learning about this history, and some sympathizing with it, is encouraging. When I was younger I expected and demanded that these people know and understand the history of this land and the Dakota Oyate who were exiled from it; now I simply hope for understanding. This simple hope is not a concession but an awareness that people, no matter their color, culture, religion, or other classification, cannot be forced to care about or consider history or place. Each individual must make a conscious decision about whether history and knowledge of the land are important. The confusion, anger, resentment, and sadness that encompassed my childhood in Mankato have transformed into pride as I have gained a better understanding of myself and the place I lived. Yes, I grew up in an area that has a horrific history, but as a Dakota person my presence in that area was a testament of resilience.

This project has unquestionable significance for its addition to the written record of the land base of Minnesota. As we have come together, Dakota and non-Dakota, to research and write "Mni Sota," we have attempted to present not just one understanding of the land and history but many. We often get caught up in one way of telling stories, thinking there is the white history and the Dakota history. History and memory are complex and deep. Understanding the Dakota presence is essential to understanding the history and land of Minnesota. The land holds memories of all that has happened here, and those memories are intertwined with Dakota culture and language. Too often, Dakota people are not included or are afterthoughts in histories and events relating to Minnesota. Without the Dakota presence, we are left with partial histories. Whether we are Dakota or Minnesotan, if we continue to accept only partial histories we will continue to limit our understanding of them and their effects on us. Limitations such as these do not allow us to face history and may tempt us to write it off as "in the past." By providing a space for Dakota voices and perspectives, this body of work includes our past, our present, and our future. I am proud to have contributed to it.

ERIN GRIFFIN is an enrolled member of the Sisseton-Wahpeton Dakota Oyate, Ḣeipa district. She received her MA in sociocultural anthropology from the University of Oklahoma in 2009 and currently works for the Sisseton-Wahpeton Oyate tribal government. She is an accomplished beadwork and quillwork artist.

THOMAS G. SHAW

There is no dispassionate way to say this: being a member of the Dakota Lands Project was a once-in-a-career delight. Even today I can't quite believe I was granted this privilege.

The working group brought together scholars from a diversity of background, interest, and perspective that one seldom has the opportunity to work with. I had collaborated with Bruce and Howard before on projects for Historic Fort Snelling. I had never met Gwen or Glenn. Sheldon and I had crossed paths a few times but had never worked together before.

At the beginning it was unclear how we would work together and how our separate interests could be leveraged to create something useful. We had no idea what form the end product would take and no understanding of how it would be used by the Indian Land Tenure Foundation. I suspect Syd, Bruce, and Gwen didn't know any of this either, but their choice of collaborators suggested they had some inkling that our association might produce something worthwhile and unexpected.

Our monthly meetings were surprising to say the least. For one thing, many of them were video recorded. I've never seen these recordings, but I wager they would be pretty startling to an outsider. The meetings were certainly startling to me as an insider. Of course we each gave a report on our work since the previous meeting. All of us would speak at greater length about something in our work that might be of special interest to the group. But it was the discussion around these routine items that was arresting. We talked about metaphysics, religion, addiction, French cartography, perceptions of time and language.

The nature of my work in the group was to provide information that could inform the work of others. In the course of our monthly meetings, thanks to the insight and candor of the other members, I discovered new ways of viewing the raw material I looked at every day. A lot of it did not make its way into the final product, but my association with the Dakota Lands Project has affected all aspects of my professional life.

The book we produced through the generosity of the people of Minnesota reflects a small part of what the group accomplished. Perhaps we will find other ways to bring this work to the public in the future. The genuine value is in making us all look at landscape and see the humans in it. Some of the landscapes are invisible because they have been profoundly altered. Others are invisible because they are part of our everyday routine. Still others are very remote. As a group we tried to recover not the landscapes themselves—they can never be completely expunged—but the meanings attached to them by humans. We enriched ourselves through fruitful, unexpected revelations. I hope the product of our work will enrich the reader and help form a closer attachment to the land that nurtures us.

THOMAS SHAW served the Minnesota Historical Society for twenty years as the assistant site manager at Historic Fort Snelling. He is a longtime student of U.S. Indian policy and the St. Peters Indian Agency.

HOWARD J. VOGEL

As a fifth-generation descendant of German-speaking immigrants who first came to the Dakota homeland in the mid-1850s, prior to its incorporation as the State of Minnesota, I heard stories about my ancestors who settled in the Minnesota River valley, where I played as a child. Thus, I heard that Margaretha Serr, my great-grandmother, who arrived with her parents in 1854 as a seven-year-old girl and settled on a small farm in Milford Township, less than two miles upriver from the town site selected for New Ulm, had "played with the Indians."

During the Dakota–U.S. War of 1862, on the first day of the first attacks in Milford Township, Margaretha Serr left a farmhouse a quarter mile from her home when the family she was visiting sat down for the noontime meal. Shortly thereafter two men were killed at the dinner table as fourteen-year-old Margaretha was walking home. Later she was one of the women and children who fled to New Ulm and gathered with dynamite in the basement of a building located in town, intent on blowing themselves to death if the warriors broke through the barricades.

As a child I also learned that Joseph P. Vogel, who would marry Margaretha Serr in 1866 and become my great-grandfather, arrived in 1856 as an eighteen-year-old boy along with his parents and settled on a small farm just south of New Ulm near the Cottonwood River, where I also played as a child. It was said that he participated in the defense of New Ulm during the 1862 war and later was present at the mass execution of thirty-eight Dakota men that took place in Mankato on December 26, 1862. These few stories of "Indians" were all told from within the settlers' experience of what they called "the Sioux Massacre of 1862."

Over the years the way the stories of the war were framed began to gradually change to eventually include references to the facts of Dakota experience in dealing with the United States. Today I refer to it, as some Dakota people do, as the "Dakota–U.S. War of 1862" to acknowledge that the Dakota were provoked to start a war by the broken treaty promises of the United States.

My understanding of the treaty negotiations has also changed over the years. During my work as a legal scholar researching the Dakota treaties for this project, I learned much while listening to the stories of the Dakota homeland told by my Dakota colleagues as well as listening to the account of the careful rereading of the written documentary record by my historian colleagues. I now understand the complex story of the negotiations at the treaty table as one marked by a clash of world views about land. Taking the story of this clash seriously reveals the treaties in a new light that is both exciting in its newness and disturbing in its details, as we have tried to make clear in Chapter 4.

I am grateful to librarians Barbara Kallusky and Megan Jens of the law library of Hamline University School of Law and to Hamline law student research assistants Chelsea Hanson and Autumn Baum.

HOWARD J. VOGEL is a Professor of Law Emeritus, Hamline University School of Law.

We are especially grateful to the following Dakota people who have shared their knowledge of Dakota history and their love of Mni Sota Makoce: Connie Big Eagle, Celine Buckanaga, Tannis Bullard, Curtis Campbell, Clifford Canku, Gary C. Cavender, Francis L. Crawford, Darell Decoteau, Harley Eagle, Emmett Eastman, Gus High Eagle, Melissa Hotain, Walter "Super" LaBatte, Chris Leith, Aaron McKay, Carl Mazawasicuna, Mikey Peters, Caroline Renville, Phyllis Redday Roberts, Clayton Sandy, Carolynn Cavender Schommer, Danny Seaboy, Kenny Seaboy, Gabrielle Tateyuskanskan, Redwing Thomas, Bob Wasicuna Wanbdi Wakiṭa, Dr. Tina Wasicuna, Glenn Wasicuna, Waziyatawiŋ, Wayne Wells.

Notes

Abbreviations used in notes:

DCB   *Dictionary of Canadian Biography*

LAC   Library and Archives of Canada, Ottawa

MHS   Minnesota Historical Society

NAM   National Archives Microfilm

NARG   National Archives Record Group

SWJP   *The Papers of Sir William Johnson*

WHC   *Wisconsin Historical Collections*

NOTES TO INTRODUCTION

1. A microfilm copy of the circa 1720 document is found in LAC, F-123, vol. 122; translation in Ames, "The Sioux or Nadouesis." Marin, "Journal," 279–81.

2. Keating, *Narrative of an Expedition,* 1:406; *Dakota Friend,* May 1851; Riggs, *Dakota Grammar,* 164. The same belief about the mouth of the Minnesota River was mentioned in Neill, *History of Minnesota,* 1.

3. 1825 treaty journal, 11, 32–33, in NAM T494, R. 1. The leader is mentioned as Standing Bull in the Taliaferro journal, June 3, 22, 1835, and as Tartunca nasiah in table of chiefs visiting the agency starting Sept. 1, 1823. See also Anderson, *Kinsmen of Another Kind,* 236. For the corrected spelling, see Riggs, *Dakota-English Dictionary,* 340, 462.

4. 1825 treaty journal, 33, 35; Taliaferro journal, June 1, 1831. See also the printed version of this council in *Niles' Register,* Nov. 19, 1825, 190. On the name of Çaŋ Sagye, see Riggs, *Dakota-English Dictionary,* 86, 430.

5. 1851 treaty journal, 15–17, 18, in NAM T494, R. 4.

6. 1851 treaty journal, 56–69.

7. Deloria, *The Dakota Way of Life,* 69; Anderson and Woolworth, *Through Dakota Eyes,* 291–95.

8. Casey, "How to Get from Space to Place," 44. Casey argued that a people's experience of space arises from their collective knowledge of specific places. Ryden, *Mapping the Invisible Landscape,* 38.

NOTES TO CHAPTER ONE

1. Wilson, *Remember This!,* 12–13.

2. The oral traditions and histories are presented here as a continuous Dakota narrative from creation to the arrival of the first Europeans. All interviewees are acknowledged for their contributions and cited in the sources for this book. Information in print or video format is cited in the standard format.

3. Riggs, "Mythology of the Dakotas," 147; Wallis, *Beliefs and Tales of the Canadian Dakota,* 12–13.

4. This multilayered story is related in many versions through a number of sources. In each version, the four young men spend a long time listening as this "strange" man explains many sacred mysteries, such as the creation of the solar system, the gift of horses from the Creator, the importance of the language, the use of medicines, and others. See in particular Waziyatawiŋ, *Remember This!* Quotation below from 74–86.

5. Uŋkteȟi are considered to be powerful underwater spirits or forces. Samuel W. Pond reported that Dakota "had seen bones of the mammoth, pieces of which they had in their possession" and "concluded that their dwelling place was in the water." *Dakota or Sioux in Minnesota,* 87.

6. Eastman and Eastman, *Smoky Day's Wigwam Evenings,* 92.

7. Public Broadcasting System, *The Elegant Universe: String Theory.*

8. A microfilm copy of the 1720 document is found in LAC, F-123, vol. 122; for a translation see Ames, "The Sioux or Nadouesis." Riggs, *Dakota Grammar.*

9. Sioux Valley Nation, *Wakan ye wiconi o iye: The Story of Our People.*

10. Others such as Riggs suggest that Isanti was derived from Isan-ta-mde, or Knife Lake, a source for sharp flint stone.

11. Elias, *The Dakota of the Canadian Northwest,* 5, 6.

12. Wambdi Oḳiya to Thomas Williamson, Apr. 1837, Franz Boas Papers.

13. White, "Encounters with Spirits." There are several descriptions of what wašicuŋ means, including "mysterious" and "fat-takers"; however, an older meaning for the word is "someone who has done well for himself, who has much to share with others," Glenn Wasicuna, conversation with Gwen Westerman, 16 Feb. 2005.

NOTES TO CHAPTER TWO

1. Birmingham and Eisenberg, *Indian Mounds of Wisconsin,* 13–36; Kane, Holmquist, and Gilman, *Northern*

Expeditions of Stephen H. Long, 146–51, 279; Lewis, *Valley of the Mississippi Illustrated,* 132.

2. Bond, *Minnesota and Its Resources,* 358–61; also *Minnesota Historical Collections* 1:149–52.

3. Gibbon, *The Sioux,* 22, 27–30; Gibbon and Anfinson, *Minnesota Archaeology,* ch. 21; Riggs, *Dakota-English Dictionary,* 425.

4. For this and paragraph below, see Anfinson, "Cultural and Natural Aspects of Mound Distribution in Minnesota," 23, 25, 27.

5. Mather, "The Headless Bison Calf."

6. Arzigian and Stevenson, *Minnesota's Indian Mounds and Burial Sites,* 335; *Dakota Friend,* July 1851; reprinted in the *Minnesota Democrat,* Aug. 19, 1851.

7. Nicollet, *On the Plains and Prairies,* 253; Warren, *History of the Ojibwe People,* 83; see also Hodge, *Handbook of American Indians,* 1:376.

8. A similar point was made in White, *Grand Portage as a Trading Post,* 22.

9. Thwaites, *Jesuit Relations and Allied Documents* (1898) 23: 224–27.

10. Walker, *Lakota Myth,* 130–33; Mather, *Archaeological Overview,* 23, 36, 45–46, 69; Densmore, *Chippewa Customs,* 123; Whelan, "Late Woodland Subsistence Systems and Settlement Size in the Mille Lacs Area," 72; Grieve, *A Modern Herbal,* 1:30, 189, 365–66; Angier, *Field Guide to Edible Plants,* 88, 126; Bronson, "The Earliest Farming," 25–26, 29; Kreidberg, *Food on the Frontier,* 15–18, 86–87, 115.

11. Throughout this chapter and elsewhere in the book, English translations not obtained from the cited sources were translated from the original French sources by Bruce White. Perrot's memoirs were first published in 1864 and reprinted in 1973. An English version of a portion of them was published in Blair, *Indian Tribes of the Upper Mississippi Valley,* 1:31–272.

12. Perrot, *Mémoires sur les Moeurs,* 85–86. The Dakota phrase for a gun includes maza, "iron," and wakaŋ: Riggs, *Dakota-English Dictionary,* 310, 311. The attitudes of Dakota toward the French and their merchandise is discussed in more detail in White, "The Fear of Pillaging."

13. Perrot, *Mémoires sur les Moeurs,* 886–87.

14. Perrot, *Mémoires sur les Moeurs,* 886–87.

15. Perrot, *Mémoires sur les Moeurs,* 88.

16. Perrot, *Mémoires sur les Moeurs,* 88–91.

17. Radisson, *Voyages of Peter Esprit Radisson,* 207–20; see also White, "Encounters with Spirits," 382–84.

18. For a discussion of the Feast of the Dead involving Radisson, see Witgen, *An Infinity of Nations,* 61–64; Warren, *History of the Ojibwe People,* 164–69.

19. Nute, *Caesars of the Wilderness,* 55–56; Radisson, *Voyages of Pierre Esprit Radisson,* 219–20.

20. La Potherie, *Histoire de l'Amerique Septentrionale,* 2: 61–62. The reference to growing corn is ambiguous in La Potherie's account; it might be interpreted that Dakota grew these crops. However, the arrangement of the sentences and a reference to the group forgetting its homeland—a statement he had made earlier about the Ojibwe who left Sault Ste. Marie—makes clear that he is referring to the Ojibwe, not to the Dakota. The region of Chequamegon Bay is known to have its own warmer microclimate that makes corn growing less precarious than in inland areas to the south; see White, *The Middle Ground,* 54.

21. Thwaites, *Jesuit Relations and Allied Documents* (1899) 51:52–55.

22. Thwaites, *Jesuit Relations and Allied Documents* (1899) 54:190–94, 55:168–71.

23. "The Pageant of 1671," in Kellogg, *Early Narratives of the Northwest,* 213–20; French version in Gagnon, *Louis Jolliet,* 49. For a discussion of the meaning of this event, see Witgen, "The Rituals of Possession."

24. Seed, *Ceremonies of Possession,* 41–68. On the manufacture of consent, see 56–63.

25. In French legal cases, a procès-verbal is a statement of facts in a particular case. See Robert, *Le Petit Robert,* 1396. On the Doctrine of Discovery, see Wilkins and Lomawaima, *Uneven Ground,* 19–63, where it is argued that the doctrine, though sometimes misconstrued, was largely a fiction.

26. Dulhut to the Marquis de Seignelay, undated, copy in MHS P1301; "Memoire du Sr. Daniel Greysolon du Luth, 1685," LAC F-414; English version in "Memoir of Duluth on the Sioux Country, 1678–1682," in Kellogg, *Early Narratives of the Northwest,* 325–34. See also letter of Dulhut to Frontenac, Apr. 5, 1679, in MHS P1301.

27. As will be discussed later, there is archaeological evidence, at least a thousand years old, of fortified villages around Mille Lacs. See Mather, *Archaeological Overview,* 67–68; Upham, *Minnesota Geographic Names,* 249, 531; Riggs, *Dakota-English Dictionary,* 206.

28. Some have suggested the name Songaskitons is a version of the later recorded name for the Sisituŋwaŋ, but the speculation is tenuous since the sounds and meanings of the two seem to have no relationship. Edward Neill stated that he arrived at the conclusion that this

group was the modern Sisituŋwaŋ by a process of elimination, since no early French sources referred to any other similar name and because a village of Sisituŋwaŋ at Lake Traverse in the 1850s had a similar name. Unfortunately, no other source has been found for the latter information. See Neill, "Dakota Land and Dakota Life," 260. Dulhut to the Marquis de Seignelay, n.d., copy in MHS P1301; Memoire du Sr. Daniel Greysolon du Luth, 1685, LAC F-414.

29. Dulhut to the Marquis de Seignelay, n.d., copy in MHS P1301; Memoire du Sr. Daniel Greysolon du Luth, 1685, LAC F-414.

30. Hennepin, *Description of Louisiana,* 124–25.

31. Hennepin, *Description of Louisiana,* x. Hennepin's alleged captivity is discussed in White, "Encounters with Spirits," 388.

32. Hennepin, *Description of Louisiana,* 92.

33. Hennepin, *Description of Louisiana,* 114; Upham, *Minnesota Geographic Names,* 347; Riggs, *Dakota-English Dictionary,* 563. See Wazikute, Pine Shooters, a branch of the Yankton; Riggs, *Dakota Grammar,* 160. See also Nicollet, *On the Plains and Prairies,* 256, 258. See also the original French version of Hennepin's narrative, *Description de la Louisiane,* 260.

34. Hennepin, *Description of Louisiana,* 108; Riggs, *Dakota Grammar,* 101; Riggs, *Dakota-English Dictionary,* 200; Walker, *Lakota Belief and Ritual,* 78.

35. Hennepin, *Description of Louisiana,* 90, 94, 106, 108, 116, 118–20, 125.

36. Hennepin, *Description of Louisiana,* 90, 125.

37. Zoltvany in DCB, vol. 2.

38. Margry, *Découvertes et Établissements des Français* (1877), 2:186–93; English version in WHC 11 (1888): 29–35.

39. Margry, *Découvertes et Établissements des Français* (1877), 2:186–93; English version in WHC 11 (1888): 29–35.

40. Prise de Possession, May 8, 1689, F-10, fol. 208–14v, LAC; Perrot in DCB, vol. 2. For çoka, see Riggs, *Dakota-English Dictionary,* 102.

41. "Memoires de Mr. Le Sueur," 42, 46, 48; Witgen, *An Infinity of Nations,* 251, gives the names of the two chiefs as Zhingobiins (Little Balsam Fur) and Tiyoskate (Plays in the Lodge). For the account of the event, see LAC F-14, fol. 80–80v, F-13, fol. 231. The French word used for settlements was *habitations.* O'Callaghan, New York Colonial Documents, 9:570.

42. LAC F-13, fol. 228–34v; O'Callaghan, New York Colonial Documents, 9:609–12.

43. "Memoires de Mr. Le Sueur," 42. A nineteenth-century copy of Delisle's tracing of the original Franquelin map is found in the Newberry Library, Ayer MS map 61. A copy of the Delisle map is found in the Library of Congress, Map Collection, and is available online.

44. "Memoires de Mr. Le Sueur," second unnumbered page, a, 1, 7, 46.

45. "Memoires de Mr. Le Sueur," 41–45.

46. "Memoires de Mr. Le Sueur," 43, 52.

47. "Memoires de Mr. Le Sueur," 43, 95; Riggs, *Dakota-English Dictionary,* 401, 516, 563; Upham, *Minnesota Geographic Names,* 11, 174.

48. "Memoires de Mr. Le Sueur," 48. Le Sueur gave the French name of the river as R. aux roches plattes, or "river of the flat rocks." For the dates, see La Harpe's narrative, translated into English and published in WHC 16:184. See also Upham, *Minnesota Geographic Names,* 11; Farmington Area Historical Society, "Inyan Bosdata."

49. "Memoires de Mr. Le Sueur," 49, 95.

50. "Memoires de Mr. Le Sueur," 46, 95; Riggs, *Dakota-English Dictionary,* 316, 438.

51. "Memoires de Mr. Le Sueur," 49, 52–53; WHC 16:187.

52. "Sacred birth": from wakaŋ, "sacred," toŋpi, "birth"; Riggs, *Dakota-English Dictionary,* 479, 507. See also Coues, *Expeditions of Zebulon Montgomery Pike,* 1:88; Anderson, *Kinsmen of Another Kind,* 37. "Memoires de Mr. Le Sueur," 52, 57. The name Ouiatespouitons may be from the Dakota words oyate, "a people, nation, tribe, band," and pawi, "a great many"; Riggs, *Dakota-English Dictionary,* 397, 416.

53. "Memoires de Mr. Le Sueur," 93. The word Le Sueur used for forts appears to be the abbreviation for "forter." which signifies "forteresses," meaning fortresses. Wilson, *Remember This!,* 75–82.

54. La Harpe, *Journal Historique,* 68.

55. "Memoires de Mr. Le Sueur," 52, 56. According to Le Sueur, they were called the Village of the Rock "because of a mine of red stone that is located with them in the middle of a prairie," from i-haŋ'-ke, "on the end"; Riggs, *Dakota-English Dictionary,* 184. The name means "end village." On the winter count, see Howard, *Yanktonai Ethnohistory,* 24.

56. The Dakota name that Le Sueur gave for the Blue Earth River, Outabea inpacchan, does not resemble any other known record of the river's Dakota name. "Memoires de Mr. Le Sueur," 96. Williamson's English-Dakota dictionary gives *to* for blue and green but offers separate terms, relating to specific English uses of the words,

for example in the case of green, to the state of having new leaves or being unripe. See Williamson, *English-Dakota Dictionary*, 19, 77. Riggs, *Dakota-English Dictionary*, 472, defines to as "blue; green, and the intermediate shades." The Ojibwe also used the same word for green and blue, according to Coleman, *Decorative Designs of the Ojibwa*, 61.

57. Featherstonaugh, *Canoe Voyage up the Minnay Sotor*, 1:281, 302, 304.

58. "Memoires de Mr. Le Sueur," 76; Riggs, *Dakota-English Dictionary*, 401, 497.

59. Margry, *Découvertes et Établissements des Français* (1883), 5: 418–19; "Memoires de Mr. Le Sueur," 76; Mather, *Archaeological Overview*, 14, 66; Mather and McFarlane, *Gii-maajaa'ind A'aw Makwa*.

60. "Memoires de Mr. Le Sueur," 52, 92.

61. Le Sueur made a point of telling one of the DeLisles in 1699 that "one should not put ouadeba for ouateba, since ouadeba means I sleep and ouateba, river": "Memoires de Mr. Le Sueur," 96. The legend on the left side of Franquelin's map translates the name Quiocpeton as "Nation renfermé," which means much the same thing. Mather, *Archaeological Overview*, 67–68. See also "Memoires de Mr. Le Sueur," 52.

62. Tangaps sinton or Psinutanghihintons, both described as "nation of the large wild rice." Le Sueur gives the name as "the village of the large wild rice," possibly from the words taŋ'-ka, large, psiŋ, wild rice, found in different forms in both names; Riggs, *Dakota-English Dictionary*, 425, 457. Village dispersed in little bands; village of the hearth; possibly from oyate, "a people, nation, tribe, band," and pa-wi, "a great many"; Riggs, *Dakota-English Dictionary*, 397, 416.

63. Birk, "Putting Minnesota on the Map," 20. A microfilm copy of the document is found in LAC, F-123, vol. 122. Early Minnesota historian Edward Neill obtained a copy of the document around 1890 and had it translated. He also sent the translation to the missionary John P. Williamson, who had grown up with his missionary father, Thomas, in Minnesota and followed the Dakota into exile in 1863. Williamson pointed out the inaccuracies, at least from a nineteenth-century point of view. See Ames, "The Sioux or Nadouesis."

64. For a discussion of the issue of clans among the Dakota, see Stipe, "Eastern Dakota Clans"; Dorsey, "The Place of Gentes."

65. LAC, F-123, vol. 122.

66. See Oneroad and Skinner, *Being Dakota*, 188–90.

67. Notes about the Sioux, Apr. 29, 1727, C11, Vol. 49, fol. 580v-81; WHC 17:7–9; see also letter of Longueuil, July 25, 1726, LAC F-48, fol. 395. Articles of a trading company for the post among the Sioux, June 6, 1727, LAC F-414; Margry, *Découvertes et Établissements des Français*, 6:547–52, WHC 17:10–15.

68. Relation of Father Guignas, sent to French Minister by Beauharnois, Oct. 3, 1728, LAC F-51, fol. 442–45v; Dupuy to French minister, Sept. 25, 1728; Margry, *Découvertes et Établissements des Français*, 6:545–46, 552–58, WHC 17:15–17; Relation of Father Guignas to Beauharnois, May 29, 1728; also another version in LAC F-414, fol. 112–17v. In one version of the Guignas narrative the post was "on the shore of Lake Pepin, on the north side [costé] . . . on a low point with excellent terrain." Another version states that the fort was at Lake Pepin, "on its shore, near the middle of the north side [côté], on a low point, the terrain of which is excellent." In both cases, it is possible that the term *costé* or *côté* (the more usual modern spelling) could refer not just to the side of the river but to the northern area or end of the lake, which flows in a southeasterly direction. Thus it is unclear whether Guignas meant to refer to the north side of the Mississippi River, possibly near present-day Stockholm, Wisconsin, or the north end of Lake Pepin, on the south shore, near present-day Frontenac. Conversely, if Guignas had referred to the word *côte*, meaning "coast or shore," rather than *costé*, the location would have been more clearly on the north shore of the lake. See first version in Relation of Father Guignas to Beauharnois, May 29, 1728, LAC F-51, fol. 444–44v; the other version in LAC F-414, fol. 112–17v; see also Margry, *Découvertes et Établissements des Français*, 6:552–58; Kellogg, "Fort Beauharnois," 239; Birk and Posely, *The French at Lake Pepin*, 32–51.

69. Boucherville, "Account," 3:13 (June). The use of the letters *au* in recording this name may accurately reflect the way the Dakota ŋ in wakaŋ was heard by the French.

70. Boucherville, "Account," 3:13 (June); Guignas to Beauharnois, Sept. 19, 1728, LAC F-51, fol. 438–39v; Beauharnois and Hocquart to French Minister, LAC F-51, fol. 22–28v; also O'Callaghan, New York Colonial Documents, 6:1016–27; Margry, *Découvertes et Établissements des Français*, 6:559–65; WHC 17:60, 67, 77–80; Beauharnois to French minister, Sept. 1, 1729, LAC F-51, fol. 135; Beauharnois and Hocquart to French minister, Oct. 25, 1729, LAC F-51, fol. 22.

71. Boishebert to Beauharnois, Feb. 28, 1732, C11, vol. 57, fol. 298; WHC 17:148–52, 230; Beauharnois to French minister, Oct. 15, 1732, C11, vol. 57, fol. 95; WHC

17:168–69; Hocquart letter, Oct. 26, 1735, C11, vol. 63; MHS M85, R2, Vol. 4, Journal 3, pp. 774–80.

72. LAC, F-66, fol. 236–56v, particularly fol. 240–40v, 251; English version of the second version, with some gaps, in O'Callaghan, New York Colonial Documents, 9:1052–58; WHC 17:245–52.

73. Relation du Sieur de Saint-Pierre, LAC F-67, fol. 172–75, also LAC F-475, xi, 9, P.; Margry, Découvertes et Établissements des Français, 6:575–80; WHC 17:269–74.

74. Birk, "Putting Minnesota on the Map," 254.

75. Paroles des Sioux, etc., July 18, 24, 25, 1742, F-77, fol. 214–15; Paroles de deux Chefs Scioux, Mar. 9, 1740, F-74, fol. 85.

76. Nichols and Nyholm, Concise Dictionary of Minnesota Ojibwe, 101, 194; Baraga, Dictionary of the Ojibway Language, 1:131, 272, 2:289; Warren, History of the Ojibwe People, 219.

77. Paroles des Sioux, etc., July 18, 24, 25, 1742, F-77, fol. 214–15; WHC 17:330, 396–97, 402–4. Expenditures for the Dakota on their return trip are recorded in LAC F-79, 230, F-80, fol. 197, F-81, fol. 360, 366; LAC F-77, fol. 235–36v.

78. WHC 17:422, 425; LAC F-79, fol. 120–21v.

79. LAC F-79, fol. 122–22v, 122–25v, 123–24v.

80. Beauharnois to French minister, Oct. 28, 1746, LAC, F-85, fol. 227–27v; O'Callaghan, New York Colonial Documents, 10:34, 37.

81. WHC 18:33, 61, 63, 66, 76–79.

82. Diedrich, Famous Dakota Chiefs, 111; LAC F-95, fol. 191–92v.

83. Speeches of the Sauteux of Chaguoamigon, July 1750, LAC F-95, fol. 192v, 246–47v.

84. Jonquière to French minister, Sept. 16, 1751, LAC, F-97, fol. 65; WHC 18:79.

85. The original of the journal is in the Henry E. Huntington Library, San Marino, CA. A published version in French is found in Marin, "Journal."

86. Marin, "Journal," 250.

87. Marin, "Journal," 256, 263; Nute, "Marin versus La Verendrye," 226–38.

88. Marin, "Journal," 264–69.

89. Marin, "Journal," 276, 277, 278, 279–81.

90. Marin, "Journal," 282.

91. Marin, "Journal," 282–83, 294–95; See Riggs, Dakota-English Dictionary, 308, 462. See also Diedrich, Famous Dakota Chiefs, 34–35; Coues, Expeditions of Zebulon Montgomery Pike, 1:88.

92. Nute, "Marin versus La Verendrye," 226–38.

93. Lotbinière in LAC MG18 L4, vol. 3, no. 18; copy in MHS P849.

94. White, Grand Portage as a Trading Post.

95. SWJP, 3:758; White, "The Fear of Pillaging."

96. Carver, Journals, 90–91; Carver, Travels, 56, 58, 59–62.

97. Carver, Journals, 91–92; Carver, Travels, 63–65.

98. Carver, Journals, 108–11; Riggs, Dakota-English Dictionary, 87.

99. Carver, Journals, 92–93; Carver, Travels, 66–72.

100. Carver, Travels, 73; Carver, Journals, 94.

101. Carver, Travels, 80; Carver, Journals, 100.

102. Carver, Journals, 95–96, 108, 116–20.

103. Gates, Five Fur Traders of the Northwest, 45.

104. Gates, Five Fur Traders of the Northwest, 52–56.

105. Journal of Mons. Gautier in MHS M89, Haldimand Papers.

106. Amable Curot to Daniel Robertson, Feb. 2, 1783, copy and translation in MHS P849, Box 6.

107. Cormier, Jean-Baptiste Perrault, 67, 69–75; Diedrich, Famous Dakota Chiefs, 111; Diedrich, Little Crow and the Dakota War, 13; Kane, Holmquist, and Gilman, Northern Expeditions of Stephen H. Long, 57.

NOTES TO CHAPTER THREE

1. Folwell, A History of Minnesota, 1:51–52, 71–72.

2. Jackson, Journals of Zebulon Montgomery Pike, 1:26–27, including notes 48, 239.

3. Jackson, Journals of Zebulon Montgomery Pike, 1: 25–28, 34, 35, 229–30; Neill, "A Memoir of Joseph Renville," 196–206.

4. Jackson, Journals of Zebulon Montgomery Pike, 1:36, 37.

5. Jackson, Journals of Zebulon Montgomery Pike, 1:118, 120, 126, 221. Pike mistakenly called Red Thunder Yankton in his narrative, although he correctly identifies him in a table. On Red Thunder's Dakota name, see Riggs, Dakota Grammar, 185.

6. Jackson, Journals of Zebulon Montgomery Pike, 1:277, 279.

7. WHC 9:158–60.

8. WHC 9:163.

9. WHC 9:159–73. Joseph Nicollet refers to a group of Yanktons known as Toshu henuapi, "those who bring the poles of lodges, because there is no wood in their country," also known as Wattapaatidan, "those who

put their lodges on rivers": Nicollet, *On the Plains and Prairies,* 256.

10. WHC 9:174, 177–78, 183–84. Anderson gives Dakota names for some of these chiefs, including Whoo-pah-edutah (Ḣupaḣu Duta) for Red Wing, Onketah en-dutah (Uŋkteḣi [which actually refers to a powerful underwater spirit, not a whale] Duta) for Red Whale, Shockope (Śakṗe) for the Six, and Kahhaigegad, possibly from Kaŋġi, (which is translated as raven or crow) for Little Crow. Anderson also refers to Thunder as Red Thunder. On these names see also Riggs, *Dakota-English Dictionary,* 106, 108, 168, 260, 440, 458.

11. WHC 9:189–92.

12. WHC 9:166, 192–204, 212, 220.

13. Kappler, *Indian Affairs: Laws and Treaties,* 2:113, 114, 128–30; Taliaferro journal, Mar. 19, 20, 1829. Taliaferro provided his version of the Dakota name with the note "alias Red Wing."

14. Janet Spector, based on a statement of Stephen R. Riggs, calls these villages "spring planting villages": Spector, *What This Awl Means,* 56, 76–77.

15. Riggs, *Dakota Grammar,* 165; Whelan, "Dakota Indian Economics."

16. Pond, *Dakota or Sioux in Minnesota,* 30.

17. Whelan, "Dakota Indian Economics," 250.

18. Pond, "Two Missionaries in Sioux Country," 28; Riggs, *Dakota-English Dictionary,* 565.

19. Schoolcraft, *Indian in His Wigwam,* 138; Hickerson, *Southwestern Chippewa,* 19, 29; Taliaferro journal, Aug. 10, 1836, in "Reply of the Agent," Aug. 18, Sept. 9, 1836.

20. Taliaferro journal, Sept. 30, 1821.

21. Taliaferro journal, Jan. 9, 1826, Dec. 15, 1827, Mar. 12, 1828, Jan. 21, 1829, Jan. 17, 1831, Dec. 17, 1835, Jan. 24, 1836; Kane, Holmquist, and Gilman, *Northern Expeditions of Stephen H. Long,* 67.

22. Taliaferro journal, Feb. 1, 1828, Jan. 25, 1831, Dec. 20, 1835, Jan. 18, 1836; Pond, "Two Missionaries in Sioux Country," 29.

23. Nicollet spells the term for the headwaters of the rivers "Mini Akipan Kaduza": Nicollet, *On the Plains and Prairies,* 23; Riggs, *Dakota-English Dictionary,* 28, 247; Taliaferro journal, Aug. 6, 1829, June 14, Aug. 16, 19, 30, 1835.

24. Hennepin, *Description of Louisiana,* 118; Pond, *Dakota or Sioux in Minnesota,* 45.

25. Nicollet, *On the Plains and Prairies,* 125–26. In 1836 Taliaferro wrote, at Fort Snelling, that "the buffalo have been within 40 miles of this Post from the Des Moines this season & are now but a few miles upon Cannon River": Taliaferro journal, Dec. 18, 1836.

Taliaferro journal, June 11, 1827. The name of the individual known as Wabasha's son-in-law is not known. Later on he was suspected of setting fire to the council house at the Indian agency. See Taliaferro journal, Sept. 11, 1830.

Taliaferro journal, Aug. 11, 1827. At this time Taliaferro seems to have suspected the chief of "stirring up the Sioux against us." Taliaferro journal, Aug. 17, 1827.

26. Taliaferro journal, Sept. 10, 1835.

27. Frazer, *Iron Face,* xx, 24, 54–58, Taliaferro journal, June 18, 1835.

28. Taliaferro journal, July 19, 20, 1831.

29. Taliaferro journal, Aug. 28, Sept. 22, Oct. 5, 1835. Kaṗoża was sometimes referred to as Nine Mile Village because of its distance from Fort Snelling.

30. Taliaferro journal, Mar. 3, 1828, Oct. 5, 1835.

31. Taliaferro journal, Jan. 22, 28, 1826, Feb. 5, Mar. 7, 1836, Aug. 20, 1838.

32. Taliaferro journal, Dec. 6, 1827.

33. Pond, *Dakota or Sioux in Minnesota,* 52–53.

34. Taliaferro journal, Mar. 5, 1828, Mar. 1, 1829, Jan. 19, 1831, Feb. 22, Mar. 29, 1836; see also Aug. 23, 1829.

35. Pond, *Dakota or Sioux in Minnesota,* 53.

36. Taliaferro journal, Mar. 13, 1829. There are many accounts of making vinegar from maple sap, in Minnesota and elsewhere. See Kreidberg, *Food on the Frontier,* 101; Johnston and Gass, "Vinegar," 61. Taliaferro journal, Mar. 15, 1829.

37. Holcombe and Bingham, *Compendium of History,* 63, 155. An early commentator stated that the painting resembled very much a site on Nicollet Island: McDermott, *Seth Eastman,* 81n14. Taliaferro journal, Apr. 13, 1829, Mar. 19, 1836; Curtiss-Wedge, *History of Wright County,* 269, 279.

38. See also Taliaferro journal, Feb. 29, 1828; Pond, *Dakota or Sioux in Minnesota,* 56.

39. Taliaferro journal, Apr. 14, 1826, Mar. 7, 1828.

40. Numerous references in Taliaferro's journal show how wild fowl served as a seasonal marker. Taliaferro reports in his journal, Mar. 27, 1829: "Geese wild—Saw four this evening the first this season." See also Mar. 27, 1826. For fall references, see Taliaferro journal, Sept. 25, 1821, Sept. 15, 1829.

41. Lockwood, "Early Times and Events in Wisconsin," 181.

42. Nicollet, *On the Plains and Prairies,* 43, 257; Nicollet also applies this name to the people of Penichon's vil-

lage. Taliaferro journal, Apr. 10, 14, 1829. Taliaferro refers to the chief as "Kocomoko" or "the drifter."

43. Taliaferro journal, Oct. 15, 1821.

44. Taliaferro journal, May 11, 1836.

45. Nicollet, *Journals,* 210: see also Taliaferro journal, Feb. 19, 20, 23, Mar. 6, May 6, 17, 1826, Mar. 1, 1831, Feb. 7, May 31, 1836.

46. Taliaferro journal, Apr. 19, 21, 23, 1826; Pond, "Dakota Superstitions," 120.

47. Taliaferro journal, Apr. 23, 1826, Mar. 20, 1828.

48. Taliaferro journal, Oct. 23, 1827.

49. Pond, *Dakota or Sioux in Minnesota,* 56. Such structures resembled the bark houses of the Ojibwe, often used in sugaring camps or "in places where the people might wish to stay for a time." Densmore, *Chippewa Customs,* 27.

50. Kane, Holmquist, and Gilman, *Northern Expeditions of Stephen H. Long,* 67; Keating, *Narrative of an Expedition,* 1:299; Taliaferro journal, July 7, 1834. Name of Kaȟboka, see Diedrich, "A 'Good Man' in a Changing World"; Riggs, *Dakota-English Dictionary,* 251; Taliaferro journal, June 10, 1821, May 11, 1826, July 1, 1831. For the name of Wambdi Taŋka, which Taliaferro spelled in various ways, see Riggs, *Dakota-English Dictionary,* 251; Diedrich, "A 'Good Man' in a Changing World," 12; Taliaferro journal, June 27, 1829; see also July 20, 1831.

51. Taliaferro journal, July 31, 1827; Keating, *Narrative of an Expedition,* 1:345; Featherstonhaugh, *Canoe Voyage up the Minnay Sotor,* 1:284.

52. Taliaferro journal, June 21, 1829, July 11, 13, 1831, June 24, 1835.

53. Pond, *Dakota or Sioux in Minnesota,* 28; Riggs, *Dakota-English Dictionary,* 425–26, 470. On the use of the pṡiŋčiŋča, see also Taliaferro journal, June 13, 1832.

54. Taliaferro journal, June 6, 1834, July 3, 4, 9, 1835, June 21, 1839; Catlin, *Letters and Notes,* 2:134, plates 235–36.

55. Pond, *Dakota or Sioux in Minnesota,* 27.

56. Taliaferro journal, Sept. 4, 1830, July 31, 1831, July 7, 1834.

57. Taliaferro journal, July 14, Oct. 3, 1836; G. Pond to Ruth Pond, Sept. 17, 1839, MHS P437, Box 2, File 2. See also typed version in MHS P489, Box 7.

58. Kreidberg, *Food on the Frontier,* 15–18, 86–87, 115; Pond, *Dakota or Sioux in Minnesota,* 57. Taliaferro makes several references to Mud Lake in his journal which suggest its location. See Taliaferro journal, Sept. 4, 1835, May 31, 1839. See also Taliaferro's map, ca.

1835, which identifies Mud Lake as the lake farthest east along Minnehaha Creek: MHS G4144 .M5 2F39 1835 .T334. For a discussion of the map, see Roads, "The Fort Snelling Area in 1835," 23.

59. Taliaferro journal, June 14, 1835, May 25, 1836; Treaty of Nov. 30, 1836, in Kappler, *Indian Affairs: Laws and Treaties,* 2:481–82. The Dakota leader's name may be related to ṡkaŋ ṡkaŋ yaŋ, "moving, in motion": Riggs, *Dakota-English Dictionary,* 446.

60. Taliaferro journal, Aug. 25, 1835, Feb. 11, Mar. 8, May 1, 1836. Wambdi Taŋka and his son had made similar inquiries in 1826: Taliaferro journal, May 28, 1826, Mar. 8, May 1, 1836.

61. Thomas S. Williamson to David Greene, May 16, 1836, MHS P489, Box 4; Pond, *Two Volunteer Missionaries,* 160; Thomas Williamson, Camp Coldwater, to David Greene, May 5, 1843, MHS P489, Box 10.

62. S. R. Riggs to David Greene, Sept. 27, 1839, MHS P489, Box 7; Treaty of 1837, Article 2, in Kappler, *Indian Affairs: Laws and Treaties,* 2:493–94.

63. Taliaferro journal, Sept. 1, 1821, Sept. 2, 1823, Aug. 21, 1827, Aug. 19, 1829, Sept. 9, 1830, Aug. 18, 1831; Riggs, *Dakota-English Dictionary,* 564.

64. Taliaferro journal, Apr. 28, 1826; see list of goods in Taliaferro journal, 15:140; *Minnesota Chronicle & Register,* Sept. 22, 1846.

65. Taliaferro journal, Sept. 28, 1821, June 10, 1834; Pond, *Dakota or Sioux in Minnesota,* 59.

66. On the begging dance, see Riggs, *Dakota Grammar,* 224.

67. Taliaferro journal, Oct. 13, Nov. 4, 1835.

68. Riggs, *Dakota-English Dictionary,* 454, 461. The French word refers to the hooped club used in the sport.

69. Marin, "Journal," 264–69; Jackson, *Journals of Zebulon Montgomery Pike,* 1:125–26.

70. This and paragraphs below are from Pond, *Dakota or Sioux in Minnesota,* 113–16. Jackson, *Journals of Zebulon Montgomery Pike,* 1:125.

71. Samuel Pond, *Dakota or Sioux in Minnesota,* 115.

72. Pond, *Two Volunteer Missionaries,* 43.

73. Pond, *Two Volunteer Missionaries,* 174.

74. J. D. Stevens to David Greene, June 26, 1838, MHS P489, Box 5. On June 21, 1839, Taliaferro noted that Little Crow's band played Shakopee's band at the place known as Lands End, a few miles up the Minnesota River. He wrote: "all the Ladies & gentlemen of the Post ride out 1½ miles to witness the play." Until 1827, this location, near present-day Post Road on the prop-

erty of the Minneapolis–St. Paul International Airport, had been the major regional post of the Columbia Fur Company. Taliaferro journal, May 24, 1829.

75. Taliaferro also referred to this village playing ball in his journal on March 1, 1836, mentioning a hand injury sustained by a man named Kah Rhee dah. Catlin, *Letters and Notes,* 2:134, plates 235–36. Taliaferro journal, July 3, 4, 1835.

76. Catlin, *Letters and Notes,* 2:145–46.

77. Taliaferro journal, July 9, Dec. 17, 1835.

78. Taliaferro journal, Feb. 22, 1836.

79. Catlin, *Letters and Notes,* 2:145–46.

80. McDermott, *Seth Eastman,* plate 46, "Ball Play of the Squaws on the Prairie," oil, Peabody Museum, Harvard University; Eastman, *Dahcotah,* 43–45; see also Mayer, *History of the Santee Sioux,* 150, 152.

81. Landes, *Mystic Lake Sioux,* 43–45.

82. See Neill, *History of Minnesota,* 75; Pond, *Dakota or Sioux in Minnesota,* 10–11.

83. Frazer, *Iron Face,* 112–13.

84. This paragraph and those that follow are based on "A Midsummer Feast" in Eastman, *Indian Boyhood,* 30–37. Anderson, *Kinsmen of Another Kind,* 234–35.

85. The first part of the name Chakpee-yuhah may be from the word caŋḣpi, which Riggs translates as war-club or tomahawk, while yuha means "to have, own, or possess." See Riggs, *Dakota-English Dictionary,* 89, 622. On Eastman's first name, see Eastman, *Indian Boyhood,* 4. Riggs, *Dakota-English Dictionary,* 122, gives the word hakakta, meaning "last, the last, the youngest." The word ohiya means "to win," according to Riggs, 352.

86. Upham, *Minnesota Geographic Names,* 350, 553; Riggs, *Dakota-English Dictionary,* 127; S. R. Riggs, Lac qui Parle, to David Greene, May 16, 1839, MHS P489, Box 7; Nicollet, *On the Plains and Prairies,* 258. The name of Star Face was recorded as "Witcharpihiteton": Nicollet, *On the Plains and Prairies,* 256. See also Riggs, *Dakota-English Dictionary,* 182, 216, 305, 568. Taliaferro also referred to these Sisituŋwaŋ in that way: see Taliaferro journal, May 28, June 12, 1836. Nicollet said in separate places in his notes that Wanata was a member of the Wazikute and Cuthead bands of Ihanktoŋ: Nicollet, *On the Plains and Prairies,* 256, 258. The lake today is 16.5 miles long, though it is currently dammed for the purpose of flood control.

87. Upham, *Minnesota Geographic Names,* 53; Riggs, *Dakota-English Dictionary,* 201, 223, 486. However, the Little Minnesota River enters from the northeast, having its source near the Coteau de Prairie in South

Dakota. Nicollet, *On the Plains and Prairies,* 256, 279. Taliaferro also mentioned a leader from Big Stone Lake called Lowing or Bellowing Buffalo, or Lowing Cow; Taliaferro journal, Oct. 14, 1835. He referred to the Little as this band's chief. Riggs later described a spiritual leader at Lac qui Parle named Ptahotonpe or Lowing Buffalo; Riggs, "Dakota Portraits," 2:513–17. Nicollet spelled Upi Iyahdeya's name, variously, as Opiyande, Opiyahande, and Up Hendeya.

88. Nicollet said the leader's name was "Nonpakie, He who speaks twice." Nicollet, *On the Plains and Prairies,* 256; Riggs, *Dakota-English Dictionary,* 169, 312. See Treaty of 1825, in Kappler, *Indian Affairs: Laws and Treaties,* 2:254; Taliaferro journal, June 23, 1838.

89. Upham, *Minnesota Geographic Names,* 593, 595, 596; Nicollet, *On the Plains and Prairies,* 112–13; Anderson, *Kinsmen of Another Kind,* 210, 234–35.

90. Upham, *Minnesota Geographic Names,* 448–49; Keating, *Narrative of an Expedition,* 1:363; survey map, MHS, T113N R36, Minnesota Secretary of State; Nicollet, *On the Plains and Prairies,* 113.

91. Upham, *Minnesota Geographic Names,* 456; Riggs, *Dakota-English Dictionary,* 459; Meyer, *History of the Santee Sioux,* 274–75.

92. Nicollet, *On the Plains and Prairies,* 52, 115, 256; spelling from Riggs, *Dakota-English Dictionary,* 162, 209; Pond, *Dakota or Sioux in Minnesota,* 6, 14. The name of the village was recorded as "Mayakichakse." Nicollet gives the name as Kanwhymentoka. The French name for Raven Man is "Male de Corbeau." Corbeau can be translated as either crow or raven, as can the Dakota word Kaŋġi. See Riggs, *Dakota-English Dictionary,* 260, 313. Also: Riggs, *Dakota-English Dictionary,* 303, 387. Another version of the Dakota name for Swan Lake is "Marha Tanka Otta Mde." Riggs, "Dakota Portraits," 484.

93. Nicollet, *On the Plains and Prairies,* 48–49, 256; Riggs, *Dakota-English Dictionary,* 106, 309, 359, 436; Taliaferro also refers to this location as a meeting place for the Sisituŋwaŋ. Taliaferro journal, Sept. 9, 1821. Riggs later wrote about Big Walker, a member of a band that later became Red Iron's band. See Riggs, "Dakota Portraits," 502–5; S. R. Riggs, Traverse des Sioux, to David Greene, Nov. 18, 1843, MHS P489, Box 10. On Tataŋkamani, see Pond, *Dakota or Sioux in Minnesota,* 6; for Big Walker, see Taliaferro journal, Aug. 16, 1835, June 11, 1838.

94. Nicollet, *On the Plains and Prairies,* 46; Taliaferro journal, June 13, 14, Aug. 7, 1835, Nov. 10, 1836, June 11, Aug. 27, 1838; Riggs, *Dakota-English Dictionary,* 508.

95. The creek now flows north through Louisville Swamp and enters the Mississippi a few miles below Little Rapids. An account of the change in the course of Sand Creek is found in Inter-Fluve, *Sand Creek, MN*, 41–42. This lower waterway may have been identified on a list by an unknown author of the French names of various rivers along the Minnesota, now in the papers of Joseph Nicollet (MHS M30, R. 2). The name given is Petite Rivière du Marais des Grès, meaning "little river of the sandstone swamp," a description that fits the geography of the present Louisville Swamp, which contains many outcrops of sandstone. Geologist George William Featherstonhaugh, who passed through the area in 1835, described a river the French called Le Grand Grès, meaning "large sandstone." He reported that the river got its name from a pillar of rock located thirty miles from its mouth, in the middle of a large prairie. In fact there is a large glacial boulder in the middle of the Louisville Swamp, in a grassy plain above the wetlands, though it does not appear to be of sandstone. At the same time, Featherstonhaugh could also have confused the site with Iŋyaŋ Bosdatu (Castle Rock), which is located along the Cannon River, in the middle of a prairie, forty miles east of Sand Creek's mouth. Durand, *Where the Waters Gather*, 36, states that another name for Sand Creek is Izuza Wakpa, meaning "whetstone" or "sandstone river," although it is not clear whether this refers to the creek's current or former course. See Featherstonhaugh, *Canoe Voyage up the Minnay Sotor*, 1:290, 42; Riggs, *Dakota-English Dictionary*, 100, 201; U.S. Fish and Wildlife Service, *Minnesota Valley Wildlife Refuge*. Taliaferro spells the name Batture au Fevre. Taliaferro journal, May 30, Aug. 6, 1827, Feb. 8, 1828; Nicollet, *On the Plains and Prairies*, 45–46; Riggs, *Dakota-English Dictionary*, 106, 389, 581; Kane, Holmquist, and Gilman, *Northern Expeditions of Stephen H. Long*, 288n41; Upham, *Minnesota Geographic Names*, 84, 511; Spector, *What This Awl Means*, 10–12, 80–93.

96. Nicollet, *On the Plains and Prairies*, 276; for Wahnacsonto, see Taliaferro journal, Mar. 14, 1828. Also: Taliaferro journal, June 13, 1835, Oct. 14, 1838.

97. Taliaferro journal, Aug. 29, 1821, Aug. 15, 1829. The Dakota name of Red Eagle is sometimes given as "Keyah." Nicollet, *On the Plains and Prairies*, 47; Riggs, *Dakota-English Dictionary*, 75, 109, 289, 304, 468, 526. Nicollet gives the name of the prairie as Marhaborhpa, which, as suggested by Durand, *Where the Waters Gather*, 89, appears to be a contraction of Maġaska, "swan," and boħpa, meaning "to shoot something down."

98. Taliaferro journal, Aug. 20, 1827, June 14, 1835.

99. The whole band located at these two villages was the largest Bdewakaŋtuŋwaŋ band in the 1830s, including, in 1839, 333 people consisting of 87 men, 76 women, and 170 children. See 1839 annuity rolls and population figures compiled for this project. Upham, *Minnesota Geographic Names*, 512; Nicollet, *On the Plains and Prairies*, 44, 45, 257; Riggs, *Dakota-English Dictionary*, 169, 389, 402, 468. Keating in his account of the journey referred to scaffolds for drying corn at what may be the same village. Kane, Holmquist, and Gilman, *Northern Expeditions of Stephen H. Long*, 158; Keating, *Narrative of an Expedition*, 1:343. Taliaferro journal, July 17, 1835. Nicollet appears to have believed that Eagle Head's band was a separate Bdewakaŋtuŋwaŋ band. Taliaferro journal, June 12, July 23, Oct. 21, 1827, Mar. 8, 1828, June 14, 1829, July 21, 1839; Nicollet gives the name as "Rhuya-pha."

100. Its location may have varied since Taliaferrro sometimes referred to it as "seven mile village": Taliaferro journal, Aug. 12, 1831; Pond, *Dakota or Sioux in Minnesota*, 11. Nicollet, *On the Plains and Prairies*, 43, 255, 257; Coues, *Expeditions of Zebulon Montgomery Pike*, 86n2. On the name for the village site, see Riggs, *Dakota-English Dictionary*, 294, 447, 454, 600, taku, "something," kokipa, "fear," šni, "not," woźupi, "field or garden." Also: Riggs, *Dakota-English Dictionary*, 397, 433. Nicollet also stated that the people who lived in this village, like the people of Black Dog village, were called "Marhayouteshni," "those who do not eat geese," although this is not confirmed in other places in his journals. Nicollet gives the name of the chief as Tachanku waste. For a standardized spelling, see Riggs, *Dakota-English Dictionary*, 90, 451, 537.

101. Nicollet, *On the Plains and Prairies*, 43, 256–57; Hohaanskae, Ohaŋska from haŋska, meaning "long": Riggs, *Dakota-English Dictionary*, 124; White, "Eligibility." On May 6, 1829, Taliaferro referred to the "Avenue Band of Medwakantong Sioux"; see also May 3, 1828; Fred Pearsall notes in MHS P1100.9. For more on Pearsall, see his letter to T. J. Mann, Dec. 26, 1918, in Pipestone Indian School and Agency Records, NARA-Kansas City, Decimal Correspondence Box 16, Censuses. Taliaferro journal, Oct. 19, 1827, July 28, Sept. 7, 1830.

102. "Indian Burial Place near Fort Snelling," original in MHS, AV1991.85.34.

103. *Harper's New Monthly Magazine*, July 1853, 185.

104. Pond, *Dakota or Sioux in Minnesota*, 5, Riggs, *Dakota Grammar*, 157; Nicollet, *On the Plains and Prairies*, 256–57; Upham, *Minnesota Geographic Names*, 170, 442, 443.

105. Keating, *Narrative of an Expedition*, 1:298; Kane, Holmquist, and Gilman, *Northern Expeditions of Stephen H. Long*, 67.

106. Taliaferro journal, May 7, 1829, May 19, 1836. On Taliaferro's name for the village, see entry for June 29, 1831. Nasiampah and "the Spotted Body" appear to have been the leaders of this community.

107. Riggs, *Dakota-English Dictionary*, 164; Riggs, *Dakota Grammar*, 157; Nicollet, *On the Plains and Prairies*, 255; Taliaferro journal, Sept. 28, 1829; Lewis, *Valley of the Mississippi Illustrated*, 115.

108. Taliaferro journal, Aug. 4, Sept. 3, 1827, Mar. 20, 1829.

109. The younger chief appears to have been the nephew of the older chief. Taliaferro referred to Wahcoota as both the son and the nephew of the older leader. Historian Mark Diedrich said the old chief was the younger chief's uncle and stepfather, after the death of his father in Dakota tradition. Taliaferro journal, July 21, 30, 31, 1829, Aug. 15, 1830, Aug. 11, 1835; Diedrich *Famous Dakota Chiefs*, 51. On the "Grand Encampment," see Kane, Holmquist, and Gilman, *Northern Expeditions of Stephen H. Long*, 61.

110. "Reminiscences by Mr. Henry P. McIntire, Read before the Goodhue County Historical Society," Jan. 6, 1927, 2, MHS, Frances Densmore Papers.

111. Riggs, *Dakota-English Dictionary*, 292–93; Upham, *Minnesota Geographic Names*, 581; Durand, *Where the Waters Gather*, 72; Keating, *Narrative of an Expedition*, 1:399

112. An article in *The Dakota Friend*, Sept. 1851, gives the English version of the third Wabasha's name as Bounding or Whipping wind, which suggests the Dakota translation Tate apa s'a, from tate, "wind," apa, "to strike," s'a, "to hiss or roar"; Riggs, *Dakota-English Dictionary*, 41, 430, 462; Taliaferro journal, Oct. 15, 1838. On the death of the second Wabasha, see Taliaferro journal, June 30, 1836.

113. Taliaferro journal, May 6, 7, 22, 1836; H. Hill and Co., *History of Winona and Olmsted Counties*, 276–77.

NOTES TO CHAPTER FOUR

1. For an example of the beginning of a Dakota speech employing this terminology, see Wilson, *In the Footsteps of our Ancestors*, 67. See also Riggs, *Dakota-English Dictionary*, 353, 455.

2. Williams, *The American Indian in Western Legal Thought*, 13–93; Miller, *Native America, Discovered and Conquered*, 9–17.

3. Williams, *The American Indian in Western Legal Thought*, 13–93; Miller, *Native America, Discovered and Conquered*, 1–58.

4. Prise de Possession, May 8, 1689, LAC F-10, fol. 208–14v.

5. Folwell, *A History of Minnesota*, 1:78–79.

6. Johnson v. M'Intosh, 21 U.S. 543 (1823); Cherokee Nation v. Georgia, 30 U.S. 1 (1831); Worcester v. Georgia, 31 U.S. 515 (1832).

7. Cherokee Nation v. Georgia, 30 U.S. 1 (1831); Williams, *The American Indian in Western Legal Thought*, 31–39.

8. Tulee v. Washington, 315 U.S. 681 (1942); Carpenter v. Shaw, 280 U.S. 363 (1930); Minnesota v. Mille Lacs Band of Chippewa Indians, 526 U.S. 172 (1999); Choctaw Nation v. Oklahoma, 397 U.S. 620 (1970); Worcester v. Georgia, 31 U.S. 515 (1832); Wilkinson and Volkman, "Judicial Review of Indian Treaty Abrogation."

9. Jackson, *Journals of Zebulon Montgomery Pike*, 1:37.

10. Kappler, *Indian Affairs*, 2:1031.

11. Jackson, *Journals of Zebulon Montgomery Pike*, 1:37–38.

12. *American State Papers: Indian Affairs* 1:755 (no. 122).

13. Kappler, *Indian Affairs*, 2:1031.

14. Jackson, *Journals of Zebulon Montgomery Pike*, 1:38.

15. Jackson, *Journals of Zebulon Montgomery Pike*, 1:243–44.

16. Jackson, *Journals of Zebulon Montgomery Pike*, 1:244–45.

17. Folwell, *A History of Minnesota*, 1:136.

18. Folwell, *A History of Minnesota*, 1:135–38, 143–45.

19. Taliaferro journal, Mar. 8, 1829.

20. Taliaferro journal, June 15, 1829.

21. Taliaferro journal, Sept. 16, 1829, Sept. 7, 1830.

22. Taliaferro journal, Sept. 7, 1830. Taliaferro returned to this point about Leavenworth on June 18, 1836.

23. Taliaferro journal, Sept. 7, 1830.

24. Taliaferro journal, Sept. 7, 1830.

25. Taliaferro journal, June 9, 1835.

26. Taliaferro journal, June 18, 1836, Oct. 15, 1838.

27. Davenport to Adjutant General, May 27, 1837, NA, QMG, CCF, reprinted in Bloom, *Territorial Papers*, 27: 792–95.

28. *House Executive Documents*, 40 Cong., 3rd sess., serial 1372, 23–24.

29. Meyer, *History of the Santee Sioux*, 38–39; Taliaferro, "Auto-biography," 203–6; Taliaferro to Dodge, Mar. 12, 1837, MHS M105; Taliaferro journal, "Note" prior to Jan. 19, 1828.

30. Folwell, *A History of Minnesota,* 1:146; Quote from Taliaferro, "Auto-biography," 206.

31. Meyer, *History of the Santee Sioux,* 40; 1825 treaty journal, 16, in NAM T494, R. 1.

32. Meyer, *History of the Santee Sioux,* 40; 1825 treaty journal, 38–39.

33. 1825 treaty journal, 20, 43–44.

34. 1825 treaty journal, 30.

35. In this case the chief was called by his French name, Petit Corbeau; 1825 treaty journal, 31–32.

36. 1825 treaty journal, 11, 32–33. The leader is mentioned in the treaty journal as Tatuncanashia, Standing Buffalo, and as Standing Bull in the Taliaferro journal, June 3, 22, 1835, and Tartunca nasiah in table of chiefs visiting the agency, starting Sept. 1, 1823. See also Anderson, *Kinsmen of Another Kind,* 236. For the corrected spelling, see Riggs, *Dakota-English Dictionary,* 340, 462.

37. The chief is named Tau sa gie in the 1825 treaty journal, 35. See also Taliaferro journal, June 1, 1831, and the printed version of this council in *Niles' Register,* Nov. 19, 1825, 190.

38. 1825 treaty journal, 28–29.

39. Anderson, *Kinsmen of Another Kind,* 123; Kappler, *Indian Affairs,* 2:251–52.

40. 1825 treaty journal, 49–50; Anderson, *Kinsmen of Another Kind,* 122–23. On the continuing problems with the boundary involving the Waḣpekuṭe, see Taliaferro journal, June 1833.

41. Folwell, *A History of Minnesota,* 1:147; Kappler, *Indian Affairs,* 2:250–55; Taliaferro journal, June 15, 1829, June 6, 1832.

42. Folwell, *A History of Minnesota,* 1:147–48n; Dodge to Harris, May 16, 1837, MHS M105; Taliaferro journal, Nov. 4, 1835.

43. Kappler, *Indian Affairs,* 2:305–10; 1830 treaty journal, 19, 26, 29, in NAM T494, R. 2; Taliaferro journal, memorandum, Aug. 1830, July 26, 1831. He stated, "Now a similar arrangement ought to be made without loss of time—between the Chippeways & Sioux—to my suggestion—by a letter to Genl Clark." See also Taliaferro journal beginning May 13, 1829. Taliaferro mentioned Chief Wiash ho ha on numerous occasions: see journal, May 29, 1821, Apr. 4, 1826. He noted that French Crow died in August 1835: see journal, Sept. 3, 1835.

44. Folwell, *History of Minnesota,* 1:324–25. A discussion of the term *relations* is found in a petition addressed by people of mixed Dakota-European ancestry addressed to Henry Dodge, Aug. 15, 1837, in MHS M105.

45. 1830 treaty journal, 21, 23; Kappler, *Indian Affairs,* 2:305–10; other treaty signers were Yanktons or Ihanktuŋwaŋ and Santies, usually a reference to Waḣpekute or Bdewakaŋtuŋwaŋ living in the region of the western Dakota; Denig, *Five Indian Tribes,* 39–40.

46. Taliaferro to Dodge, Feb. 12, 1837, MHS M105; Meyer, *History of the Santee Sioux,* 55–56.

47. Taliaferro journal, Dec. 7, 1835.

48. Taliaferro journal, May 30, June 6, 1836; Taliaferro to Harris, July 24, 1837, MHS M105.

49. Folwell, *A History of Minnesota,* 1:159–60; Taliaferro journal, Nov. 30, 1836; Kappler, *Indian Affairs,* 2:491–93.

50. Taliaferro to Dodge, Aug. 2, 1837, MHS M105; Aug. 6, 1837, W281, MHS M175, NAM M234, R. 758; Dousman to Crooks, Aug. 10, 1837, MHS M151, R. 25, p. 2959.

51. Sibley Papers, MHS M164, R. 22, V. 24, f. 213; the invoice also includes a long list of merchandise including two dozen looking glasses, a variety of cloth, clothing, and blankets: RG 217, entry 525, #1296, box 225; Nute, "Calendar of the American Fur Company's Papers," 2:2925. The date of August 18 is inferred from the departure Taliaferro announced to military officers at the time; see Taliaferro to Scott, Aug. 16, 1837, MHS M175, NAM M234. However, Sibley's invoice of goods supplied to Taliaferro for the delegation notes that he was paid for these items by Taliaferro on August 20, which may mean the delegation did not leave until this date; Neill, "Occurrences in and around Fort Snelling," 132; Neill's account appears to be based on Taliaferro, "Auto-biography," 219.

52. See invoice for steamboat *Ariel* for transporting a "Delegation of 26 of the Mdewakanton, the Sisseton, Wahpeton and Wapoakoota tribes of Sioux," Aug. 29, 1837, in NARG 217, entry 525, #1296, box 225; Kappler, *Indian Affairs,* 2:493–94; Taliaferro to Dodge, Aug. 2, 1837, MHS M105.

53. Taliaferro to Dodge, Aug. 21, 1837, W304, MHS M175, NAM M234; see also Taliaferro to Dodge, written at Trempealeau, Aug. 20, 1837, MHS M105.

54. NARG 217, entry 525, #1296, box 225; Meyer, *History of the Santee Sioux,* 57; the outline of the treaty is undated, but it appears to accompany a statement of proposed "Annuity & Treaty Stipulations," Sept. 20, 1837, MHS M105.

55. Anderson, *Kinsmen of Another Kind,* 153.

56. 1837 treaty journal, 1–2, in NAM T494, R. 3.

57. 1837 treaty journal, 2–3.

58. 1837 treaty journal, 4. Here Ehake's name was given as "O hah kaa how, the one that comes last."

59. 1837 treaty journal, 5. In this case Ehake's name was spelled Ee hah kaa kow.

60. 1837 treaty journal, 5–6, 11–12, 25.

61. 1837 treaty journal, 12–18.

62. 1837 treaty journal, 19–20, 25. Bad Hail's Dakota name was given in the treaty journal as Wasson Wachushtishnee. See Riggs, *Dakota-English Dictionary,* 535, 569.

63. Riggs, *Dakota-English Dictionary,* 305, 340.

64. Kappler, *Indian Affairs,* 2:493–94.

65. Sibley to Crooks, Sept. 29, 1837, MHS M151, R. 25.

66. Sibley to Crooks, Oct. 9, 1837, MHS M151, R. 25.

67. Kappler, *Indian Affairs,* 2:495–98; see complaints by Big Thunder about settlement and logging taking place prior to the treaty proclamation, Taliaferro journal, June 9, 1838. Folwell, *A History of Minnesota,* 1:227.

68. Taliaferro journal, May 28, 29, 31, June 3, 1838.

69. Clemmons, "We Will Talk of Nothing Else," 173, 178, 180, 182; Kappler, *Indian Affairs,* 2:493.

70. 1837 treaty journal, 6, 11, 24.

71. Clemmons, "We Will Talk of Nothing Else," 173, 178, 180, 182.

72. The population estimates for Dakota and other groups are based on figures for the late 1840s in White, "The Power of Whiteness," 30–31. For the white population, see Folwell, *A History of Minnesota,* 1:351.

73. Gilman, "A Northwestern Indian Territory," 18; treaty text in Snyder, *The 1851 Treaty of Mendota,* 154–60.

74. Snyder, *The 1851 Treaty of Mendota,* 155, 158.

75. *Madison Express,* Jan. 31, 1842, 1; Gilman, *Henry Hastings Sibley,* 84; Gilman, "A Northwestern Indian Territory," 19–20.

76. Folwell, *A History of Minnesota,* 1:236–39; Meyer, *History of the Santee Sioux,* 75.

77. Meyer, *History of the Santee Sioux,* 75; Ramsey to Sibley, Sept. 21, 1849, MHS M164, R. 6; Folwell, *A History of Minnesota,* 1:273–74.

78. Snyder, *The 1851 Treaty of Mendota,* 170, 175.

79. Folwell, *A History of Minnesota,* 1:274; Sibley to Chouteau and Company, Nov. 3, 1850, Sibley Letter Book, no. 1; quoted in Kane, "The Sioux Treaties and the Traders," 66; original in MHS M164, R. 29.

80. Ramsey and Sibley to Brown, Dec. 10, 1849, MHS M175, NAM M234, R. 760; Folwell, *A History of Minnesota,* 1:275, 277; Meyer, *History of the Santee Sioux,* 77.

81. Meyer, *History of the Santee Sioux,* 78.

82. Folwell, *A History of Minnesota,* 1:282.

83. Meyer, *History of the Santee Sioux,* 78.

84. Mayer, *With Pen and Pencil on the Frontier,* 146; 1851 treaty journal, 2, in NAM T494, R. 4; Folwell, *A History of Minnesota,* 1:278.

85. 1851 treaty journal, 7–8.

86. 1851 treaty journal, 9–10.

87. 1851 treaty journal, 10, 11.

88. In this case the Dakota name of Star Face was given as Wee-tchan-h' pee-ee-tay-toan; 1851 treaty journal, 14.

89. 1851 treaty journal, 15–17.

90. 1851 treaty journal, 17–18.

91. 1851 treaty journal, 18.

92. 1851 treaty journal, 18, 19.

93. 1851 treaty journal, 21. Upi Iyahdeya's name was given here as Oo-pee-ya-hen-day-a.

94. 1851 treaty journal, 21.

95. 1851 treaty journal, 21.

96. 1851 treaty journal, 22.

97. Running Walker's name was given as Een-yang-manee, but the treaty journal stated that he was "known among the whites" as "The Big Gun"; 1851 treaty journal, 23; "Proposition of the Mendaywakanton and Wakpakoota Sioux to the U.S. Commissioners," MHS M164, R. 8. Lea and Ramsey to Stuart, Aug. 6, 1851, filed with 1851 treaty journal, in NAM T494, R. 4.

98. 1851 treaty journal, 23.

99. 1851 treaty journal, 24–25.

100. 1851 treaty journal, 25–26.

101. In this case, Upi Iyahdeya's name was given as Oo-pee-ya-hen-day-a, or Extending His Train.

102. Meyer, *History of the Santee Sioux,* 80; Kappler, *Indian Affairs,* 2:594–96.

103. Gilman, *Henry Hastings Sibley,* 126.

104. Folwell, *A History of Minnesota,* 1:282–83. Various versions of these schedules survive in Sibley's papers, some of them in Sibley's own handwriting. See MHS M164, R. 8 for July and August 1851.

105. Folwell, *A History of Minnesota,* 1:283–84.

106. 1851 treaty journal, 34–37.

107. On these waterways, see Upham *Minnesota Geographic Names,* 455, 457; for the Dakota names, see Riggs, *Dakota-English Dictionary,* 73, 96, 99.

108. 1851 treaty journal, 37–40.

109. 1851 treaty journal, 41–42.

110. 1851 treaty journal, 43–45.

111. McClurken, *Fish in the Lakes,* 211; Babcock, "With Ramsey to Pembina," 2.

112. 1851 treaty journal, 45–46.

113. 1851 treaty journal, 47–48.

114. 1851 treaty journal, 48–49.

115. 1851 treaty journal, 49–51.

116. 1851 treaty journal, 51–54.

117. 1851 treaty journal, 55; MHS M164, R. 8.

118. 1851 treaty journal, 56.

119. 1851 treaty journal, 59.

120. One possibility for Big Lake on Falls Creek is Lake Minnetonka, which literally meant "big lake" and from which flowed Minnehaha Creek, known to the Dakota as "little creek," on which was located Minnehaha Falls, sometimes known as "little falls." However, this location is clearly outside the territory that was being discussed. For that and Little Rock Creek, see Upham, *Minnesota Geographic Names,* 224, 230, 374. 1851 treaty journal, 56–69.

121. 1851 treaty journal, 47, 64–65. At at least one point in the treaty journal, the chief was identified by a version of his grandfather's name, Çetaŋ Wakuwa Mani.

122. Folwell, *A History of Minnesota,* 1:286–87; Annuity Roll, Aug. 8, 1851, NARG 217, Entry 525, Box 670, Account no. 12,826-C, 1852.

123. Folwell, *A History of Minnesota,* 1:284.

124. Folwell, *A History of Minnesota,* 1:288–89; Trennert, *Indian Traders on the Middle Border,* 177–93.

125. Folwell, *A History of Minnesota,* 1:289–90.

126. Folwell, *A History of Minnesota,* 1:290–91.

127. Folwell, *A History of Minnesota,* 1:291, 292, 295.

128. Folwell, *A History of Minnesota,* 1:296.

129. Folwell, *A History of Minnesota,* 1:209–303; on Red Iron, see Riggs, "Dakota Portraits," 495n22; Riggs, *Dakota-English Dictionary,* 309, 440.

130. Sibley to Dousman, July 5, 1853; Kane, "The Sioux Treaties and the Traders," 80. On the investigation, see Folwell, *A History of Minnesota,* 1:462–70.

131. Kappler, *Indian Affairs,* 2:781–89.

132. Folwell, *A History of Minnesota,* 2:109–17, 190, 255

133. Folwell, *A History of Minnesota,* 2:190–211, 249, 251–55, 262, 263; Henry Sibley to Tatanka Nazin et al., Sept. 24, 1862, Henry H. Sibley Papers.

134. *Statutes at Large,* 12:652–54; Meyer, *History of the Santee Sioux,* 140–41; Folwell, *A History of Minnesota,* 2:258.

1. Meyer, *History of the Santee Sioux,* 89–91; Gorman to Commissioner of Indian Affairs, Aug. 23, 1853, NAM M234, R. 761; Gorman to COIA, Nov. 15, 1853, in NAM M234, R. 761.

2. Gorman to COIA, Sept. 13, Nov. 15, 1853, NAM M234, R. 761.

3. Meyer, *History of the Santee Sioux,* 92, 93–94.

4. Ramsey and Neill to COIA, Feb. 14, 1853, NAM M234, R. 761. Many volumes of the work edited by Schoolcraft were entitled *Historical and Statistical Information Respecting the History, Condition and Prospects of the Indian Tribes of the United States.*

5. *Dakota Friend,* Mar. 1851.

6. *Dakota Friend,* May 1851.

7. Riggs, *Dakota Grammar,* 182–83.

8. Meyer, *History of the Santee Sioux,* 145; "John P. Williamson to his Mother, May 13, 1863," *Minnesota History* 2 (1918): 422–25.

9. Anderson, "Dakota Identity in Minnesota," 240–51; "Census of Medawakanton Sioux of Minnesota James McLaughlin, U.S. Indian Inspector, March 15/17 1899, Approved by Department, March 29, 1899, See 14542 March 30, 1899," original in NARG 75, Washington, DC, microfilm copy in MHS, M405, R. 1. See also McLaughlin to Secretary of Interior, Mar. 17, 1899, in NAM M1070, R. 24.

10. Meyer, *History of the Santee Sioux,* 278, 350–53; "Memorandum to Indian Organization," Jan. 25, 1936, NARG 75, CCF-Pipestone, Box 3, File 9645-A.068; John O. Crow, Acting Commissioner of Indian Affairs, to Congressman Albert H. Quie, Apr. 19, 1961, copy in Dakota County Historical Society, South St. Paul, MN.

11. Woolworth, *Santee Dakota Indian Legends.*

12. See Martinez, *Dakota Philosopher,* for an interpretation of Eastman's career that makes clear his vision of Minnesota.

13. Eastman, *Indian Boyhood,* 29, 30–37, 64.

14. Neill and Williams, *History of Washington County,* 460.

15. Deloria, *Dakota Way of Life,* 69.

16. Werner, *Burial Places of the Aborigines of Kaposia,* 3, 5, 6.

17. Arzigian and Stevenson, *Minnesota's Indian Mounds and Burial Sites,* 371; Peterson, *Minnesota Trunk Highway Archaeological Reconnaissance Survey,* 98–105.

18. Helmen, "Salvage Archaeology at the Science Museum," 10–12; *St. Paul Dispatch,* July 12, 1968, sec. 2; Leslie D. Peterson, "Amendment to Report on Investigations at

Black Dog," Mar. 25, 1977, in file for archaeological site 21-DK-25, Minnesota Office of State Archaeologist; see also Edith J. Cavender, Minnesota Sioux Inter-Tribal, Inc., Apr. 8, 1977, with resolution, in Minnesota Indian Affairs Council records, MHS; Bob Dodor, "Report on Indian Burial Grounds," ca. Feb. 1977, Minnesota Indian Affairs Council records, MHS.

19. Dodor, "Report on Indian Burial Grounds"; Minnesota Statutes 307.08.

20. Dodor, "Report on Indian Burial Grounds"; Gurnoe, "Minnesota Human Burial Law," 151; Peterson, "Amendment to Report on Investigations at Black Dog."

21. Don Gurnoe to Alfred Polk, Aug. 26, 1977, Don Gurnoe to Les Peterson, Sept. 6, 1977, Minnesota Indian Affairs Council records, MHS.

22. In a speech at the Cooperative Stewardship Workshop at Prairie Island, in February 2006, Gurnoe stated that his mother's family was from Santee. See "Summary for Proposed 1978 Legislation," Oct. 25, 1977, in notes and drafts on burial legislation, in Minnesota Indian Affairs Council records, MHS; Gurnoe. "Minnesota Human Burial Law," 151.

23. Gurnoe. "Minnesota Human Burial Law," 150–52.

24. *Minnesota History* 8 (1927): 281–82; Tishler and Luckhardt, "H. W. S. Cleveland," 289–90; Landscape Research, *Henry H. Sibley House*, 43–46; White and Woolworth, "Oheyawahi/ Pilot Knob," 12; Fridley, "Fort Snelling from Military Post to Historic Site," 178–92.

25. Losure, *Our Way or the Highway*, 6.

26. Losure, *Our Way or the Highway*, 70; McLaughlin to Secretary of Interior, Mar. 17, 1899, in NAM M1070, R. 24.

27. Losure, *Our Way or the Highway*, 87–90, 215.

28. Hotopp, et al, *Cultural Resource Assessment*, 60–61; King, *Cultural Resource Laws and Practice*, 258–60, 381.

29. Losure, *Our Way or the Highway*, 227; White and Woolworth, "Oheyawahi/ Pilot Knob," 15, 17.

30. Darlene St. Clair, conversations with Bruce White, Feb., June 2011.

31. Notes of the Oct. 4, 2009, event in research collection of Bruce White; Chris Leith interview with Bruce White and Bob Brown, Apr. 29, 2003, tape and transcript in research collection of Bruce White.

32. Summit Envirosolutions and Two Pines Resource Group, *The Cultural Meaning of Coldwater Spring*, 79–80.

33. Summit Envirosolutions and Two Pines Resource Group, *The Cultural Meaning of Coldwater Spring*, 61–62.

34. Letter of JoAnn M. Kyral to Stanley R. Crooks and other tribal leaders, in Summit Envirosolutions and Two Pines Resource Group, *The Cultural Meaning of Coldwater Spring*, Appendix B.

35. Waziyatawiŋ, *What Does Justice Look Like?*

36. Parker and King, *Guidelines for Evaluating and Documenting Traditional Cultural Properties*; King, "Beyond Bulletin 38"; see also King, *Places That Count*, 256–57.

37. King, "Beyond Bulletin 38."

38. Norder, "Creation and Endurance of Memory and Place."

39. Leith interview, Apr. 29, 2003.

40. Eastman, *Indian Boyhood*, 87–96. Inspiration for this paragraph and those below came from conversations with Sheldon Peters Wolfchild during the course of the Dakota Lands Project.

41. Conversations with Sheldon Wolfchild, Dakota Lands Project.

42. Anfinson, "Maka Yusota"; conversations with Sheldon Wolfchild, Dakota Lands Project.

43. Wilson, *Remember This!* 24.

44. Kappler, *Indian Affairs*, 2:1031.

45. Videos of the speakers were recorded by Bruce White and are in his possession. National Park Service, MNRRA, News Release Jan. 2010, copy in possession of the authors.

46. Marin, "Journal," 279–81.

47. Charles Eastman, *The Soul of an Indian*, 5.

NOTES TO CHAPTER ONE SIDEBARS

i. Riggs, *Dakota Grammar*, 44, 156, 164; Anderson, "Dakota Identity in Minnesota," 22, 24; Pond, *The Dakota or Sioux in Minnesota*, 174.

ii. Tateyuskanskan, "The Terrible Truth of a Beautiful Landscape," 1, 167, in Wilson, *In the Footsteps of Our Ancestors*; Wilson, *In the Footsteps of Our Ancestors*, 114; Woolworth, *Santee Dakota Indian Legends*, 9; Riggs, *Dakota Grammar*, 1, 164; Anderson, "Dakota Identity in Minnesota," 74; Pond, *The Dakota or Sioux in Minnesota*, 4, 15; Wilson, *Remember This!* 4.

iii. Deloria, *Speaking of Indians*, 25, 26–27; Diedrich, *Old Betsey*, 11.

iv. Curtis Campbell interview with Glenn Wasicuna and Gwen Westerman, 1–2 Jan. 2009, recording and transcript in research collection of Gwen Westerman.

v. Riggs, *Dakota Grammar*, 164; see also *Dakota Friend*, May 1851, and Neill, *History of Minnesota*.

vi. Lockwood, "Early Times and Events in Wisconsin," 195.

vii. An aerial photograph from around 1935 shows the mouth of the Minnesota River prior to construction of the new channel. See MHS MD2.1B p12, Negative no. 94794.

viii. Transcript of Feb. 26, 1999, news conference in research collection of Bruce White. See also affidavits of Gary Cavender, Oct. 3, 1998, Jan. 5, 1999, in U.S. Department of Transportation and Minnesota Department of Transportation, *A Cultural Resource Assessment.*

ix. Pipestone National Monument, www.nps.gov/pipe; Nicollet, *On the Plains and Prairies,* 77; "Memoires de Mr. Le Sueur," 52.

x. Carver, *Journals,* 138–39; Carver, *Travels,* 101–2; Nicollet, *On the Plains and Prairies,* 73–85; "The Minnesota Marker in the Washington Monument," *Minnesota History* 8: 176–77; Folwell, *History of Minnesota,* 1:119–21.

xi. Kappler, *Indian Affairs: Laws and Treaties,* 2:776–81; Theodore L. Nydahl, "The Pipestone Quarry and the Indians," *Minnesota History* 31 (1950): 193–208; Harvard University, Pluralism Project, Research report on Pipestone, available: http://pluralism.org/reports /view/50.

xii. Riggs, *Dakota Grammar,* 157; Walker, *Lakota Myth,* 132–33.

xiii. Upham, *Minnesota Geographic Names,* 249; Riggs, *Dakota-English Dictionary,* 206.

xvi. White, "Ojibwe-White Conflicts over Land and Resources on the Mille Lacs Reservation"; Whelan, "Late Woodland Subsistence Systems and Settlement Size in the Mille Lacs Area," 73.

xv. Brower Papers, MHS M330, R. 2, Vol. 13.

xvi. Birk and Johnson, "The Mdewakanton Dakota and Initial French Contact," 216–17; also supported by Whelan, "Late Woodland Subsistence Systems and Settlement Size in the Mille Lacs Area," 66.

xvii. Hennepin, *Description of Louisiana,* 117.

xviii. Carver, *Journals,* 92–93; Carver, *Travels,* 66–72.

xix. Pond, "Dakota Superstitions," 120.

i. Durand, *Where the Waters Gather,* 30; Upham, *Minnesota Geographic Names,* 164–65; Farmington Area Historical Society, "Inyan Bosdata"; Taliaferro journal, Aug. 7, 1831, MHS, M35, M35-A.

ii. Upham, *Minnesota Geographic Names,* 207; Durand, *Where the Waters Gather,* 108; Riggs, *Dakota-English Dictionary,* 316, 438; 1851 treaty journal, 56–69, in NAM T494, R. 4; survey notes for T109N R14W, in MHS, U.S. Office of Surveyor General of Minnesota, land survey field notes; Frazer, *Iron Face,* 54–58. Wakute's name is sometimes spelled Wacouta.

iii. Despite the abundance of rice found in the Rice Creek lakes throughout the nineteenth century, place-name historian Warren Upham insists the creek was named for Henry Rice, who owned property along it, rather than for the resource the Dakota had made use of for hundreds of years; Upham, *Minnesota Geographic Names,* 25. Durand spells the name Otonwe Wakpadan: Durand, *Where the Waters Gather,* 67.

iv. Gibbon, *The Sioux,* 38–52.

v. Reprinted in *Minnesota Democrat,* Aug. 19, 1851.

vi. Neill and Williams, *History of Washington County,* 460.

vii. The version of the name given here is from Durand, *Where the Waters Gather,* 25–26. Neill and Williams, *History of Washington County,* 177, gave the name as Hogan-wahnkaykin. See also Riggs, *Dakota-English Dictionary,* 525. "Memoires de Mr. Le Sueur," 95; Carver, *Journals,* 90–91.

viii. Carver, *Travels,* 477–78; Brick, "Serpent God of the Iron Cave," 63–67.

ix. *Dakota Tawaxitku Kin,* or *The Dakota Friend,* Jan. 1851; also quoted in Neill and Williams, *History of Washington County,* 177.

x. In a version of the story recorded in Oneroad and Skinner, *Being Dakota,* 176, editor Laura Anderson explains the events in terms of "the second of the ten rules of life," which remind one that "water is sacred and, therefore, requires a red-feather sacrifice before dipping it up for the medicine feast. If this ceremony is omitted, it is cautioned that a pickerel will swallow the offender or drag him into the water." See also *Dakota Friend,* Jan. 1851; also quoted in Neill and Williams, *History of Washington County,* 177. Terrell, "Determination of the Eligibility of Carver's Cave," 65.

xi. Laframboise reprinted in Woolworth, *Santee Dakota Indian Legends,* 83–84. Ramsey, "Address," 51; it is unclear where Ramsey obtained this information, though it may have been from his secretary, Thomas Foster, who had an interest in ethnography. Winchell, *The Aborigines of Minnesota,* 270–71; Brower field notebook, Apr. 13–15, 1902, MHS, M330, R3, Vol. 21.

xii. Hennepin referred to the St. Croix as the "river of the tomb," which may also refer to the dead Frenchman. See "Memoires de Mr. Le Sueur," 49; Upham, *Minnesota Geographic Names,* 10.

i. Carroll, "Who Was Jane Lamont?" 189.

ii. Nicollet's importance as an ethnographer and map-maker is discussed in the introductions to *Journals* and *On the Plains and Prairies*. A reprint of his map was also produced by the Minnesota Historical Society in 1976, under its original 1843 title, "The Hydrographical Basin of the Mississippi River."

iii. See Taliaferro journal, "List of presents made to Sioux Chiefs & head men at St Peters at the dates Specified and During the 1st & 2 Qr of the year 1820."

iv. Taliaferro journal, June 28, 1831.

v. Taliaferro journal, June 17, 1823. Anthropologist Ruth Landes, who visited the Prairie Island Dakota in the 1930s, recorded a traditional account describing a very similar peace ceremony involving Dakota and Ojibwe leaders near Fort Snelling: Landes, *Mystic Lake Sioux*, 85.

vi. Warren, *History of the Ojibwe People*, 49–50.

vii. Taliaferro himself made the point about his involvement in bringing about the treaty. See Taliaferro journal, Apr. 7, 1826: "It may be hereafter said that the Late Treaty at Prairie du Chiens [*sic*]—originated with some other person & in some other Quarter—than at this agency. Look at my letters to the Supt of Ind[ia]n affairs at St Louis—also records in the War Dept—See my Journal for 1820–21–22–23–24—all of which will prove that I was the prime mover and it was to effect a general meeting of all the Tribes." Kappler, *Indian Affairs: Laws and Treaties*, 251–52.

viii. Taliaferro journal, May 7, Sept. 5, 1827, May 5, 1829, Aug. 7, 1830.

ix. For references to Dakota and Ojibwe dancing at each other's camps while at Fort Snelling together, see Taliaferro journal May 31, 1829, June 27, 29, 1831, May 17, 1832, July 13, 1835, June 23, 1839. Not all the entries state explicitly that the Ojibwe were encamped at Coldwater when this occurred. However, Taliaferro mentions the camping place of the Ojibwe as being at Coldwater on Aug. 7, 1830, July 15, 1835, Sept. 28, 1836, and July 14, 1838. At other times he mentions them being at Baker's trading post, which was located at Coldwater; Taliaferro journal, Sept. 21, 25, 1833 (letter of H. Groom), Aug. 3, 1838. The Ojibwe were also known to have camped at Coldwater when negotiating their Treaty of 1837; Taliaferro, "Auto-biography," 216. All of these entries establish Coldwater as the usual camping place of the Ojibwe while at Fort Snelling.

Conveyance, Elias Langham to Louis Massey, Jan. 26, 1831, MHS P2689.

x. Ollendorf and Anderson, "Traditional Cultural Property," 4–5; *Dakota Friend*, Mar. 1852; Pond, "Dakota Superstitions," 220.

xi. Transcript of Feb. 26, 1999, news conference in research collection of Bruce White. See also affidavits of Gary Cavender, Oct. 3, 1998, Jan. 5, 1999, in U.S. Department of Transportation and Minnesota Department of Transportation, *A Cultural Resource Assessment*.

xii. Hotopp, et al., *Cultural Resource Assessment*. Taliaferro arrived at St. Peters early that summer. He did not record a narrative of what occurred, but he did leave a record of presents given to Dakota leaders starting in June 1820. See Taliaferro journal, "List of presents made to Sioux Chiefs & head men at St Peters at the dates Specified and During the 1st & 2 Qr of the year 1820."

xiii. Schoolcraft, *Historical and Statistical Information*, 339, 352–53.

xiv. Schoolcraft, *Narrative Journal*, 199–200, 433; Taliaferro journal, Jan. 22, 1828, June 28, 1831; Landes, *Mystic Lake Sioux*, 85–86.

xv. Transcript in U.S. Department of Transportation and Minnesota Department of Transportation, *Cultural Resource Assessment*, 316–18. The last part of Benton-Banai's name is misspelled as "Bonet" in the transcript; see also Benton-Banai, *The Mishomis Book*.

xvi. The plaque was erected by the Daughters of the American Colonists in 1930; see *Minnesota History* 12 (1931): 80.

xvii. 1839 Annuity Roll, NARG 217, Entry 525, Box 314, settlement no. 4050. This lake is now known as Lake Calhoun, named in honor of former secretary of war John C. Calhoun: Upham, *Minnesota Geographic Names*, 229.

xviii. Pond, *Dakota or Sioux in Minnesota*, 10–11. According to Taliaferro, the village was founded on August 15, 1829: Taliaferro journal, Sept. 4, 1830.

xix. Pond, *Dakota or Sioux in Minnesota*, 11

xx. Taliaferro journal, Sept. 4, 1830.

xxi. Taliaferro journal, Sept. 7, 1835.

xxii. Anderson, *Kinsmen of Another Kind*, 107

xxiii. Diedrich, "A 'Good Man' in a Changing World."

xxiv. Among Maḣpiya Wiċaṡta's descendants was the Dakota writer Charles Eastman, who in his own way integrated change with a firm belief in Dakota traditions. See Chapter 5.

xxv. Keating, *Narrative of an Expedition,* 1:298; Upham, *Minnesota Geographic Names,* 570–71.

NOTES TO CHAPTER FOUR SIDEBARS

i. King, *Truth about Stories.*

ii. Ewick and Silbey, "Subversive Stories and Hegemonic Tales," 197.

iii. Taliaferro journal, Dec. 12, 1828.

iv. Winchell, *The Aborigines of Minnesota,* 286.

v. 1851 treaty journal, 24–25. A Dakota version of the Traverse des Sioux treaty was also printed in *The Dakota Friend*, August 1851, with a similar version of the Mendota treaty the following month. Compared to the manuscript version shown below, the printed version of the first treaty contains typographical errors and missing lines.

vi. Quotations are from Schommer's introduction to a reprint of Riggs, *Dakota-English Dictionary,* vii-viii.

vii. Pond, *Dakota Life in the Upper Midwest,* xii; "The Dakota Dictionary and Grammar," appendix 3 in Folwell, *History of Minnesota,* 1:347–52.

viii. The Dakota-language version of the Treaty of 1851 at Traverse des Sioux is found on NAM T494, Roll 10.

ix. Riggs, *Dakota-English Dictionary,* 573, 596.

x. Riggs, *Dakota-English Dictionary,* 115, 348.

xi. For discussions of the mixed economy of the Great Lakes fur trade, of which the Dakota were a part, see White, "Encounters with Spirits," "The Trade Assortment," and "Balancing the Books." On the beginning of Dakota participation in a cash economy, see Hyman, *Dakota Women's Work,* 39-66.

xii. Riggs, *Dakota-English Dictionary,* 115.

xiii. Riggs, *Dakota-English Dictionary,* 236, 582.

xiv. Anderson and Woolworth, *Through Dakota Eyes,* 291–95.

xv. White and Woolworth, "Oheyawahi/ Pilot Knob," 4–5; Durand, *Where the Waters Gather,* 64; Nicollet, *Journals,* 199–211.

xvi. Chris Leith interview with Bruce White and Bob Brown, Apr. 29, 2003, tape and transcript in possession of Bruce White; White and Woolworth, "Oheyawahi/ Pilot Knob," 17; *South West Review*, Apr. 4, 2004.

xvii. White and Woolworth, "Oheyawahi/ Pilot Knob."

NOTES TO CHAPTER FIVE SIDEBARS

i. From *The Word Carrier* 1.9, Dakota Myths No. VI.

ii. Transcript of Feb. 26, 1999, news conference in research collection of Bruce White. See also affidavits of Gary Cavender, Oct. 3, 1998, Jan. 5, 1999, in U.S. Department of Transportation and Minnesota Department of Transportation, *A Cultural Resource Assessment.*

iii. Terrell, "Determination of the Eligibility of Carver's Cave," 35–39, 65; Carver, *Journals,* 91–92, 108–11; Carver, *Travels,* 63–65.

iv. Terrell, "Determination of the Eligibility of Carver's Cave," 67, 78.

v. Waziyatawiŋ interview with Erin Griffin, 2007; Basso, *Wisdom Sits in Places,* 7.

vi. Meyer, *History of the Santee Sioux,* 262.

Bibliography

ORAL HISTORIES AND INTERVIEWS

Unless otherwise indicated, interviews were conducted by Glenn Wasicuna and Gwen Westerman; recordings and transcripts in research collection of Gwen Westerman.

Big Eagle, Connie. Good Thunder, MN. Aug. 22, 2010.

Buckanaga, Celine. Sisseton, SD. July 27 and Dec. 7 and 30, 2008.

Bullard, Tannis. Good Thunder, MN. Aug. 22, 2010.

Campbell, Curtis. Welch, MN. Jan. 1–2, 2009.

Canku, Clifford. Sisseton, SD. Dec. 6, 2008, Jan. 30, 2009.

Cavender, Gary C. Granite Falls, MN. Jan. 31, 2009.

Crawford, Francis L. Sisseton, SD. Jan. 30, 2008.

Decoteau, Darell. Sisseton, SD. Interview with Glenn Wasicuna. Nov. 5, 2010.

Eagle, Harley. Lower Sioux Indian Community, Morton, MN. Interview with Gwen Westerman. Nov. 8, 2008.

Eastman, Emmett. Upper Sioux Indian Community, Granite Falls, MN. Aug. 2, 2008.

High Eagle, Gus. Sisseton, SD. July 4, 2009, July 3, 2010.

Hotain, Melissa. Prairie Island Indian Community, Welch, MN. July 12, 2008.

LaBatte, Walter "Super." Mankato, MN. Sept. 18, 2010.

Leith, Chris. Prairie Island Indian Community, Welch, MN. July 13, 2008.

McKay, Aaron. Good Thunder, MN. June 5, 2011.

Mazawasicuna, Carl. Sisseton, SD. July 4, 2008.

Peters, Mikey. Sisseton, SD. Nov. 19, 2010, Feb. 25, 2011.

Renville, Caroline. Sisseton, SD. Dec. 6, 2008.

Roberts, Phyllis Redday. Sisseton, SD. July 5 and 26 and Nov. 7, 2008.

Sandy, Clayton. Sisseton, SD. Feb. 21, 2009.

Schommer, Carolynn Cavender. Upper Sioux Indian Community, Granite Falls, MN. July 3, 2008, Jan. 31, 2009.

Seaboy, Danny. Sisseton, SD. Interview with Glenn Wasicuna. Dec. 4, 2010.

Seaboy, Kenny. Sisseton, SD. Aug. 9 and Nov. 13, 2008.

Tateyuskanskan, Gabrielle. Mankato, MN. Interview with Gwen Westerman. Nov. 9, 2008.

Thomas, Redwing. Brookings, SD. Feb. 19 and May 14, 2011.

Wanbdi Wakiṭa, Bob Wasicuna. Sisseton, SD. Feb. 21, 2009.

Wasicuna, Dr. Tina. Good Thunder, MN. Nov. 27, 2009.

Wasicuna, Glenn. Conversation with Gwen Westerman. Feb. 16, 2005.

Waziyatawiŋ. Interview with Erin Griffin. 2007.

Wells, Wayne. Prairie Island Indian Community, Welch, MN. Jan. 1, 2009.

BOOKS, ARTICLES, AND REPORTS

Ames, John H., trans. "The Sioux or Nadouesis." *Minnesota Archaeologist* 39.4 (1980): 199–206.

Anderson, Carolyn Ruth. "Dakota Identity in Minnesota, 1820." PhD diss. Indiana University, 1997.

Anderson, Gary Clayton. *Kinsmen of Another Kind: Dakota-White Relations in the Upper Mississippi Valley, 1650–1862.* Lincoln and London: University of Nebraska Press, 1984.

———. *Little Crow: Spokesman for the Sioux.* St. Paul: Minnesota Historical Society Press, 1986.

Anderson, Gary Clayton, and Alan R. Woolworth. *Through Dakota Eyes: Narrative Accounts of the Minnesota Indian War of 1862.* St. Paul: Minnesota Historical Society Press, 1988.

Anderson, Thomas G. "Narrative of Thomas G. Anderson." *Wisconsin Historical Collections* 9 (1909): 136–206.

Anfinson, Scott. "Cultural and Natural Aspects of Mound Distribution in Minnesota." *Minnesota Archaeologist* 43 (1984): 3–30.

Anfinson, Scott F. "Maka Yusota." National Register of Historic Places Registration Form (2002). On file at the State Historic Preservation Office, St. Paul, MN.

Angier, Bradford. *Field Guide to Edible Plants.* Mechanicsburg, PA: Stackpole Books, 1974.

Arzigian, Constance M., and Katherine P. Stevenson. *Minnesota's Indian Mounds and Burial Sites: A Synthesis of Prehistoric and Early Historic Archaeological Data.* St. Paul: Minnesota Office of the State Archaeologist, 2003.

Babcock, Willoughby. "Louis Provençalle, Fur Trader." *Minnesota History* 20 (1939): 259–68.

———. "Sioux Villages in Minnesota Prior to 1837." *Minnesota Archaeologist* 11.4 (1945): 126–46.

———. "With Ramsey to Pembina in 1851: A Treaty-Making Trip in 1851." *Minnesota History* 38 (1962): 1–10.

Bacqueville de la Potherie, Claude Charles Le Roy. *Histoire de l'Amerique Septentrionale.* Vol. 2. Paris: Nyon Fils, 1753.

Baraga, Frederic. *A Dictionary of the Ojibway Language.* 2 vols. Reprint, St. Paul: Minnesota Historical Society Press, 1992.

Basso, Keith H. *Wisdom Sits in Places: Landscape and Language among the Western Apache.* Albuquerque: University of New Mexico Press, 1996.

Bean, William L. Eastman. *Cloud Man, Many Lightnings: An Anglo-Dakota Family.* Flandreau, SD: For the Eastman Family Reunion, July 6, 1989.

Benton-Banai, Edward. *The Mishomis Book: The Voice of the Ojibway.* N.p.: Indian Country Press, Inc., 1979.

Birk, Douglas A. "Putting Minnesota on the Map: Early French Presence in the Folle Avoine Region Southwest of Lake Superior." *Minnesota Archaeologist* 51 (1992): 7–26.

Birk, Douglas A., and Elden Johnson. "The Mdewakanton Dakota and Initial French Contact." In *Calumet and Fleur-de-Lys: Archaeology of Indian and French Contact in the Midcontinent,* edited by John A. Walthall and Thomas E. Emerson, 203–40. Washington, DC: Smithsonian Institution Press, 1992.

Birk, Douglas A., and Judy Posely. *The French at Lake Pepin: An Archaeological Survey for Fort Beauharnois.* St. Paul: Minnesota Historical Society and Minnesota Department of Natural Resources, 1978.

Birmingham, Robert A., and Leslie E. Eisenberg. *Indian Mounds of Wisconsin.* Madison: University of Wisconsin Press, 2000.

Bishop, Harriet E. *Floral Home; or, First Years of Minnesota.* New York: Sheldon, Blakeman and Company, 1857.

Blair, Emma H. *The Indian Tribes of the Upper Mississippi Valley and Region of the Great Lakes: as Described by Nicolas Perrot, French Commandant in the Northwest; Bacqueville de la Potherie, French Royal Commissioner to Canada; Morrell Marston, American Army Officer, and Thomas Forsyth, United States Agent at Fort Armstrong.* 2 vols. Cleveland, OH: Arthur H. Clark Co., 1911.

Blegen, Theodore C., ed. "Two Missionaries in the Sioux Country." *Minnesota History* 21 (1940): 15–32, 158–75, 272–83.

Bloom, John Porter, ed. *The Territorial Papers of the United States.* Vols. 27–28, Wisconsin Territory. Washington, DC: National Archives, 1969, 1975.

Boehme, Sarah P., Christian F. Feest, and Patricia Condon Johnston. *Seth Eastman: A Portfolio of North American Indians.* Afton, MN: Afton Historical Society Press, 1995.

Bond, J. Wesley. *Minnesota and Its Resources.* New York: Redfield, 1853.

Boucherville, Pierre Boucher de. "Account of Monsieur de Boucherville." *La Biblioteque Canadienne* (1826).

Brick, Greg A. "St. Paul Underground—What Happened to Fountain Cave—The Real Birthplace of St. Paul?" *Ramsey County History* 29 (1995): 4–15.

———. "The Serpent God of the Iron Cave: Hydromythology of the Dakota Indians." *Minnesota Speleology Monthly* (2005): 63–67.

Bronson, Bennet. "The Earliest Farming: Demography as Cause and Consequence." In *Origins of Agriculture,* edited by Charles Reed. The Hague: Mouton, 1977.

Brooks, Lisa. *The Common Pot: The Recovery of Native Space in the Northeast.* Minneapolis and London: University of Minnesota Press, 2008.

Bushnell, David I., Jr. "Tribal Migrations East of the Mississippi." *Smithsonian Miscellaneous Collections* 89.12 (1934).

Callahan, Kevin L. "Dakota Sacred Stones and Spirit Island, Mille Lacs, Minnesota: The Boulder Island that Moves." *Minnesota Archaeologist* 60 (2001): 137–42.

Carroll, Jane Lamm. "Who Was Jane Lamont? Anglo-Dakota Daughters in Early Minnesota." *Minnesota History* 59 (2005): 184–96.

Carver, Jonathan. *The Journals of Jonathan Carver and Related Documents, 1766–1770.* Edited by John Parker. St. Paul: Minnesota Historical Society Press, 1976.

———. *Travels through the Interior Parts of North America.* Reprint, Minneapolis, MN: Ross & Haines, Inc., 1956.

Casey, Edward. "How to Get from Space to Place in a Fairly Short Stretch of Time: Phenomenological Prolegomena." In *Senses of Place,* edited by Stephen Feld and Keith Basso, 13–52. Santa Fe, NM: New School of American Research Press, 1997.

Catlin, George. *Letters and Notes on the Manners, Customs, and Conditions of the North American Indians.* 2 vols. Reprint, New York: Dover Publications, Inc., 1973.

Clemmons, Linda M. "'We Will Talk of Nothing Else': Dakota Interpretations of the Treaty of 1837." *Great Plains Quarterly* 25 (2005): 173–85.

Coleman, Sister Bernard M. *Decorative Designs of the Ojibwa of Northern Minnesota.* Washington, DC: The Catholic University of America Press, 1947.

Cormier, Louis P., ed. *Jean-Baptiste Perrault marchand voyageur parti de Montreal le 28e de mai 1783.* Montreal: Boreal Express, 1978.

Coues, Elliott. *The Expeditions of Zebulon Montgomery Pike.* 3 vols. in 2. Reprint, Minneapolis, MN: Ross & Haines, Inc., 1965.

Cruikshank, Julie. *Do Glaciers Listen? Local Knowledge, Colonial Encounters, and Social Imagination.* Seattle: University of Washington Press, 2005.

Curtiss-Wedge, Franklyn. *History of Wright County Minnesota.* Chicago: H. C. Cooper, Jr. & Co., 1915.

Deloria, Ella Cara. *Dakota Texts.* Lincoln and London: University of Nebraska Press, 2006.

——. *The Dakota Way of Life.* N.p.: Mariah Press, 2007.

——. *Speaking of Indians.* Lincoln and London: University of Nebraska Press, 1998.

Denig, Edwin Thompson. *Five Indian Tribes of the Upper Missouri.* Norman: University of Oklahoma Press, 1961.

Densmore, Frances. *Chippewa Customs.* Reprint, St. Paul: Minnesota Historical Society Press, 1979.

Dictionary of Canadian Biography. Toronto: University of Toronto Press, 1981– .

Diedrich, Mark. "A 'Good Man' in a Changing World: Cloud Man, the Dakota Leader, and His Life and Times." *Ramsey County History* 36.1 (2001): 4–24.

——. *The Chiefs Wapahasha: Three Generations of Dakota Leadership, 1740–1876.* Rochester, MN: Coyote Books, 2004.

——. *Famous Dakota Chiefs.* Revised ed. Vol. 1. Rochester, MN: Coyote Books, 1999.

——. *Little Crow and the Dakota War (The Long Historical Cover-ups Exposed).* Rochester, MN: Coyote Books, 2006.

——. *Old Betsey: The Life and Times of a Famous Dakota Woman and Her Family.* Rochester, MN: Coyote Books, 1995.

Dorsey, James Owen. "The Place of Gentes in Siouan Camping Circles." *American Anthropologist* (1889) 2:375–79.

Durand, Paul C. *Ta-Ku-Wa-Kan Ti-Pi "Dwelling Place of the Gods": The Dakota Homeland in the Twin Cities Metropolitan Area.* Prior Lake, MN: The author, 1982.

——. *Where the Waters Gather and the Rivers Meet: An Atlas of the Eastern Sioux.* Faribault, MN: The author, 1994.

Eastman, Charles A. *Indian Boyhood.* New York: McClure, Phillips & Company, 1902.

——. *The Soul of an Indian.* Boston and New York: Houghton Mifflin Company, 1911.

Eastman, Charles A., and Elaine Goodale Eastman. *Smoky Day's Wigwam Evenings.* New York: Little, Brown, 1928.

Eastman, Mary Henderson. *Dahcotah or, Life and Legends of the Sioux around Fort Snelling.* Afton, MN: Afton Historical Society Press, 1995.

Elias, Peter Douglas. *The Dakota of the Canadian Northwest: Lessons for Survival.* Winnipeg: University of Manitoba Press, 1988.

Ewick, Patrick and Susan S. Silbey. "Subversive Stories and Hegemonic Tales: Toward a Sociology of Narrative." *Law & Society Review* 29 (1995): 197.

Farmington Area Historical Society. "Inyan Bosdata: Rock-Standing-On-End." *Over the Years* 45.3 (2004): 1–8.

Featherstonhaugh, George William. *A Canoe Voyage up the Minnay Sotor.* 2 vols. Reprint, St. Paul: Minnesota Historical Society Press, 1970.

Folwell, William Watts. *A History of Minnesota.* Vols. 1–3. Reprint, St. Paul: Minnesota Historical Society Press, 1956–69.

Forsyth, Thomas. "Journal of a Voyage from St. Louis to the Falls of St. Anthony, in 1819." *Report and Collections of the State Historical Society of Wisconsin* 6 (1872): 188–219.

Frazer, Joseph Jack. *Iron Face: The Adventures of Jack Frazer, Frontier Warrior, Scout, and Hunter; A Narrative Recorded by "Walker-in-the-pines" (Henry Hastings Sibley).* Edited by Theodore C. Blegen and Sara A. Davidson. Chicago: Caxton Club, 1950.

Fridley, Russell W. "Fort Snelling from Military Post to Historic Site." *Minnesota History* 35 (1956): 178–92.

Gagnon, Ernest. *Louis Jolliet: Découvreur du Missisipi et du Pays des Illinois, Premier Seigneur de l'ile d'Anticosti: étude biographique et historiographique.* Montreal: Beauchemin, 1946.

Gates, Charles M. *Five Fur Traders of the Northwest*. Reprint, St. Paul: Minnesota Historical Society, 1965.

Getches, David H., Charles F. Wilkinson, and Robert A. Williams, Jr. *Federal Indian Law*. 5th ed. St. Paul, MN: West Thomson, 2005.

Gibbon, Guy. *The Sioux: The Dakota and Lakota Nations*. Malden, MA: Blackwell Publishing, 2003.

Gibbon, Guy, and Scott F. Anfinson. *Minnesota Archaeology: The First 13,000 Years*. (Minneapolis: University of Minnesota) *Publications in Anthropology* 6 (2008). Online: http://anthropology.umn.edu/labs/wlnaa/first/contents/contents.html.

Gilman, Rhoda R. *Henry Hastings Sibley: Divided Heart*. St. Paul: Minnesota Historical Society Press, 2004.

———. "A Northwestern Indian Territory—The Last Voice." *Journal of the West* 39 (2000): 16–22.

Goodrich, Albert M. "Early Dakota Trails and Settlements at Centerville, Minn." *Collections of the Minnesota Historical Society* 15 (1915): 315–22.

Grieve, Mrs. M. *A Modern Herbal*. Reprint, New York: Dover Publications, Inc., 1971.

Gurnoe, Donald G., Jr. "The Minnesota Human Burial Law." *Minnesota Archaeologist* 39.3 (1980): 150–54.

Helmen, Vernon R. "Salvage Archaeology at the Science Museum." *Museum Observer* (St. Paul: Minnesota Science Museum) 3.2 (1963): 10–12.

Hennepin, Father Louis. *Father Louis Hennepin's Description of Louisiana*. Minneapolis: University of Minnesota Press, 1938.

Hickerson, Harold. *The Southwestern Chippewa: An Ethnohistorical Study. American Anthropologist* 64.3 (1961): Part 2, Memoir 92.

Hill, H. H., and Co. *History of Winona and Olmsted Counties*. Chicago: H. H. Hill and Co., 1883.

Hodge, Frederick Webb. *Handbook of American Indians North of Mexico*. 2 vols. Washington, DC: Smithsonian Institution, Bureau of American Ethnology, Bulletin 30, 1912.

Holcombe, R. I., and William H. Bingam, eds. *Compendium of History and Biography of Minneapolis and Hennepin County, Minnesota*. Chicago: Henry Taylor & Co., 1914.

Hopkins, George E. *Bloomington Historic Sites*. Bloomington, MN: Bloomington Historical Society, n.d.

Hotopp, John, and Randall Withrow, et al. *A Cultural Resource Assessment of the Proposed Reroute for Trunk Highway 55, 54th Street to County Road 62, Hennepin County, Minnesota*. Marion, IA: The Cultural Resource Group, Louis Berger & Associates, Inc., prepared for the U.S. Department of Transportation Federal Highway Administration and the Minnesota Department of Transportation, St. Paul, MN, 1999.

Howard, James H. *Yanktonai Ethnohistory and the John K. Bear Winter Count*. Memoir 11, *Plains Anthropologist* (1976): 21–73, pt 2.

Hyman, Colette A. *Dakota Women's Work: Creativity, Culture, and Exile*. St. Paul: Minnesota Historical Society Press, 2012.

Inter-Fluve. *Sand Creek, MN: Final Report—Fluvial Geomorphic Assessment*. Prepared for Scott [County] Watershed Management Center, 2008.

Jackson, Donald, ed. *The Journals of Zebulon Montgomery Pike with Letters and Related Documents*. 2 vols. Norman: University of Oklahoma Press, 1966.

Janis, Mark W. *An Introduction to International Law*. 4th ed. New York: Aspen Publishers, 2003.

Johnson, Sir William. *The Papers of Sir William Johnson*. 13 vols. Albany: The University of the State of New York, 1921–62.

Johnston, Carol S., and Cindy A. Gaas. "Vinegar: Medicinal Uses and Antiglycemic Effect." *Medscape General Medicine* 8.2 (2006): 61.

Kane, Lucile M. "The Sioux Treaties and the Traders." *Minnesota History* 32 (1951): 65–80.

Kane, Lucile M., June D. Holmquist, and Carolyn Gilman. *The Northern Expeditions of Stephen H. Long: The Journals of 1817 and 1823 and Related Documents*. St. Paul: Minnesota Historical Society Press, 1978.

Kappler, Charles J., comp. and ed. *Indian Affairs: Laws and Treaties*. Vol. 2. Washington, DC: Government Printing Office, 1904.

Keating, William H. *Narrative of an Expedition to the Source of the St. Peter's River*. 2 vols. in 1. Reprint, Minneapolis, MN: Ross & Haines, Inc., 1959.

Kellogg, Louise Phelps. *Early Narratives of the Northwest, 1634–1699*. New York: Charles Scribner's Sons, 1917.

———. "Fort Beauharnois." *Minnesota History* 8 (1927): 232–46.

King, Thomas. *The Truth about Stories: A Native Narrative*. Minneapolis: University of Minnesota Press, 2003.

King, Thomas F. "Beyond Bulletin 38: Comments on the Traditional Cultural Properties Symposium." *CRM* Special Issue 16 (1993).

———. *Cultural Resource Laws and Practice*. Walnut Creek, Lanham, NY, Oxford: Altamira Press, 2008.

———. *Places That Count: Traditional Cultural Properties in Cultural Resource Management*. Walnut Creek, Lanham, NY, Oxford: Altamira Press, 2003.

Kreidberg, Marjorie. *Food on the Frontier: Minnesota Cooking from 1850 to 1900, with Selected Recipes*. St. Paul: Minnesota Historical Society Press, 1975.

La Harpe, Bernard de. *Journal Historique de l'Établissement des Français à la Louisiane*. New Orleans: A.-L. Boimare, 1831.

Landes, Ruth M. *The Mystic Lake Sioux: Sociology of the Mdewakantonwan Santee*. Madison, Milwaukee, and London: University of Wisconsin Press, 1968.

Landscape Research. *The Henry H. Sibley House: Historic Structure Report*. Prepared for the Minnesota Historical Society, 1997.

Lass, William E. *The Treaty of Traverse des Sioux*. St. Peter, MN: Nicollet County Historical Society Press, 2011.

Lewis, Henry. *The Valley of the Mississippi Illustrated*. St. Paul: Minnesota Historical Society, 1967.

Lockwood, James H. "Early Times and Events in Wisconsin." *Wisconsin Historical Collections* 2 (1903): 98–196.

Losure, Mary. *Our Way or the Highway: Inside the Minnehaha Free State*. Minneapolis: University of Minnesota Press, 2002.

McClurken, James M., comp. *Fish in the Lakes, Wild Rice, and Game in Abundance: Testimony on Behalf of Mille Lacs Ojibwe Hunting and Fishing Rights*. East Lansing: Michigan State University Press, 2000.

McDermott, John Francis. *A Glossary of Mississippi Valley French*. Washington University Studies, New Series, *Language and Literature* 12. St. Louis, MO: Washington University, 1941.

———. *Seth Eastman: Pictorial Historian of the Indian*. Norman: University of Oklahoma Press, 1961.

———. *Seth Eastman's Mississippi: A Lost Portfolio Recovered*. Urbana, Chicago, Lincoln: University of Illinois Press, 1973.

Margry, Pierre. *Découvertes et Établissements des Français dans l'Ouest et dans le Sud de l'Amerique Septentrionale, 1614–1754*. 6 vols. Paris: D. Jouast, 1876–86.

Marin, Joseph. "Journal de Marin, Fils, 1753–1754." *Rapport des Archives du Quebec* 41 (1963): 237–308.

Martínez, David. *Dakota Philosopher: Charles Eastman and American Indian Thought*. St. Paul: Minnesota Historical Society Press, 2009.

Mather, David. *Archaeological Overview of the Mille Lacs Locality*. Minneapolis: Loucks and Associates, Loucks Project Report 96506-2. Prepared for the Minnesota Department of Transportation, 2000.

———. "The Bear's Funeral: Archaeological Expressions of Bear Ceremonialism in Minnesota." Paper presented in advance of preliminary oral examination, PhD program in Interdisciplinary Archaeological Studies, University of Minnesota, 2004.

———. "The Headless Bison Calf: An Archaeological Mystery." *The Rake* [Minneapolis, MN] (December 2004).

Mather, David, and Joseph McFarlane. Gii-maajaa'ind A'aw Makwa: *Phase II and Phase III Archaeological Investigations at the Elders' Site (21 ML 68), Mille Lacs County, Minnesota*. Minneapolis, MN: Loucks & Associates, Inc., Loucks Project Report 98510, 1999.

Mayer, Frank Blackwell. *With Pen and Pencil on the Frontier in 1851*. Edited by Bertha L. Heilbron. St. Paul: Minnesota Historical Society, 1932.

Meyer, Roy W. *History of the Santee Sioux: United States Indian Policy on Trial*. Revised ed. Lincoln and London: University of Nebraska Press, 1986.

Miller, Robert J. *Native America, Discovered and Conquered: Thomas Jefferson, Lewis and Clark, and Manifest Destiny*. Lincoln: University of Nebraska Press, 2008.

"The Minnesota Marker in the Washington Monument," *Minnesota History* 8: 176–77.

"Mission to the Indians." *Niles' Register,* Nov. 19, 1825. Reprinted from the *National Journal*.

Neill, Edward D. "Dakota Land and Dakota Life." *Collections of the Minnesota Historical Society* 1:254–294.

———. *The History of Minnesota from the Earliest French Explorations to the Present Time*. Minneapolis: Minnesota Historical Company, 1882.

———. "A Memoir of Joseph Renville." *Collections of the Minnesota Historical Society* 1 (1872): 196–206.

———. "Occurrences in and around Fort Snelling, from 1819 to 1840." *Minnesota Historical Collections* 2 (1889): 102–42.

Neill, Edward D., and J. Fletcher Williams. *History of Washington County and the St. Croix Valley.* Minneapolis, MN: North Star Publishing Company, 1881.

Nichols, John D., and Earl Nyholm. *A Concise Dictionary of Minnesota Ojibwe.* Minneapolis: University of Minnesota Press, 1995.

Nicollet, Joseph N. *Joseph N. Nicollet on the Plains and Prairies: The Expeditions of 1838–39 with Journals, Letters, and Notes on the Dakota Indians.* Reprint, St. Paul: Minnesota Historical Society Press, 1976.

———. *The Journals of Joseph N. Nicollet: A Scientist on the Mississippi Headwaters with Notes on Indian Life.* St. Paul: Minnesota Historical Society Press, 1970.

Nilles, Myron A. *A History of Wapasha's Prairie, 1660–1853 (First Called Keoxa, Later Winona, Minneesota).* 2nd ed. Winona, MN: Winona County Historical Society, 2005.

Norder, John. "The Creation and Endurance of Memory and Place Among First Nations of Northwestern Ontario, Canada." *International Journal of Historical Archaeology* 16.2 (June 2012).

Norgren, Jill. *The Cherokee Cases: Two Landmark Federal Decisions in the Fight for Sovereignty.* Norman: University of Oklahoma Press, 2004.

Nute, Grace Lee. *Caesars of the Wilderness: Médard Chouart, Sieur des Groseillers and Pierre Esprit Radisson, 1618–1710.* Reprint, St. Paul: Minnesota Historical Society Press, 1978.

———. "Calendar of the American Fur Company's Papers." *Annual Report of the American Historical Association,* Vols. 2–3. Washington, DC: Government Printing Office, 1945.

———. "Marin versus La Verendrye." *Minnesota History* 32 (1951): 226–38.

Nydahl, Theodore L. "The Pipestone Quarry and the Indians." *Minnesota History* 31 (1950): 193–208.

O'Callaghan, E. B., ed. (New York Colonial Documents) *Documents Relative to the Colonial History of the State of New York.* Vol. 9. Albany: State of New York, 1855.

Ollendorf, Amy L. and Carolyn R. Anderson. "Traditional Cultural Property and National Register of Historic Places Eligibility Assessment for Taku Wakan Tipi (Morgan's Mound), Hennepin County, Minnesota." N.p.: Peterson Environmental Consulting, 2004.

Oneroad, Amos, and Alanson Skinner. *Being Dakota: Tales and Traditions of the Sisseton and Wahpeton.* Edited by Laura L. Anderson. St. Paul: Minnesota Historical Society Press, 2003.

Parker, Patricia, and Thomas F. King. *Guidelines for Evaluating and Documenting Traditional Cultural Properties.* National Register Bulletin 38 (1998).

Perrot, Nicolas. *Mémoires sur les Moeurs, Coustumes et Relligion des Sauvages de l'Amerique Septentrionale.* Edited by R. P. J. Tailhan. 1864. Reprint, Montreal: Éditions Élysée, 1973.

Peterson, Leslie D. *The Minnesota Trunk Highway Archaeological Reconnaissance Survey, Annual Report.* St. Paul: Minnesota Historical Society, 1977.

Pond, Gideon H. "Dakota Superstitions." *Minnesota Historical Society Collections* 2 (1889): 215–55.

Pond, S. W., Jr. *Two Volunteer Missionaries among the Dakotas, or the Story of the Labors of Samuel W. and Gideon H. Pond.* Boston and Chicago: Congregational Sunday-School and Publishing Society, 1893.

Pond, Samuel W. *The Dakota or Sioux in Minnesota as They Were in 1834.* Reprint, St. Paul: Minnesota Historical Society Press, 1986.

———. "Two Missionaries in Sioux Country." *Minnesota History* 21 (1940): 17–32, 158–75, 272–83.

Prescott, Philander. *The Recollections of Philander Prescott, Frontiersman of the Old Northwest, 1819–1862.* Lincoln: University of Nebraska Press, 1966.

Prucha, Francis Paul. *American Indian Treaties: The History of a Political Anomaly.* Berkeley: University of California Press, 1994.

Public Broadcasting System. *The Elegant Universe: String Theory.* Sept. 2007.

Radisson, Pierre. *Voyages of Peter Esprit Radisson.* 1885. Reprint, New York: Burt Franklin, 1967.

Ramsey, Alexander. "Address of Gov. Alex. Ramsey, President of the Society, Before Its Annual Meeting, Jan. 13, 1851." *Collections of the Minnesota Historical Society* 1 (1902): 43–52.

Riggs, Maida Leonard. *A Small Bit of Bread and Butter: Letters from Dakota Territory, 1832–1869.* South Deerfield, MA: Ash Grove Press, 1996.

Riggs, Stephen R. *A Dakota-English Dictionary.* St. Paul: Minnesota Historical Society Press, 1992.

———. *Dakota Grammar, Texts, and Ethnography.* Reprint, Minneapolis, MN: Ross & Haines, 1973.

———. "Dakota Portraits." *Minnesota History* 2 (1918): 481–568.

———. "Mounds of the Minnesota Valley." *Collections of the Minnesota Historical Society* 1 (1872): 149–52.

———. "Mythology of the Dakotas." *The American Antiquarian* 5.2 (1883): 147.

Roads, James B. "The Fort Snelling Area in 1835: A Contemporary Map." *Minnesota History* 35 (1956): 22–29.

Robert, Paul. *Le Petit Robert: Dictionnaire Alphabétique & Analogique de la Langue Française.* Paris: S. N. L., 1973.

Robertson, Lindsay G. *Conquest by Law: How the Discovery of America Dispossessed the Indigenous Peoples of Their Lands.* New York: Oxford University Press, 2005.

Ryden, Kent C. *Mapping the Invisible Landscape: Folklore, Writing, and the Sense of Place.* Iowa City: University of Iowa Press, 1993.

Schoolcraft, Henry R. *Historical and Statistical Information Respecting the History, Condition and Prospects of the Indian Tribes of the United States.* Part 1. Philadelphia: Lippincott, Grambo & Company, 1851.

———. *The Indian in His Wigwam, or Characteristics of the Red Race of America.* Buffalo, NY: Derby & Hewson, Publishers, 1848.

———. *Schoolcraft's Narrative Journal of Travels.* Reprint, East Lansing: Michigan State University Press, 1992.

Seed, Patricia. *Ceremonies of Possession: Europe's Conquest of the New World, 1492–1640.* Cambridge: Cambridge University Press, 1995.

Singer, Joseph William. *Introduction to Property.* 2nd ed. New York: Aspen Publishers, 2005.

Sioux Valley Nation. *Wakan ye wiconi o iye: The Story of Our People.* Sioux Valley, Manitoba: Sioux Valley Nation, n.d.

Skinner, Alanson. *Medicine Ceremony of the Menomoni, Iowa, and Wahhpeton Dakota. Indian Notes and Queries* 4. New York: Museum of the American Indian, Heye Foundation, 1920.

———. "A Sketch of Eastern Dakota Ethnology." *American Anthropologist* New Series 21 (1919): 164–74.

Snelling, William Joseph. *Tales of the Northwest.* Minneapolis, MN: Ross & Haines, Inc., 1971.

Snyder, Rebecca. *The 1851 Treaty of Mendota.* South St. Paul, MN: Dakota County Historical Society, 2002.

Spector, Janet D. *What This Awl Means: Feminist Archaeology of a Wahpeton Dakota Village.* St. Paul: Minnesota Historical Society Press, 1993.

Stipe, Claude E. "Eastern Dakota Clans: The Solution of a Problem." *American Anthropologist* New Series 73 (1971): 1031–35.

Summit Envirosolutions, Inc., and Two Pines Resource Group, LLC. *The Cultural Meaning of Coldwater Spring: Final Ethnographic Resources Study of the Former U.S. Bureau of Mines Twin Cities Research Center Property, Hennepin County, Minnesota.* Prepared for the National Park Service Mississippi National River and Recreation Area, 2006.

Sundstrom, Linea. "Sacred Islands: An Exploration of Religion and Landscape in the Northern Great Plains." In *Islands on the Plains: Ecological, Social, and Ritual Use of Landscapes,* edited by Marcel Kornfeld and Alan J. Osborn. Salt Lake City: University of Utah Press, 2003.

Taliaferro, Lawrence. "Auto-biography of Major Lawrence Taliaferro: Written in 1864." *Collections of the Minnesota Historical Society* 6 (1894): 189–255.

Terrell, Michelle M. "Determination of the Eligibility of Carver's Cave and Dayton's Bluff Cave, Bruce Vento Nature Sanctuary Project, St. Paul, Ramsey County, Minnesota." St. Paul: The 106 Group, 2003.

Thwaites, Reuben Gold, ed. *The Jesuit Relations and Allied Documents.* 73 vols. Cleveland: Burrows Brothers, 1896–1901.

———. *New Voyages to North-America: by the Baron de Lahontan.* 2 vols., Chicago: A. C. McClurg, 1905.

Tishler, William H., and Virginia S. Luckhardt. "H. W. S. Cleveland: Pioneer Landscape Architect to the Upper Midwest." *Minnesota History* 49 (1985): 281–91.

Trennert, Robert A., Jr. *Indian Traders on the Middle Border: The House of Ewing, 1827–54.* Lincoln: University of Nebraska Press, 1981.

U.S. Department of Transportation and Minnesota Department of Transportation. *A Cultural Resource Assessment of the Proposed Reroute of Trunk Highway 55, 54th Street to Route 62, Hennepin County, Minnesota.* Vol. 2, parts 1–2. 1999.

U.S. Fish and Wildlife Service. *Minnesota Valley Wildlife Refuge: Louisville Swamp Unit Trail Map.* n.d.

Upham, Warren. *Minnesota Geographic Names: Their Origin and Significance.* Reprint, St. Paul: Minnesota Historical Society Press, 1969.

Vadnais, Cynthia E. *Looking Back at White Bear Lake: A Pictorial History of the White Bear Lake Area.* N.p., 2004.

Vennum, Thomas. *American Indian Lacrosse: Little Brother of War.* Baltimore, MD: Johns Hopkins University Press, 1994.

Vogel, Howard J. "The Clash of Stories at Chimney Rock: A Narrative Approach to Cultural Conflict over Native American Sacred Sites on Public Land." *Santa Clara Law Review* 41 (2001): 757. Online: http://law.hamline.edu/files/Vogel_Clash.pdf.

Walker, James R. *Lakota Belief and Ritual*. Lincoln and London: University of Nebraska Press, 1991.

———. *Lakota Myth*. Lincoln and London: University of Nebraska Press, 1983.

Wallis, Wilson D., ed. *Beliefs and Tales of the Canadian Dakota*. St. Paul, MN: Prairie Smoke Press for Sisseton-Wahpeton Sioux Tribe, 1999.

Warren, William W. *History of the Ojibway People*. St. Paul: Minnesota Historical Society Press, 1985.

Waziyatawiŋ [Waziyatawiŋ Angela Wilson]. *What Does Justice Look Like? The Struggle for Liberation in Dakota Homeland*. St. Paul, MN: Living Justice Press, 2008.

Wedel, Mildred Mott. "The Ioway, Oto, and Omaha Indians in 1700." *Journal of the Iowa Archaeological Society* 28 (1981): 2–11.

———. "Le Sueur and the Dakota Sioux." In *Aspects of Upper Great Lakes Archaeology: Papers in Honor of Lloyd A. Wilford*, edited by Elden Johnson. St. Paul: Minnesota Historical Society, 1974.

Werner, Reinhold O. *Burial Places of the Aborigines of Kaposia*. South St. Paul, MN: The Kaposia Press, 1974.

Whelan, Mary K. "Dakota Indian Economics and the Nineteenth-Century Fur Trade." *Ethnohistory* 40 (1993): 246–76.

———. "Late Woodland Subsistence Systems and Settlement Size in the Mille Lacs Area." In *The Woodland Tradition in the Western Great Lakes: Papers Presented to Elden Johnson*, edited by Guy E. Gibbon, 55–75. Minneapolis: University of Minnesota Publications in Anthropology 4 (1990).

White, Bruce. "Balancing the Books: Trader Profits in the British Lake Superior Fur Trade." In *New Faces of the Fur Trade: Selected Papers of the Seventh North American Fur Trade Conference*, edited by Jo-Anne Fiske, Susan Sleeper-Smith, and William Wicken, 175–92. East Lansing: Michigan State University Press, 1998.

———. "Eligibility under the 1888, 1889, and 1890 Federal Appropriations for the Mdewakanton Sioux of Minnesota." Report prepared for the Organization of Mendota Dakota. St. Paul, MN: Turnstone Historical Research, 2006.

———. "Encounters with Spirits: Ojibwa and Dakota Theories about the French and Their Merchandise." *Ethnohistory* 41 (1994): 369–405.

———. "The Fear of Pillaging: Economic Folktales of the Great Lakes Fur Trade." In *The Fur Trade Revisited: Selected Papers of the Sixth North American Fur Trade Conference, Mackinac Island, Michigan, 1991*. East Lansing: Michigan State University Press, 1994.

———. *Grand Portage as a Trading Post: Patterns of Trade at "the Great Carrying Place."* Grand Marais, MN: National Park Service, Grand Portage National Monument, 2005.

———. "Minnesota's Disappearing Mounds." (July 11, 2005). Online: http://www.minnesotahistory.net/MHNet18.htm.

———. "Ojibwe-White Conflicts over Land and Resources on the Mille Lacs Reservation, 1855–1923." Report prepared for the Mille Lacs Band of Ojibwe, 2003.

———. "The Trade Assortment: The Meanings of Merchandise in the Ojibwa Fur Trade." In *Vingt ans après* Habitants et marchands *Twenty Years Later*, 115-37. Montreal and Kingston: McGill-Queens University Press, 1998.

———. "What Happened at Black Dog in 1977: A Cautionary Tale." (January 16, 2006). Online: http://www.minnesotahistory.net/MHNet21.htm.

White, Bruce, and Alan Woolworth. "Oheyawahi/ Pilot Knob: A Hill of State & National Significance in Dakota County." *Over the Years* 45.2 (2004):1–24.

White, Richard. *The Middle Ground: Indians, Empires, and Republics in the Great Lakes Region, 1650–1815*. Cambridge, New York, Port Chester, Melbourne, Sydney: Cambridge University Press, 1991.

Wilford, Lloyd A. "Indian Burials near Black Dog's Village." *Minnesota Archaeologist* (July 1944): 92–104.

Wilkins, David, and K. Tsianina Lomawaima. *Uneven Ground: American Indian Sovereignty and Federal Law*. Norman: University of Oklahoma Press, 2001.

Wilkinson, Charles F., and John M. Volkman. "Judicial Review of Indian Treaty Abrogation: 'As Long as Water Flows or Grass Grows Upon the Earth'—How Long a Time is That?" *California Law Review* 63 (1975): 601, 608–19.

Williams, Robert A. Jr. *The American Indian in Western Legal Thought: The Discourses of Conquest*. New York: Oxford University Press, 1990.

Williamson, Andrew W. "Minnesota Geographical Names Derived from the Dakota Language." *Minnesota Archaeologist* 35.4 (1976): 15–23.

Williamson, John P. *An English-Dakota Dictionary*. St. Paul: Minnesota Historical Society Press, 1992.

———. "John P. Williamson to His Mother, May 13, 1863." *Minnesota History* 2 (1918): 422–25.

Wilson, Waziyatawiŋ Angela. *In the Footsteps of Our Ancestors: The Dakota Commemorative Marches of the 21st Century*. St. Paul, MN: Living Justice Press, 2006.

———. *Remember This! Dakota Decolonization and the Eli Taylor Narratives.* Lincoln & London: University of Nebraska Press, 2005.

Winchell, Newton H. *The Aborigines of Minnesota: A Report on the Collections of Jacob V. Brower, and on the Field Surveys and Notes of Alfred J. Hill and Theodore H. Lewis.* St. Paul: Minnesota Historical Society, 1911.

Wingerd, Mary Lethert. *North Country: The Making of Minnesota.* Minneapolis: University of Minnesota Press, 2010.

Wisconsin, State Historical Society of. *Collections of the State Historical Society of Wisconsin.* 31 vols. Also known as *Wisconsin Historical Collections* and *Publications of the State Historical Society of Wisconsin.* Madison, WI: The society, 1881–1931.

Witgen, Michael. *An Infinity of Nations: How the Native New World Shaped Early North America.* Philadelphia: University of Pennsylvania Press, 2012.

———. "The Rituals of Possession: Native Identity and the Invention of Empire in Seventeenth-Century Western North America." *Ethnohistory* 54.4 (2007): 639–68.

Wood, W. Raymond, and Douglas A. Birk. "Pierre-Charles Le Sueur's 1702 Map of the Mississippi River." *Minnesota Archaeologist* 60 (2001): 31–35.

Woolworth, Alan R., comp. *Santee Dakota Indian Legends.* St. Paul: Prairie Smoke Press, for Sisseton-Wahpeton Sioux Tribe, 2003.

Zellie, Carole. "From Palisade Head to Sugar Loaf: An Inventory of Minnesota's Geographic Features of Historic and Cultural Significance." Prepared for the Minnesota State Historic Preservation Office, St. Paul, MN, 1989.

MANUSCRIPTS

American Philosophical Society, Philadelphia, PA.
  497.3:B63c. Franz Boas Papers.

Library and Archives of Canada, Ottawa.
  MG1. Fonds des Colonies. Série C11A. Correspondance générale; Canada. Microfilm Rolls F-48, 49, 51, 66, 67, 69, 71, 74, 77, 79, 80, 85, 89, 93, 95, 97, 118, 119, 120, 123, 197, 198, 201, 202, 414. Some of the documents on these microfilms have been scanned and are available, in varying quality, on the Library and Archives of Canada website, http://collectionscanada.gc.ca/lac-bac/search/all.

  MG2. Fonds de la Marine. Service hydrographique de la Marine. Sous-série 3JJ. Microfilm Roll F-475. "Mémoires de Mr. Le Sueur."

Library of Congress, Washington, DC, Map Collection.
  G4042.M5 1702 .L5 Vault. Carte de la rivière de Mississipi : sur les mémoires de Mr. Le Sueur qui en a pris avec la boussole tous les tours et detours depuis la mer jusqu'à la rivière St. Pierre, et a pris la hauteur du pole en plusieurs endroits / par Guillaume de L'Isle geographe de l'Academie des Sciences. 1702. Online: http://memory.loc.gov/cgi-bin/query/h?ammem/gmd:@field%28NUMBER+@band%28g4042m+ct000665%29%29.

Minnesota Historical Society.
  M30. Joseph Nicollet Papers.
  M35, M35-A. (Taliaferro journal) Lawrence Taliaferro, Manuscripts. As part of this project a scanned version of the Taliaferro journal was prepared using optical character recognition software from typed transcripts done in the 1930s and 1940s by MHS staff. Although the transcript contains many errors, it allowed for extensive use of the journal.
  M89. Sir Frederick Haldimand Papers.
  M105. Selected letters and other documents relating largely to the St. Peters Indian Agency.
  M164. Henry H. Sibley Papers, Microfilm.
  M330. Jacob V. Brower Field Notebooks.
  P489. Manuscripts Relating to Northwest Missions.
  P763. Frances Densmore Papers.
  P849. Montreal Merchants Collection.
  P1100.9. Fred Pearsall. Sioux Geographic Names.
  P1301. Daniel Greysolon Duluth, Letters, 1679, 1685.
  United States. Office of Surveyor General of Minnesota, land survey field notes, 1848–1907.

National Archives, Washington, DC.
  NAM M234, Rolls 757–64. Letters Received. St. Peters Agency.
  NAM M668. Ratified Indian Treaties.
  NAM T494. Documents Relating to the Negotiation of Ratified and Unratified Treaties with Various Indian Tribes. Many treaty negotiation journals have been scanned and are online at http://uwdc.library.wisc.edu/collections/History/IndianTreatiesMicro.
  NARG 75. Office of Indian Affairs.
  NARG 217. General Accounting Office. Second Auditor. Entry 525. Indian Accounts.

National Archives and Records Administration, Kansas City, MO.
  NARG 75. Pipestone Indian School and Agency Records.

Newberry Library, Chicago. Map Collections.
  Ayer MS map 61. Cours du grand fleuve Missisipi : depuis sa source jusqu'a son embouchure avec toutes les rivieres qui y tombent ou est compris la decouverte du Sr. le Sueur qui se rent sur les pays et nations del l'est et de l'ouest de ce fleuve à prendre depuis la Riviere Ouisconsing en montant jusqu'a la source du même fleuve. Tracing made ca. 1850 by historian Pierre Margry from 1697 manuscript by French royal geographer Jean Baptiste Louis Franquelin.

Index

Image Credits

"C" refers to the color section that begins after page 120.

PAGES 12, 20 BOTTOM	T. H. Kirk, *Illustrated History of Minnesota* (St. Paul: D. D. Merrill, 1887), 51.
PAGES 18, C12, C13	Smithsonian American Art Museum, gift of Mrs. Joseph Harrison, Jr.
PAGE 22	Valdimir Il'yin/ dreamstime.com
PAGES 24, 25, 46 TOP AND BOTTOM, 48, 88	Library of Congress
PAGE 35	Gilcrease Museum, Tulsa, OK
PAGES 47 TOP AND BOTTOM, 53, 170, 181	Photos courtesy of the Newberry Library
PAGES 105, 145, 146, 177	National Archives
PAGES 110, 120	Keating, *Narrative of an Expedition,* frontispiece.
PAGES 122–23	David Deis, Dreamline Cartography
PAGES 128 RIGHT, 187	Bruce White
PAGE 151	James Otto Lewis, *The Aboriginal Portfolio* (Philadelphia: J. O. Lewis, 1835–[36]).
PAGE 193	National Anthropological Archives, Smithsonian Institution [03651]
PAGE 194	Sioux delegation to Washington, 1858. Standing left to right: Akipa, Wambdi Upi Duta (Scarlet Eagle Tail), Maza Ša (Red Iron), Aŋpetu Tokca (Other Day), Mazakutemani, and Charles Crawford. Seated left to right, Mazamani, He Hu Tani (Stumpy Horn), Wasuiciyapi (Sweet Corn), and Upi Iyahdeya. MHS collections
PAGE 206	National Anthropological Archives, Smithsonian Institution [03462]
PAGE 215	Gwen Westerman
C-01	W. Duncan and Nivin MacMillan Foundation
C-03	Collection of the U.S. House of Representatives
C-11	Schoolcraft, *Historical and Statistical Information,* 339, 352–53.

All others from Minnesota Historical Society collections

Mni Sota Makoce: The Land of the Dakota was designed
by Cathy Spengler and set in type by Judy Gilats.
The text face is Minion Pro and the display face is Ideal Sans.
The book was printed by Thomson-Shore, Dexter, Michigan.